D1476185

The Edinburgh Companion to
Twentieth-Century Literatures in English

The Edinburgh Companion to Twentieth-Century Literatures in English

Edited by Brian McHale and Randall Stevenson

'The moment for this book is absolutely perfect . . . It instructs both by its programmatic statements and by the success of its examples. The book stands to make a genuinely outstanding contribution.'

Bruce Robbins, Department of English, Columbia University

'This intriguing and informative book rides the updraught provided by the continuing popularity of guides and companions, but also performs some surprising and fascinating new mid-air manoeuvres with the form. The . . . reshuffling of the literary-historical deck in this volume is refreshing and illuminating for student readers too.'

Steven Connor, School of English and Humanities, Birkbeck College, University of London

An imaginatively constructed new literary history of the twentieth century.

In an era suspicious of grand narratives, when consensus lies beyond reach and alternative histories proliferate, literary history has become more exciting, challenging – and problematic – than ever. The usual forced march through the decades, genres and national literatures no longer seems adequate. A reference work for the new century, the present *Companion* cuts across these familiar categories, focusing instead on 'hot spots' – crossroads in space and time around which the products and movements of the literary imagination can be seen to arrange themselves: Freud's Vienna and Conrad's Congo in 1899, Chicago and London in 1912, the Somme in July 1916, Dublin, London and Harlem in 1922, and so on, down to Bradford and Berlin in 1989 (the *fatwa* against Salman Rushdie, the new digital media), Stockholm in 1993 (Toni Morrison's Nobel Prize) and September 11, 2001.

Twenty-one chapters, commissioned from specialists in various sub-fields of twentieth-century literary studies, each target one of these seminal times and places, ranging widely around them to gather in broad swathes of culture and context. Framed by the editors' introduction and conclusion, the essays collectively offer a complex, interlocking and overlapping 'group portrait' of twentieth-century literatures in context.

This is a companion with a difference which sets a controversial new agenda for literary-historical analysis and will remain a point of reference and discussion within English Studies for years to come.

Brian McHale is Distinguished Humanities Professor in English at the Ohio State University. Randall Stevenson is Professor of Twentieth-Century Literature in the University of Edinburgh.

The Edinburgh Companion to Twentieth-Century Literatures in English

Edited by Brian McHale and Randall Stevenson

Edinburgh University Press

Edinburgh University Press Ltd
22 George Square, Edinburgh

Typeset in 10/12 Goudy
by Servis Filmsetting Ltd, Manchester, and
printed and bound in Great Britain by
The Cromwell Press, Trowbridge, Wilts

A CIP record for this book is available from the British Library

ISBN-10 0 7486 2011 7 (hardback)
ISBN-13 978 0 7486 2011 1

Contents

Acknowledgements

This volume might well have been entitled 'The Macclesfield Companion to Twentieth-Century Literatures in English', as it was imagined and shaped at the kitchen table of John and Alison Cartmell's house near Macclesfield, Cheshire, in the spring of 2003. Since then, the editors have worked at other tables in various places, together and apart, but never under friendlier or more hospitable circumstances. The editors are grateful, too, to the Royal Society of Edinburgh and the School of Literatures, Languages and Cultures in the University of Edinburgh for their generous financial support. We are also grateful to all who contributed essays to the volume, and to the imagination and commitment of Edinburgh University Press, both in first commissioning it, and in supporting us in the enjoyable but demanding process of its completion. Many thanks, too, to Cairns Craig and Colin Nicholson for generous help in the late stages of completion.

BMcH and RS

Introduction

On or about December 1910, London

Brian McHale and Randall Stevenson

Stories of the Street

> One dream in particular . . . he would find himself alone in a long street in the middle of the night . . . This street stretched as far as one could see. It had on either side lamp-posts which burned with a steady staring illumination, long rows of lamp-posts that converged in the farthest distance.
>
> (Mackenzie 1983: 45)

Repeatedly endured by Compton Mackenzie's hero in *Sinister Street* (1913–14), this dream seems to recur for the central characters in Thomas Pynchon's *V.* (1963), disturbed by the prospect of an

> abstracted Street . . . [of] mercury-vapor lamps, receding in an asymmetric V to the east where it's dark . . . the street of the 20th Century, at whose far end or turning – we hope – is some sense of home or safety. (Pynchon 1973: 2, 303)

Visions of a dark, 'abstracted street', dotted with pools of clear illumination, turn up significantly often in the half-century separating *Sinister Street* and *V.* They figure in the regularly spaced, talkative streetlamps described in T. S. Eliot's 'Rhapsody on a Windy Night' (1917), for example, and perhaps in the 'series of gig-lamps symmetrically arranged' Virginia Woolf mentions a few years later in her essay on 'Modern Fiction' (1919/1925; Woolf 1986–94: 4: 160). Graham Greene's *It's a Battlefield* (1934) likewise envisages a 'battlefield' indefinite in dimensions and area, and 'made up of nothing except small numberless circlets commensurate with such ranges of vision as the mist might allow at each spot' (Greene 1980: 5). Further down the century, William Gibson's *Neuromancer* (1984) continues to describe 'clusters and constellations of data' in cyberspace as 'Like city lights, receding' (Gibson 1984: 67).

Looking back now, from the 'far end, or turning' Pynchon anticipated, the recurrence of such dreams and images seems one of many symptoms of fragmentation, of fracturing of vision or illumination, so central to the century just completed, and so distinctive in its art. For Mackenzie, doodling the names of First World War battlefields in the margins of his manuscript while finishing *Sinister Street*, or for Pynchon, following the century's experience as far as the Second World War and Suez in *V.* – or for a great many other writers – such fragmentation was primarily, obviously, historic in its origins. For others among the century's major novelists, there were further sources too, including a rapidly developing technology. In *A la recherche du temps perdu* (1913–27), for example, Marcel Proust regularly reflects on the fractured images of life imposed on imagination by early forms of the cinematograph. Virginia Woolf's hero/heroine in *Orlando* (1928) experiences a comparable 'chopping up small of identity' when she drives out of London, finding that the still-newish experience of motoring leaves

> long vistas steadily shrunk together . . . nothing could be seen whole or read from start to finish. What was seen begun . . . was never seen ended. After twenty minutes the body and mind were like scraps of torn paper tumbling from a sack.

Orlando finds herself as a result 'a person entirely disassembled . . . [with] seventy-six different times all ticking in the mind at once' (Woolf 1975: 216–17).

Woolf and her modernist contemporaries were committed to developing literary forms adequate to the demands of a new age of speed, fragmentation and uncertainty. Yet, 'seeing whole' nevertheless remained an aim, however tentative – a residual possibility that reassemblage of self and vision might be achievable through deeper delvings into consciousness, or through subtler myths and structures, subtending the often-fractured surfaces of their work. By the latter part of the century, however, the modernist sense of 'obligation toward the difficult whole' (Venturi 1977: 88) had largely (though not universally) given way to a postmodernist scepticism of wholeness that expressed itself through disassemblage rather than reassemblage. A later hero of Pynchon's, Tyrone Slothrop of *Gravity's Rainbow* (1973), is sent into the Zone of Occupied Germany to witness 'his own assembly – perhaps, heavily paranoid voices have whispered, *his time's assembly*' (Pynchon 2000: 752). But he is disassembled instead, and his 'time' with him: on a street of the Zone, as if finding one of Orlando's 'scraps of torn paper', he picks up a fragment of newsprint reporting the destruction of Hiroshima (707). In the work of many other postmodernist writers, new textual forms found further means of emphasising the absence of faiths, coherences or 'grand narratives' from contemporary life. Even among authors apparently uninvolved in the formal invention distinguishing modernist and postmodernist writing, there seemed little evidence of the 'sense of home or safety' Pynchon had hoped to find at the far end of the twentieth century – still less after the shattering events of 11 September 2001, which seemed at a stroke to realise much of the preceding half-century's 'imagination of disaster'.

Twentieth Century

The sinister street that haunts the twentieth-century literary imagination provokes reflections on the writing of literary history. The street and its streetlamps offer a figure of time, perceived not as a continuum, but as points of illumination dotting a void. This was part of the modernists' vision of the street, developed more fully in the work of postmodernists after them. It is in the spirit of this vision that the Italian postmodernist Italo Calvino concludes in *If on a Winter's Night A Traveller* (1979) that 'the dimension of time has been shattered, we cannot love or think except in fragments of time each of which goes off along its own trajectory' (Calvino 1981:13). Time, Gabriel García Márquez suggests in *One Hundred Years of Solitude* (1967), 'had accidents and could therefore splinter and leave an eternalised fragment in a room' (Márquez 1977: 322). Perhaps as a result, the gypsy Melquíades is able to concentrate 'a century of daily episodes in such a way that they coexisted in one instant' (Márquez 1977: 382) – or at any rate within the span of a middle-sized novel. For literary history, there might be obvious advantages in thinking, or studying, a century in the terms in which it thought or understood itself: fragments reflecting its fractured history may also offer the sharpest, most incisive way of anatomising it. The question, then, is how to write literary history in fragments, without ceasing to write literary *history* altogether? In other words, how are we to reconcile these rival stories of the street, the street as continuous vs. the street as punctuated?

One method is suggested by the innovative *New History of French Literature*, edited by Denis Hollier and others (1989). Hollier's *New History* comprises a series of essays, each keyed to a particular event in literary, cultural, or political history, but moving out from that event to sweep in large swathes of past, future and contemporary developments. These key events, captured in dated 'headlines' at the top of each essay, are sometimes 'properly' literary (publication dates of key texts, premières of plays, deaths of authors), sometimes reflect the intersection of literature and other social institutions (for example, the 1857 trials of Gustave Flaubert's *Madame Bovary* and Charles Baudelaire's *Les fleurs du mal*, the appointment of André Malraux as Minister of Cultural Affairs, the 500th broadcast of the televised book-chat show *Apostrophes*), and sometimes highlight non-literary events with more or less profound literary repercussions (for example, the canonisation of Jeanne d'Arc, the Dreyfus Affair, the First World War, the *événements* of May 1968). In justifying their calculatedly discontinuous approach to literary history, the editors write, 'The juxtaposition of these events is designed to produce an effect of heterogeneity and to disrupt the traditional orderliness of most histories of literature' (Hollier 1989: xix). This is one of our models in the present *Companion*.

Literatures in English

Those visions of the street also provoke reflection on the space of literary history. Woolf's *Orlando* finds innumerable new identities, vistas, time-scales, paces of imagination developing as soon as she departs from the metropolis. When Slothrop ventures into the Zone, he too undergoes disassembly, and the space of the Zone with him. On a far greater scale, 'English' itself underwent comparable dispersal and dissemination throughout the twentieth century.

Once, perhaps, it had seemed unproblematic to speak of 'the literature of England' or of 'America'. Looking back, however, it became clear how violent an imposition these territorial categories had been, how they ignored or absorbed national differences (Wales, Scotland, Ireland, the 'rest' of the Americas) and linguistic diversity (the minority languages in the British Isles; Spanish, native, and immigrant languages in the United States; 'non-standard' regional varieties and dialects everywhere). In any case, in the course of the twentieth century such territorial designations became progressively less tenable, as literature in English increasingly 'internationalised' itself. In the first decades of the century, modernism was already an international affair, conducted by Americans in London and Paris, British expatriates, Irishmen in exile, and speakers of English as a second language. After the middle of the century, it became increasingly difficult to ignore the Empire that by then had already been 'writing back' to the mother countries for some time. The discipline of 'Commonwealth Literature' arose in response to this situation, serving to contain and manage the fractious diversity of English literatures abroad – but only briefly, breaking down, as the Commonwealth itself did, into a multiplicity of postcolonial successor-disciplines (Caribbean literature, South Asian literature in English, etc.)

At the turn of the millennium, international English had become an instance, perhaps *the* paradigmatic instance, of the paradoxes of globalisation. Carried to every continent by British imperialism, consolidated by US neo-imperialism as the international language of mass entertainment, commerce, advanced research and the internet, global English is simultaneously uniform and diverse, local and planetary, metropolitan and peripheral, centripetal and centrifugal, singular and plural. The literatures erected on these international Englishes reflect both heterogeneity and globe-spanning unity. Our title, *Twentieth-Century Literatures in English*, is simultaneously presumptuous and an admission of limitations: presumptuous in its ambition to address (however incompletely and imperfectly) the global distribution and cultural diversity of literature in English in the twentieth century; limited in its focus on a single (albeit protean) language in a century that has become increasingly translinguistic and transcultural. While we have encouraged our contributors to take into account exchanges with literatures in other languages (bilingual or multilingual situations, exile and expatriation, translation) and non-English or non-standard literatures within English-speaking territories (Scots; Yiddish in New York; 'Black British' dialects), there was no question of our undertaking a *Companion to Twentieth-Century Literatures in All Languages*, however desirable that might be.

That project will have to be left to editors with different competencies and ambitions, and with many more pages at their disposal. Meanwhile, an Edinburgh Companion may offer an unusually appropriate perspective on the century's diverse English literatures, especially in light of UNESCO's nomination of Edinburgh as the first 'World City of Literature' in 2005. The designation helped to identify qualities highly specific, yet also broadly representative. Capital city of one of the peripheral nations of the United Kingdom, Edinburgh's situation is paradigmatic of tensions and coalescences between centre and periphery, mainstream and margin, local and global, in evidence everywhere across the increasingly globalised imagination of writing in English.

A Companion

Companions to literature abound these days, as do encyclopedias, handbooks, concise introductions, idiots' guides – all the genres and sub-genres of paraliterary reference works. Dictated largely, no doubt, by marketing considerations, this proliferation of reference works also reflects a generational changing of the guard, as a younger cohort of scholars displaces an older one, and takes its turn at creating updated 'standard authorities' for the use of students, researchers and others. Whatever its causes, the recent proliferation of literary reference works suggests that there would need to be good reasons for creating yet another. Our determination to do so arises from a conviction that many recent reference works are underwritten by a surprisingly retrograde, uncontemporary understanding of literary historiography.

Those visions of the twentieth-century street – receding to an indeterminate vanishing-point – confront us with problems of delimiting an appropriate historical interval to be 'covered', fixing its beginning- and end-points, and then dividing that interval into shorter units. Conventional divisions are available – centuries, decades, canonical periods – but suspect. When, notoriously, Woolf locates the onset of modern consciousness 'on or about December 1910', she is foregrounding the arbitrariness of periodisation (Woolf

1986–1994: 3: 421). Recent historicists likewise urge us to think outside the little boxes of conventional periodisation, and to engage with longer durations of history, 'long centuries' that overrun merely calendrical limits ('1800', '1900', '2000'). Yet readers of literary history are often still conscripted into a forced march through national literatures, centuries, decades, arbitrarily divided periods and genres – British and American, Romantic, Victorian and Modern, lyric, novel and drama, etc. – as though there were nothing problematic about what are actually much-contested categories. Typically, too, conventional histories have tended to separate 'background' from the 'properly' literary or aesthetic foreground, as though the perspective space implied by the metaphor of background and foreground had never been thrown into doubt by modernist practice in the visual arts. Texts remain at the centre of attention, as though the opposition between text and context had never been subjected to deconstruction. If we have learned anything from the past several decades of intense theoretical self-reflection, it is that categories and distinctions such as these – foreground vs. background, text vs. context, etc. – while they cannot be done without, also can no longer be taken for granted.

We tried to re-imagine what a companion to literature could be. We envisioned a series of essays in which, instead of being kept hierarchically separate, literary backgrounds and foregrounds, texts and contexts were braided or folded together to constitute *thick descriptions* (to use the ethnographer Clifford Geertz's term) of literary phenomena. The ultimate aim would be, not 'coverage' in temporal or spatial breadth, but *involution*, revealing literary works' involvement with and situatedness within the material cultures, societies and histories which produced them. Woolf's conclusion that 'on or about December 1910 human character changed' also poses an exemplary challenge to think through, thoroughly, what was happening in a particular month, not only within the literary sphere, but also well beyond it. Many critics have construed that 'beyond' in narrowly aesthetic terms, referring only to the opening of Roger Fry's Post-Impressionist exhibition in London at the time. Commentators have too rarely gone on to assess contemporary developments in suffragism, trade unionism, or in the Liberal government's threats to the House of Lords, with all that those implied about weakening class hierarchies. Woolf's conviction that 'all human relations have shifted' is after all based largely on the behaviour of her cook, apparently content no longer with 'the lower depths' either of the house or of her conventional social station.

Woolf insisted that life is *not* a series of lamps, but a 'luminous halo'. Accordingly, every essay in the *Companion* would, we hoped, throw a firmly directed, 'steady, staring' light on its subject, but one which might also reach towards the territory of its neighbours, even illuminating this diverse century generally. Instead of seeking to ensure that our contributors' stories would dovetail neatly together to form a single integrated narrative, one that gave the illusion of exhaustiveness, we would seek multiplicity and heterogeneity, and acknowledged incompleteness. Our *Companion* would honour the principle enunciated by Siegfried Schmidt some twenty years ago: 'Literary histories exist but not *literary history*' (Schmidt 1985: 294) – a multiplicity of stories of the street, but no unitary story.

How to accomplish these things? Not, surely, by asking our contributors to 'cover' a region or decade or movement or genre, or any of the other familiar categories by which literary histories are typically organised – that would only have meant encouraging them to produce a narrative of a more or less familiar kind. Instead, taking Hollier *et al.*'s *New History of French Literature* as our model, we invited them to begin from a starting-point – a time, a place (or places), and an event or complex of events, captured in a kind of dateline: *1912, London, Chicago, Florence and New York* (the disappearance of the magazine

The Freewoman and the founding of *Poetry*), or *1936, Madrid* (the Spanish Civil War), or *1989, Bradford and Berlin* (the *fatwa* against Rushdie, the fall of the Wall). We conceived of these as 'hot spots,' spatial and temporal crossroads on the twentieth century's sinister street, around which the activities and products of the literary imagination might be seen to arrange themselves – not, by any means, the only such 'hot spots' one might identify, though neither were they merely arbitrary choices. We hoped, at least, that our contributors would find the datelines provocative, using them as jumping-off points for excursions of greater or lesser scope into literary-historical space-time, exploring the nature and operations of literary development, diversification and change. Inevitably, our sampling of 'hot spots' does not yield the sort of 'coverage' of key figures, genres or national literatures that one might expect from a more conventional narrative history. We thought that any loss of conventional 'coverage' would be compensated for by the variegated illumination that our contributors would shed on the century, and we have not been disappointed in that expectation.

Apart from the Hollier literary history, our methodological inspirations have included Michael North's monograph, *1922: A Return to the Scene of the Modern* (1999), which undertakes to reconstruct (however partially) the universe of books and reading in the year of T. S. Eliot's *The Waste Land* and James Joyce's *Ulysses*, including some, at least, of the books permanently overshadowed by those modernist monuments. In effect, North poses a thought-experiment: what might a reader find in a well-stocked bookstore in 1922, and how would such a reader understand what he or she found there? We envisioned the present *Companion*, on the model of North's book, as a collection of essays each of which might be entitled, '1899 (or 1912, 1916, 1993, 2001, etc.): A Return to the Scene of the Modern (or Postmodern)'.

Another relevant model – from another of our contributors – is Cary Nelson's *Repression and Recovery: Modern American Poetry and the Politics of Cultural Memory, 1910–1945* (1989) and its sequel (so to speak), his *Oxford Anthology of Modern American Poetry* (2000). Aiming to capture the 'historical simultaneity of modern poetry's diversity', Nelson seeks to recover writers 'lost' in the process of literary canonisation, as well as the range of alternative criteria for valuing these 'lost' figures (Nelson 1989: xii). In his book-length essay, as in his anthology, he juxtaposes poets familiar and unfamiliar, canonical and uncanonical, avowedly political and supposedly apolitical, much as they might have appeared in the pages of the era's little magazines and other periodicals. Indeed, the little magazines serve as a model for Nelson's project, both in their mingling of poets who only later would be marshalled into supposedly distinct groups, and in their still unfixed and exploratory sense of modernism's potential (Nelson 1989: 230). A contemporary equivalent of the modernist-era little magazine might be the World Wide Web, and it is surely no coincidence that Nelson's *Oxford Anthology* is associated with a web-site (www.english.uiuc.edu/maps) that actualises in its hypertextual form the proliferation of alternative narratives to which Nelson is committed. One might think of the present *Companion* as similarly hypertextual and cross-linked, though its medium is the printed page rather than the internet.

A well-stocked bookstore, a little magazine, a web-site, a newspaper page (see the essay below on the year 1916), a modernist or postmodernist novel: these are the sorts of analogues that come to mind for the essays assembled in this *Companion*. These, and of course also the street of the twentieth century itself, simultaneously continuous and punctuated, receding into indeterminate darkness but dispersedly illuminated, momentarily elucidated.

References

Calvino, Italo (1981) *If on a Winter's Night a Traveller*, London: Pan

Gibson, William (1984) *Neuromancer*, London: Pan

Greene, Graham (1980) *It's a Battlefield*, Harmondsworth: Penguin

Hollier, Denis *et al.* (1989) *A New History of French Literature*, Cambridge, MA: Harvard University Press

Mackenzie, Compton (1983) *Sinister Street*, Harmondsworth: Penguin

Márquez, Gabriel García (1977) *One Hundred Years of Solitude*, Harmondsworth: Penguin

Nelson, Cary (1989) *Repression and Recovery: Modern American Poetry and the Politics of Cultural Memory, 1910–1945*, Madison, WI: University of Wisconsin Press

North, Michael (1999) *1922: A Return to the Scene of the Modern*, New York: Oxford UP

Pynchon, Thomas (1973) *V.*, New York: Bantam

——(2000) *Gravity's Rainbow*, New York: Penguin

Schmidt, Siegfried (1985) 'On Writing Histories of Literature: Some Remarks from a Constructivist Point of View', *Poetics* 14, 279–301

Venturi, Robert (1977) *Complexity and Contradiction in Architecture*, 2nd edn, New York: Museum of Modern Art

Woolf, Virginia (1975) *Orlando*, Harmondsworth: Penguin

——(1986–94) *The Essays of Virginia Woolf*, vols 1–4, ed. Andrew McNeillie, London: Hogarth Press

I: The First Moderns

Chapter 1

1899, Vienna and the Congo: The Art of Darkness

Vassiliki Kolocotroni

On 21 April 1896, Dr Sigmund Freud presented his recent findings on 'The Aetiology of Hysteria' to the Society for Psychiatry and Neurology in Vienna, beginning with an explication of his new diagnostic method:

> I should like to bring before you an analogy taken from an advance that has in fact been made in another field of work.
>
> Imagine that an explorer arrives in a little-known region where his interest is aroused by an expanse of ruins, with remains of walls, fragments of columns, and tablets with half-effaced and unreadable inscriptions. He may content himself with inspecting what lies exposed to view, with questioning the inhabitants – perhaps semi-barbaric people – who live in the vicinity, about what tradition tells them of the history and meaning of these archaeological remains, and with noting down what they tell him – and he may then proceed on his journey. But he may act differently. He may have brought picks, shovels and spades with him, and he may set the inhabitants to work with these implements. Together with them he may start upon the ruins, clear away the rubbish, and, beginning from the visible remains, uncover what is buried. If his work is crowned with success, the discoveries are self-explanatory: the ruined walls are part of the ramparts of a palace or a treasure-house; the fragments of columns can be filled out into a temple; the numerous inscriptions, which, by good luck, may be bilingual, reveal an alphabet and a language, and, when they have been deciphered and translated, yield undreamed-of information about the events of the remote past, to commemorate which the monuments were built. Saxa loquuntur! [Stones speak!] (Freud 1962: 192)

The other 'field of work' which Freud instances is of course that of archaeology, the dashing endeavour that, in the latter part of the nineteenth century, had yielded so many 'treasures' both cultural and scientific. One imagines Freud's flourish striking a chord with the gathering of cultured Europeans who were his audience that day. Drawn from the senior ranks of the University of Vienna, they would surely have been familiar with such celebrated figures as Heinrich Schliemann, the enterprising German who discovered Troy in the 1870s, and Vienna's own Emanuel Löwy – epigrapher, excavator of Trysa, and the first Professor of Art and Archaeology at the University of Rome. According to one commentator on his work, Freud himself 'appears to have suffered throughout most of his professional life from a kind of "spade envy"' (Armstrong 2005: 112), and to have constructed in his fascination with archaeological success an 'alternative ego', 'a kind of fantasy-figure for an alternative life [he] could vicariously experience' (Armstrong 2005: 118). Freud's archaeological metaphors at any rate reappear, famously, as late as 1930, in *Civilization and Its Discontents*:

> in mental life nothing which has once been formed can perish . . . everything is somehow pre-
> served and . . . can once more be brought to light. Let us try and grasp what this assumption
> involves by taking an analogy from another field. We will choose as an example the history of
> the Eternal City . . . suppose that Rome is not a human habitation but a psychical entity with
> a similarly long and copious past . . . in which nothing that has once come into existence will
> have passed away and all the earlier phases of development continue to exist alongside the
> latest one. (Freud 1985a: 256, 257)

At the time of his lecture on 'The Aetiology of Hysteria', fame and success were still in the future, and Freud was still struggling to impress. He had to wait another six years before the significance of his own 'discoveries' was to be recognised by his peers – officially, in the form of his election to the post of Associate Professor, in 1902. Personally, Freud had been encouraged a little earlier by the publication of *The Interpretation of Dreams* – issued in the last months of 1899, though the publishers chose to front the volume with the epochal date '1900'. Its successful completion led to identification with another 'alternative ego', or 'fantasy-figure'. Famously, Freud idolised throughout his life a string of conquering and colonising heroes – Alexander the Great, Hannibal, Cromwell, Napoleon, Bismarck (Jones 1964; Schorske 1980; Marcus 1984). In a letter of 1 February 1900 to Wilhelm Fliess – a steady confidant during crucial, heroic, early years of personal and professional exploration – he declares:

> I am actually not at all a man of science, not an observer, not an experimenter, not a thinker.
> I am by temperament nothing but a conquistador – an adventurer, if you want it translated –
> with all the curiosity, daring, and tenacity characteristic of a man of this sort. (Freud 1985b: 398)

Written barely two months after the publication of *The Interpretation of Dreams*, the letter's triumphant tone is in stark contrast to the agonised litany of self-doubting statements in the month when his 'child of sorrow' (Freud 1985b: 359) was about to be delivered. In September 1899, Freud fired off a flurry of letters to Fliess with comments ranging from the defensive through the defiant to the downright depressed. On the 6th, for example, he records 'I am afraid it is – bunk', ending with the plea 'if only someone could tell me whether there is any real value to the whole thing!' (Freud 1985b: 369–70).

Such uncertainties were probably inevitable. More often than not, his pioneering explor- ations in the 'little-known region' of mental ruins had met with the psychiatric establish- ment's stony indifference. They had also required of Freud new tactics of spade-work and surveying; often in dark or difficult areas, alternately daunting and exciting. On the one hand, letters to Fliess seem keenly aware of the excitement and potential of transposing his studies of hysteria towards the analysis of dreams. In January 1898, for example, he records that 'all sorts of little things are teeming; dream and hysteria fit together ever more neatly': hysterical speech had taught Freud a language, a decipherable and translatable idiom, with its own grammar and laws (Freud 1985b: 294). Other communications nevertheless suggest challenges as well as excitement. In December 1896, Freud had offered Fliess one of the 'mottoes' of his work: 'the psychology of hysteria will be preceded by the proud words, *Introite et hic dii sunt* [from Aristotle's *De partibus animalium*, I: 5, "Enter – for here too are gods"]' (Freud 1985b: 205). Another classical allusion, this time in the epigraph of *The*

Interpretation of Dreams itself, characterises the territory of gods that Freud intended to enter and explore. Juno's 'proud words' from Virgil's *Aeneid* – '*Flectere si nequeosuperos, Acheronta movebo*' ['if I cannot bend the higher powers I will move the infernal regions'] – confirm Freud's determination to enter and excavate regions both dark and, at the turn of the century, still largely unknown.

Further ambitions accompanied these entries into dark regions. Two years after H. G. Wells published *The Time Machine* (1895), Freud conceived journeys into the under-world of dream as a kind of time-travel. Going inside also meant going back and forward in time to meet the residual force at the back of reason. Describing 'the latest product of my mental labor' in an excited note to Fliess in December 1897, Freud explains that

> The dim inner perception of one's own psychic apparatus stimulates thought illusions, which of course are projected onto the outside and, characteristically, into the future and beyond. Immortality, retribution, the entire beyond are all reflections of our psychic internal [world] . . . Psychomythology. (Freud 1985b: 286)

Freud's 'psychomythology' crucially links the past, present and future of mental processes, and with a single strike of the spade uncovers the loquacious ruins of a personal and collect-ive prehistory. He displays this significant find in Chapter VII of *The Interpretation of Dreams*:

> dreaming is on the whole an example of regression to the dreamer's earliest condition, a revival of his childhood, of the instinctual impulses which dominated it and of the methods of expres-sion which were available to him. Behind this childhood of the individual we are promised a picture of a phylogenetic childhood – a picture of the development of the human race of which the individual's development is in fact an abbreviated recapitulation influenced by the chance circumstances of life . . . we may expect that the analysis of dreams will lead us to a knowledge of man's archaic heritage, of what is psychically innate in him. Dreams and neuroses seem to have preserved more mental antiquities than we could have imagined possible. (Freud 1965: 587–8)

Freud's accounts of early, formative journeying in time and space offer points of entry of other kinds. The huge later impact of his thinking makes the appearance of *The Interpretation of Dreams* an appropriate marker, generally, for the opening of the twentieth century. But his early work also defines a particular domain of metaphors and structures which extend throughout the imagination of later decades. Images of excavation, of recov-ering 'events from the remote past', anticipate many twentieth-century narratives in which archaeology figures prominently, often within a textual practice itself sedimenting or inter-weaving numerous historical layers. Archaeology features centrally in this way in James Joyce's mythic method in *Ulysses* (1922), his continuous and systematic parallelism between contemporary Dublin life on a June day in 1904 and an 'underlying' stratum of events from the *Odyssey* of Homer. It features, too, in the poetry of T. S. Eliot and Ezra Pound. As in Freud's Rome, 'earlier phases of development continue to exist alongside the latest one' in much of Pound's poetry. 'We sit here . . . /there in the arena . . .' he remarks in Canto IV, emphasising simultaneities of past culture and present audience. These extend throughout *The Cantos* (1925–70), both in regular description of literal ruins – of 'the old sarcophagi,/ such as lie, smothered in grass, by San Vitale' (IX), for example – and in Pound's continual references to past culture and writing, fracturing his text into innumer-able allusive fragments (Pound 1967: 19, 27).

For Eliot, too, throughout *The Waste Land* (1922), allusions to earlier culture and writing offer fragments which can be shored against a ruinous phase of contemporary civilisation – practising possibilities Eliot had recently theorised in his essay 'Tradition and the Individual Talent' (1919). This 'archaeological' sense of the past's presence just under the surface, or ruinously visible in plain sight, persists throughout the century's poetry in the wake of Eliot and Pound, for instance in the long poem *Trilogy* (1944–6) by H.D. (Hilda Doolittle), and in Basil Bunting's *Briggflatts* (1965) and Geoffrey Hill's *Mercian Hymns* (1971), two 'pocket epics' excavating the English past. Other instances appear in the American Charles Olson's *Maximus Poems* (1950–70); in the Irish poet Seamus Heaney's 'bog poems' from his collections *Wintering Out* (1972) and *North* (1975), which meditate on ancient murder – evidenced by corpses exhumed from long-preserving peat – in the context of contemporary violence in Northern Ireland; and even in the pseudo-archaeological installations and mock ruins of the Scottish poet Ian Hamilton Finlay's garden of concrete poetry at Little Sparta.

Emerging during or immediately after the First World War, such interests in 'archaic heritage' might in Freud's terms be described as 'phylogenetic'. They were concerned, in other words – as Freud himself came to be in *Beyond the Pleasure Principle* (1920) and later works – with the difficult current state of the 'human race' and its history, at any rate in the West, and with redemptive recuperation of 'remains' and traditions. Contemporaries of Pound and Eliot – novelists especially – were often more disposed to share Freud's interest in 'what is psychically innate' not in the race as a whole but in individuals – in their present experience, and in its manifold connections with a recovered or revisited past. Many influences (see also Chapter 3 below) encouraged emphases on memory in modernist fiction – and its corresponding readiness to depart from linear narrative structures – but some correspond closely with Freud's exploration of an archaeology of consciousness. His description of the mind as an Eternal City, in which 'nothing that will have come into existence will have passed away' is echoed, for example, in D. H. Lawrence's description of Gudrun in *Women in Love* (1921), on the verge of sleep but

> conscious of everything – her childhood, her girlhood, all the forgotten incidents, all the unrealized influences and all the happenings she had not understood, pertaining to herself, to her family, to her friends . . . it was as if she drew a glittering rope of knowledge out of the sea of darkness, drew and drew and drew it out of the fathomless depths of the past, and still it did not come to an end, there was no end to it . . . she must haul and haul . . . from the endless depths of the unconsciousness. (Lawrence 1971: 391)

Lawrence's simile of a 'rope of knowledge' is close to Virginia Woolf's – of memory as a 'seamstress', threading together disparate parts of characters' experience, and of course of the novels in which they appear. Each image would be still more representative of modernist practice if less suggestive of deliberately chosen entries to the past. Such entries more often occur involuntarily in modernist fiction, in terms perhaps closer to Freud's 1899 account of 'Screen Memories' (Freud 1995: 117–26). 'Earlier phases of development' regularly connect with 'the latest one' almost without a stroke of the spade – through the kind of instant association Marcel Proust identifies in showing how a whole past landscape 'sprang into being, town and gardens alike', stimulated only by a madeleine cake his hero happens to taste (Proust 1985: I: 51).

'How could the literature of description possibly have any value, when it is only beneath the surface . . . that reality has its hidden existence', Proust also wonders in *A la recherche du temps perdu* (1913–27), adding that 'really everything is in the mind'

(Proust 1985: III: 930, 950). As his remarks confirm, Freud's significance for literature, in the years following his pioneering work at the turn of the century, is scarcely confined to matters of memory or the archaeological survival of the past in present consciousness. Instead, as critics regularly remark, Freud's work is paradigmatic of an age, and a literature, generally disposed towards expanding interests in individual psychology, and in exploring experience beneath the immediate surface of life. Literary developments early in the century could even be pictured much as Freud described his explorer's activities in 1896. The century's first decade, in this model, remains content with 'beginning from the visible' and 'inspecting what lies exposed to view' (Freud 1962: 192), typically in the social realism of fiction by Arnold Bennett, H. G. Wells, and John Galsworthy. By the 1920s, this 'literature of description' had been replaced by tactics better equipped to take narrative 'beneath the surface'. These included the free indirect discourse of D. H. Lawrence, mingling authorial tones with the inner voice of characters; the interior monologues of Virginia Woolf; or the streams of consciousness developed by Dorothy Richardson in the early volumes of *Pilgrimage* (1915–67), as well as by Joyce in *Ulysses* and William Faulkner in novels such as *The Sound and the Fury* (1929).

It was at any rate in terms of this shift in priorities, between visible and 'buried' worlds, that novelists emerging in the second and third decades of the century sought to distinguish themselves from their predecessors. D. H. Lawrence, for example, complained in 1928 about an excess of 'social being' in Galsworthy's fiction, to the detriment of the 'psychology of the free human individual' (Lawrence 1955: 121, 120). Woolf, famously, dismissed Edwardian novelists as materialists, explaining in her 'Modern Fiction' essay, first published in 1919, that 'for the moderns . . . the point of interest, lies very likely in the dark places of psychology' (Woolf 1986–94: 4: 162). In a draft, unpublished form of another essay, 'Mr Bennett and Mrs Brown' (1924), Woolf toyed with the idea that this change had occurred due to 'scientific reasons' such as the influence of Freud. She might plausibly have gone on to refer to a further mid-1890s scientific encouragement to probe beneath the surface – Wilhelm Röntgen's 1895 discovery of X-rays, later greatly to interest authors including Joseph Conrad and Thomas Mann. Yet Woolf also ponders 'how much we can learn' and 'make our own from science' (Woolf 1986–94: 3: 504). Any assessment of the significance of Freud's thinking for writers early in the twentieth century might likewise question how far, or how altogether directly, their innovations were indebted to his.

There were certainly direct connections. Though first translated into English only in 1909, Freud's work was rapidly popularised by his introductory *Five Lectures on Psycho-Analysis*, published the following year. By 1913, May Sinclair was helping establish the first psychoanalytic clinic in London, her awareness of Freud's theories later shaping novels such as *Mary Olivier* (1919) and *Life and Death of Harriet Frean* (1922). Dorothy Richardson was another early initiate: many others were soon alerted to Freud's theories of mind by the need to treat traumatised victims of the First World War – Rebecca West's *The Return of the Soldier* (1918) and Woolf's *Mrs Dalloway* (1925) examining forms of treatment for shell-shock which developed as a result. A general atmosphere of 'Freudianity', in Richardson's description, had evolved by the end of the war, and as Richard Aldington suggests in *Death of a Hero* (1929), partly because of it. By the early 1920s, in *Fantasia of the Unconscious and Psychoanalysis and the Unconscious* (1923), Lawrence similarly concluded – despite scepticisms of his own about psychoanalysis – that Freud was 'on the brink of a *Weltanschauung* [worldwide creed]' (Lawrence 1961: 198).

The power and eventual influence of Freud's thinking inevitably invites analysis of its own relations with power, in ways sharply focused by his early self-image as explorer or conquistador. One implication of his metaphors of exploration and archaeology is that the natives – or the analysand – may not be trusted, their 'tradition' offering only a screen, an unreliable or false consciousness. If the explorer is lucky, translation, truth and reconstruction may reward the journey. Where there was a ruin, a city may rise again, or at least, re-imagine itself intact. Fragments once hidden or unintelligible may then be exposed and collected, meaningfully, to be displayed in the museum of the cured mind. Yet in describing this enlightening pursuit of truth, understanding and reconstruction, Freud extends uncritically the language of late nineteenth-century imperialism; of Europe's exploitative encounter with 'perhaps semi-barbaric people'. The commentator who identified Freud's 'spade envy' therefore raises – referring to Britain's imperial appropriation of Greek antiquities – an apt if 'impertinent question: to what extent does the analysand lose her Elgin marbles in the course of Freud's scientific expedition?' (Armstrong 2005: 121). The licence to journey, unearth and preserve is backed, both literally and metaphorically, by political power:

> For the stones are made to speak by those with the power to do so; that is, those who can erect temples, mausoleums, and triumphal arches, and those who can recover and reconstruct them. In the nineteenth century at least, only empires excavated empires. (Armstrong 2005: 122)

*

Powers of empire, and cryptic encounters with 'semi-barbaric people', were central issues in another highly influential publication in the last year of the nineteenth century: Joseph Conrad's *Heart of Darkness*, serialised in *Blackwood's Magazine* in 1899 before publication as a novella in 1902. Like Freud in Vienna, Conrad's narrator begins by describing little-known regions to an audience of cultured, distinguished Europeans – the Lawyer, the Accountant and the Director of Companies who 'hear about one of Marlow's inconclusive experiences' at nightfall on the Thames (Conrad 1988: 11). This twilit setting immediately suggests a shady complicity between colonised territories and the centre of empire – once itself 'one of the dark places of the earth', Marlow suggests, when it was a subject of imperial rule, in Roman times, and not its principal agent and beneficiary (Conrad 1988: 9). Further complicities are soon established between his civilised audience on the Thames and the processes of empire Conrad most deplored. Marlow breaks off his narrative of the Congo to address his listeners directly, describing their various professions as no more than the performance of 'monkey tricks . . . on respective tight-ropes' for 'half-a-crown a tumble'. Though the description elicits a growled 'try to be civil, Marlow' from one of its targets, for Conrad, as for his narrator, a cynical materialism had become almost a defining characteristic of 'civil' society in Europe at the turn of the century (Conrad 1988: 36). 'Il n'y a plus d'Europe' [Europe no longer exists] Conrad remarked in 1905, 'there is only an armed and trading continent, the home of slowly maturing economical contests for life and death, and of loudly proclaimed worldwide ambitions' (Conrad 1925: 112). Enthralled to 'the supremacy of material interests', individual nations in this 'armed and trading continent' compete with each other in Africa primarily for 'spheres of trade' and for the self-serving 'privilege of improving the nigger (as a buying machine)' (Conrad 1925: 107).

    The novel Conrad published the previous year, *Nostromo* (1904), had also been centrally concerned with 'material interests', tracing their corruption of individuals, and eventually of an entire country, helped by a 'capitalist of shrewd mind' – the San Francisco financier, Holroyd, committed to 'the religion of silver and iron' (Conrad 1969: 66, 71). Alert to incipient US economic imperialism in *Nostromo*, Conrad's strongest criticism of empire and its material imperatives nevertheless already appears in *Heart of Darkness*. Though ready to favour the 'real work' done in British territories – even what he calls 'an idea at the back of it' which might conceivably 'redeem' imperialism itself – Marlow generally dismisses empire as a matter of 'conquerors . . . brute force . . . robbery with violence, aggravated murder on a great scale' (Conrad 1988: 10, 6). His narrative also shows a native population reduced not even to 'buying machines', but rather to a kind of scrapyard of inert mechanical components. On first landing at his Company's African station, he immediately encounters 'a boiler wallowing in the grass . . . an undersized railway truck lying there on its back with its wheels in the air . . . pieces of decaying machinery'. Soon after, he meets the 'black shadows of disease and starvation . . . moribund shapes' of a group of discarded, 'inefficient', native workers. An interchange of attributes connects the two encounters: the overturned truck looks like the 'carcass of some animal'; the skeletal natives merely like 'bundles of acute angles' (Conrad 1988: 19–21). While imperial materialism confers animate or zoological characteristics on machinery, it imposes an inert mechanical geometry on the human.

Grimly evident among victims of empire, the same processes nevertheless threaten its agents, too. Marlow's next encounter is with the 'amazing', dandified figure of the Company's chief accountant, immediately reminding him of 'a hairdresser's dummy' (Conrad 1988: 21). This is appropriate, for the accountant is his first source of information about the 'chief of the Inner Station', Kurtz, who turns out to be a kind of dummy, too – not the presumed 'emissary of pity, and science, and progress' but eventually a 'hollow sham', committed only to 'something that is really profitable': the ivory trade (Conrad 1988: 28, 67). Alone and bereft of ideals, Kurtz had 'looked within' and 'gone mad', finding the wilderness 'echoed loudly within him because he was hollow at the core' (Conrad 1988: 65, 58). The description makes him a prototype for a long line of Conradian 'hollow men' or semi-automata. This begins as early as 1896 in 'An Outpost of Progress' – a Congo tale broadly anticipating *Heart of Darkness* – with central figures who 'lived like blind men in a large room, aware only of what came in contact with them (and that only imperfectly), but unable to see the general aspect of things' (Conrad 1998: 253). Later examples include the spiritually bankrupt mining engineer, Gould, in *Nostromo*, and the aptly named financier, de Barral, in *Chance* (1913). Verloc, in *The Secret Agent* (1907), is another, described as resembling 'a mechanical figure', with 'an automaton's absurd air of being aware of the machinery inside him' (Conrad 1967: 162) Not surprisingly, Conrad himself expressed a peculiar interest in marionettes – 'especially those of the old kind, with wires, thick as my little finger, coming out of the top of the head' – described as 'superhuman, fascinating' in a letter of 1897 (Taxidou 1998: 87).

As a tone of gothic anticipation in its early pages suggests, Conrad's concerns in *Heart of Darkness* extend well beyond the reifying effects material interests impose on both coloniser and colonised. Marlow's journey into what 'had become a place of darkness' begins with an 'eerie' encounter in the Company's European office with two 'uncanny and fateful' figures. 'Often far away', he recalls,

> I thought of these two, guarding the door of Darkness, knitting black wool as for a warm pall, one introducing, introducing continuously to the unknown, the other scrutinizing the cheery and foolish faces with unconcerned old eyes. *Ave!* Old knitter of black wool. *Morituri te salutant.* [Hail! Those who are about to die salute you.] Not many of those she looked at ever saw her again. (Conrad 1988: 12–14)

If not a god, certainly two of the ancient Fates are in attendance here, weaving Marlow's destiny out of black wool: an introduction to a 'place of darkness' comparable to Freud's anticipated entry into 'infernal regions' and into negotiations with the deities who inhabit them. Later experiences in these regions lead Marlow to views about the 'psychically innate' – about 'phylogenetic childhood . . . the development of the human race' – potentially as disturbing, at the turn of the century, as Freud's. Marlow eventually finds himself concerned less by complicities with the material interests of empire than by affinities with the 'black and incomprehensible frenzy' of 'prehistoric' natives encountered while travelling upriver, into what he describes as 'a night of first ages'. He claims to view these frenzied natives 'as sane men would . . . an enthusiastic outbreak in a madhouse'. But he also acknowledges 'the thought of their humanity – like yours – the thought of your remote kinship with this wild and passionate uproar', concluding that 'the mind of man is capable of anything – because everything is in it, all the past as well as all the future' (Conrad 1988: 37–8).

The erosion of distinctions between civilisation and barbarism, reason and anarchy, intelligence and instinct which his vision implies remained a concern throughout the twentieth century, often grimly confirmed by a history in which 'il n'y a plus d'Europe' seemed a more and more just evaluation. In this and other ways, *Heart of Darkness* remained an example, or an influence, for many narratives of empire which followed, including E. M. Forster's *A Passage to India* (1924); Graham Greene's *The Heart of the Matter* (1948); and even *Dispatches* (1977), an account of the American war in Vietnam by the journalist Michael Herr, who also contributed material to the script of Francis Ford Coppola's Vietnam film *Apocalypse Now* (1978). In 1899, however, Conrad's dark assessment of Europe's relations with its empire distinguished him sharply from other authors of colonial experience among his acquaintances, such as Rider Haggard and Rudyard Kipling – both, incidentally, appreciated by Freud. Conrad's views were still further from other contemporary novelists working in popular or 'adventure' modes. Such novelists of 'imperial adventure' are more obviously vulnerable to criticism expressed in late twentieth-century postcolonial analysis – that Europeans consolidated a sense of superiority, during the period of empire, by ascribing their own negative characteristics to the colonised native, simultaneously stressing their absolute separateness from the native so characterised. Yet as the Nigerian novelist Chinua Achebe famously pointed out, Conrad himself might be susceptible to the same kind of criticism in a different form (see Achebe 2001). While acknowledging an atavistic affinity with 'black and incomprehensible frenzy', Marlow simply perpetuates the patronising assumption that frenzy and the irrational are particular prerogatives of the natives, making darkness or blackness their defining quality metaphorically as well as literally. Like Freud in 1896, even while pursuing better understanding of the 'civilised' mind, Conrad may extend some of the assumptions of imperialism and of Europe's continuing encounter with supposedly 'semi-barbaric people', sharing, too, in doing so, its rhetoric of 'niggers' and 'savages'. As the critic Terry Eagleton succinctly suggests, in showing that 'Western civilisation is at base as barbarous as African society', *Heart of Darkness* 'disturbs imperialist assumptions to the precise degree that it reinforces them' (Eagleton 1990:135).

Conrad's interests, of course, were not only 'phylogenetic', or even concentrated primarily on Western or African society in general. On the contrary, as critics have extensively discussed, Marlow's journey into the interior is an exploration not only into the base of Western civilisation, but principally into the depths of the narrator himself. Little credence accrues to his opening disclaimer, 'I don't want to bother you much with what happened to me personally'. Instead, his journey to 'the farthest point of navigation and the culminating point of my experience' offers striking parallels with Freud's closely contemporary explorations into the darker phases of the individual's mind (Conrad 1988: 11). It also has interesting implications for ways a new and deeper archaeology of consciousness figured in fiction in the first decades of the twentieth century. Marlow's first-person, ostensibly oral narrative – supposedly improvised on the spot out of a set of more or less distant recollections – obviously facilitates the kind of interests in memory, and reliance on it as a structuring device for fiction, discussed above. This is an opportunity Conrad exploited more fully in the novel he was writing alongside *Heart of Darkness*, *Lord Jim* (1900), and one later extended still further by his erstwhile collaborator, Ford Madox Ford, in *The Good Soldier* (1914). In some ways, the idea in all these novels of compressing a story into a single evening of telling extended still further – into 1920s fiction such as Joyce's *Ulysses* (1922) or Woolf's *Mrs Dalloway* (1925), each concentrated on one day of present experience, with characters' memories used to stitch in the past.

Heart of Darkness makes fuller use of another opportunity offered by a fictionalised oral narrative – the opportunity to discuss the tactics and problems of storytelling directly with an immediate audience, located within the novel. For Marlow, these problems are substantial, extensively discussed, and further comparable with some of Freud's interests at the time – particularly those expressed in that 1896 account of the difficulties of 'a little-known region'. For Marlow, Kurtz himself is 'a little-known region', just as much as the territory he inhabits, neither offering much in terms of 'what lies exposed to view'. At one point in his narrative, he explicitly complains that the distraction of 'mere incidents of the surface' ensures that 'the reality . . . fades. The inner truth is hidden' (Conrad 1988: 36). At another, he questions whether his listeners can 'see' Kurtz at all, adding

> Do you see the story? Do you see anything? It seems to me I am trying to tell you a dream – making a vain attempt, because no relation of a dream can convey the dream-sensation . . . that notion of being captured by the incredible which is the very essence of dreams . . .
>
> No, it is impossible; it is impossible to convey the life-sensation of any given epoch of one's existence – that which makes its truth, its meaning . . . We live, as we dream – alone. (Conrad 1988: 30)

Marlow, in other words, and by extension his audience, share some of the puzzlement of Freud's explorer, confronted by an intermingled 'dream-sensation' and 'life-sensation', and by the lonely, impenetrable particularity of individual consciousness.

Apart, that is, from an opportunity Marlow emphasises immediately after questioning his audience's chances of seeing anything at all. Following a moment's reflection, he adds 'of course in this you fellows see more than I could then. You see me, whom you know'. This is literally true for his immediate circle of listeners, on their yacht at nightfall on the Thames. But it is also true for the wider audience of Conrad's novel, a readership able to 'see more' than Marlow could himself by interpreting the hesitations, problems, particularities and oversights in his narrative. Part of 'the essence of dreams' is their frequent opacity to the dreamer, and many aspects of Marlow's experience in *Heart of Darkness* – such as the scale of his identification with Kurtz – invite the deductive intervention of readers to provide interpretations he cannot produce for himself. When Marlow describes his impression of seeing Kurtz looking at him out of the 'glassy panel' of his fiancée's door in Brussels, for example, readers are left to work out that he may be seeing a reflection of himself, and to assess for themselves all this implies.

In concentrating interpretive faculties on the psychology of an individual in this way, Conrad's tactics bear comparison with others developing in turn-of-the-century fiction.

Marlow's suggestion that his audience 'see more than I could' recalls *The Ambassadors* (1903) by Conrad's friend, the expatriate American novelist Henry James, in which the central character, Strether, remarks of his experience 'You see more in it than I', to which his confidant replies, 'of course I see you in it' (James 1973: 46). Unlike Marlow, Strether is not a narrator, though he is a character whose point of view – James's tactics ensure – readers almost completely share. In each case, James and Conrad present narratives in which, rather like the fiancée's door, the thoughts and motives of central characters or narrators are comprehensively reflected. Instead of a straightforward 'life-sensation', each author traces complex inscriptions of experience 'beyond the visible', within individual minds and responses, anticipating much modernist writing developing in the next decades (see Stevenson 1996)

On the Thames, however, fading twilight leaves Marlow less than fully visible to his listeners, one of whom remarks that

> it had become so pitch dark that we . . . could hardly see one another. For a long time already he, sitting apart, had been no more to us than a voice . . . I listened, I listened on the watch for the sentence, for the word, that would give me the clue to the faint uneasiness inspired by this narrative that seemed to shape itself without human lips in the heavy night-air of the river.

Marlow himself sometimes finds words equally mysterious, equally fugitive in providing a 'clue' about the meaning of experience: recalling one stage of his difficulties in 'seeing' Kurtz, he mentions that the latter was 'just a word for me' (Conrad 1988: 29). Faint uneasiness of this kind is a predecessor of further features of twentieth-century writing. While Conrad's work, like James's, is a precursor of modernist writing's growing concentration on processes of mind, it also anticipates modernism's need to develop a language and a style able to reflect inner workings of the self – ones potentially lying beyond the reach of words or even rational consciousness itself. Like Freud's explorer, writers early in the century therefore had to develop 'an alphabet and a language' in order to 'yield undreamed of information' about the self. Sometimes evident as a problem in Lawrence's writing, this need is in one way eventually answered by Joyce in *Finnegans Wake* (1939), in the 'curios of signs' and 'allaphbed' he invents to represent the dreaming mind (Joyce 1975: 18). In other ways, darkling communication described in the passage above might be seen to have still further resonances with later writing. Marlow's dubious musings on his storytelling powers are subtly metafictional, reflecting on and challenging the validity of narrative even while continuing to engage in it. Along with uneasiness expressed about words, this anticipates the self-conscious scrutiny of artistic language and strategies characteristic of modernist writing, Joyce's particularly. There is also an anticipation of deeper doubts about the reliability of narrative in a late twentieth-century postmodern age – one whose uncertainties about selfhood and identity included the possibility that it is language that speaks the self, as if out of the darkening air, rather than vice versa.

Conrad's own language, like Freud's, further demonstrates difficulties of moving towards the priorities of a new century. Though each anticipates so broadly the outlook of a new age, each is also, as discussed earlier, still confined by the vision of the old: enthralled by late nineteenth-century archaeology, or inadvertently enwrapped in the rhetoric and assumptions of an imperialism repudiated consciously. In this and other ways, even apart from its extensive direct or indirect influences, the work of each vividly characterises the opening of the century and the changing priorities of that moment. Some of these changes are summed up in Marlow's conversation with the Company's Doctor, an amateur 'alienist' or psychiatrist who examines him before he sets out on his fateful journey:

'I always ask leave, in the interests of science, to measure the crania of those going out there,' he said. 'And when they come back, too?' I asked. 'Oh, I never see them,' he remarked, 'and, moreover the changes take place inside, you know'. (Conrad 1988: 15)

References

Achebe, Chinua (2001) 'An Image of Africa: Racism in Conrad's *Heart of Darkness*' (1975), in Vincent B. Leitch, gen. ed., *The Norton Anthology of Theory and Criticism*, New York and London: W. W. Norton, 1783–96

Armstrong, Richard H. (2005) *A Compulsion for Antiquity: Freud and the Ancient World*, Ithaca, NY, and London: Cornell University Press

Conrad, Joseph (1998) 'An Outpost of Progress', in Elleke Boehmer, ed., *Empire Writing*, Oxford: Oxford University Press, 248–70

——(1925) *Notes on Life and Letters*, Edinburgh and London: John Grant

——(1967) *The Secret Agent*, Harmondsworth: Penguin

——(1969) *Nostromo*, Harmondsworth: Penguin

——(1988) *Heart of Darkness: An Authoritative Text, Backgrounds and Sources, Criticism*, ed. Robert Kimbrough, New York and London: W. W. Norton

Eagleton, Terry (1990) *Criticism and Ideology: A Study in Marxist Literary Theory*, London: Verso

Freud, Sigmund (1962) 'The Aetiology of Hysteria', *The Standard Edition of the Complete Psychological Works of Sigmund Freud*, vol. 3, trans. and ed. James Strachey, London: Hogarth Press, 191–221

——(1965) *The Interpretation of Dreams*, trans. and ed. James Strachey, New York: Avon Books

——(1985a) *Civilization, Society and Religion: Group Psychology, Civilization and Its Discontents and Other Works* (The Pelican Freud Library, vol. 12), trans. James Strachey, ed. Albert Dickson, Harmondsworth: Penguin

——(1985b) *The Complete Letters of Sigmund Freud to Wilhelm Fliess 1887–1904*, trans. and ed. Jeffrey Moussaieff Masson, Cambridge, MA, and London: The Belknap Press

——(1995) 'Screen Memories', in *The Freud Reader*, ed. Peter Gay, London: Vintage, 117–26

James, Henry (1973) *The Ambassadors*, Harmondsworth: Penguin

Jones, Ernest (1964) *The Life and Work of Sigmund Freud*, ed. and abridged Lionel Trilling and Steven Marcus, Harmondsworth: Penguin

Joyce, James (1975) *Finnegans Wake*, London: Faber and Faber

Lawrence, D. H. (1955) 'John Galsworthy', in *Selected Literary Criticism*, ed. Anthony Beal, London: Heinemann, 118–31

——(1961) *Fantasia of the Unconscious and Psychoanalysis and the Unconscious*, London: Heinemann

——(1971) *Women in Love*, Harmondsworth: Penguin

Marcus, Steven (1984) *The Culture of Psychoanalysis: Studies in the Transition from Victorian Humanism to Modernity*, Boston, MA: George Allen and Unwin

Pound, Ezra (1967) *Selected Cantos of Ezra Pound*, London: Faber and Faber

Proust, Marcel (1985) *Remembrance of Things Past*, trans. C. K. Scott Moncrieff and
    Terence Kilmartin, 3 vols, Harmondsworth: Penguin
Schorske, Carl E. (1980) *Fin-de-Siècle Vienna: Politics and Culture*, London: Weidenfeld and
    Nicolson
Stevenson, Randall (1996) 'The Modern Novel', in Richard Bradford, ed., *Introducing
    Literary Studies*, Hemel Hempstead: Harvester Wheatsheaf, 439–80
Taxidou, Olga (1998) *The Mask: A Periodical Performance by Edward Gordon Craig*,
    Amsterdam: Harwood Academic Publishers
Woolf, Virginia (1986–94) *The Essays of Virginia Woolf*, vols 1–4, ed. Andrew McNeillie,
    London: Hogarth Press

Chapter 2

1912, London, Chicago, Florence, New York: Modernist Moments, Feminist Mappings

Linda A. Kinnahan

Imagine a moment in 1912 London, picking up a copy of the *Poetry Review*, published in conjunction with the new Poetry Society of England and founded by editor Harold Monro in January of that year. It is May, and the issue on the stands is a special edition of 'Women-Poets', evidence of Monro's championing of this undervalued group. Given two decades of incessant talk of the 'New Woman' in Europe and America and ten years of increased militancy – labelled 'feminism' by 1910 – the focus of this issue is not entirely surprising. Women are, after all, constantly in the news with their protests and parades and activism for the vote; women have themselves produced copious volumes of writing in regard to women and economics, sex, family, labour and political rights. Networks of feminists and their organisations cross lines of class and nationality, creating a truly international movement focused on myriad issues of suffrage, sexuality, birth control, education reform, civil rights, labour reform and economic equality. A wave of activism suffuses 1912 and the years just prior, so an issue of a new journal claiming to promote new forms of poetry that heralds the contributions of women seems perfectly a part of the moment. Open the pages and read the preface (probably written by Monro), and feel somehow knocked off keel, especially if you are one of those new women:

> He [the Great Poet] has represented Woman so adequately in poetry that there seemed scarcely any call for her to represent herself. Now at last, however, some change is taking place. Woman, late though it be, is becoming conscious of herself. . . . *Despite all emancipation*, Woman still lives in a garden and we must receive her verses gift-wise, as we might some fine broidery. She will play with a fancy as lovingly as with a child; she enjoys delicacy in her verse, and soft light shades: she loves especially a gentle hopefulness. Her poetry is the expression of personal moods, or of the mystical and apparently supernatural: it is remarkable how seldom she may be reckoned a whole poet. ('Women-Poets'1912: 199–200, emphasis added)

That women should be graciously acknowledged for their efforts while simultaneously excluded from aesthetic formations of poetry, particularly those taken seriously within evolving articulations of modernism, colours these comments and undercuts Monro's modernising claims for *Poetry Review*. Monro had already published another such voice articulating the need to modernise poetry: Ezra Pound's 'Prologomena (sic)', which appeared in Monro's second issue. Now absorbed into literary history as signalling a wake-up call to abandon the old and invent the new, this is, not uncharacteristically, a thinly disguised condemnation of the 'old' as feminine (sentimental, emotional) and the 'new' as masculine (hard, vigorous), demanding a poetry 'free from emotional slither' and from 'blurry', 'messy' and 'sentimentalistic' failings, and equating the new and the modern with a 'harder and saner' poetry (Pound 1912: 75–6). To read Pound's poetic proclamations alongside the editorial introduction to the 'Women-Poets' issue – which inevitably although unintentionally describes women's poetry in terms that Pound has condemned – is to get a foretaste of the gender politics of modernist histories that perpetuate underlying cultural assumptions. In doing so, they diminish, erase and marginalise the pioneering work of women poets, editors and commentators in creating new forms, supporting modernist projects and advancing new ideas about poetry. That their ideas have often preceded, influenced or enabled the modernist innovations attributed most often to men like Pound, Joyce or Eliot; or that their experiments offer alternative versions of modernist poetics; or that their publishing and editing energies kept something called 'modernism' alive are factors all too often treated superficially, if at all, in conventional modernist histories.

London and Chicago: *The Freewoman/The New Freewoman*

A strong anxiety over women's ascending ambitions accompanied the increasingly public debate over suffragism and feminism. The threat of radical feminist discourse underscores a buried but significant modernist moment in October 1912 when *The Freewoman: A Humanist Weekly* was silenced. The publisher, W. H. Smith, rejected it for its scandalous ideas about women, resulting in its banning from bookshops (Green 2003: 226). Begun a year earlier, in late 1911, under the name of *The Freewoman*, the journal responded to the conservatism of the suffrage movement alleged by its founding editors, Dora Marsden and May Gawthorpe, who themselves had taken part in militant protests and hunger strikes on behalf of the movement.

The suffragist movement in Britain depended, in the first decade of the twentieth century, upon strategies of spectacle and shock, intending to generate public visibility through consciously 'unladylike' stunts such as hunger striking, public protests and other spectacles. The militant turn in the movement, spearheaded by suffrage leaders, Emmeline, Christabel and Sylvia Pankhurst, accompanied intensified international activism among American, British and European suffragists and increased their visibility. In 1912, for example, the woman's popular American magazine *Good Housekeeping* ran an article on Emmeline Pankhurst by feminist journalist Rheta Dorr (Adickes 1997: 40). For all of their unorthodox uses of public spectacle, however, the Pankhurst organisation and the suffrage movement attracted criticism from more radical elements of a newly emerging feminist movement that increasingly expanded the discussion of the women's rights into arenas of sexuality, birth control, labour and economics, offering critiques of traditional social institutions of family and religion. Seen by the new feminists as too conservative and morally timid, the focus on the vote to the exclusion of more far-reaching ideas of women's equality motivated Marsden and Gawthorpe to advocate a bolder intellectual, economic, and sexual agenda for women's liberation.

Joined by nineteen-year-old Cicely Fairfield as Assistant Editor, *The Freewoman* included essays by notably radical feminists such as Theresa Billington Greig, who would also write for *The Woman Rebel*, Margaret Sanger's organ of the birth control movement in America. Fairfield adopted her better known literary name of Rebecca West in 1912 to spare her family embarrassment over her feminist publications. Writing a few years after the journal's demise, West asserted that the 'greatest service that the paper did its country was through its unblushingness' about sexuality, for it

> mentioned sex loudly and clearly and repeatedly and in the worst possible taste . . . [provid-ing] an immense service to the world by shattering, as nothing else would, as not the mere cries of intention towards independence had ever done, the romantic conception of women. (West 1926: 648–9)

Writing also for the socialist *Clarion*, West carried her feminist banner to diverse audiences during this time (Green 2003: 228–31). Like other new feminists in Britain, America, and elsewhere, by 1912 she was espousing a view of women's rights that demanded a 'shatter-ing' of traditional androcentric structures and assumptions about society, art, and the human self, a breaking and restructuring urgently necessitated by the modern moment.

When the journal re-launched itself in June 1913 as *The New Freewoman: An Individualist Review*, West soon sought literary input from Ezra Pound. Pound came to the journal through a network of literary feminist friends, meeting West through writer Violet Hunt (and her husband Ford Madox Ford), who in turn had met him through the poet and novelist May Sinclair, who befriended him in 1909. Sinclair's 1912 pamphlet publication 'Feminism' situates her clearly within the new, more radical wave of British feminists. Three years into her friendship with Pound, Sinclair also published *The Three Brontës*, a study of the nineteenth-century women novelists suggesting the need for women writers to know a tradition of women predecessors. Virginia Woolf would later articulate this need in *A Room of One's Own* (1929), implicitly questioning modernism's obsession with trad-ition as male histories, forms and voices. Sinclair's feminist interests, combined with her focus on women's literary traditions and the relation between her own poetic work and gender, intertwine modernism's beginnings with an insistence – as early as 1912 – upon women as active makers of culture, not passive objects marked by culture.

Indeed, Pound was in the midst of women making culture in the early teens, benefiting from their efforts. With the 1912 inception of Harriet Monroe's *Poetry, A Magazine of Verse*, Pound quickly moved from contributor/supporter to the position of foreign correspondent, shortly thereafter beginning his involvement with *The New Freewoman*. His use of both magazines to promote his own ideas about poetry and to support poets he admired is well documented, and the significance of Pound's efforts should not be underestimated in understanding how modernist poetry came to construct itself and its readership. However, the 'Pound Era' or 'Men of 1914' narratives that inform literary histories of modernist poetry remove Pound from both a literal feminist context and a history of women advan-cing ideas of the 'new' in poetry and society. To consider these contexts asks us to think of modernism as prefaced and infused by the most unsettling challenge to gender ideas ever played out upon the international western scene. Such a reading of modernist literary his-tories suggests a continual appropriation of women's revolutionary ideas and efforts along-side the concomitant erasure of the women themselves. The example of *The New Freewoman*'s evolution into the modernist journal *The Egoist* is a case in point of such appropriation and erasure.

Upon meeting West, Pound offered to republish pieces from *Poetry* in *The New Freewoman*, most notably a selection of his 'Imagist' poems in 1913, introduced by a short essay by West. Pound's involvement coincided with a shift in Dora Marsden's own inter-ests toward the philosophy of egoism espoused by German philosopher Max Stirner (which had informed her ideas about women virtually from the start) and away from political feminism, a shift that seems to have crystallised during *The Freewoman*'s period of dormancy in 1912. West would later describe *The Freewoman* as

> coming to an end psychically when it came to an end physically . . . due to the fact that Dora Marsden started on a train of thought which led her to metaphysics. She began to lose her enthusiasm for bringing women's industry on equal terms with men. . . . I waged war with her on this point. (West 1926: 648–9)

The serendipitous – for Pound – loosening of the feminist focus allowed him to advance his literary goals, an ambition that involved, intentionally or not, encouraging the suppression of the feminist agenda. This ambition, in West's eyes, was an 'ambition to benefit his friends' (West 1970: 12).

In the course of its run, from June until December 1913, *The New Freewoman* diluted the feminist radicalism of its earlier incarnation and increased the 'individualist' philosophical/metaphysical component. This was encouraged by Marsden's own trajectory from a hunger-striking suffragist to an advocate for individual power who disdained the 'weakness' of the socially oppressed, ideas embracing the philosophy of egoism and spurring the landmark name-change of the journal to *The Egoist*. However, the involvement of men – particularly Pound – clearly contributed to Marsden's announcement in the issue of 15 December 1913 (Vol. 1, No. 13) that 'it has become clear that its present title can be regarded only as a serious handicap'. Persuaded by a (male) group of 'regular contributors' who included Pound, Allen Upward, Richard Aldington, Huntly Carter and Reginald W. Kauffman, Marsden included in the announcement a letter from these self-described 'men of letters' requesting 'another title which will mark the character of your paper as an organ of individualists of both sexes' and would eliminate any confusion of the journal 'with organs devoted solely to the advocacy of an unimportant reform in an obsolete political institution'. Marsden announced that the first issue of 1914 would bear the new 'neutral title' of *The Egoist*. This would become one of the most significant modernist little magazines of the 1910s, and as early as 1914 would begin serialising fiction such as Joyce's *A Portrait of the Artist as a Young Man*, and, immediately afterwards, Wyndham Lewis's *Tarr*, novels which became cornerstones of a male-dominated modernist canon.

While an increasing emphasis on literary content accompanied these developments, West's own disappointment with the altered social stance would eventually combine with her dissatisfaction over the increasing involvement of Pound and the poet and novelist Richard Aldington in literary editing. Soon after the name-change, West resigned, claiming in not-so-veiled terms that there was 'an *arriviste* American poet who intended to oust me, and his works and those of his friends continually appeared in the paper without having passed me. This was unbearably irritating . . .' (West 1926: 649). Aldington replaced West as literary editor, while Harriet Shaw Weaver (who had been involved with *The Freewoman* since its 1911 inception) took over as editor. Marsden stepped back to the position of contributing editor so that she might continue to submit columns on individualism and egoism.

What would prove to be a temporary failure of the feminist magazine nonetheless held the seeds for its eventual transformation into *The Egoist* and its role in asserting a modern movement clustered around Ezra Pound – and later, T. S. Eliot. The customary association of *The Egoist* with these writers displaces its publication history as a feminist journal (Levenson 1984: 63–79; Benstock 1986: 364–5; Kinnahan 1994: 22–6; Clarke 1996; Morrison 2001: 84–132). Moreover, centralising Pound and Eliot obscures the space that *was* given to women poets and writers in *The Egoist*, which did publish and review work by new women artists. Marianne Moore's first published poems, outside of publications at her alma mater Bryn Mawr College, appear in 1915 and include the staunchly anti-war poem 'To Military Progress'. H.D. (Hilda Doolittle) regularly published poems and reviews, including significant reviews of other women such as Moore. Her 1916 review of Charlotte Mew's *The Farmer's Bride* praised Mew as the best of her generation working with dramatic monologue. Between 1913 and 1916, this British writer pioneered experiments with stream of consciousness in verse, and the poem from which *The Farmer's Bride* takes its name was published in 1912 in the *Nation* (Dowson 2002: 181). Mew's early experiments with poetic form and stream of consciousness have remained relatively ignored, despite her recognition by other poets at the time.

Chicago and London: Imagism and *Poetry*

While successfully helping to persuade Marsden to change the name of *The New Freewoman* to *The Egoist*, Pound was also aggressively battling with Harriet Monroe, by December 1913, over altering *Poetry* magazine, which had been published for a little more than a year – since October 1912. The story of *Poetry*'s beginnings, so often foregrounding Pound's early involvement as the foreign correspondent, reveals multiple narrative threads linking the magazine's inception in 1912 with the efforts of women in relation to an incipiently self-conscious modernist poetics, foregrounding the creative innovations and traditions involving women at this time.

Born and raised in Chicago, Harriet Monroe was fifty-one when she decided in 1911 to turn her own poetic ambitions toward the lofty goal of creating a literary magazine promoting a new American poetry. She sent letters to Chicago businessmen inviting financial patronage and wrote to poets in the course of 1911 and 1912, including Amy Lowell, whose first book of poetry, *A Dome of Many-Colored Glass*, appeared in 1912. Lowell's enthusiasm and support for the magazine was immediate and enduring, and correspondence between Lowell and Monroe over the years yields insight into women's infamous struggles with Pound, as well as their ideas about the scope of poetic innovation. As a subscriber to *Poetry* from the start, Lowell responded to the January 1913 issue with particular enthusiasm, reading the poetry of H.D. for the first time and recognising her own poetic proclivities to be similarly 'imagiste'. Wanting to contact the group of poets that *Poetry* introduced as Imagists (Pound, Richard Aldington, H.D.), Lowell travelled to England to meet them and affirm her affiliation. Her subsequent efforts in support of modern poetry included close correspondences with H.D., after that first London visit, and with Margaret Anderson when she began the *Little Review* in 1914. More famously, it also included her publication of three Imagist anthologies in the 1910s.

As part of a network of women promoting new poets and their work, Lowell laboured behind the scenes to advance the cause of Imagism, and Pound (who had included her 'In the Garden' in *Des Imagistes*, his 1913 anthology of Imagist poets) invited her in 1914 to consider becoming editor of *The Egoist*, in part to help bolster the financial situation of the journal through monetary contribution (Pound 1971: 31–4). Women could be useful to Pound, especially when they supported his causes financially and/or editorially (as he expected from Marsden, Monroe and West at this time). Correspondence ensued over the invitation during February and March, following on the heels of Pound's complaints to Lowell about Monroe's running of her magazine and his threats to resign in disgust over her editorial decisions. Receiving an unexpected monetary contribution in March, the journal was able to survive without Lowell's help, and Pound withdrew the offer. However, one must wonder how Lowell reacted to the bashing of Monroe: writing to Aldington in 1915, she defended Monroe in the face of the 'young, vigorous' and implicitly condescending 'artistic principles' of the younger poets who were disgruntled with Monroe's poetic divergences from their own sense of progressive poetic form (in Scott 2004: 151).

Lowell's entrance into the international discussions of modern poetry, enabled by the appearance of *Poetry*, eventuates most famously in a schism with Pound over the Imagist movement each is trying to promote. The story has most often been told, following Pound's own lead, as one in which Lowell poaches upon Pound's territory without a bone of poetic talent in her body – producing 'Amygism', rather than Imagist poetry, claimed Pound derisively. But Lowell's experience is narrated differently in her own poetry, and in recent scholarship that revisits this famous modernist moment, recasting Lowell's valuable contributions to other poets and to the poetic sense of the modern. Poems such as 'Astigmatism' (a 1914 parody of Pound), 'A Critical Fable', and 'The Sisters' – all composed in the 1910s or early 1920s – investigate attitudes toward women writers and traditions associated with them (Donaldson 2004: 27–42): dismissive and silencing attitudes that Lowell knew well from the 1912 publication of her first book until her death in 1925. Her writings on poetry in *Six French Poets* (1915) and *Tendencies in American Poetry* (1917), her vigorous, controversial lectures defending the 'New Poetry' to (often unreceptive) American audiences (1915–19), her three anthologies of *Some Imagist Poets* (1915, 1916 and 1917), and her involvement with little magazines like *Poetry*, the *Little Review*, and even *The Egoist* all established her centrality to efforts both to historicise and theorise modernist poetry during the 1910s. Receiving dubious praise from J. G. Fletcher in the May 1915 issue of *The Egoist* – one that focused on the Imagist poets and featured both Lowell and H.D. – in which he claimed her best poems were good enough to be 'male-authored', Lowell and her achievements have been all but forgotten (Dowson 2002: 140). Yet her experiments with polyphonic prose, begun in 1914, constitute a significant 'formal literary innovation' that cannot 'be easily subsumed' under Poundian notions of Imagism (Thacker 2004: 104–19). Revolutionary lyric inflections of sexuality join with works such as Gertrude Stein's in charting a lesbian poetics that links the woman's body, poetic production and sexual energy to the generation of a new poetry (Donaldson 2004: 27–42). Moreover, Lowell's claim to traditions of women's poetry, including Sappho, Elizabeth Barrett Browning and Emily Dickinson, indicates an early 'consciousness of how the sexual economy of the poetic voice shapes women writers' (Donaldson 2004: 28). Indeed, her critical attention to a poet such as H.D., in *Tendencies in American Poetry*, links the modernist woman poet with a preceding tradition through a consciousness of the lyric's gendered structures of desire and expression.

Lowell's writings on the poet H.D., indeed, prove significant in the history of modernist poetry, in part through alerting the young British writer Winifred Ellerman – who came to be known as Bryher – to the writings of H.D. Having written a letter of appreciation to Lowell for her critical acumen, Bryher requested a reading list, which subsequently included H.D.'s *Sea Garden* (1916). Bryher would seek out H.D. – obtaining her address from May Sinclair – and, subsequently, live out her life with her. The intertextual relation between Bryher, Lowell and H.D. continued until Lowell's death, with poetic encouragement and reciprocal appraisals (Radford 2004: 43–58; Marek 2004: 154–7; Thacker 2004: 49–59). Regarding Lowell as a central figure in modernist poetry, Bryher would write a critical appreciation of her in 1918, in which she credited Lowell with opening a 'new world' of poetry for her (in Radford 2004: 47). Lowell and H.D. remained close after their 1913 meeting in London, and H.D. joined Lowell's effort to disengage 'imagism' from Pound's control. Both H.D. and Aldington worked with Lowell to produce the three Imagist anthologies that ostensibly severed the relationship of Pound and Lowell. Objecting to the latter's use of the term, Pound was angered to find Lowell promoting herself or her projects as 'Imagist' without his permission (see Pound's letters to Lowell of 12 August, 12 October and 19 October 1914), or turning Imagism into what he angrily termed, in a January 1915 letter to Monroe, 'a democratic beer-garden' without the standards of selectivity he demanded (Pound 1971: 38; 41–3, 48). Certainly, it infuriated Pound to see Lowell referred to as the 'foremost member of the "Imagists"' in advertising copy promoting her 1914 volume, *Sword Blades and Poppy Seed* (Pound 1971: 43). Although invited by Lowell to take part in the anthology project that resulted in the three volumes of *Some Imagist Poets*, Pound objected to the enterprise and to the use of the term for it, although the poets originally associated with the movement – H.D., Aldington, Fletcher – were all involved in shaping and choosing the contents of the volumes. Whether to include the term 'Imagist' in the title engaged the contributors in collective debate, for they were keenly aware of Pound's sense of proprietorship. Indeed, Pound's claim to the term motivated Fletcher to provide Lowell with evidence that the term originated with T. E. Hulme, opening it to 'collective access' (Scott 2004: 142–3).

While Monroe prepared to publish her first issue of *Poetry*, H.D. was travelling to London and by 1912 taking part in vigorous conversations about new poetry among a group that included Pound, Aldington and F. S. Flint (whose essay 'Imagisme', actually ghost-written by Pound, appeared alongside the latter's 'A Few Don'ts by an Imagiste' in the March 1913 issue of *Poetry*). The group explored T. E. Hulme's ideas of the image and a more concrete modern poetry. The story is often told of the October 1912 meeting in a tea shop in which Pound, having read some of Hilda Dollitle's poetry of that year, declares her an 'imagiste' and, crossing out her name on the poems, reinscribes her as 'H.D.'. Having been in correspondence with Harriet Monroe since her enquiry into his interest in the journal that summer, he had sent her already a trio of his poems that would appear in the first October issue, and had begun attempts to recruit other poems for her from the likes of W. B. Yeats. Upon reading H.D.'s poems in October, including 'Priapus' and 'Hermes of the Ways', he sent them directly to Monroe, with great enthusiasm:

> I am sending you some *modern* stuff by an American, I say modern, for it is in the laconic speech of the Imagistes. . . . this is the sort of American stuff that I can show here and in Paris without its being ridiculed. Objective – no slither; direct – no excessive use of adjectives, no metaphors that won't permit examination. It's straight talk, straight as the Greek! And it was only by persistence that I got to see it at all. (Pound 1971: 11)

Later claiming to have invented Imagism to promote H.D. – and, in effect, to have created H.D. – Pound established the standard narrative of Imagism's origin as one in which the male poet holds Pygmalion-like powers over the woman, who is both muse and material to mould (Pondrom 1990: 104; Pound 1971: 288). At the same time, Pound's narrative credits himself with the discovery of poetic Imagism, a claim amplified by his later reactions to Lowell's poetic and editorial energies. Within this version of Imagism's contribution to modernist poetry, H.D. figures – as she does most infamously in Hugh Kenner's influential critical homage to Pound, *The Pound Era* (1971) – as a minor poet crippled by a neurotic attachment to Pound.

Careful consideration of the composition dates of Pound's poems of this period and of H.D.'s leads to the conclusion not only that Pound did *not* 'create' H.D., but, instead, that her poems were the model upon which Pound articulates his ideas of Imagism and in the light of which he transforms his own poetry to Imagist standards (Pondrom 1990). Looking at the first issue of *Poetry*, one encounters the poems that Pound sent to Monroe in August of 1912, two months before reading H.D.'s poetry. Although claiming to have sent Monroe a poem that he calls an 'over-elaborate post-Browning "Imagiste" affair' (Pound 1971: 10), their wordiness and sentimental turns of phrase makes them far from recognisable as 'Imagist'. H.D.'s poems of 1912, on the other hand, have achieved the sparseness and clarity of image that Pound and Flint would espouse shortly thereafter in respective pieces in *Poetry* (March 1913), although Pound especially would receive credit for creating the poetic model for Imagism, particularly with the now iconic poem, 'In a Station of the Metro'. However, it seems most likely that Pound did not write this poem until late December of 1912, *after* reading the poems of H.D.'s that would appear, under the banner of 'imagiste', in January 1913 in *Poetry*.

New York/Florence/New York

By the end of the 1910s, Alfred Stieglitz's avant-garde journal *Camera Work* was actively advancing new ideas and practices in art, bringing to Americans a sense of the European art scene. Having already introduced American readers to Cubist painting in the pages of *Camera Work* and the shows of his Photo-Secession Gallery in New York, Stieglitz devoted a special issue in 1912 to Gertrude Stein, publishing her portraits of Picasso and Matisse alongside artwork by each of the painters. Stein's radical language innovations, first evidenced in the publication in 1909 (to little acclaim) of *Three Lives*, drew attention to modern art's possibilities for literary experimentation, and Steiglitz positioned Stein as a leading pioneer in this inter-arts infusion. His opening editorial asserts that the 'the *raison d'être* of this special issue' is the 'articles themselves, and not either the subjects with which they deal or the illustrations that accompany them', for Stein employs the 'raw material of words' and the 'technical manipulation' of their 'medium' to express 'the Post-Impressionist spirit . . . in literary form' (in Brogan 1991: 285–6).

At the time of the appearance of her portraits of Matisse and Picasso in *Camera Work*, Stein was in the process of writing *Tender Buttons*, which she had begun in the year previous and would complete in 1913. A modernist *tour de force* that superimposes the 'raw material of words' upon the domestic realm of food, interior spaces, and their objects, *Tender Buttons* carries her experiment in parataxis (juxtaposition) to extremes that expose and explore the operations of language and its relation to social inscriptions of gender. Her associations with women and her exposure to widespread, radical ideas about women infuse her artistic ambition to create a new 'composition' that accurately expresses the new composition of the age, as she would define formal innovation in her later essay, 'Composition as Explanation' (1926). Moreover, the international debates about women's suffrage, sexuality and rights constituted an insistent part of the era from which Stein's 'composition' would be drawn. With Alice B. Toklas, she visited during the summer of 1912 a particularly receptive pair of women whose respective roles in fusing feminism, modernist art and literature would energise New York avant-garde circles. Mina Loy and Mable Dodge were among a colony of expatriate writers and artists clustered around Florence, exploring new ideas of psychology (especially the French philosopher Henri Bergson), spirituality sexuality, and art, intermingling with artists, intellectuals and radicals (including Dodge's lover John Reed, a leading American socialist) at the villa Stein would immortalise in the 'Portrait of Mable Dodge at the Villa Curonia', written after her visit in 1912. An English woman of Jewish descent who had studied art in Paris and moved to Florence with her husband Stephen Hawais in 1907, Loy thrived intellectually and artistically in this environment even as her marriage dissolved, and her friendship with Dodge enabled her literary beginnings as an important early innovator of modern poetry. Dodge also became the conduit through which ideas of American feminism travelled to Loy, beginning later in 1912 when Dodge left Florence to return to America.

Loy and Dodge read and enthusiastically discussed Stein's work during her summer visit, and she sent them copies of *Camera Work* when it appeared later that year, along with her portrait of Dodge. Stein credited Loy and her husband as 'among the very earliest to be interested in the work of Gertrude Stein', although when Hawais suggested that Stein use commas, Stein contrasted Loy's modern prescience with her husband's traditional reading: 'Mina Loy equally interested was able to understand without the commas. She has always been able to understand' (in Burke 1996: 129–30). Taking Stein's portraits as a model, Loy would herself write a portrait (undated) of Dodge from this period, positing creativity in decidedly gendered terms. Imagination and body are interlinked in explicitly womanly evocations, as Loy describes Dodge as 'more organically conscious than most women' and longing 'to stuff everything into her vulva to see what marvelous creative modification it has undergone in the process' (in Burke 1996: 134).

Indeed, it is during this period that the various strands of Loy's modernism coalesce, preparing the way for striking innovations in form and radical expressions of feminist consciousness that would attract even the attention of the *New York Sun* by 1917, in an article on Loy as the exemplary 'New Woman'. The article reflects upon the congruence of the 'New Woman' and the new poetry, commenting that 'some people think that women are the cause of modernism, whatever that is', and remarking upon the 'new female perspective' of Loy's 'original kind of free verse' (Burke 1985: 37). By the time that this newspaper article was written, reflecting the popular level of discussion about feminism at the time, Loy had moved to New York, preceded by the publication of her poetry in numerous avantgarde journals, beginning with *Camera Work*'s 1914 printing of her 'Aphorisms on Futurism', and including *Rogue*, *Others* and *Trend*. Incorporating techniques of parataxis, fragmentation and simultaneity, her work translated these techniques from the European art scene and (like Stein, an important formal influence) applied them to language, significantly helping introduce American audiences to the vital interactions of art and poetry that increasingly marked modernist experimentation, especially in the 1910s. Loy's work began to appear soon after the 1913 Armory Show in New York City, the first major exhibition in America of modern European Post-Impressionist and Cubist art. It had shocked the public, including the poet William Carlos Williams, who experienced a conversion to modernism after seeing it. Mabel Dodge kept Loy abreast of the American attitudes toward the show, which she had helped organise upon returning from Europe to America in the autumn of 1912. Stein's portrait of Dodge was distributed at the Armory Show, along with a March 1913 article on Stein by Dodge, published in *Arts and Decoration*, which claimed that 'Gertrude Stein is doing with words what Picasso is doing with paint. She is impelling language to induce new states of consciousness, and in doing so language becomes with her a creative art rather than a mirror of history' (Dodge 1913: n.p.).

Loy was witness, in 1912, to Roger Fry's second Post-Impressionist exhibition in London, which she attended while travelling to her own one-woman show at the Carfax Gallery.

Impressed by Wyndham Lewis's *Timon of Athens* and its explosive use of geometric space, Loy would be drawn to the elements of movement and simultaneity advocated by the Italian Futurists during these years. After Dodge left for America and Hawais left for the South Seas, Loy found friendship with the young American art student, Frances Simpson Stevens, who rented a studio from her. Together, the women developed an interest in the Italian Futurists, studying their manifestoes and works and meeting them upon their arrival in Florence in 1913. Loy grew close to major Futurist writers Filippo Marinetti and Giovani Papini, absorbing the movement's ideas about dynamism but rejecting the misogyny underlying their celebration of motion and energy. By the time Loy's works come to be published, their coalition of Futurism, feminism and modern art marks them as utterly new in form and content (Kouidis 1980; Burke 1985 and 1996). Her treatment of women's cultural and economic confinement, in poems such as 'Virgins Plus Curtains Minus Dots', of bodily female experience in 'Parturition', or of heterosexual institutions in 'The Ineffectual Marriage' or 'Three Moments in Paris', explicitly introduce feminist critique into avantgarde experimentation – a radical poetics enabled by sympathetic readings of Stein; by friendships with American women such as Dodge, Muriel Draper, Frances Stevens; by reactions to Futurist misogyny; and by exposure to feminism. For Loy, proclaiming female sexuality and experience as a basis for poetic form and subject matter in the early 1910s gained her both notoriety and the respect of fellow modernists. In 1918, theorising a component of modern poetry that he described as the dance of the intellect among words, Pound would identify Loy, along with Moore, as a practitioner of 'logopeoia', and Williams' patronage of Loy's work, through the journals *Others* and *Contact*, insured her regular appearance in these literary magazines between 1915 and 1921. Indeed, Williams chose to initiate each of these journals with poems by Loy, including 'Love Songs I–IV' in the first issue of *Others* (1916), and a printing of the entire poem 'Love Songs to Joannes, I–XXXIV' in 1917. Loy's poetry exemplified the gendered difference that *Others* contributor and guest editor Helen Hoyt argued was needed in modern women's poetry when, in October 1916, she edited a special 'Woman's Number'. In her preface, she claimed,

> At present most of what we know, or think we know, of women has been found out by men. We have yet to hear what woman will tell of herself, and where can she tell more intimately than in poetry? (Hoyt 1916: n.p.).

The clamour to 'hear what woman will tell of herself' reached unprecedented proportions in prewar America, leading *Harper's Weekly* to call the feminist movement 'the stir of new life, the palpable awakening of conscience' (in Cott 1987: 14). For Mabel Dodge and her Greenwich Village compatriots, the 'new stir' involved the volatile commingling of arts, activism, politics and new ideas that the feminist movement helped invigorate. Indeed, Loy's works both drew from and were read within the hotbed of American feminism located in Greenwich Village by 1912, culminating most explicitly in her 'Feminist Manifesto', sent to Dodge in America in 1914 and stimulated by news she was receiving from her American friend about the feminist movement. Attracting socialists, feminists, artists and writers to her salon gatherings in Greenwich Village, Dodge interacted with birth-control campaigner Margaret Sanger (who held her own activist gatherings in Greenwich Village), John Reed, socialist and editor Max Eastman, feminist and lawyer Crystal Eastman, anarchist Emma Goldman, and other central voices in the era's radical movements. Dodge absorbed feminist ideas, also, from her membership in Heterodoxy, a feminist club founded in 1912 and 'composed of women whose names were known' – such as writers Charlotte Perkins Gilman and Susan Glaspell – but who were 'unorthodox women, women who did things and did them openly' (Dodge 1936: 143). That feminist ideas from such sources resonate within Loy's poetry illuminates the reciprocity of artistic and social radicalism energising much early modernist poetry.

In the modernist decades following 1912, as proponents of a separation of art from social forces increasingly define the poetic field, socially-committed poets the likes of Lola Ridge, Genevieve Taggard or Muriel Rukeyser are relegated to relative critical obscurity. Just as the year 1912 marks a high point in feminist activism and discussion, it also registers the ongoing power of backlash moments to silence that discussion. These reactionary moments have largely succeeded in effacing or trivialising women's roles in modernist literary history. Countering such moments requires a reframing of modernism in terms of 'other' moments that richly illuminate women as innovative bearers of the new in 1912 and beyond.

References

Adickes, Sandra (1997) *To Be Young Was Very Heaven: Women in New York Before the First World War*, New York: St Martin's Press

Benstock, Shari (1986) *Women of the Left Bank: Paris, 1900–1940*, Austin, TX: University of Texas Press

Brogan, Jacqueline Vaught (1991) *Part of the Climate: American Cubist Poetry*, Berkeley, CA: University of California Press

Burke, Carolyn (1985) 'The New Poetry and the New Woman: Mina Loy', in *Coming to Light: American Women Poets in the Twentieth Century*, ed Diane Middlebrook and Marilyn Yalom, Ann Arbor, MI: University of Michigan Press, 37–57

——(1996) *Becoming Modern: The Life of Mina Loy*, New York: Farrar, Straus, and Giroux

Clarke, Bruce (1996) *Dora Marsden and Early Modernism: Gender, Individualism, Science*, Ann Arbor, MI: University of Michigan Press

Cott, Nancy (1987) *The Grounding of Modern Feminism*, New Haven, CT, and London: Yale University Press

Dodge, Mabel (1913) 'Speculations, or Post-Impressionism in Prose', in *Arts Decoration*, March: www.clpgh.org/exhibit/neighborhoods/northside

—— [under the name of Mabel Dodge Luhan] (1936) *Intimate Memories*, Vol. III: *Movers and Shakers*, New York: Harcourt, Brace and Co.

Donaldson, Elizabeth J. (2004) 'Amy Lowell and the Unknown Ladies: The Caryatides Talk Back', in Munich and Bradshaw (2004), 27–42

Dowson, Jane (2002) *Women, Modernism and British Poetry, 1910–1939: Resisting Femininity*, Aldershot, Hampshire: Ashgate Press

Green, Barbara (2003) 'The New Woman's Appetite for "Riotous Living": Rebecca West, Modernist Feminism, and the Everyday', in Ann L. Ardis and Leslie W. Lewis, eds, *Women's Experience of Modernity, 1875–1945*, Baltimore, MD, and London: Johns Hopkins University Press, 221–36

Hoyt, Helen (1916) 'Retort', in *Others* 3.3: n.p.

Kinnahan, Linda A. (1994) *Poetics of the Feminine: Authority and Literary Tradition in William Carlos Williams, Mina Loy, Denise Levertov, and Kathleen Fraser*, Cambridge: Cambridge University Press

Kouidis, Virginia (1980) *Mina Loy, American Modernist Poet*, Baton Rouge, LA: Louisiana State University Press

Levenson, Michael H. (1984) *A Genealogy of Modernism: A Study of English Literary Doctrine 1908–1922*, Cambridge: Cambridge University Press

Marek, Jayne E. (2004) 'Amy Lowell, *Some Imagist Poets*, and the Context of the New Poetry', in Munich and Bradshaw (2004), 154–66

Morrison, Mark S. (2001) *The Public Face of Modernism: Little Magazines, Audiences, and Reception 1905–1920*, Madison, WI: University of Wisconsin Press

Munich, Adrienne, and Melissa Bradshaw, eds (2004) *Amy Lowell, American Modern*, New Brunswick, NJ, and London: Rutgers University Press

Pondrom, Cyrena N. (1990), 'H.D. and the Origins of Imagism', in *Signets: Reading H.D.*, ed. Susan Stanford Friedman and Rachel Blau DuPlessis, Madison, WI: University of Wisconsin Press, 85–109

Pound, Ezra (1912) 'Prologomena [sic]', in *Poetry Review* 1.2, February: 72–6. Reprinted as 'Prolegomena' in Pound (1954), 8–9

——(1954) *Literary Essays of Ezra Pound*, ed. T. S. Eliot, London: Faber and Faber

——(1971) [1950] *The Selected Letters of Ezra Pound 1907–1941*, ed. D. D. Paige, New York: Faber and Faber

Radford, Jean (2004) 'A Transatlantic Affair: Amy Lowell and Bryher', in Munich and Bradshaw (2004), 43–58

Scott, Bonnie Kime, ed. (1990) *The Gender of Modernism*, Bloomington, IN: Indiana University Press

——(2004) 'Amy Lowell's Letters in the Network of Modernism', in Munich and Bradshaw (2004), 136–53

Thacker, Andrew (2004) 'Unrelated Beauty: Amy Lowell, Polyphonic Prose, and the Imagist City', in Munich and Bradshaw (2004), 104–20

West, Rebecca (1926) 'The "Freewoman"', in *Time and Tide*, July: 648–9. Reprinted in Scott (1990), 573–7

——(1970), 'Spinster to the Rescue', in *Sunday Telegraph*, 11 November: 12. Reprinted in Scott (1990), 577–80

'Women-Poets' (1912), *Poetry Review*, May: 199–200

Chapter 3

1916, Flanders, London, Dublin: 'Everything Has Gone Well'

Randall Stevenson

Human character may have changed, as Virginia Woolf claimed, 'on or about December 1910' (Woolf 1986–94: 3: 421). But it changed more radically at 7.30am on Saturday, 1 July 1916, with the beginning of the offensive on the Somme – a battle which eventually wiped out more than a million human characters, around half of them British. Fundamental changes in human communication, too, were in evidence over that weekend. The language and even the page-layout of *The Times* on Monday 3 July – when the battle was first reported in the London daily press – indicate areas involved. Other events and publications in 1916 further highlight new influences on the age and its writing: 1916 offers both a half-way stage and a defining moment in the emergence of modernist literature between 1900 and 1930.

Pages in *The Times*, first of all, confront readers with some odd contrasts between columns, and between war and non-military life. Headed 'Roll of Honour', page 12 is devoted almost entirely to an immense list of military casualties – more than 1,500 names – yet contains in the middle a brief 'Oxford Honours List', naming recent graduates alongside the recently dead or wounded. In this brief column, the name 'A. L. Huxley' appears in 'Class I' of English Language and Literature graduates – the novelist Aldous Huxley, whose first book, a collection of poems, was published two months later. A still stranger contrast appears on page 10 (Fig. 3.1). In a column on the left, fighting on the Somme is described as 'of the most desperate character . . . fierce beyond description . . . a sight of pure horror'. Four inches to the right, a Kodak advertisement invites readers to turn 'this year's holiday' into a 'picture-story of every sunny hour'. Though seldom so bizarre, juxtapositions of this kind were becoming almost familiar in the modern age. Less than 2 per cent of the population read newspapers in 1850, but the introduction of faster, cheaper rotary presses helped raise this figure to 20 per cent even by the end of the century. Wider circulation was further encouraged by replacement of old-fashioned, print-saturated pages with more reader-friendly, headline-based layouts – often including graphic advertising, capitalising on expanding readerships.

Reshaped encounters with newsprint had resonances in modernist fiction, figuring in both the subject and style of its outstanding achievement, James Joyce's *Ulysses* (1922). When work as an advertising man takes Bloom to the newspaper office in the 'Aeolus' chapter (7), the text itself reproduces the kind of headlines beginning to dominate contemporary journalism. It also describes Bloom watching the printing presses and worrying that 'machines. Smash a man to atoms' and may 'Rule the world one day' (Joyce 1992: 150). Similar fears of 'flesh turned to atoms' (1973: 150), in a new machine age, figure in Virginia Woolf's references to the war in *To the Lighthouse* (1927). But *Ulysses* principally reflects another atomisation: the print media's new powers in fragmenting the

Figure 3.1.   Page from *The Times*, 3 July 1916

Figure 3.2.   Page from *The Times*, 3 July 1916

language through which the world and its news is recorded. Joyce's unprecedented use of disparate styles for individual chapters of *Ulysses* seemed disturbing, at the time, even to his admirers. Yet it was also thoroughly contemporary, reflecting and exploring the intimate antinomies of subject and style, horror and sunshine, death and learning, which early twentieth-century readers were beginning to encounter in their newspapers everyday.

Those pages of *The Times* reflect other recent pressures on language, print and communication. A report on page 8 (Fig. 3.2) that 'the glorious defenders of Verdun have won back again the rubbish-heap of ruins which once was Thiaumont' appears under the headline 'GOOD NEWS FROM OTHER THEATRES' – ironically juxtaposed, in this case, with a column advertising stage productions in London theatres. Significantly, one of these theatres, the Scala, has replaced dramatic performances with showings of 'the finest war films ever seen'. This 'interesting spectacle', the Earl of Derby attests in the advertisement, will 'bring home to the people more than it has ever been brought home to them before what our men are doing'. A few weeks later, on 10 August, the same theatre premièred *The Battle of the Somme*, a film seen by huge audiences throughout Britain in the autumn of 1916. These included some of the combatants themselves, and at least one civilian diarist who followed the Earl of Derby in suggesting that nothing could have brought home more vividly 'the realities of the war' (Brown 2002: 265). This claim was nevertheless a contradictory one for a newspaper to publicise, suggesting that film, and not print – despite further increases in newspaper sales encouraged by the war – could best communicate what was going on at the front. Along with Kodak's cheery emphasis on 'picture-story', this suggests how far the written word in the early twentieth century was pressured by new media and technologies.

Such pressures also contributed to the formal innovations distinguishing modernism. At the end of the nineteenth century, Joseph Conrad still stressed in his preface to *The Nigger of the 'Narcissus'* (1897) 'the power of the written word . . . before all, to make you *see*' (Conrad 1968: 13). A decade or so afterwards, involvement in opening the first cinema in Dublin particularly equipped Joyce to recognise ways this power had been overtaken – an encounter with film which a later experimental novelist, B. S. Johnson, considered 'of crucial significance in the history of the novel' (Johnson 1973: 11). If a picture is worth a thousand words, a motion picture or Kodak 'picture-story' may be worth many thousands more. As Johnson suggests, this encouraged modernist novelists to shift attention away from the visible world and towards inward experiences cameras are less able to capture. In her essay on 'Modern Fiction', first published in 1919, Virginia Woolf stressed a contemporary need to 'look within' and 'examine . . . the mind': by that date, writers including Joyce and Dorothy Richardson had already begun to develop the stream-of-consciousness and interior monologue styles characteristic of modernist fiction (Woolf 1986–94: 4: 160).

Another pressure on contemporary language was simply the nature of experiences it had to represent. The reporter quoted above records 'pure horror' witnessed on the Somme as 'beyond description': again, a contradictory comment for a newspaper to allow. Yet other *Times* reports repeatedly exhibit a language torn and tormented beyond any decency or decorum words conventionally offered. Mention of 'glorious' struggle for the ruined rubbish-heap of Thiaumont offers one example. Another appears on page 8, under the headline 'EVERYTHING HAS GONE WELL', in a report recording that

> Many interesting novelties have been introduced, such as the massacre of Drachen observation balloons, by which the Germans are deprived of some of their eyes . . . the Flying Corps has been as active as ever, while the cavalry in this country have more chance of bearing a hand, and, in short, all the means of modern war can be profitably employed.

Mention of cavalry taking part in 'modern war' along with the Flying Corps incidentally highlights conflicts between old and new, tradition and a machine age, typical of the early twentieth century. More sinisterly, mention of 'interesting novelties' and their 'profitable' employment confirms the capacities of an age of new technologies and mass communications to recuperate even 'pure horror' as 'interesting', saleable spectacle. The report's language seems unwittingly infected by the destructive, reifying forces of this age, reproducing lexically the shattering, atomising effects of war on human flesh: soldiers are anatomised, in glib synecdoche, in terms of their functions, as eyes, and the cavalry as hands. Heightened by the idea of massacring balloons, or of hands borne on horseback, the effect is nearly surreal, as if derived from the first experiments of the Dadaists, a few months earlier, in the Cabaret Voltaire in Zurich, in February 1916. By July, newspapers and Dada alike were responding to murderous insanities, in an age of supposed reason and technological progress, through a language collapsing towards absurdity.

Yet much the most important effect of war *The Times* illustrates was not in making language surreal, but simply *un*real in what it conveys. That Saturday morning on the Somme saw the death or mutilation of 60,000 soldiers between 7.30 and 11am: the greatest disaster the British army has ever experienced, before or since. Yet Monday's *Times* recorded that the British commander-in-chief Sir Douglas Haig 'telegraphed last night that the general situation was favourable'. Other reports claimed that 'as far as can be ascertained our casualties have not been heavy', and talked of 'a good beginning' and of the British army 'winning new glory' (pp. 8, 9, 10). *The Times* of 3 July, in other words, demonstrated at least on a *scale* new in history the capacity of language to remain perfectly plausible, grammatical, and self-consistent, yet sustain little connection with truth or reality. This capacity, of course, has been thoroughly confirmed in later decades. As the historian Paul Fussell suggests in *The Great War and Modern Memory* (1973):

> A lifelong suspicion of the press was one lasting result of the ordinary man's experience of the war. It might even be said that the current devaluation of letterpress and even of language itself dates from the Great War. (Fussell 1979: 316)

Looking back on the 'nightmare' period of the war, Richard Aldington talks in *Death of a Hero* (1929) of 'the limitless Cant, Delusion, and Delirium let loose on the world during those four years', exceeding anything that memory could retain, or 'pen portray' (Aldington 1984: 223). Suspicion of the press, and ultimately of language itself, was naturally strongly evident among modernist writers, such as Aldington, who had directly experienced military action themselves. In *The Good Soldier* (1915), set and written largely before the war, Ford Madox Ford's narrator still considers that 'for all good soldiers . . . their profession . . . is full of the big words, courage, loyalty, honour, constancy' (Ford 1977: 31). In *A Farewell to Arms* (1929), on the other hand, Ernest Hemingway's narrator records that war experience has left him 'embarrassed by the words sacred, glorious, and sacrifice and the expression in vain . . . the things that were glorious had no glory . . . abstract words such as glory, honour, courage or hallow were obscene' (Hemingway 1977: 202). Similar embarrassment figures in Hemingway stories such as 'Soldier's Home' (1926), concerned with the impossibility of communicating experience of the war, or even 'Hills Like White Elephants' (1928), its heroine longing for silence instead of a language of evasion and covert compulsion.

As the latter story suggests, suspicion of a 'devalued' language in the war's aftermath extended well beyond contexts affected immediately or directly by its violence. Taking 'glorious' as one of his examples, Stephen Dedalus remarks in *Ulysses*, 'I fear those big words . . . which make us so unhappy' (Joyce 1992: 38). Similar concerns shape the entire 'tragic age' D. H. Lawrence envisages in *Lady Chatterley's Lover* (1928). Ruined by the 'cataclysm' of the war, this age also experiences a ruination of language. 'All the great words . . . were cancelled for her generation', Lady Chatterley concludes: 'love, joy, happiness, home, mother, father, husband, all these great dynamic words were half dead now'. These 'half-dead' or 'cancelled' words, she adds, are 'always coming between her and life', occluding the experience they were once supposed to represent (Lawrence 1982: 5, 64, 96). Such views of language as a screen, as occlusion rather than transparency, were explored more fully by Stephen Dedalus in an earlier incarnation, in Joyce's *A Portrait of the Artist as a Young Man*. Marking the major novelistic debut of 1916, *Portrait* indicates the origin of further modernist interests in the medium of language, concurrent with those discussed above. 'Words. Was it their colours?' Stephen asks, thinking about 'a day of dappled seaborne clouds' and its literary description. 'No, it was not their colours', he adds,

> it was the poise and balance of the period itself . . . was it that, being as weak of sight as he
> was shy of mind, he drew less pleasure from the reflection of the glowing sensible world through
> the prism of a language many-coloured and richly storied than from the contemplation of
> an inner world of individual emotions mirrored perfectly in a lucid supple periodic prose?
> (Joyce 1973: 166–7)

In one way, Stephen seems to confirm modernism's characteristic preference for an 'inner world', and for representing the outer one not directly but subjectively. 'Those mirrors, the minds of men', as Virginia Woolf called them, are likewise shown in *To the Lighthouse* to be preferable to external reality, stained by experience of the war (Woolf 1973: 150). Yet the passage indicates another dimension in such preferences, suggesting that it is not only Stephen but language itself which has become 'weak of sight' – a 'prism' of fractured if colourful refractions, rather than a reliable reflector of the world beyond the mind. By the time he wrote *Heart of Darkness* (1899), Conrad was already beginning to doubt language's power to 'make you *see*'. Joyce's *Portrait* expands such doubts, envisaging language no longer as an inert or invisible communicative medium, but one drawing attention towards autonomous properties of its own; towards balances, powers and periods not only reflecting experience, but shaping, constructing, and potentially distorting it.

Stephen's remarks thus anticipate the prism, or even prison, that language so often came to seem for late twentieth-century literature, and for literary theory, increasingly oriented towards linguistic issues after the 1970s. Yet *Portrait* points back as well as forwards, indicating that new attitudes to language did not originate entirely in 1916, however sharply they were focused by events in that year. Joyce's novel, after all, was begun long previously, serialised earlier in *The Egoist*, and published entire in 1916 – almost simultaneously with the Somme, and scarcely as its consequence. The war may have finally shattered confidence in communication for Fussell's ordinary man, and for many modernist authors, but in certain quarters such confidence had begun to wane long before 1916. As another combatant, J. B. Priestley, later concluded, the war worked decisively 'to widen and deepen splits in the Western mind', but it was not always responsible for initiating them (Priestley 1960: 327). Friedrich Nietzsche defined one of these splits in 1880, suggesting that 'mankind set up in language a separate world beside the other world', realising 'a great deal later – only now' that this 'belief in language . . . propagated a tremendous error' (Nietzsche 1986: 16). Part of a wider shift in turn-of-the-century epistemology, similar scepticism extended among philosophers such as William James, convinced that 'language works against our perception of the truth' (James 1890: I, 241), and Henri Bergson, finding 'no common measure between mind and language' (Bergson 1971: 165). Confidence in language – or in the rational, word-generating intellect generally – was also undermined by Sigmund Freud's identification of deeper, pre-verbal mental activity in studies such as *The Interpretation of Dreams* (1899). Adding to modernist fiction's determination to 'examine the mind', Freud also focused attention on 'unspeakable communication', as Lawrence describes it in *Women in Love* (1921): in 'vital, sensual reality that can never be transmuted into mind content, but remains outside, living body of darkness and silence' (Lawrence 1971: 360).

By the early years of the century, linguisticians themselves were introducing comparable doubts into their field of study. These were influentially summarised in Ferdinand de Saussure's *Cours de linguistique générale*, first published in 1916 – especially in his renowned conclusion that 'the bond between the signifier and the signified is arbitrary . . . *the linguistic sign is arbitrary*'. Any idea, Saussure suggests, could just as well be represented in language by a different sequence of sounds, a possibility confirmed by 'differences among languages and by the very existence of different languages' (Saussure 1960: 67–8). His comments identify another source of linguistic interest among modernist authors – many of whom were exiles, daily encountering such 'differences' – and particularly illumine Joyce's early, long-sustained and pre-eminent concern with the prism of words. The very last line of *Ulysses* is in this way among the most significant in the novel: not Molly Bloom's famously affirmative concluding repetitions of 'yes', but the dateline appended beneath them, '*Trieste–Zürich–Paris*, 1914–1921'. Residence abroad before and during the First World War – including periods working as an English-language teacher in Trieste – sharpened Joyce's awareness of language and its shifty reshaping of the world, later highlighted in his panoply of parodies throughout *Ulysses*.

Linguistic objectivity of this kind was also forced on Joyce by an earlier form of exile or estrangement – by the kind of formative experiences his autobiographical hero Stephen describes in *Portrait*, at a time when Dublin was still ruled from London. Stephen's interests on his 'day of dappled seaborne clouds' appear in a new light in a later, more celebrated passage in the novel, when he concludes of an encounter with an English priest that

> The language in which we are speaking is his before it is mine. How different are the words *home*, *Christ*, *ale*, *master*, on his lips and on mine! I cannot speak or write these words without unrest of spirit. His language, so familiar and so foreign, will always be for me an acquired speech. I have not made or accepted its words. My voice holds them at bay. My soul frets in the shadow of his language. (Joyce 1973: 189)

'Unrest' of this kind figures in modernist writing from other peripheral nations in the British Isles – in the 'fretting' of Scots against standard English in Hugh MacDiarmid's 1920s poetry, or in Lewis Grassic Gibbon's trilogy *A Scots Quair* (1932–4), for example – and in Lawrence's use of dialect in novels such as *Lady Chatterley's Lover* (1928). It also anticipates the areas of development and innovation in later twentieth-century literature recently discussed in postcolonial criticism. As a legacy of the colonial period – of 'a century of displaced persons' – Salman Rushdie identifies in *Imaginary Homelands* (1991) a 'migrant sensibility' which in some ways further extends modernist writers' experience of exile, difference, and linguistic estrangement. Finding themselves living among languages, cultures or systems of power often more foreign than familiar, Rushdie's migrants inevitably experience a necessity 'to make a new imaginative relationship with the world' (Rushdie 1991: 124, 125). A new, postcolonial phase of literary innovation and cultural re-invention was one of the consequences.

Significantly, Stephen later finds mingled familiarity and foreignness make him a *better* speaker of English than the Englishman he encounters. For Joyce himself, unlike some of his modernist contemporaries, linguistic 'fretting' and a language 'devalued' in its conventional roles likewise proved more productive than problematic – offering new freedoms for the increasingly extravagant linguistic experiment and innovation of his later writing. Parodic highlighting of words' prismatic aspects makes *Ulysses* a novel less realistic than *Portrait* – one still concerned with the life and geography of Dublin, but also, self-consciously, with the language used to represent it. The latter concern expands in Joyce's 'Work in Progress' of the later 1920s and 1930s, eventually published as *Finnegans Wake* in 1939. In a way, this most challenging of modernist narrative experiments extends to new limits its urge to look within the mind, creating a stream of *un*consciousness. But Joyce's playful, inexhaustible linguistic inventiveness focuses attention, above all, on the written word, rather than its powers to reflect experience, conscious or otherwise. As *Finnegans Wake* itself suggests, Joyce's later writing is primarily 'graphique', writing for itself: not 'por daguerre', nor a 'picture story' of any other kind (Joyce 1971: 339). Samuel Beckett emphasised this role in 1929, in an early volume of commentary on 'Work in Progress', remarking that Joyce's writing 'is not *about* something; *it is that something itself*'. Another commentator in the same volume, Eugene Jolas, confirmed that Joyce's work showed that

> the real metaphysical problem today is the word. The epoch when the writer photographed the life about him with the mechanics of words redolent of the daguerreotype, is happily drawing to its close. The new artist of the word has recognised the autonomy of language. (Beckett *et al.* 1972: 14, 79)

Defining in 1916 pressures which led towards a postcolonial age, *Portrait* also anticipated directions followed by a postmodern one, further shaped by Joyce's later writing and the linguistic self-consciousness of Beckett's work around mid-century. Increasingly pressured by the powers of media and advertising, writers in later decades concerned themselves more and more frequently with the problem of the word, the unstable nature of fictional worlds it creates, and the 'autonomy' of a language detached from long-established realist conventions of representation. Such problems had begun to acquire the metaphysical aspect Jolas mentions even by the end of the nineteenth century, through the work of the philosophers mentioned. Events early in the twentieth century – the war particularly – ensured that the problem of the word was also inescapably historical and political.

*

Authors early in the century might scarcely have anticipated how long the problems of the word, so sharply focused in 1916, would continue to dominate thinking in later years. Nevertheless 1916 seemed a thoroughly epochal year even at the time. Abroad, the Russian Revolution soon confirmed the end of old worlds and old regimes. For many writers, decisive change was in other ways already inescapably evident at home. 'It was in 1915 the old world ended', D. H. Lawrence remarked:

> in the winter 1915–1916 . . . the integrity of London collapsed, and the genuine debasement began, the unspeakable baseness of the press and public voice, the reign of that bloated ignominy, *John Bull*.

No man who has really consciously lived through this can believe again absolutely in democracy. (Lawrence 1960: 220)

His views were widely shared among contemporaries. For many, the Defence of the Realm Act (DORA) and legislation which followed had terminated long-standing decencies of civil society, sanctioning new state controls over public life, and over the life – and death – of the individual. The introduction of conscription in March 1916, in particular, decisively ended the spirit of enthusiasm, patriotism, honour and other 'big words' with which the war had begun. 'Never such innocence again', Philip Larkin later remarked of huge queues of army volunteers in 1914, in a poem whose very title – 'MCMXIV' (1964) – highlights an older-fashioned accounting of historical time. Yet a certain innocence continued beyond 1914 – even the sense Larkin talks of, in 'MCMXIV', of war as 'August Bank Holiday lark' (Larkin 1985: 28). The utter loss of an 'innocent' *belle époque* occurred not at the war's beginning but nearly two years later, when the Somme finally wiped out the volunteer armies of 1914. 'Horrors that make the old tragedies seem no more than nursery shows' – as Rebecca West describes them in *The Return of the Soldier* (1918) – could no longer be entirely disguised, even by mendacious reporting and the propaganda of those 'interesting' films (West 1980: 63). As the First World War historian John Keegan records, 'the Somme marked the end of an age of vital optimism in British life that has never been recovered' (Keegan 1998: 321). 'The watershed of the Somme', Henry Williamson likewise records in *The Golden Virgin* (1957), part of his *Chronicle of Ancient Sunlight* sequence, marked 'not only the end of the old order, but the end of ideas that had endured a thousand years' (Williamson 1957: 340). Nor can the circumstances of this loss be forgotten. 'The Somme is like the Holocaust', the novelist Pat Barker still considered in the 1990s: 'it revealed things we cannot come to terms with and cannot forget. It never becomes the past' (Jaggi 2003: 16). In Barker's own trilogy of First World War novels, *Regeneration* (1991–5), the temporary, traumatic loss of speech of a central character continues to represent vividly, for a later age, the unspeakable nature of the war and its reductive effects on language itself.

Further state intrusions into everyday life, also long influential later in the twentieth century, were instituted by DORA and the circumstances of war. Fears about the economy and the cost of the war, for example, led to the abandonment of the gold standard and the steady replacement of coinage with paper money. While the currency of language was devalued by the war, so was the language of currency – newly arbitrary in its relations between signifier and signified, with mere promissory notes replacing metal bearing some at least of the value it proclaimed, and without any ultimate or secure standard of value. Much else once solidly central to everyday life soon melted into air, or into new forms of accounting. New artificiality, and new forms of state authority, were particularly evident in computation of the dimension of time. Concerns about industrial efficiency and the sobriety of workers encouraged government regulation of licensing hours: that ominous call, 'HURRY UP PLEASE ITS TIME', resounding in T. S. Eliot's *The Waste Land*, was first heard during the war and still a relative novelty when the poem was published in 1922. Similar concerns about productivity led to the introduction of daylight saving and British Summer Time – the last of a series of rationalisations of temporality, stretching back through the institution of Greenwich Mean Time in 1884 to the standardisations required by the railway companies in the 1840s. Implemented in 1916, the Summer Time Act made temporality still less the province of natural movements of the sun and stars, still more a convenient commodity in a clocked-in industrial age, increasingly regulated by the 'time is money' principles introduced to factory work by F. W. Taylor and Henry Ford.

In the circumstances, it was ironic – or appropriate – that Albert Einstein's General Theory of Relativity was published in the same year. A huge vogue for Einstein followed widely publicised confirmation of his ideas three years later. D. H. Lawrence remarked in the early 1920s that 'everybody catches fire at the word Relativity. There must be something in the mere suggestion which we have been waiting for'. This 'something', he added, was offered by relativity's replacement of 'absolute central principle governing the world' with a sense that 'in itself each individual living creature is absolute: in its own being . . . all things in the universe are just relative to the individual living creature' (Lawrence 1961: 177–9). As Lawrence suggests, relativity offered just the kind of message contemporary society did want to hear, at least in the loose formulations in which Einstein's work reached the general public. Revaluation of individual beings as 'absolute' and irreducibly particular in their perspectives was peculiarly necessary in an age increasingly governed by state powers and controls, by time-and-motion regulation of the industrial life of the masses, and by military precision coordinating the exact, 7.30am start of mass slaughter on the Somme.

This need contributed to new emphases on the 'inner world of individual emotion', discussed above, in the interior monologues favoured by modernist fiction. It also encouraged modernist novelists to favour 'time in the mind', as Virginia Woolf calls it in *Orlando* (1928), rather than 'time on the clock' (Woolf 1975: 69). Focalisation within individual consciousness facilitated abandonment of conventional chronology: the 'appalling narrative business of the realist' – tainted by complicities with Victorian ideas of progress the war had destroyed – which Woolf also repudiated in her diary in 1928 (Woolf 1980: 209). Instead, fiction could rely on the 'seamstress' Woolf recommended, stitching episodes into single days of consciousness through the fickle associations of memory, connecting events and moments of being through mutual significance rather than mere historical succession. Memory also served a natural contemporary inclination towards nostalgia. In West's *The Return of the Soldier*, the hero's shell-shock in 1916 takes the form of complete mental reversion to a happier life, fifteen years earlier. Much modernist fiction follows a similar path, with *Ulysses* set in 1904, Marcel Proust's *A la recherche du temps perdu* recovering in memory the lost time of the *belle époque* years, and Woolf looking back in the first part of *To the Lighthouse* to the relative tranquillity of 1910. With its short, sharp middle section, set in the war years, and its sad postwar conclusion, *To the Lighthouse* illustrates especially clearly, at a formal level, the divisive, fragmenting effects on contemporary experience which Richard Aldington describes, in *Death of a Hero*, leaving 'adult lives . . . cut sharply into three sections – pre-war, war and post-war' (Aldington 1984: 199).

To the Lighthouse indicates a number of other influences extending from the war – sometimes from its Home Front – into the writing of later years. Stringent state controls, ending an epoch in 1915–16, reflected not only military pressures abroad but the anxieties of a government troubled by various threats within the British Isles. A renewed focus for these anxieties in 1916 was the women's suffrage movement. Divided between patriotism and criticism of the war, the suffragists had largely renounced militancy since its outbreak. But 20,000 people turned up in Trafalgar Square on 9 April 1916 to hear the suffragette leader Sylvia Pankhurst and to protest at restrictions imposed by DORA. Part of the crowd was hostile to the suffragettes, and a near-riot ensued – an episode described in another volume of Williamson's *Chronicle of Ancient Sunlight*, *A Fox under my Cloak* (1955), though assigned to a slightly earlier date. Though the vote was virtually promised by August 1916, suffragist demands remained a concern for the rest of the war, strongly reinforced by women's expanding employment as military auxiliaries, and in munitions and other industries.

Economic factors, as much as direct agitation, refocused attention on women's roles, and on issues of gender and justice generally. Variously evident in modernist writing, this attention was once again particularly influential on literary language and form. In *The Tunnel* (1919), an early volume of her *Pilgrimage* sequence (1915–67), Dorothy Richardson shows her heroine Miriam striving towards new freedoms but still disturbed that 'in speech with a man, a woman is at a disadvantage – because they speak different languages. She may understand his. Hers he will never speak nor understand . . . she must therefore, stammeringly, speak his'. Yet no woman, Miriam adds, can ever reveal 'her mental measure . . . even the fringe of her consciousness' through using the language of men. Since culture is constructed in what Miriam considers effectively a foreign language, she finds 'nothing to turn to. Books were poisoned. Art. All the achievements of men' (Richardson 1979: 2: 210, 222).

In *A Room of One's Own* (1929), Woolf reached much the same conclusion: that for a woman novelist

> it is useless to go to the great men writers for help . . . the first thing she would find, setting pen to paper, was that there was no common sentence ready for her use . . . a man's sentence . . . was unsuited for a woman's use (Woolf 1974: 76).

Yet typically of modernist literature – perhaps of all literature – conditions restrictive culturally and politically proved enabling, or compelling, imaginatively and artistically. Positioned culturally in ways more 'alien and critical' (Woolf 1974: 96) than their male counterparts, in Woolf's view, women were more disposed, like exiles, towards reconstructing the culture in which they found themselves. Women writers, in particular, contributed crucially to modernist fiction's most characteristic movement: towards the 'room of one's own' of inner consciousness, and away from rationalised, alienating, state-controlled public and social worlds. Early volumes of *Pilgrimage* employed the first extended form of stream-of-consciousness writing in English, and the inner voice and language of fiction subsequently developed particularly strongly in the work of May Sinclair, Virginia Woolf and eventually Jean Rhys.

Disturbed by suffragette riots early in April, the government found that worse was to follow a fortnight later: the Easter Rising in Dublin, its consequences still of grave concern in *The Times* on 3 July. Its outbreak was all the more shocking because it was so unexpected – despite long-standing Irish agitation – even among those in Dublin who might have been likeliest to anticipate it. One of these was W. B. Yeats, whose early poetry – recently in 'September 1913' – had often exhumed a heroic or mythic Irish past as an incentive to political action in the present. Yet Yeats's 'Easter 1916' reflects a response to such action, when it actually occurred, characterised by bewilderment, regret and an implicit self-criticism, evident in his naming of the revolutionaries in the poem's concluding lines:

> I write it out in a verse –
> MacDonagh and MacBride
> And Connolly and Pearse
> Now and in time to be,
> Wherever green is worn,
> Are changed, changed utterly:
> A terrible beauty is born.

(Yeats 1971: 205)

Like that *Times* reporter a few months later, Yeats envisages events that may lie beyond description, or at any rate beyond art. He apparently chooses instead to record only the names of the dead, like those wartime casualty lists in *The Times*, anticipating the unadorned naming, without 'abstract words', later favoured by Hemingway's narrator in *A Farewell to Arms*. Yet this record, of course, itself remains in verse, an element of 'beauty' – formal order, at any rate – still sustained despite its tensions with death and terror. Yeats's 'I write it out in a verse' in this way both emphasises, directly and declaratively, the responsibilities which replaced his early romanticism, yet tentatively anticipates later poems such as 'Sailing to Byzantium', or 'Byzantium', which envisage willing withdrawal from the world and its 'dying generations' in favour of eternal, stable, consoling orders of beauty and art.

Movement in this direction is paradigmatic of modernist writing's response to the period of war and revolution it surveyed. Adept in finding within individual consciousness, or memory, spaces freer of the pressures of the modern world, modernist literature was also readier than its predecessors to draw explicitly, sometimes self-referentially, on art and aesthetic order as antidotes to an intolerable actuality. The artist figure in *To the Lighthouse*, Lily Briscoe, emphasises this possibility when she refers to her brush as 'the one dependable thing in a world of strife, ruin, chaos' (Woolf 1973: 170). It is developed further by Woolf's tactics in the novel, formally analogous with Lily's painting in its tri-partite structure, and in its repeated depiction of ephemeral human moments framed artistically through doors or windows. Following Joyce's interest in the aesthetic, and in self-representation, in *A Portrait of the Artist as a Young Man*, similarly self-reflexive tactics figure throughout modernist fiction, often through reference to artists and painting: for example, in D. H. Lawrence's *Women in Love*, in Richardson's *Pilgrimage*, and in Wyndham Lewis's *Tarr* (1918) and *The Apes of God* (1930). Much modernist poetry was shaped, like Yeats's, by comparable concerns. When T. S. Eliot praised Joyce's Homeric allusions in *Ulysses*, as a way of shaping and controlling experience of an anarchic contemporary world, he might almost have been describing his own strategies in *The Waste Land* – or Ezra Pound's in *The Cantos* (1925–70), reliant throughout on allusion to earlier art and culture.

Later critics have hesitated between praising modernist strategies as new ways of ordering a threatening contemporary history, or criticising them as a new means simply of evading responsibility for it. Georg Lukács took the latter view in his essay 'The Ideology of Modernism' (1957). For critics such as Fredric Jameson, modernist emphases on the inner self, artistic order, freer temporality and the pleasures of memory offered forms of 'Utopian compensation', sustaining at least in imagination exactly the qualities most threatened in contemporary life (Jameson 1986: 42, 236). A reading of 1916 – of *The Times* of 3 July – neither resolves such issues of evaluation, nor exhausts the complexities of modernist invention occasioning them. Yet it does focus the problems and shaping challenges modernist writers encountered, highlighting reasons innovation and new imagination seemed so necessary to them. 'The herbage was soaking with dew', a *Times* correspondent recorded of the hours before the Somme offensive began. 'It was a lovely morning, the sun, still low, shining directly in our faces . . . a beautiful summer day, with promise of great heat . . . the sky above is clear blue, flecked with dazzling white islands of cloud'. After 7.30am, never such innocence again: not among words, not among men. Instead, history as the 'nightmare' Richard Aldington describes, and literary imagination straining in response towards ghostlier consolations, keener forms.

References

Aldington, Richard (1984) *Death of a Hero*, London: Hogarth Press

Beckett, Samuel, *et al.* (1972) *Our Exagmination Round His Factification for Incamination of Work in Progress*, London: Faber and Faber

Bergson, Henri (1971) *Time and Free Will*, trans. F. L. Pogson, London: George Allen and Unwin

Brown, Malcolm (2002) *The Imperial War Museum Book of the Somme*, London: Pan

Conrad, Joseph (1968) *The Nigger of the 'Narcissus', Typhoon and Other Stories*, Harmondsworth: Penguin

Ford, Ford Madox (1977) *The Good Soldier*, Harmondsworth: Penguin

Fussell, Paul (1979) *The Great War and Modern Memory*, Oxford: Oxford University Press

Hemingway, Ernest (1977) *The Essential Hemingway*, London: Panther

Jaggi, Maya (2003) 'Dispatches from the Front', *Guardian* Review, 2 August 2003, 16–19

James, William (1890) *The Principles of Psychology*, 2 vols, London: Macmillan

Jameson, Fredric (1986) *The Political Unconscious*, London: Routledge

Johnson, B. S. (1973) *Aren't You Rather Young to be Writing Your Memoirs?*, London: Hutchinson

Joyce, James (1971) *Finnegans Wake*, London: Faber and Faber

——(1973) *A Portrait of the Artist as a Young Man*, Harmondsworth: Penguin

——(1992) *Ulysses*, Harmondsworth: Penguin

Keegan, John (1998) *The First World War*, Oxford: Oxford University Press

Larkin, Philip (1985) *The Whitsun Weddings*, London: Faber and Faber

Lawrence, D. H. (1960) *Kangaroo*, London: Heinemann

——(1961) *Fantasia of the Unconscious* and *Psychoanalysis and the Unconscious*, London: Heinemann

——(1971) *Women in Love*, Harmondsworth: Penguin

——(1982) *Lady Chatterley's Lover*, Harmondsworth: Penguin

Nietzsche, Friedrich (1986) *Human, All Too Human*, trans. R. J. Hollingdale, Cambridge: Cambridge University Press.

Priestley, J. B. (1960) *Literature and Western Man*, London: Heinemann

Richardson, Dorothy (1979) *Pilgrimage*, 4 vols, London: Virago

Rushdie, Salman (1991) *Imaginary Homelands: Essays and Criticism 1981–1991*, London: Penguin/Granta

Saussure, Ferdinand de (1960) *Course in General Linguistics*, trans. Wade Baskin, London: Peter Owen

West, Rebecca (1980) *The Return of the Soldier*, London: Virago

Williamson, Henry (1957) *The Golden Virgin*, London: MacDonald

Woolf, Virginia (1973) *To the Lighthouse*, Harmondsworth: Penguin

——(1974) *A Room of One's Own*, Harmondsworth: Penguin

——(1975) *Orlando*, Harmondsworth: Penguin

——(1980) *The Diary of Virginia Woolf*, vol. 3: 1925–1930, ed. Anne Olivier Bell and Andrew McNeillie, London: Hogarth Press

——(1986–94) *The Essays of Virginia Woolf*, vols 1–4, ed. Andrew McNeillie, London: Hogarth Press

Yeats, W. B. (1971) *Collected Poems*, London: Macmillan

Chapter 4

1922, Paris, New York, London: The Modernist as International Hero

Michael North

One of the very first literary events of 1922 was an unusual dinner party in Paris, at which Ezra Pound played host to T. S. Eliot, James Joyce and the American publisher Horace Liveright (Dardis 1995: 86–92; Rainey 1998: 82). Eliot, on his way back from a rest-cure in Lausanne, was in possession of a manuscript not yet entitled *The Waste Land*, and Joyce had just scrambled his way through the final revisions to *Ulysses*, which was to appear a month later. Liveright, who had been turning his firm into one of the major American outlets for daring and experimental writing, was prowling Europe in search of authors just like Eliot and Joyce. It must have seemed, even at the time, like a millennial conjunction of literary planets, since all the participants were aware that these still unpublished works would make 1922 the first year in an entirely new literary calendar.

In the end, only Eliot actually published any major work with Liveright, who issued *The Waste Land* in December 1922. In later years the three writers themselves became more distant and estranged, as Pound, who at one-time had both *The Waste Land* and *Ulysses* passing through his hands, came to find Joyce's new work too radical and Eliot's too conservative. Even though it did not yield the results Pound apparently had in mind, however, this extraordinary social occasion does reveal a great deal about the modern movement that was to make its public mark so auspiciously in 1922. It might seem, in fact, to expose modernism as an artistic cartel, with Pound its chief monopolist. In this light, the celebrated difficulty of works like *The Waste Land* and *Ulysses* seems part of an elaborate sales job, as if they were never meant to be read but just admired from a distance.

What this argument suggests, in short, is that literary modernism enters the world of commerce only to secure itself all the more completely from competition. But the very site of this meeting tells a different story. Three Americans and an Irishman meet in Paris to discuss the future of English literature because that future was to be made by travellers such as themselves, moving through cities like Paris in a process of constant cultural exchange. Americans of this era were drawn to Paris because, in addition to legal alcohol and low rents, it offered culture, but that culture was to a surprising extent based on American materials. The French avant-garde was fascinated by American skyscrapers, American cars, even American plumbing. As Edmund Wilson marvelled in *Vanity Fair*, 'Young Americans going lately to Paris in the hope of drinking culture at its source have been startled to find young Frenchmen looking longingly toward America' (Wilson 1922: 49). In Paris, international modernism self-reflexively celebrated its own internationalism and the translation of ideas from place to place, language to language, medium to medium. Even if Pound had wanted to establish modernism as a closed shop, his very ability to do so would have depended on the free exchange that brought his principals together in Europe.

To Liveright, Pound seemed the very centre of the Parisian whirlwind, as together they called on Igor Stravinsky, Constantin Brancusi, Eric Satie and Pablo Picasso (Dardis 1995: 88). In point of fact, however, Pound was a marginal and almost comically anachronistic figure in the Paris of 1922, and his most significant work of the year was done on a research trip to Italy, where he began work toward the Malatesta Cantos. But the familiarity was not entirely a pose, and Pound was involved in one of the most bizarrely significant events of 1922, the Congress for the Determination of the Directives and the Defence of the Modern Spirit, announced in February by André Breton. At least, Pound's name is enlisted in support of the Congress by Francis Picabia, who had sided with Breton against Tristan Tzara in a conflict that led within a year to the break that created the Surrealist movement (Dachy 1990: 152–7; Alexander 1985: 98). The Congress of Modernism, which was to have demonstrated the unified front of all the tendencies gathered in Paris, was instead a chaotic disaster, but it was no less significant for having disintegrated. For 1922 was a banner year for congresses and international exhibitions, most of which managed to find the chaos lurking within their catholicity.

The first of these was the Congress of International Progressive Artists, convened in Düsseldorf in May, in conjunction with what was billed rather grandly as the First International Exhibition (Benson 2002: 35–7; Dachy 1990: 162). Predictably, the Dadaists refused to participate in the more organised aspects of the congress, and a rather considerable group of the more radical participants broke away from the congress altogether and reconstituted itself as the 'International Faction of Constructivists', taking its name from the art that El Lissitzky had recently brought from Russia. This group then convened its own congress, called the International Congress of Constructivists and Dadaists, in Weimar that September, in conjunction with its own exhibition of Constructivist art (Lodder 2002: 172–3, 178; Benson 2002: 37–8; Dachy 1990: 162–3). The internationalisation of the Constructivist movement continued with the First Russian Art Exhibition, held in Berlin from October to December (Lodder 2002: 176).

In a way, these various congresses might be considered large, contentious, public versions of the private congress convened by Pound in the same year, for they signified, even in their social arrangements, the same dual tendencies of dispersal and concentration. The urge to convene, to hold congresses, to enlist individuals under common banners, suggests a widespread sense of a growing common effort that linked individuals, styles, art forms, languages and countries, while at the same time the very tendencies that brought these groups together propelled them beyond their initial unity into new factions. There was a general belief in internationalism at these congresses, a general dedication to an international style, even a conviction that artists could perfect a new international language, comprehensible to all.

It may not seem so ironic, therefore, that Gilbert Seldes came to Europe at the end of 1922 to finish *The Seven Lively Arts*, his book on American popular culture. Seldes had been publishing articles on topics like slapstick, vaudeville and the comics throughout the year, while also serving as managing editor of *The Dial*, where he oversaw publication of *The Waste Land* in November. Travelling in Europe, he inhabited a similar cultural sphere, made up of modernist art on the one hand and popular culture on the other. He dined and drank with e. e. cummings, whose work of the year included vaudeville drawings for *The Dial* as well as *The Enormous Room*, published by Liveright. He met Gertrude Stein and

Picasso, who, among many other things, shared a lively interest in Katzenjammer Kids cartoon-strips, and Stravinsky, who was increasingly interested in jazz. He also met and struck up a friendship with Clive Bell, whose own work of this year lamented Joyce, Woolf and Eliot as artists nearly corrupted by jazz (Kammen 1996: 78–9, 94; Bell 1922: 222). Seldes was able to complete his book in Europe because the popular culture he celebrated had become an international fascination.

Sometime during Seldes' absence in Europe *The Dial* rejected some short stories submitted by an unknown young writer named Ernest Hemingway, who had moved to Paris a year earlier. Convinced that the rejection had come from Seldes, Hemingway established in himself a deep, lifelong antipathy for the other man (Kammen 1996: 53–4). The irony, of course, is that Hemingway and Seldes were so much alike, having been brought to Paris by similar impulses, to meet and learn from the same artists and writers. In fact, Hemingway spent much of 1922 covering the Genoa Conference with Seldes' brother George, from whom he apparently acquired some of the information sent out over the wires as if it were his own (Mellow 1992: 180). It was also at this time that Hemingway announced the new style of 'cablese', suggesting that the discipline of writing news dispatches for the telegraph had created in him 'a *new* language'. Hemingway actually wrote very little for the telegraph, and it is likely that his conviction that it had created a new language is derived as much from the European avant-garde as it is from the newspapers (North 2005: 188). But it is significant nonetheless that a fascination with new technological languages, especially with their ability to overcome distances and differences, manages to link even Seldes and Hemingway, despite their hostility.

One concrete link between the two men, as between so many other expatriates in Paris at this time, was Gertrude Stein, who published *Geography and Plays* in 1922. Most of the pieces in this collection had been written years earlier, and few of them show any of the technological idolatry so common in the little magazines of that year. Later, however, in 'Portraits and Repetition', Stein claimed to have been doing 'what the cinema was doing'. Though she does not remember having seen any actual movies, Stein maintains that she and they were both in the business of 'series production', by which she apparently means the process of generating infinite, incrementally different repetitions that add up, like the frames of a film, to a single continuous picture (Stein 1935: 176–7). The term 'series production' has an oddly industrial air to it, and it suggests the repetitive, formulaic nature of many popular films. As Wendy Steiner suggests, however, Stein was concerned to rehabilitate repetition, but not by subverting it or detaching it from its inevitably mechanical connotations (Steiner 1985: xiv). Stein seems to have realised that even if a machine repeats itself exactly it nonetheless repeats quite differently from the way a human being would and thus tends to thwart human habits and perceptions.

Unlike organic creatures, machines build up wholes out of discrete and discontinuous parts, and one of Stein's most effective literary strategies seems to rely on purposeful interference between machinic systems and supposedly organic ones. In the middle of 'Sacred Emily', for example, the word 'Door' is repeated as 'Do or', almost as if there has been a typographical mistake, a slippage in the gears of literary production (Stein 1922: 187). What appears in the crack between syllables, however, is the oddly arbitrary relationship of parts to wholes within words, even words as simple as *door*. In one sense, 'do' and 'or' are the parts that make up the word *door*, but not in any sense that a linguist might recognise. What, exactly, is the socio-psychological process that makes independent entities such as 'do' and 'or' disappear in larger entities like *door*, with which they have apparently very little to do? As she asks in 'Advertisements': 'why can I read it if I know page to page what is coming if I have not read it before. Why can I read it. I do' (Stein 1922: 341). The process of reading is apparently not one of finding meaning but rather of imposing it, taking the oddly assorted symbols of our language and forcing them into lockstep.

Americans, with their shallow history and arbitrary social associations, raise similar questions about the family of nations. As Stein puts it in 'The Gradual Making of The Making of Americans':

> think of anything, of cowboys, of movies, of detective stories, of anybody who goes anywhere or stays at home and is an American and you will realize that it is something strictly American to conceive a space that is filled with moving, a space of time that is filled always filled with moving . . . (Stein 1935: 161).

Like many European intellectuals of the time, Stein apparently considers Americans to be intrinsically cinematic, which is to say that they constitute a series of repetitive instances that somehow doesn't become a conventional whole. Americans thus raise questions about nationality, which becomes one of the major issues in *Geography and Plays*. In particular, the piece entitled 'Americans' is obsessed with the odd differences between a whole and the sum of its parts. What, for example, is the difference between a bale and the hay that makes it up: 'Bale, bale is a thing that surrounding largely means hay, no hay has any more food than it needs to weigh that way henceforward and not more that most likely' (Stein 1922: 39–40). In 'England', the statement 'Kindling is wood and coal is tonny' (Stein 1922: 87), seems a bit of charming nonsense until one reflects that the kindling and the ton bear the same relationship to their constituents that Englishness does to the individual citizen. 'Startling and true the same are few' (Stein 1922: 87) might be the truism on which the whole collection is founded, even when it deals with the system of nations, which often depends on the assumption of sameness.

Geography and Plays thus turns out to be an appropriate reflection on this particular international moment, with all its hopes for world understanding, its faith in new machine-made languages, and its giddy pop modernism of 'cowboys, of movies, of detective stories'. In America itself, however, there was also a very different mood. One of the more notorious American publications of this year was Harold Stearns' collection, *Civilization in the United States*, the contributors to which attacked the 'emotional and aesthetic starvation' of their home country (Stearns 1922: vii). Certain European visitors to the United States tended to agree with Stearns' estimate of his country, if for rather different reasons of their own. G. K. Chesterton's teasingly titled *What I Saw in America*, for instance, rails against advertisements, mass production, immigration, fads and moving pictures, which together make up a force called 'Americanisation' that was just as fearsome for him as it was attractive to the Dadaists (Chesterton 1922: 14). Chesterton was joined by the far more liberal Clive Bell, whose book *Since Cézanne* also decried the influence of America's non-culture on the rest of the world.

Works like this, with their American counterparts such as Lothrop Stoddard's *Revolt against Civilization*, make it clear that 1922 marked a kind of crisis in the social and aesthetic influence of American modernisation. In addition, they provide a context for certain American novels of the time, the more prominent of which seem to feature crisis and collapse and not the heady optimism of the European avant-garde. The most enduring bestseller of the year has been Sinclair Lewis's *Babbitt*, which seems at times almost to be an exposition in fictional form of the claims of *Civilization in the United States* or even *What I Saw in America*. The same kind of verbal repetition that opens up such odd possibilities for

Stein rules the consciousness of George Babbitt, gradually draining it of everything genuine. The empty oratory of the after-dinner speech and the sales pitch has so thoroughly infiltrated Babbitt's mind that he uses it even in private. Both Stearns and Chesterton identify standardisation as one of the chief threats of and to American life, and Babbitt seems their perfect case study. His greatest moment, in fact, is the after-dinner speech in which he extols the virtues of 'our Standardized Citizen' (Lewis 1922: 182). Even Babbitt's later rebellion against the conformity of middle-class life is but a different kind of conformity, and he is brow-beaten by jazz and late-night drinking just as surely as he had been brow-beaten by early rising and hard work.

Babbitt is interesting, of course, because he does not precisely fit into this world, and yet it is never quite clear why. At times it seems as if Lewis is claiming that Babbitt has unsatisfied emotional and aesthetic needs that mercantile America simply cannot meet. At other times, however, it seems as if Babbitt is too sturdy and old-fashioned for a newly bewildering world in which style and appearance matter more than substance. Even the advertising men of this time, according to Roland Marchand, were somewhat suspicious of their trade, dimly conscious of a shift toward style that threatened to leave utility behind (Marchand 1985: 158). In 1922, the advertising trade journal *Printer's Ink* announced 'The Dawn of the Distribution Age', the point at which the shift from production to consumption would put advertising in the dominant role previously occupied by industry itself (Marchand 1985: 6). Babbitt is a perfect representative of the bewilderment of this moment, which turned even some of its proponents into instant anachronisms.

In this sense, Babbitt displays an intriguing resemblance to a character who might otherwise seem his exact opposite: Anthony Patch, who is the focus of *The Beautiful and Damned*, F. Scott Fitzgerald's major publication of this year. One of Anthony's more dismal failures in the world of work is his foray into sales, which degenerates, as so many of Anthony's efforts do, into a drunken shouting match. It seems quite natural, in fact, that Anthony, a cosmopolitan aesthete, should fail at such work, and yet he is not as exceptional as he seems. He and his wife Gloria are actually ideal consumers, since they do nothing else. They are the nuclear family of the 'Distribution Age', producing nothing, not even offspring. Basic wants satisfied by a small inheritance, they are even incapable of producing sufficient desire to make it from day to day. On the surface an indictment of the idle rich, *The Beautiful and Damned* is actually an exposé of middle-class consumerism, which founders because the imperative to buy is too empty to sustain itself alone.

At the same time, however, Fitzgerald seems to suggest that Anthony and Gloria are much *less* substantial than the vast middle class. Anthony differs markedly and interestingly from Joseph Bloeckman, the movie mogul who delivers the most humiliating blows to his pride. Quite against the anti-Semitic stereotypes of the times, Bloeckman is portrayed as solid and manly, and his increasing refinement is played against Anthony's progressive vulgarisation, almost as if they were related as cause to effect. Racial anxieties that were to come out more fully in Fitzgerald's later novel *Tender Is the Night* (1934) are obviously at work here, as are doubts about the fate of the literary in a world dominated by film. Together they put the narrative in an almost masochistic position, as Anthony lashes out against Bloeckman and is righteously thrashed for it. It is an uncomfortably complex moment, as Anthony lies on the pavement before his stronger and more successful antagonist, a moment in which the narrative itself displays a mixture of prejudice and envy, hatred and self-disgust, and it suggests, distorted and dreamlike though it is, some of the difficulty of American racial relations in this year.

The year was marked, in fact, by significant controversies around race and immigration. A number of books, including Kenneth Roberts' *Why Europe Leaves Home* and Lothrop Stoddard's *Revolt against Civilization*, were written to alarm the populace about the threat of immigration. Debate in Congress about the Dyer Anti-Lynching Law, though it did not finally lead to legislation, focused attention on the epidemic of racial violence in the South. At the same time, the first significant steps were taken in establishing the literary movement that was to be known as the Harlem Renaissance. Rather quietly, Zora Neale Hurston made her literary debut with three poems in the *Negro World*. Much more publicly, James Weldon Johnson published *The Book of American Negro Poetry*, which was widely reviewed along with another collection, *Harlem Shadows* by Claude McKay. Both of these collections were actually retrospective, and they were generally rather conservative in style and tone. Even McKay's angrier and more defiant poems were framed as sonnets, with a rhetoric self-consciously modelled on that of Milton and Wordsworth. But the two books were taken by the press to have inaugurated something significant, and they made public a growing literary cohort, with a topic that held the literary and artistic interest of the country throughout the 1920s. In many cases, however, celebrity only complicated the already difficult situation of African-American writers. McKay, in fact, left the country late in 1922 to travel in the Soviet Union, having finally reached the breaking point in his relations with *The Liberator*, which had been his chief literary and financial supporter.

A month or two after McKay departed from the United States, one of his *Liberator* contributors delivered a manuscript entitled *Cane* to Horace Liveright. Parts of this book had been appearing all over the literary landscape of 1922: in *The Liberator* in September and October; in *The Crisis* in June; in the *Little Review* and the *Double Dealer* in the autumn; in *Broom* in December. The very range of the publications is intriguing, for there can have been few writers of the time who appeared almost simultaneously in *The Crisis* and in *Broom*. The author, Jean Toomer, was in fact an uncommon individual and the book he delivered to Liveright in 1922 was quite literally unique, but together they carried for a brief time the literary hopes of a wide range of American writers, from Alain Locke to Sherwood Anderson.

Toomer was self-consciously heir to the transnationalism of Randolph Bourne and *Seven Arts*, which had been transmitted to him in part by his friend Waldo Frank. Convinced that his racially mixed background made him an entirely new kind of American, Toomer attempted to create a literary form equivalent to his character. Originally conceived as a short-story cycle, something like *City Block*, which Frank published at this time, *Cane* ultimately became a quintessentially super-generic modernist work, mixing poetry, prose, and a short closet drama, 'Kabnis', transformed uneasily into fiction as a finale. Its three-part structure was intended to resolve all sorts of social and psychological divisions: between the North and the South; between city and country; between races; and between men and women. But 'Kabnis' is hardly a happy or successful resolution. Dramatically, it demonstrates the tensions that make life in the South virtually impossible for its title character, and generically it shows how difficult it is to patch over the inherent differences between a play and a short story.

The reception that *Cane* received also demonstrated how utopian were Toomer's hopes for a new pan-racial Americanism. Though he was hailed in the landmark anthology *The New Negro* (1925) as 'the very first artist of the race', Toomer refused to be celebrated solely as an African-American writer and ultimately ceased to identify himself as African-American at all (Brathwaite 1968: 44). Some of this reluctance may have been due to the extensive advertising campaign carried on by Liveright, which emphasised 'the real human interest value' of Toomer's racial background, and to the reaction even of his close friends among the literary avant-garde, who tended to view him as something of a curiosity (Soto 2001: 162–87). *Cane*, which might have functioned as a real bridge between literary and racial communities instead demonstrated the very real distances between them.

At this time, though, Toomer expressed to Liveright his enthusiasm about coming 'into the fold' with the other Liveright authors such as Eliot, and it is intriguing to imagine him as a fourth guest at Pound's momentous dinner party (North 1994: 147). It is also enlightening to realise how thoroughly that dinner party could have dominated Anglophone literature of the time without including any British writers at all. Liveright did spend considerable time in England during 1922, and he had fond hopes of peeling away from the British literary establishment certain of its more prominent iconoclasts, including H. G. Wells and George Bernard Shaw (Dardis 1995: 109). But, in fact, the most lasting works of this year were contributed by an American and an Irishman, and this simple fact in itself makes 1922 the first year in an entirely new kind of British literary history.

In one sense, 1922 seemed to mark for the British a return to normalcy after the massive dislocations of the First World War. It was, according to the *Daily Mail*, the first real postwar year (North 1999: 5). Even the fall of Lloyd George's government might have signalled a new beginning, especially since the elections of 1922 made Labour into the strongest opposition party (Lucas 1999: 145). But the prevailing mood was instead dour and fearful, epitomised perhaps by C. E. Montague's *Disenchantment*. The Washington Naval Conference formally recognised the end of Britain's domination of the world's oceans; the relinquishment of control over Egypt began the retreat of Britain's empire; the establishment of the Irish Free State marked a loss for Great Britain itself (Russell 1922a: 70–2). As the nature, the powers, and even the boundaries of Great Britain began to alter, the very notion of what it meant to be British came under unprecedented scrutiny.

In this context, the Bloomsbury group, named after all for a smallish neighbourhood in London, may seem almost deliberately out of step. Certainly, academic criticism of the group, led by Hugh Kenner's *A Sinking Island* (1987), has tended in the past to see it as insular in character as well as in fact. A look at the actual whereabouts of significant Bloomsburyites in 1922 might tell a different story, however. E. M. Forster returned from his second extended visit to India at the end of 1921, and most of his publications of the next year are about political and social problems in the subcontinent. Bertrand Russell was listed as 'Sometime Professor of Philosophy in the Government University of Peking' on the title page of his 1922 publication *The Problem of China* (Russell 1922b). This book is all about the virtues of comparing an alien culture with one's own because it forces a scrutiny of basic values and assumptions. D. H. Lawrence spent much of 1922 on the road, pursuing a great circumnavigation that took him from Italy to Ceylon, then on to Australia and finally the southwest United States. Of his novels, only *Aaron's Rod*, set in Italy, appeared in 1922, but his Australian novel *Kangaroo*, mostly written in 1922, was published in the next year, as was *Studies in Classic American Literature*, in the US. Another significant publication of the year, Katherine Mansfield's *The Garden Party*, was by a New Zealander who had in a sense reversed Lawrence's route between England and the South Pacific.

In comparison, Virginia Woolf, who spent much of the year cooped up in the country, may seem like something of a recluse (Lee 1997: 453). In fact, her novel of this year, *Jacob's Room*, is quite deliberately housebound. Britain's losses in the war come to be symbolised by an empty room, its vanished occupant surviving only in bits and pieces of domestic memory. It is a very significant difference, therefore, that Woolf's next work, *Mrs Dalloway*, which she started to work on in 1922, begins with its title character flinging open the door.

Woolf's own delight in London life is expressed in the peripatetic construction of this book, much of which takes place in the street. There is a significant correlation as well between the dramatic construction, which begins quite literally on the threshold, and the mobile, flexible style of indirect discourse that Woolf adopts for this occasion. 'Mrs Dalloway said she would buy the flowers herself' is an opening sentence that sends the main character out the door on an errand and simultaneously suspends the narrative between the first-person and the third, between subjective reflection and objective description (see also Chapter 5 below). Woolf constructs the rest of this novel by teasing out these relations: her characters spend so much time musing in the street because she thinks of them as subjectivities made up of the objective, social presences around them. 'Stream of consciousness', the term often applied to such writing, is a misnomer insofar as it implies a static consciousness with ideas streaming through it. *Mrs Dalloway* shows instead how necessary mobility is to thought; ideas and impressions come to Woolf's characters only when they move out of the house and into the world, which they travel just as adventurously as Forster in India or Lawrence in Ceylon.

It is no sign of disrespect to Woolf to suggest that much of the difference between the novel published in 1922 and the one begun in that year is due to *Ulysses*, parts of which she had seen as early as 1918, when it was suggested that the Hogarth Press might be its publisher (Lee 1997: 385). At first blush, Woolf found Joyce's novel smutty, but she paid concerted attention to it and gave Joyce pride of place in 'Modern Fiction', the essay she wrote and rewrote between 1919 and 1925. And it is certainly clear that *Mrs Dalloway* owes a great deal of its basic structure to *Ulysses*: both novels take place in a single day; both follow dual main characters as they manage not to meet; both rely on restless urban walking to propel the stream of consciousness of their main characters. In a sense, then, *Mrs Dalloway* is one of the first and one of the finest analyses of *Ulysses*, and it is instructive to see what parts of that great novel another great novelist found useful for her work.

Significantly, Woolf did not find it useful or interesting to pursue Joyce's celebrated 'mythic method'. The rather shaky scaffolding provided by the *Odyssey* appealed to Eliot because it seemed to offer a method of 'controlling' the chaos of the modern world, but Woolf is far less interested in control than she is in connections. The ability of one consciousness to dimly sense another through all the barriers of space and social distance becomes an ethical fact for her, as it is for Joyce as well. One of the most significant facts about Joyce's hero, Leopold Bloom, is that he can often think his way into the minds of others, swimming in a different stream of consciousness, as he does on the very first page of his account when he hears the cat's purr as if it were a sentence: 'Scratch my head' (Joyce 1986: 45). Bloom's sympathy is the basis of Joyce's literary method, allowing him to expand the story of a single, rather eccentric individual until it becomes the story of Dublin as a whole.

Franco Moretti has called *Ulysses* a 'world text', not just because it seems to sum up a world, but more importantly because it is written '*for* the world' (Moretti 1996: 222). *Ulysses* is meant to be read variously, and it shows the way by reading itself variously, repeating and reinterpreting the same details from a variety of different perspectives. Bloom, it is often noticed, is intrigued by the idea of parallax (see also Chapter 5), which comes to his mind as he watches a distant clock mark the time. Woolf puts a similar scene at the beginning of *Mrs Dalloway*, as dozens of urban spectators watch a sky-writer, each of them reading the puffed-out letters in a different way. The scene seems a comic demonstration of the distortions of perspective, but it is also a very early look at a new form of commonality. 1922 is also the birth-year of broadcasting, with the establishment of the BBC, and

Joyce and Woolf seem to be forecasting how that establishment will bring about huge new aggregates of experience, larger, stronger, and swifter than any possible before. But it will still be possible to receive and interpret these experiences in various ways, to hear or see the broadcast differently. *Ulysses* seems most modern not just in those places where it comments on such experiences, as in Bloom's musings on parallax, but also in its very form, which offers an aesthetic model for them.

In 1945, Delmore Schwartz would say something similar about *The Waste Land*: 'The reader of T. S. Eliot by turning the dials of his radio can hear the capitals of the world, London, Vienna, Athens, Alexandria, Jerusalem' (Schwartz 1945: 199). Eliot was also in close touch with Woolf during 1922, and from her perspective he apparently seemed painfully provincial. Years later, though, Schwartz was to look back on *The Waste Land* and see it as a kind of passport.

> Modern life may be compared to a foreign country in which a foreign language is spoken. Eliot is the international hero because he has made the journey to the foreign country and described the nature of the new life in the foreign country. (Schwartz 1945: 206).

In this analysis, modern life is in essence international, and *The Waste Land* is the truly inaugural poem of the modern because it puts its readers in touch with the foreignness of the international experience. Thus it is the confusion of the poem, and not its schemes for order, that really matter, and the untranslated languages, annoying to so many readers, that are its main contribution to the modern style. Eliot's own pained experience as a foreigner in London, so evident in all its disadvantages to Woolf, became the basis for a style as powerful in its reach and influence as the radio. It is certainly in this sense that *Ulysses* and *The Waste Land* are the defining works not only of 1922, a year marked by so much significant travel, but also perhaps of the rest of the twentieth century as well.

References

Alexander, John (1985) 'Parenthetical Paris, 1920–1925', in *Pound's Artists: Ezra Pound and the Visual Arts in London, Paris and Italy*, London: Tate Gallery, 81–120

Bell, Clive (1922) *Since Cézanne*, London: Chatto and Windus; New York: Harcourt, Brace

Benson, Timothy O. (2002) 'Exchange and Transformation: The Internationalization of the Avant-Garde[s] in Central Europe', in *Central European Avant-Gardes: Exchange and Transformation, 1910–1930*, ed. Timothy O. Benson, Los Angeles: Los Angeles County Museum of Art/Cambridge: MIT Press, 34–67

Brathwaite, William Stanley (1968) 'The Negro in American Literature', in *The New Negro*, ed. Alain Locke, New York: Atheneum, 29–44

Chesterton, G. K. (1922) *What I Saw in America*, New York: Dodd, Mead

Dachy, Marc (1990) *The Dada Movement, 1915–1923*, New York: Rizzoli

Dardis, Tom (1995) *Firebrand: The Life of Horace Liveright*, New York: Random House

Joyce, James (1986) *Ulysses*, New York: Viking Penguin

Kammen, Michael (1996) *The Lively Arts: Gilbert Seldes and the Transformation of Cultural Criticism in the United States*, New York: Oxford University Press

Kenner, Hugh (1987) *A Sinking Island*, Baltimore, MD: Johns Hopkins University Press

Lee, Hermione (1997) *Virginia Woolf*, New York: Knopf

Lewis, Sinclair (1922) *Babbitt*, New York: Harcourt, Brace

Lodder, Christina (2002) 'Art into Life: International Constructivism in Central and Eastern Europe', in *Central European Avant-Gardes: Exchange and Transformation, 1910–1930*, ed. Timothy O. Benson, Los Angeles: Los Angeles County Museum of Art/Cambridge: MIT Press, 172–98

Lucas, John (1999) *The Radical Twenties: Writing, Politics, and Culture*, New Brunswick, NJ: Rutgers University Press

Marchand, Roland (1985) *Advertising the American Dream: Making Way for Modernity, 1920–1940*, Berkeley, CA: University of California Press

Mellow, James R. (1992) *Hemingway: A Life without Consequences*, Boston, MA: Houghton Mifflin

Moretti, Franco (1996) *Modern Epic: The World System from Goethe to García Márquez*, London: Verso

North, Michael (1994) *The Dialect of Modernism: Race, Language, and Twentieth-Century Literature*, New York: Oxford University Press

——(1999) *Reading 1922: A Return to the Scene of the Modern*, New York: Oxford University Press

——(2005) *Camera Works: Photography and the Twentieth-Century Word*, New York: Oxford University Press

Rainey, Lawrence (1998) *Institutions of Modernism: Literary Elites and Public Culture*, New Haven, CT: Yale University Press

Russell, Bertrand (1922a) 'Hopes and Fears as Regards America', *New Republic*, 15 March, 70–2

——(1922b) *The Problem of China*, London: George Allen and Unwin

Schwartz, Delmore (1945) 'T. S. Eliot as the International Hero', *Partisan Review*, Spring, 199–206

Soto, Michael (2001) 'Jean Toomer and Horace Liveright; or, a New Negro Gets "Into the Swing of It"', in *Jean Toomer and the Harlem Renaissance*, ed. Geneviève Fabre and Michel Feith, New Brunswick, NJ: Rutgers University Press, 162–87

Stearns, Harold (1922) 'Preface', *Civilization in the United States*, Westport, CT: Greenwood Press, iii–viii

Stein, Gertrude (1922) *Geography and Plays*, Boston, MA: The Four Seas Company

——(1935) *Lectures in America*, Boston, MA: Beacon Press, 1985

Steiner, Wendy (1985) 'Introduction', *Lectures in America*, Boston, MA: Beacon Press, ix–xxvii

Wilson, Edmund (1922) 'The Aesthetic Upheaval in France', *Vanity Fair*, February, 49–51

II: Between the Wars

Chapter 5

1925, London, New York, Paris: Metropolitan Modernisms – Parallax and Palimpsest

Jane Goldman

And today, for the 165th time, Nelly has given notice – Won't be dictated to: must do as other girls do. This is the fruit of Bloomsbury. On the whole I'm inclined to take her at her word. The nuisance of arranging life to suit her fads, & the pressure of 'other girls' is too much, good cook though she is, & honest, crusty old maid too, dependable, in the main, affectionate, kindly, but incurably fussy, nervy, unsubstantial. Anyhow, the servant question no longer much worries me.

(Virginia Woolf, *Diary*, Tuesday 6 January 1925)

Virginia and Leonard Woolf saw in the New Year at Monks House, Rodmell, their country retreat, and returned on 2 January 1925 to their metropolitan home in Tavistock Square, Bloomsbury. Woolf's first diary entry for the year records another row with her cook, Nelly Boxall, whose spirited defiance Woolf recognises as partly her own doing – the 'fruit' of the Bloomsbury group's progressive, egalitarian politics and notoriously easy-going domestic arrangements (Woolf 1977–84: 3: 3). The spat with her servant forms a timely coda to Woolf's famous assertion, in 'Mr Bennett and Mrs Brown' (1924), that 'on or about December 1910 human character changed', which she illustrates with reference to the behaviour and character of 'one's cook' (Woolf 1986–94: 3: 421–2). Woolf's essay describes a shift from the Edwardian to the Georgian era, in art and life, in which 'all human relations have shifted – those between masters and servants, husbands and wives, parents and children. And when human relations change there is at the same time a change in religion, conduct, politics, and literature' (Woolf 1986–94: 3: 422). The 'Victorian cook' – 'a leviathan in the lower depths' – is surpassed by 'the Georgian cook' – 'a creature of sunshine and fresh air; in and out of the drawing room, now to borrow the *Daily Herald*, now to ask advice about a hat' (Woolf 1986–94: 3: 422) – and now to argue with her mistress.

Woolf's pronouncements about 1910 articulate a sense of change inevitably shared by many of her contemporaries. Cultural and political unrest in 1910 marked the beginning of a period which witnessed the Balkan Wars, the cataclysm of the Great War (the First World War), the Russian Bolshevik Revolution, the execution of the Tsar (1918), the creation of an Irish Free State (1922), the establishment of the Union of Soviet Socialist Republics (1923), the Teapot Dome affair (scandalising the United States in the early 1920s), the foundation of an Italian Fascist State in 1924, and, in the same year, the death of Lenin and the beginning of Stalin's dictatorship in the Soviet Union. Within Britain, there were stirrings from 'the lower depths'. In the despondent period after the Great War, industrial unrest was developing towards the General Strike of 1926, and 1924 saw the formation of the first Labour government in Britain, headed by Ramsay MacDonald, soon brought down by the infamous 'Zinoviev Letter', supposedly sent by the government of the Soviet Union.

Written in the turbulent political context of 1924, 'Mr Bennett and Mrs Brown' looks back across fourteen years of exceptional upheaval, Woolf inferring possibilities of a more egalitarian life in the mid-1920s – for her cook and others – as the direct result of cultural and political change inaugurated in 1910. The essay shuttles between literature and life, blurring boundaries and examining the interpenetration of these spheres. The transgressive cook herself bridges life and writing. Laying claim to the progressive newspaper, the *Daily Herald*, she also lays claim to literacy, education and political participation, and is herself a sort of herald, a 'sign'. While claiming equality with her mistress, her employer, she also provides an allegory for the rise of both these women from domestic to public sphere. Woolf's essay clarifies this feminist import with 'more solemn instances' of change, from the cultural, literary sphere: with a revised reading of the *Agamemnon* that turns 'sympathies [. . .] entirely' away from the murdered husband to the monstrous Clytemnestra (the murdering wife, dispatched by her son in the aftermath of the Trojan War). Clytemnestra is a literary sign whose potential meaning is transformed by the new social context and the political expectations of those who read her. Woolf switches perspective from myth to history, finding a further feminist 'instance' in 'the married life of the Carlyles'. The historical reality of Jane Carlyle's subservience to her husband – a daily and degrading domestic reality, 'chasing beetles, scouring saucepans, instead of writing books' – enabled Thomas Carlyle to sustain his voluminous literary production from the 1820s to the 1860s, but prevented Jane herself from fulfilling her potential as a writer, debarring her from proper access to the sphere of literature (Woolf 1986–94: 3: 422). How very different was the married life of the Woolfs by the 1920s. Woolf's diary is testimony to a life spent fulfilling her creative potential, buoyed by the companionship and support of her husband, albeit still dependent on truculent servants.

'Mr Bennett and Mrs Brown', of course, offers much more than an account only of shifting class or gendered hierarchies: much more, too, than an argument that literature should change only in subject matter in order to reflect social change and the new, modern experience it creates. Woolf's essay argues instead that literary form itself simultaneously undergoes radical, and turbulent, transformation: that radical literary form even *produces* change and transformation in the social sphere – in human character; in 'religion, conduct, politics' (Woolf 1986–94: 3: 422). Woolf makes the violation of 'the very foundations and rules of literary society' resonate with the sound of the destruction of society itself, as 'grammar is violated; syntax disintegrated' in everything from poetry to journalism (Woolf 1986–94: 3: 434). 'So the smashing and the crashing began', she adds. 'Thus it is that we hear all round us, in poems and novels and biographies, even in newspaper articles and essays, the sound of breaking and falling, crashing and destruction. It is the prevailing sound of the Georgian age' (Woolf 1986–94: 3: 433–4). Woolf's inclusion of newspaper articles, harbingers of destruction in the real world, emphasises the sense of radical, violating instability she posits between language and the social and political sphere. Literary work she refers to by James Joyce, T. S. Eliot and the biographer Lytton Strachey – critical of many figures he surveys in *Eminent Victorians* (1918) – further indicates modern literature's rejection of the past and vital struggle for new form. Indeed, the 'indecency' of Joyce's *Ulysses* (1922) is seen as the 'calculated indecency of a desperate man who feels that in order to breathe he must break the windows' (Woolf 1986–94: 3: 434). Woolf urges readers to 'tolerate the spasmodic, the obscure, the fragmentary, the failure' almost as if urging endurance of the hardships of war and of the turbulent postwar period itself. (Woolf 1986–94: 3: 436).

Yet in Woolf's essay the self-reflexive, fragmentary, subjective and momentary qualities of modernist writing are not only tolerated or endured, but celebrated and indeed performed – as they had come to be, much more extensively, by the mid-1920s. In 1925 Woolf published *Mrs Dalloway*, a novel, set in one metropolitan day, that reconsiders Homer over the head of Joyce's *Ulysses*, and the essays of *The Common Reader*, including the seminal 'Modern Fiction', modernism's most cited manifesto, and an early defence of *Ulysses*. Much innovative fiction was published in the same year in the United States: John Dos Passos's *Manhattan Transfer*, Theodore Dreiser's *An American Tragedy*, F. Scott Fitzgerald's *The Great Gatsby*, the expatriate Gertrude Stein's *The Making of Americans*, and her acquaintance Ernest Hemingway's story-cycle *In Our Time*. Alain Locke's edited work *The New Negro* showcased the writing of the Harlem Renaissance, and the poet William Carlos Williams ventured into prose in the essays of *In the American Grain*. It was a good year, too, for American writers from the previous century: there was a posthumous edition of Emily Dickinson's *Complete Poems*, and in Camden, New Jersey, the opening of the Walt Whitman Hotel, a community hotel established by the Greater Camden Movement (a progressive group of civic and business leaders), testimony perhaps that poetry makes some things happen.

On the British side of the Atlantic, Nancy Cunard published her long poem *Parallax*, while the Irish poet W. B. Yeats produced his mystical treatise *A Vision*, and the Scottish poets Hugh MacDiarmid and Edwin Muir some of their early work, respectively in *Sangschaw* and *First Poems*. Further afield, the Czech-Jewish novelist Franz Kafka's *The Trial* was first published in German in 1925. The same year saw the opening of *Neue Sachlichkeit* exhibition in Berlin, showing satirical work by Otto Dix, George Grosz and others which exposed the urban, industrial disaffection – more movement in 'the lower depths' – undermining postwar Germany. In Paris, the African-American entertainer Josephine Baker created a sensation in *La Revue Nègre*. Back in the United States, the blues artist Bessie Smith recorded 'St. Louis Blues' with Louis Armstrong, and found herself successful enough to buy her own Pullman railroad car. The modernist explosion of the mid-1920s also encompasses cultural milestones of the preceding year, 1924, including the First Surrealist *Manifesto*, and the first issue of the little magazine *Transatlantic Review*; Woolf's 'Mr Bennett and Mrs Brown'; T. E. Hulme's posthumous philosophical *Speculations*; the first publication in Britain of D. H. Lawrence's *Studies in Classic American Literature*; Marianne Moore's poetry *Observations*; E. M. Forster's novel of empire *A Passage to India*, and, in German, Thomas Mann's *The Magic Mountain*. The following year, 1926, saw the publication in the United States of William Faulkner's first novel *Soldier's Pay*, H.D.'s *Palimpsest*, and Ernest Hemingway's *The Sun Also Rises*; Gertrude Stein's essay 'Composition as Explanation'; and poetry and an essay by one of the Harlem Renaissance writers, Langston Hughes, in *The Weary Blues* and 'The Negro Artist and the Racial Mountain'. That same year, in Britain, Robert Graves and Laura [Riding] Jackson published their anthology *Modernist Poetry* and Hugh MacDiarmid his long work *A Drunk Man Looks at the Thistle*. Also in 1926, Sean O'Casey premièred in Dublin his play about the Easter rising of 1916, *The Plough and the Stars*; the German director Fritz Lang released his futuristic film *Metropolis*; and Woolf issued, in French, 'Time Passes', the central part of her novel, *To the Lighthouse*, published in full the following year.

1925 itself, though, was a particularly rich year, especially for the avant-garde novel, and certainly for Woolf herself. Her diary is an inviting threshold to 1925 and beyond, but it is her two great modernist landmarks, *Mrs Dalloway* and 'Modern Fiction', both in the wake of 'Mr Bennett and Mrs Brown', that dominate that year, and to an extent – along with the other outstanding novel of 1925, Dos Passos's *Manhattan Transfer* – many that follow.

Reading *Mrs Dalloway* eighty years after its first publication inevitably involves recognition of the many adaptations, imitations or reworkings it has encouraged in the intervening years. Both *Mrs Dalloway* and *Manhattan Transfer* continue to be read as both classic and essentially modern. Each reflects on and in some senses produces the transitional, transgressive and contesting subjectivities of modern urban life – increasingly, in the 1920s, a central concern of modernist fiction, and one influential on later narrative. In Michael Cunningham's filmic homage, *The Hours* (1999), *Mrs Dalloway* is transported from London to New York, in keeping with the twentieth-century's imperial power shifts. *Manhattan Transfer* remains a vital intertext for Jonathan Safran Foer's 'post 9/11' New York novel, *Extremely Loud and Incredibly Close* (2005). Foer's work also clearly readdresses Joyce's *Ulysses* and its classical allusions. Its poignant narrative of a bereaved son, negotiating New York in search of a lost father after the terrorist attack, echoes the story of Telemachus, reconsidering Homer over the head of Joyce. It views the terrorist attack on the Manhattan skyline alongside the epic devastation of Dresden and Hiroshima too.

Among other modernist novels of 1925 Gertrude Stein's epic *The Making of Americans* probably remains the least often read – probably less often than Stein's essay, 'The Gradual Making of The Making of Americans' (1935) – and is ripe in the twenty-first century to be made new. F. Scott Fitzgerald's *The Great Gatsby*, by contrast, continues to enjoy popularity, despite Francis Ford Coppola's schmaltzy film treatment in 1974. A decade earlier, in his song 'Ballad of a Thin Man' (1965), Bob Dylan had been devastatingly sceptical of the relevance of Fitzgerald's writing to contemporary counter-cultural negotiations of modernity. Despite his having been through 'all of F. Scott Fitzgerald's books', Dylan's 'Thin Man', the 'very well read' Mister Jones, crucially fails to 'know' whatever it is that 'is happening here'. What is happening here, in Dylan's lyric, is an avant-garde aesthetics that performs the failure of received knowledge, something that *The Great Gatsby* gestures towards but, for all its 'jazz age' setting, fails to enact or disclose. ('Here is your throat back/Thanks for the loan') (Dylan 1974: 307–8). Essentially conservative in his late-Romantic aesthetics, as in his narrative tactics, which had been developed a quarter-century earlier in Joseph Conrad's *Lord Jim* (1900), Fitzgerald never fully participated in the violation of the 'foundations and rules of literary society' that Woolf identified.

Avant-garde attitudes and tactics are more directly in evidence in *Mrs Dalloway* and in *Manhattan Transfer*. Thus, if the narrator of *The Great Gatsby*, nostalgic for America's lost promise, erases the obscenities scrawled on Gatsby's impossibly white steps, and, with his back to 'the dark fields of the republic', urges its boats to 'beat on . . . against the current, borne back ceaselessly into the past' (Fitzgerald 1991: 168), Dos Passos, assembling his picture from urban detritus, accuses contemporary America of betraying that promise:

> 'They are sending the Reds back to Russia . . . Deportees . . . Agitators . . . Undesirables.' . . .
> Gulls wheeled crying. A catsup-bottle bobbed gravely in the little ground-glass waves. A sound
> of singing came from the ferryboat getting small, slipping away across the water. (Dos Passos
> 2000: 263)

Over debris reminiscent of T. S. Eliot's soiled urban river in *The Waste Land* (1922), the unnamed onlookers hear the fading strains of the Internationale. A man with 'telescopes and fieldglasses' invites us to 'take a look at the undesirable aliens', and 'a girl's voice burst[s] out suddenly, "*Arise prisoners of starvation*", "Sh . . . They could pull you for that"' (Dos Passos 2000: 263). The disappearing ferry and wheeling gulls poignantly conjure the potent imagery of 'Crossing Brooklyn Ferry' (1865), Whitman's hymn to the Manhattan metropolis, and to America's democratic potential, only to have it diminish and disappear:

> At the end of a marbled wake the ferryboat was shrinking into the haze. *International . . . shall be the human race.* The singing died. From up the river came the longdrawn rattling throb of a steamer leaving dock. Gulls wheeled above the dark dingydressed crowd that stood silently looking down the bay. (Dos Passos 2000: 263)

Whitman's expansive crowd, along with his 'oscillating gulls' that 'wheel in large circles, high in the air', is much diminished too (Whitman 1973: 164). By 1925 his vision of 'a hundred years hence' has already been betrayed. Whitman envisioned a free, democratic, collective of 'Others' who, just like the poem's speaker, 'will enter the gates of the ferry, and cross from shore to shore;/Others will watch the run of the flood-tide;/Others will see the islands large and small' (Whitman 1973: 160). But not *all* 'others', it now appears, 'will enjoy the sunset, the pouring-in of the flood-tide, the falling-back to the sea of the ebb-tide' (Whitman 1973: 160). Some of Whitman's others are now undesirable aliens, Bolsheviks who might recruit, or *be*, 'one's cook'. Much had changed in society, and for its 'lower depths', between 1910 and 1925: some hierarchies nevertheless remained firmly in place.

Like *Mrs Dalloway*, the other outstanding novel of the year, *Manhattan Transfer* nevertheless illustrates particularly clearly what modernism had changed in the foundations of *literary* society by 1925. *Manhattan Transfer* is New York's first great work of literary montage, and *Mrs Dalloway* is London's, though speaking also to Paris and New York. In their montage tactics – so apt, in their juxtaposition of disparate visions, for the exploration of modern city life – both novels might equally well be described by another term gaining contemporary currency, especially following Nancy Cunard's use of it as the title of her 1925 poem: parallax. Dos Passos's borrowings from Whitman – and Virginia Woolf's, considered below – also exemplify another modernist term and tactic, highlighted in this case by H.D.'s 1926 novel title: palimpsest. Nancy Cunard's poem, the term 'parallax' itself, and the wider significance of each, are considered in the next section; H.D.'s novel, and modernist 'palimpsest' more generally, in the one following.

Parallax

In that first diary entry for 1925, Woolf moves on from 'the servant question' to discuss the 'depressing & exacting' business of final revisions to *Mrs Dalloway*, along with the conception of material – 'scenes' – for her next novel, *To the Lighthouse* (1927), and for her feminist polemic, *A Room of One's Own* (1929). Then, characteristically, she switches perspective: 'however, back to life. Where are we?' (Woolf 1977–84: 3: 3–4). Woolf answers by recounting her morning, a typical Bloomsbury morning of writing entering life, and life entering writing – a morning mixing serious scholarship, creative fomenting, intellectual exchange, gossip, financial transactions, dog walking and the tedious business of typesetting. Virginia and Leonard Woolf's Hogarth Press was just then setting up the type for a long poem by the socialite and shipping heiress, Nancy Cunard – an original of several *femmes fatales* in 1920s fiction (including Aldous Huxley's *Antic Hay* [1923] and *Point*

Counter Point [1928], and Evelyn Waugh's *Decline and Fall* [1928]). Her poem's title, *Parallax*, suggests in one way an avant-garde experimentalism matching the work of a sworn enemy of Bloomsbury, and of Roger Fry in particular – the novelist, painter and essayist Wyndham Lewis, whose 'Vortex' movement had flourished briefly in London just before the First World War.

Cunard's title also recalls the 'parallax' that 'stalks' and 'goads' through Joyce's *Ulysses*, the 'parallax or parallactic drift of socalled fixed stars' which intrigues and puzzles Bloom (Joyce 1993: 395, 651). Cunard herself, however, cites in her epigraph the seventeenth-century essayist Sir Thomas Browne: 'many things are known as some are seen, that is by Paralaxis [*sic*], or at some distance from their true and proper being'. Also a particular favourite of Woolf's, Browne amplifies in *Christian Morals* (*c.*1680), his endorsement of 'parallaxis' with the observation that 'the superficial regard of things hav[e] a different aspect from their true and central Natures' (Browne 1904: 39). As explained by Browne – or as it might have been to Bloom, had he made his projected trip to Dunsink Observatory – parallax records changes of vision induced by the shifting position or perspective of observers; involving, in literary terms, juxtaposing, distancing, or cutting between diverse texts, histories, realities. The distancing effect of parallaxis removes the deception of mere appearance, showing affinity with the kind of modern painterly aesthetics Cunard adopts and celebrates in her poem, and which her Bloomsbury publishers had notoriously promoted fifteen years earlier in the Post-Impressionist exhibition organised by Roger Fry in 1910. Indeed, Desmond MacCarthy's much-quoted attack on the exhibitors' predecessors, the Impressionist painters, for their 'passive attitude toward appearances', and his heralding of the 'disconcerting', non-realist, techniques of Post-Impressionism, have much in common with Browne's suspicion of appearances and his interest in deeper truths. The technique of the 'revolutionary' Post-Impressionist Paul Cézanne, MacCarthy explains, leads 'from the complexity of the appearance of things to the geometrical simplicity which design demands': Cézanne's own instruction, to 'treat nature by the cylinder, the sphere, the cone' opened the way for the younger Post-Impressionists, Paul Gaugin and Vincent Van Gogh (MacCarthy 1998: 176; Cézanne 1976: 301).

Parallax is itself disconcerting in design, plunging the reader first into an abstract cosmos inhabited by a 'poet-fool [. . .] halt[ing] at every tavern', then into metropolitan London, juxtaposed with scenes from the South of France, then Paris and its bohemian Left Bank. The London passages are populated by street vagrants – 'the scabrous old', 'fur-collared decreptitude', and 'derelicts' – and catalogue the 'cold muds, rains, intolerable nauseas of the street' in lines recalling the dispirited urban vision of T. S. Eliot's poetry. Eliot's personification of the street and city and his imagery of disembodied, fragmented and alienated inhabitants, in 'Preludes' and 'Prufrock' and *The Waste Land*, echo in lines such as 'Afternoon settles on the town' and 'Sunday creeps in silence/ under suspended smoke,/ And curdles defiant in unreal sleep.' Cunard's alienating city is as 'unreal' as Eliot's, haunted, like his, by the spectres of the war: 'the war's dirges/ Burning, reverberate – burning'. Cunard figures the city ablaze, razed by war – like the burning Carthage described in *The Waste Land* – and as an impacted, desiccated cemetery: 'dry graves filled in, stifled, built upon with new customs' (Cunard 1925).

By contrast, Cunard introduces Southern France, haunt of Cézanne, Van Gogh and Gauguin, with 'well, instead – / The south and its enormous days [. . .] a classic land, time-less and hot', rich with 'red earth, ripe vines and plane-trees', a land that embodies 'the dream,/ the question's answer'. Yet the poem undermines what Thomas Browne would have termed the 'superficial regard' of the art tourist's pleasure in Provence, Miramas and

Les Baux, expressing a snatch of French ennui at the death of an anonymous old local 'patriarch': 'il est fatigué, depuis douze ans toujours dans la même coin' ['he's weary, after twelve years always in the same spot']. To remain in one place is fatal. Cunard's poem communicates modernism's restlessness and its refusal to settle, performing a modernist 'parallaxis' in which both London and Provence offer necessary, illuminating, 'distance' on each other. Another revelation of the Provence landscape is that it fails to yield Cézanne to the visitor, nor has the master of modern art left any remaining visible trace on Provence: 'in Aix, what's remembered of Cézanne?/ A house to let (with studio) in a garden'. Cunard describes his art as a rural product exported to the city: 'beauty picked in a field, shaped, re-created,/ Sold and dispatched to distant Municipality –'. Cézanne's compositions on the landscape of Provence speak to this 'distant Municipality' (Paris in the first instance, then London and New York), but remain silent to the locals 'here in the Master's town' where 'an old waiter, crossly,' recalls 'a dull silent fellow,/ Dead now' (Cunard 1925).

The import of Cézanne's art is not his Provençal subject matter, then, but his modern technique, something that transcends his geographical, rural, location and speaks directly to the 'unreal', and international, cultural dimension of metropolitan centres. In this comical distancing from the local, he is paradoxically victim of his own parallactic technique – also the enabling technique of the poem itself. Cunard moves on to Paris, the primary destination and warehouse of Cézanne's and everyone else's pioneering modern art. This location is described in terms of its legendary bohemian, avant-garde associations, and the perennial, 'disparate', figure of the *flâneur*, the urban stroller of Charles Baudelaire's late nineteenth-century Parisian poetry, anticipatory of much modernist city-vision. 'Where now from the river bank?/ From the Seine, up the Quarter, homeward at last to sleep.' The modernist model of the avant-garde *bricoleur*, Baudelaire's rag-picker, is also invoked by Cunard's speaker who tells the time by the 'alarm clock [. . .] rag-man'. Baudelaire's proto-collage technique, juxtaposing the random findings of stroller or rag-man, is obviously also a kind of parallaxis. The juxtapositioning of collage forces disparate elements and surfaces against each other, an act of discontinuity and distancing. In *Parallax*, the streets of London become properly visible through the parallax of Cézanne's paintings of Provence and the Baudelairean streets of Paris.

In her January diary entry, Woolf records her own impressions of the London streets: 'it being a black grained winter day; lengths of the pavement ink black where not lighted'. Her 'ink black' epithet for the pavement connects walking the streets with the process of writing, a connection affirmed in her essay, 'Street Haunting: A London Adventure' (1927), described by the critic Rachel Bowlby as Woolf's 'walking text', in homage to her engagement with Baudelaire's *flâneurs* and passers-by (Bowlby 1997: 218). 'Never shall I describe all the days I have noticed', Woolf concludes in her diary, 'I cannot hit it off, quite, & yet perhaps if I read this again I shall see what I meant then'. Her almost incidental vision of the 'ink black' street will prompt future readings and future attempts to describe the specificity of the day. Her venture out into the dark urban winter street is more than she managed while in rural Rodmell where 'I did not see very much [. . .] having to keep my eyes on the typewriter'. On her typewriter was, of course, her *vision* of the London streets in *Mrs Dalloway*. Again, it is important for Woolf to record the exigencies of the outside world as well as the writer's interior experience of the latter stages of the compositional process:

> Rodmell was all gale & flood; these words are exact. The river over-flowed. We had 7 days rain out of 10. Often I could not face a walk. [. . .] I revised Mrs D[alloway]: the dullest part of the

whole business of writing; the most depressing & exacting. [. . .] L. read it; thinks it my best
[. . .] but is difficult owing to the lack of connection, visible, between the two themes. (Woolf
1977–84: 3: 4)

Mrs Dalloway's difficulty is in its disconnected accounts of the experiences of Clarissa
Dalloway, London society hostess, and of Septimus Smith, shell-shocked veteran of the
Great War. Their visions of the London street barely coincide. Clarissa's joyful shopping
expedition in Bond Street, punctuated by nostalgic visions of a past erotic moment, contrasts with Septimus's dreadful urban progress, haunted by the horrors of war. Yet the term
'visible' in her diary entry both suggests the blatant *lack* of connection between Clarissa
and Septimus and, paradoxically, identifies the visible realm as the very point of connection. That Clarissa and Septimus both tread the streets of London, and have visible points
of urban geography and experience in common, is the parallactic crux of the novel (and
the crux of its satire). Similarly the diary record, itself written in ink, of the visible 'lengths
of the pavement ink black' serves as the self-consciously constructed avenue back into
Woolf's experience of the day spent writing, printing and gossiping.

Woolf's writing in the mid-1920s offers further paradigms of modernist parallaxis –
textual, geographical and temporal. Completion of the almost entirely metropolitan
Mrs Dalloway in the 'gale & flood' of rural Rodmell contrasts with her experience of com-
posing in 'the heart of London' significant tracts of her next novel, *To the Lighthouse*, set in
the western isles of Scotland. 'What is so perplexing is the change of perspective', Woolf
wrote to her new lover Vita Sackville-West: 'here I'm sitting thinking how to manage the
passage of ten years, up in the Hebrides: then the telephone rings [. . .] well, am I here
[. . .] or in a bedroom up in the Hebrides?' (Woolf 1975–80: 3: 244). Woolf did not actually visit the Hebrides until 1938, eleven years after the publication of *To the Lighthouse*,
and the novel's Hebridean setting is in part a literary intertext with Samuel Johnson's and
James Boswell's accounts of their tour of the western isles in the late eighteenth century,
as well as with other Scottish texts. But if the rural location of *To the Lighthouse* is literary,
it does not follow that the metropolitan location of *Mrs Dalloway* is entirely literal. On the
contrary, Woolf's writing, autobiographical and fictional, teaches us to read geographical
location as text, as always and already literary, and to read text as location. Her ink-
inscribed vision of the modern street simultaneously transports us into both realms. Woolf's
London is a reading in the London of Johnson, Carlyle, John Keats and William Blake, to
name but a few. Of Blake, poet and visionary, Woolf suggested that he lived in London 'as
it is necessary to live somewhere [. . .] but there is no reason to think that the tree that
was filled with angels was peculiar to Peckham Rye' (Woolf 1986–94: 2: 162). While both
Blake and Woolf write specifically and compellingly about London, it would be naïve and
diminishing to ignore the imaginative and symbolic dimensions that they infuse in their
London locations.

Mrs *Dalloway* self-consciously alerts the reader to its radically distanced sense(s) of place
(social, political, geographical) in its opening lines, where Mrs Dalloway, in saying 'she
would buy the flowers herself', takes on the work of her servant: 'for Lucy had her work cut
out for her. The doors would be taken off their hinges; Rumpelmayer's men were coming'.
The removal of the doors is in preparation for Mrs Dalloway's party, the crowning scene of
the novel, but it is an image that simultaneously heralds the unhinging of the novel's own
narrative portals. Firstly it ushers in Clarissa's interior narrative: 'and then, thought
Clarissa Dalloway, what a morning – fresh as if issued to children on a beach'. Her beach
simile serves to express the quality of the present moment, Clarissa's excited anticipation

of her expedition to buy flowers being likened to the anticipation of children on a beach, but it is also unhinged, in a typical Woolfian narratorial manoeuvre, to a metaphor: 'What a lark! What a plunge!'. Clarissa is plunging into her day as the children in the simile might plunge into the sea, but the markers of simile ('as if') have been removed. Who has issued the simile, who the metaphor? In the slippery terrain of Woolf's free indirect narrative, intermingling the voices of author and character, it is difficult to decide. Clarissa, however, seems to lay claim to the day-on-the-beach simile with the metaphor, as 'What a plunge!' plunges the reader into neither sea nor shopping expedition but into Clarissa's memory of a key moment in her distant past, a moment itself of plunging: 'for so it had always seemed to her when, with a little squeak of the hinges, which she could hear now, she had burst open the French windows and plunged at Bourton into the open air' (Woolf 2000: 3).

The 'squeak of the hinges' from the past, still audible in the present, suggests unhinging the doors will open up the past moment still further. Present and past moments cohabit in Woolf's elaborate next sentence, in which the unhinged door and the plunge into sea-water figure not only Clarissa's plunge into the past, but the reader's plunge into the flapping waves of the prose itself:

> how fresh, how calm, stiller than this of course, the air was in the early morning; like the flap of a wave; the kiss of a wave; chill and sharp and yet (for a girl of eighteen as she then was) solemn, feeling as she did, standing there at the open window, that something awful was about to happen [. . .] – Peter Walsh. (Woolf 2000: 3)

This parallactic narrative is a dual portal to Clarissa's present and past, where each moment, balanced on a string of present participles, acts in distancing juxtaposition on the other. The foreboding, 'feeling as she did' applies to past and present moment; and we might wonder if the 'something awful' that 'was about to happen' did go on to happen, or is only now 'about to happen'. That squeak of the hinges – echoed throughout modernist narrative, so disposed to plunge back into its characters' recollections – ushers in Clarissa's memory of her one moment of ecstasy when she and her friend Sally Seton kissed, interrupted by Walsh who is about to interrupt again in the present. The novel explores the politics of her nostalgia for this one lesbian encounter, now distanced by a lifetime of conformity to compulsory heterosexuality. But this parallactic narrative is also a palimpsestic portal to another literary text, as well as to two other metropolitan centres.

Palimpsest

An acquaintance of Marianne Moore and William Carlos Williams – and briefly fiancée of Ezra Pound – 'H.D.' (Hilda Doolittle) is better known as a poet than a novelist, though she also wrote much fiction and autobiographical prose. Her novel *Palimpsest* defines palimpsest (in its epigraph) as 'a parchment from which one writing has been erased to make room for another'. Parallaxis cuts between diverse texts, histories, realities: palimpsest overwrites them, in a form of radical erasure which also remains implicitly citational. In exploring diverse empires, cultures, subjectivities, and sexualities, H.D.'s experimental, lyric novel is parallactic as well as palimpsestic. Its tripartite form juxtaposes three metropolitan locations, ancient and modern. The first part, set in 'War Rome (circa 75 B.C.)', explores the life and art of the Greek woman poet, Hipparchia, a vessel of waning Greek culture, attracted to Egypt, negotiating the dominance of imperial Roman culture; the second, set in 'War and post-war London (circa 1916–1926 A.D.)', explores that of an American woman poet with Hellenic and Judeo Egyptian obsessions; the synthesising third, set in 'Excavator's Egypt (circa 1925 A.D.)' explores that of an American woman archaeological assistant. The novel brilliantly delineates the sexual/textual politics of each epoch, probing the palimpsestic erotics of the hetero/sapphic sexual relations and cultural roles of the mistresses, wives and lovers of imperial soldiers in and after war, each part culminating in intense empathy between women. Amid invocations of Joyce and Einstein and declarations on 'semi-transparent' modernity and enduring antiquity, *Palimpsest* is an avant-garde war elegy:

> There were shrines beyond shrines, feet beyond feet, faces beyond faces. Faces overlaid now one another like old photographic negatives and faces whirled on and on and on and on, like petals down, down as if all those overlaid photographic negatives had been pasted together and rolled off swifter, swifter, swifter from some well controlled cinematograph. (Doolittle 1926: 224, 222)

The ancient palimpsest of parchment transposes to modern montage; the surface text of modern metropolitan London is inscribed on ancient imperial ones. The reader of *Palimpsest*, like the reader of *Mrs Dalloway*, becomes archaeologist of a dense geo-literary space.

In the course of her walk through London in *Mrs Dalloway*, Clarissa will read in a bookshop window an extract from Shakespeare's *Cymbeline*, 'fear no more the heat o' the sun/ Nor the furious winter's rages', which becomes a significant refrain in the novel. But in the opening lines we encounter a less obvious literary allusion: a fugitive, palimpsestic, citation. 'The doors would be taken off their hinges' rehearses the expansive democratic gesture of Walt Whitman's *Leaves of Grass*: 'unscrew the locks from the doors!/ Unscrew the doors themselves from their jambs!' In this passage, Whitman declares himself both 'a kosmos', a claim to universal transcendent constellated subjectivity, and 'of Manhattan the son', identifying himself specifically as a New Yorker and an American. He also celebrates himself in terms of free-roaming sensuality and sexuality: 'turbulent, fleshy, sensual, eating, drinking and breeding,/ No sentimentalist, no stander above men and women or apart from them'. He follows his injunction to remove the barriers imposed by social and political hierarchy as well as sexual propriety ('Unscrew the doors themselves from their jambs!') with the declaration of democratic solidarity: 'whoever degrades another degrades me,/ And whatever is done or said returns at last to me' (Whitman 1973: 52). Doors taken off their hinges for Mrs Dalloway's London party unhinge the text of *Mrs Dalloway* itself, opening a portal to Whitman's progressive, democratic, unhinging in Manhattan, and by extension, once again, to the shifting social hierarchies that concerned Woolf in 'Mr Bennett and Mrs Brown' in the mid-1920s.

Woolf certainly knew and admired Whitman's work. In essays such as 'American Fiction', also published in 1925, she celebrates the 'refreshing unfamiliarity' of *Leaves of Grass*, or Whitman's 'greater and greater' democratic 'power to include' (Woolf 1986–94: 3: 269; 2: 207). Woolf also acknowledges Whitman's capacity to make us 'blush', perhaps a reference to his poetry's overt celebration of homosexuality – something that D. H. Lawrence considers in his 1924 study of American literature, and that the American poet Hart Crane celebrates in his great New York work, *The Bridge*, written in 1926 (Woolf 1986–94: 2: 80). Eileen Barrett's criticism identifies Septimus Smith's 'revelation' in Regent's Park as an echo of Whitman (Barrett 1997: 153). She also identifies suppressed homosexuality as the key point of commonality between Clarissa and Septimus. While

Clarissa is nostalgic for 'the most exquisite moment of her life', kissing Sally Seton, Septimus is haunted by his feelings for his dead comrade Evans, and by his guilt over his secret homosexual 'vice' (Woolf 2000: 3, 77).

Other significances are opened up by the removal of those doors, heralding 'Rumpelmayer's men'. David Bradshaw rightly recommends extreme attention to the 'minor' details' of Woolf's novels, such as street and shop names, and directs us to 'Rumpelmayer's Tea Rooms' of St James's Street, Westminster, 'a firm of "refreshment contractors"', according to the *Post Office London Directory* for 1923 (Bradshaw 2002: 109). Rumpelmayer's men, Mrs Dalloway's caterers, were also known to Arnold Bennett. According to Woolf, Bennett was one of 'the most prominent and successful novelists in the year 1910', though one deplorably reluctant to renovate literary form in response to the radical changes she saw in 'human character' in that year (Woolf 1986–94: 3: 427, 422). He was consequently a principal target of her criticism in 'Mr Bennett and Mrs Brown', though she was more sympathetic to his journalism, warmly reviewing a collection of his writings for the *New Age* in 1917 (Woolf 1986–94: 2: 128–31). This work included Bennett's account of Rumplemayer's as a haunt of the 'prosperous crowd [. . .] called the middle-class, but it ought to be called the upper-class [. . .] well-fed, well-dressed, completely free from the cares which beset at least five-sixths of the English race'. Like Mrs Dalloway herself, this affluent crowd 'spend their lives in spending. They deliberately gaze into shop windows in order to discover an outlet for their money. You can catch them at it any day' (Bennett 1917: 89)

There was also a French Rumpelmayer's. The *salon de thé* of the French *chocolatier*, Rumpelmayer's, in the Rue de Rivoli, was likewise a haunt of the chic and the famous, and of American expatriates, perhaps including H.D. It was certainly known to Woolf, who mentions it in her letters, including one from Paris in 1923 describing a date there with Hope Mirrlees, partner of her revered intellectual mentor, Jane Harrison. A range of meanings is emerging, then, to hinge on the minor detail of Woolf's sentence, hinged itself on her trademark semi-colon: 'the doors would be taken off their hinges; Rumpelmayer's men were coming'. It signals that Mrs Dalloway's doors are opening to the kind of privileged set, accustomed to the Rumpelmayer's catering, described by Bennett. But the unhinged doors disclose a Whitmanian subtext, a palimpsest that speaks to the progressive metropolitan centre of New York, while Rumpelmayer's also discloses Woolf's Parisian rendezvous with the lesbian companion of the intellectual she most admires.

The powerful reach, the poise and delicacy of Woolf's arabesquing narrative, allow the reader to trace out from such portal moments the complex dimensions of her satire. Woolf's ambition for *Mrs Dalloway* was 'to give life & death, sanity & insanity; I want to criticise the social system, and to show it at work, at its most intense' (Woolf 1977–84: 2: 248). The satire is communicated by the matching intensity of Woolf's prose: by a palimpsestic, lyric compression of multivalent meaning in every minor detail, every apparently incidental name. These fragments of lyric compression are suspended in a syntax engineered like Thomas Browne's distancing parallax. This combination of lyric compression and parallactic technique allows us to read each detail as presenting at least two alternatives. 'The doors would be taken off their hinges; Rumpelmayer's men were coming' indicates the necessary preparations for a party to entertain the elite and privileged, structured around compulsory heterosexuality, and dependent on the suppression of homosexuality; but it also communicates an alternative democratic possibility that includes liberated sexual orientation. Just as Cézanne's Provence paintings were already in dialogue with more distant municipalities, so *Mrs Dalloway* is already in dialogue with Paris and New York, and opening doors to each.

And just as H.D.'s palimpsestic characters simultaneously inhabit modernity and antiquity, there is no reason to think that Clarissa and Septimus are entirely peculiar to the streets of London, or to 1925. Indeed, Marleen Gorris's film, *Mrs Dalloway*, starring Vanessa Redgrave, faithfully set in post-Great War London, has been criticised for its less faithful emphasis of heterosexual relations and elision of the homosexual ones of Woolf's novel. Perhaps there is more fidelity in the parallactic and palimpsestic departure of Michael Cunningham's novel, and Stephen Daldry's film, *The Hours* (2002), in transferring Clarissa and Septimus to the distant streets of New York in 2001 to explore, among other things, a nostalgia for heterosexuality in the gay and lesbian milieu of the literary scene. Whitman's pledge is appropriate here: 'I will make inseparable cities with their arms about each others necks, by the love of comrades' (Whitman 1973: 117). Whitman's is the parchment on which 1925's two finest avant-garde novels are written. Each is an outstanding demonstration of modernism's new tactics, structures and subtleties in writing life in the modern city. 1925 heralds the zenith of avant-garde techniques: parallax and palimpsest.

References

Barrett, Eileen (1997) 'Unmasking Lesbian Passion: The Inverted World of *Mrs Dalloway*', *Virginia Woolf: Lesbian Readings*, ed. Eileen Barrett and Patricia Cramer, New York: New York University Press

Bennett, Arnold (1917) *Books and Portraits: Being Comments on a Past Epoch 1908–1911*, London: Chatto and Windus

Bowlby, Rachel (1997) 'Walking, Women and Writing', *Feminist Destinations and Further Essays on Virginia Woolf*, Edinburgh: Edinburgh University Press, 191–219

Bradshaw, David (2002) '"Vanished, Like Leaves': The Military, Elegy and Italy in *Mrs Dalloway*', *Woolf Studies Annual* 8: 107–26

Browne, Thomas (1904) *Christian Morals*, Cambridge: Cambridge University Press

Cézanne, Paul (1976) *Paul Cézanne: Letters*, trans. Marguerite Kay, ed. John Rewald, 4th edn, London: Cassirer

Cunard, Nancy (1925) *Parallax*, London: Hogarth Press

Doolittle, Hilda ('H.D.') (1926) *Palimpsest*, New York: Contact

Dos Passos, John (2000) *Manhattan Transfer*, London: Penguin

Dylan, Bob (1974) *Writings and Drawings*, London: Granada

Fitzgerald, F. Scott (1991) *The Great Gatsby*, Cambridge: Cambridge University Press

Joyce, James (1993) *Ulysses*, Oxford: Oxford University Press

MacCarthy, Desmond (1998), 'The Post-Impressionists' (1910), *Modernism: An Anthology of Sources and Documents*, ed. Vassiliki Kolocotroni, Jane Goldman and Olga Taxidou, Edinburgh: Edinburgh University Press, 174–8

Whitman, Walt (1973) *Leaves of Grass*, ed. Sculley Bradley and Harold W. Blodgett, New York: W. W. Norton

Woolf, Virginia (1975–80) *The Letters of Virginia Woolf* (1888–1941), 6 vols, ed. Nigel Nicolson and Joanne Trautmann, London: Hogarth Press

——(1977–84) *The Diary of Virginia Woolf* (1915–41), 5 vols, eds. Anne Olivier Bell and Andrew McNeillie, London: Hogarth Press

——(1986–94) *The Essays of Virginia Woolf*, vols 1–4 (of 6), ed. Andrew McNeillie, London: Hogarth Press

——(2000) *Mrs Dalloway*, ed. David Bradshaw, Oxford: Oxford University Press

Chapter 6

1928, London: A Strange Interlude

Chris Baldick

Exits and Entrances

It was a year of Victorian endings and postmodern beginnings. Thomas Hardy, last of the great Victorian writers, died in January, and his career concluded later in the year with the appearance of his last volume of poems, *Winter Words*. The unfinished business of Victorian lexicography, too, terminated in the dozen enormous volumes of the *Oxford English Dictionary*, published at last after seventy years of collective toil. Havelock Ellis's tireless compendium of sexology, *Studies in the Psychology of Sex*, begun in the 1890s, was also concluded with the appearance of its seventh and final volume. Soames Forsyte, whom John Galsworthy had introduced to the world in 1905 as the irascible embodiment of Victorian high-bourgeois values, finally expired in the last of the long-running Forsyte sequence of novels, *Swan Song*. On the other hand, Andy Warhol and Stanley Kubrick were both born in 1928, which was also a breakthrough year for the nascent technology of television: the first television transmissions, including the first made across the Atlantic, were demonstrated in 1928, and the first TV sets were manufactured. Cinema was still in the throes of transition from the silent era to the new thrill of the 'talkies', and it witnessed the arrival of Walt Disney's first Mickey Mouse cartoons.

Closer to the directly literary developments of the time was the arrival in Paris of Samuel Beckett, who soon met his fellow Irishman James Joyce and became his amanuensis and general errand-boy. Meanwhile in England there emerged a fresh generation of poets and novelists who had been born in the twentieth century itself: W. H. Auden and C. Day Lewis issued their debut collections of verse in this year, while Evelyn Waugh and Christopher Isherwood published their first novels, *Decline and Fall* and *All the Conspirators*. V. S. Pritchett too brought out his first book, an account of travels in Spain. At a more modest level, one 'E. A. Blair', later George Orwell, began his journalistic career with a short article for *G.K.'s Weekly*. With these premonitory stirrings, what we now understand to be the literary 'Thirties' started two years early.

The more prominent and visible literary landmarks of the year were of course associated with the established writers of the generations between Hardy's and Auden's. This was the year of W. B. Yeats's *The Tower*, of D. H. Lawrence's *Lady Chatterley's Lover*, of Virginia Woolf's *Orlando*, of Aldous Huxley's *Point Counter Point*, of Eugene O'Neill's *Strange Interlude*, of Lytton Strachey's *Elizabeth and Essex*, of T. S. Eliot's *For Lancelot Andrewes*, of Siegfried Sassoon's *Memoirs of a Fox-Hunting Man*, and of Radclyffe Hall's *The Well of Loneliness*. And from some of these writers, significant notes of resignation, valediction and abdication were heard. The title tale of D. H. Lawrence's new collection

The Woman Who Rode Away and Other Stories is a hypnotically world-weary fantasy of symbolic racial suicide, in which an unnamed white woman willingly abandons her 'gods' and accepts her fate as a human sacrifice at the hands of a Mexican Indian tribe. In W. B. Yeats's new volume, *The Tower*, the opening poem, 'Sailing to Byzantium', is a leave-taking spoken by an aged man: 'That is no country for old men', he complains in parting. That country is often taken to be Ireland, but it is also the youth-crazed culture of the Twenties more generally, from which Yeats distances himself by assuming the identity of the wizened sage. Yeats was the surviving leader of poets born in the 1860s, while T. S. Eliot now clearly dominated those born in the 1880s. Eliot himself, though, was in the process of outgrowing and discarding his earlier selves: he dismayed many of his admirers, for whom *The Waste Land* (1922) had been the defining expression of postwar disillusionment, by declaring in the preface to his new book of essays, *For Lancelot Andrewes*, that he now regarded his position as classicist in literature, royalist in politics, and Anglo-Catholic in religion. It was a kind of abdication from the imputed leadership of a 'modern' literary generation that had too easily assumed that poetic experiment was in some way twinned with secular liberalism.

Just as bewildering to admirers of the leading modernists was the appearance in the same year of James Joyce's *Anna Livia Plurabelle*, an instalment of the 'Work in Progress' that grew into *Finnegans Wake* (1939), portions of which had been appearing in various journals since 1924. Even among admirers of Joyce's *Ulysses* (1922), some were inclined to think that with this baffling new project Joyce had taken leave of his senses. He certainly appeared to have taken leave of the vocabulary of English as now codified by the *Oxford English Dictionary*, a monumental word-hoard that Joyce melted down into an avalanche of Freudian slips crashing its way through a forest of symbols. Attacks on Joyce's obscurity and allegedly pathological obscenity were coming thick and fast by now, the latest in 1928 being Rebecca West's title essay in her critical collection *The Strange Necessity*. Joyce, thrown on the defensive, rounded up his remaining supporters and asked them to issue a collective rebuttal, which appeared in the following year as *Our Exagmination Round His Factification for Incamination of Work in Progress*.

The energetic movement of literary experiment that we now rather too tidily call modernism had, it seemed, passed its heroic phase (let us say, 1913–27), and, apparently abandoned or betrayed by its own luminaries, was subsiding into whimsy and extravagance: very few notable works of this year maintain the focus upon contemporary actuality that often stabilises earlier modernist masterpieces, and many were either fantastical (*Orlando*, *Anna Livia Plurabelle*, 'The Woman Who Rode Away', Wyndham Lewis's *The Childermass*, T. F. Powys's *Mr Weston's Good Wine*), or melodramatic (*The Well of Loneliness*, *Strange Interlude*), or satirically grotesque (*Decline and Fall*, *Point Counter Point*). In the remainder of this chapter I will offer a brief account of 1928 as a culmination of some of the dominant trends and preoccupations of Twenties writing and, more tentatively and fleetingly, as a disintegration from which germinate new 'Thirties' moods, styles, and voices. Although I will take some notice of the especially significant O'Neill play from which I take my subtitle, and of Margaret Mead's ethnographic utopia *Coming of Age in Samoa*, I shall devote most attention to the British literary scene, this being, despite significant new volumes of verse from Robert Frost and Carl Sandburg, a rather lean year in American letters (William Faulkner was still at work on *The Sound and the Fury* (1929), three chapters of which are set in 1928; Ernest Hemingway and F. Scott Fitzgerald too were 'between' books).

Swan Song of the Mandarins

The suggestion that the literary Twenties closed earlier than the calendar allowed and the Thirties began prematurely is not a new one. It was floated as long ago as 1938 by Cyril Connolly, the failed novelist and successful literary journalist who, as editor of the influential journal *Horizon*, became the dominant impresario of London literary life in the 1940s. Connolly's most important book, *Enemies of Promise* (1938; revised 1949), proposes in its opening literary-historical section a schematic account of modern literary trends, which he traces through three distinct phases. Whereas almost all literary historians since the 1970s would describe this period in terms of the vindication of 'modernism' and the discrediting of its various supposed antagonists (realist fiction, naturalistic drama, late-Romantic or 'Georgian' poetry), Connolly had the advantage of surveying the literary scene of the recent past before those academic blinkers could narrow his scope. His more catholic conception of the 'modern movement' in letters, as he calls it, is broad enough to include Bernard Shaw, H. G. Wells, John Galsworthy, Arnold Bennett, W. Somerset Maugham, Rupert Brooke and several others who are now beyond the modernist pale.

Ecumenical as Connolly's model of literary modernity is, it is by no means undifferentiated: he divides writers into two camps, not as we might be encouraged to do today by degrees of technical innovation or by imputation of a philosophy of representation, but according to their styles – and so too according to the breadth of readership they seem to address. On the one side are the 'Mandarins', devotees of exclusive, esoteric, and apolitical high art and of self-consciously polished style for the refined tastes of initiates, and on the other are the anti-Mandarins or vernacular realists, who speak plainly and with a social conscience to a broad public. In caricatured terms, the Mandarins would resemble an effete priesthood presided over by a Henry James or a Marcel Proust, the anti-Mandarins a pugnacious scrum of journalists with H. G. Wells somewhere in the front row. This central distinction underpins the chronological scheme of Connolly's that most concerns us here. His simple proposition is that literary phases and fashions define themselves in over-reaction against the excesses of their predecessors, so that the Mandarin heyday of Aestheticism, dandyism, 'decadence' and Symbolism of the 1880s and 1890s provokes a new phase of reaction, which Connolly dates from 1900 to 1918, in the form of socially committed realistic fiction and drama alongside more vernacular styles in verse, notably in realistic war poetry. This in turn exhausts itself to give way to a new Mandarin revival, associated with the fastidiousness of T. S. Eliot and of the Bloomsbury group (although among Bloomsbury-linked writers, E. M. Forster is counted as an anti-Mandarin on account of his easy colloquial prose). The year 1928 stands in Connolly's calendar as the last year of the postwar Mandarin interregnum, and the first of a new reactive phase of plainer styles and political commitments that we now associate with the works of Auden, Isherwood, Orwell and the early Graham Greene, and in the US with Hemingway, John Dos Passos and John Steinbeck, and refer to in our shorthand as 'the Thirties'. In this scheme, it should be pointed out, the succession of phases indicates only the temporary and fragile predominance of one camp over the other, not its definitive monopoly of critical or public favour. It is possible too for an individual writer to belong to both camps: James Joyce, to take the major instance only, is both demotically naturalistic and arcanely symbolistic, fusing the strengths of both traditions.

A scheme such as this is only a scheme, and should not be taken as anything more reliable. Nonetheless, Connolly's sense of the tide turning in 1928 is worth attending to as a valuable contemporary testimony. In that year, he had reached the age of twenty-five, found a niche as regular fiction reviewer for the *New Statesman* (he reviewed *Point Counter Point* and *Decline and Fall*, for instance), and was sampling the various styles of contemporary writing with an ear already finely attuned to the shifts of literary fashion. His account of 'The New Mandarins' in the seventh chapter of *Enemies of Promise* recaptures the intoxication of his own generation with the works of Joyce, Proust, Eliot, André Gide, Paul Valéry, Woolf, Lytton Strachey, Huxley and the Sitwells, as it recalls the attitudes of 'inflated' aesthetic individualism that well-read youngsters in the Twenties cultivated under those influences. The opening of his next chapter identifies the point at which youthful hero-worship turns with cruel abruptness to boredom and to rejection of former idols:

> The mass attack on the new Mandarins was launched in the late Twenties. By that time these had squandered their cultural inheritance, for their inflationary period coincided with the Boom and their adversaries were to come into their own with the Slump. In spite of their apparent success and publicity, the three great Mandarin books of 1928, *Orlando, Elizabeth and Essex, Point Counter Point,* were disappointing; they were not, except in America, popular successes and met also with considerable highbrow opposition. (Connolly 1961: 70)

'Mass attack' is of course putting it too strongly, but Connolly does trace a body of adversaries who were gathering in force in the late Twenties, including the newcomers Waugh and Isherwood, the recently emerging Hemingway, the modern mavericks Wyndham Lewis and D. H. Lawrence, and the veteran realist W. Somerset Maugham. Of the books of 1928, he nominates *Lady Chatterley's Lover, Decline and Fall*, and *All the Conspirators* as notable examples of the anti-Mandarin vernacular style, these being followed in the next year by Henry Green's *Living*, Hemingway's *A Farewell to Arms*, Robert Graves's *Goodbye to All That*, Richard Aldington's *Death of a Hero*, and Lawrence's verse collection *Pansies*. He might also have added to his 1928 list Maugham's *Ashenden*, a short-story sequence about wartime espionage that debunks the glamour of spying in a deflatory realist style which George Orwell adopted as his model of plain modern English prose. As we shall see, the predominance of war books in this new wave of vernacularist works is significant in the larger transition we are tracing from Twenties modernism to the realist revival of the Thirties.

Connolly is guilty of understating the success of Bloomsbury and of the larger Mandarinate in the late Twenties. 1928 was in some ways an *annus mirabilis* for that tendency in letters. Huxley's *Point Counter Point* was widely recognised as his most important and ambitious work to date, by Connolly himself as well as by other reviewers. Virginia Woolf had an even better year, being awarded the Femina–Vie Heureuse prize for *To the Lighthouse* (1927) in May, and being rendered still more *heureuse* herself by the unexpected warm public response to *Orlando* in the autumn. Sales of *Orlando*, especially in America, gave her her first real commercial success, and helped to stabilise the Woolfs' Hogarth Press as a viable business concern after eleven years of tight budgets. As well as bringing out Sigmund Freud's *The Future of an Illusion*, the Hogarth Press issued in 1928 several important short critical works, including Edwin Muir's *The Structure of the Novel*, Harold Nicolson's *The Development of English Biography*, Herbert Read's *Phases of English Poetry*, and Clive Bell's *Proust*. Elsewhere in the Bloomsbury circle, E. M. Forster published *The Eternal Moment and Other Stories*, Clive Bell published his book *Civilization*, and, to cap it all, Desmond MacCarthy launched a new literary monthly, *Life and Letters*, going on to edit it over the next six years as a showcase for Bloomsbury authors. It had been MacCarthy who, as literary editor of the *New Statesman*, had given Connolly his first break as a reviewer; and he now brought the younger man in as a regular contributor to *Life and Letters* too. Connolly knew well enough, then, that the Bloomsbury group not only marched vigorously into the Thirties but served as important sponsors to the emerging generation: it was the Hogarth Press that was to publish all Isherwood's books of the 1930s and the landmark verse anthology of the Auden group, *New Signatures* (1932). Mandarinism did not suffer any sudden implosion during or soon after 1928; but then Connolly is careful not to claim that it did. With the benefit of hindsight, he could see, though, that it had by the end of that year completed its most creative phase, and was receding into a new role as mentor to the younger talents.

Ten Years Ago: Aftershocks of War

After years of work on the arrangement of cemeteries along the Western Front, the Imperial War Graves Commission unveiled at the Belgian town of Ypres on 24 July 1927 a new monument commemorating those soldiers whose bodies had never been recovered from the many appalling battles along the Ypres salient. The New Menin Gate, at which the Last Post was to be sounded every evening (it still is), provided a focus for the growing numbers of British pilgrims who came to pay respects to their dead in the late Twenties. Siegfried Sassoon arrived there a day after the official unveiling, en route to a German holiday, and then composed a poem, 'On Passing the New Menin Gate', in which he scorned the monument as a 'sepulchre of crime' (Sassoon 1961: 188); it appeared in his verse collection *The Heart's Journey* in 1928. In the same year Sassoon brought out his *Memoirs of a Fox-Hunting Man*, the first volume of his selective autobiographical narrative disguised as the fictional memoirs of 'George Sherston'. Tracing the hero's passage from an idle life of country sports to the confusions and horrors of the Western Front, this book belongs to an important body of new works over the next three years that revisit the defining conflict of the age.

Whether we date the transition from the literary Twenties to the Thirties according to Connolly's scheme or by the standard calendar, the war-books boom of 1928–30 has an important place in it. The new war literature of those years represents in part a resurgence of a largely masculine vernacular realism after the introspective indulgences of the Mandarin interregnum. Some of it was indeed so vernacular in its rendition of soldiers' talk as to require bowdlerising for public consumption, as with Aldington's *Death of a Hero*, passages of Graves's *Goodbye to All That*, and Frederic Manning's *The Middle Parts of Fortune* (1930). Some of its themes, too, of comradeship and collective struggle undermined by callous authorities, feed through into the temper of Thirties writing at large, and constitute an implicit rejection of Twenties individualism. The war books paved the way for the literary Thirties, then; but they also bring prominent features of Twenties writing to a climax of satiric revulsion. One often repeated legend about the war-books boom is that it broke a ten-year silence about an event that the public did not want to read about, until the appearance in English of E. M. Remarque's *All Quiet on the Western Front* in 1929 broke the spell. In fact the literature of the Twenties is almost continuously a war literature. Even if we set aside the numerous histories of the War that appeared through the decade, we have a strong pre-1929 tradition in Wilfred Owen's *Poems* (1920), e. e. cummings's *The Enormous Room* (1922), Isaac Rosenberg's *Poems* (1922), T. E. Lawrence's *Seven Pillars of*

Wisdom (1926; abridged as *Revolt in the Desert*, 1927), R. H. Mottram's *The Spanish Farm Trilogy* (1924–7), Ford Madox Ford's historical tetralogy of 'Tietjens' novels (1924–8) later reprinted as *Parade's End*, and the war poems of Edmund Blunden scattered among several collections in that decade.

The most important war writings of 1928 itself were Sassoon's *Fox-Hunting Man*; Edmund Blunden's *Undertones of War*, a sequence of prose reminiscences to which is appended a selection of his war poems; Maugham's book of spy stories, *Ashenden*; R. H. Mottram's collection of short stories set in the war, *Ten Years Ago*; and R. C. Sherriff's trench melodrama *Journey's End*, which was first staged in December before beginning in 1929 an extraordinary West End run of 594 performances. A. P. Herbert's 1919 tragic war novel *The Secret Battle* was also reissued in 1928 with a new preface by Winston Churchill. But this list covers only the writings that directly represent experiences of the War itself. There is a much broader war literature of the Twenties that addresses the delayed effects of the war in terms of despair, disillusionment, bereavement, shell-shock, and moral dislocation, a literature that includes Eliot's *The Waste Land*, Lawrence's *Kangaroo* (1923), Woolf's *Mrs Dalloway* (1925), and her *To the Lighthouse*, for example. 1928 was especially rich in such works. Among them are Wyndham Lewis's unusual prose fantasy *The Childermass*, which is set in a kind of limbo of dead souls that resembles the devastated landscapes of No Man's Land in the Flanders battlefields; Mary Butts's strange symbolic romance *Armed with Madness*, in which a war veteran succumbs to a fit of deranged violence; and Ford Madox Ford's *The Last Post*, the final volume in his *Parade's End* sequence, in which the central figure, Mark Tietjens, brother of the earlier three novels' protagonist, lies on his deathbed refusing to speak a word, apparently in protest against the terms of the peace settlement.

Two especially important works about the war's aftermath are worth noticing here. D. H. Lawrence's *Lady Chatterley's Lover* is notorious as an explicitly erotic romance, but it is also an attempt to diagnose the social and psychic malaise of an England wounded and exhausted by the war. The country estate of Wragby in which most of the action is set has seen its woodlands ravaged to provide war supplies, and its owner, Sir Clifford Chatterley, brought back from the war paralysed from the waist down. He is the last of his dynasty, and his inability to beget an heir represents allegorically the doom of the English ruling class, while his admiration for the work of Proust represents the terminal degeneracy of Mandarin literary sensibilities. The most innovative dramatic work of 1928, meanwhile, was Eugene O'Neill's *Strange Interlude*, which ran for seventeen months and 426 performances on Broadway from January despite the exhausting six-hour length of the show (inclusive of a ninety-minute dinner break). The play won O'Neill his third Pulitzer Prize, and was a huge success in commercial terms too, going on tour for a further two years, being adapted as a film (1932) with Norma Shearer and Clark Gable in leading parts, and earning the honour of a brief spoof in the Marx Brothers' film *Animal Crackers* (1930).

Strange Interlude is notable in the history of modern drama for its technical boldness in exploiting continuously the novelistic device of interior monologue: the characters alternate dialogue with the delivery of asides to the audience – during which the other characters' movements are 'frozen' – expressing their true thoughts, often ironically undercutting their public utterances. Many of these soliloquies are also spoken in fragmented 'stream-of-consciousness' style, O'Neill being an admirer of Joyce's method in *Ulysses*. What makes *Strange Interlude* a centrally representative work of the late 1920s, however, is not so much its cumbersome transposition of novelistic devices to the stage as its plot. The play is a domestic melodrama, which some critics have characterised as a soap opera. It follows the life and loves of Nina Leeds, the daughter of a university professor, following the death of her fiancé, Gordon, an aviator shot down in flames two days before the Armistice. Nina blames both her father, who advised Gordon to delay marriage until after the war, and herself for passing up the chance of sexual fulfilment and maternity before it was too late. In Nina's case war trauma assumes the form of sexual loss, and she attempts at first to compensate by working as a nurse in a war veterans' hospital, engaging in promiscuous sex with her patients until rescued by a semi-Freudian psychiatrist, Dr Darrell, who later becomes her lover and unacknowledged father to her son, who is of course named Gordon. In fact the loss of her war-hero shapes Nina's life and that of the various men in her life over the course of at least twenty-five years, the play's time scheme requiring the central characters to stagger on into the 1940s. Other writers in the late 1920s had traced the effects of the war on their own times, but O'Neill foresees the psychic damage persisting right through to the next generation.

Let's Do It: Women, Sex and Emancipation

Following her promiscuous exploits with wounded soldiers, Nina is encouraged to settle down into marriage with a decent friend of Gordon's and have children; but she aborts her pregnancy upon discovering that her husband has congenital madness in his family line, and later persuades Dr Darrell to father a child who will be brought up as her husband's. Like *Lady Chatterley's Lover*, *Strange Interlude* captures the central obsessions of 1920s literature by pairing war-damaged men with sexually voracious women. Nina Leeds and Connie Chatterley are only the most prominent fictional adulteresses and sexual adventuresses of 1928. Elsewhere we find the cynical seductress Lucy Tantamount in *Point Counter Point*; the dejected Marya Zelli in Jean Rhys's first novel, *Postures* (later retitled *Quartet*), who is lured into an affair with a married man while her own husband is in prison; and Soames's daughter Fleur Mont in Galsworthy's *Swan Song*, who pursues and ensnares her old flame Jon Forsyte despite their respective marriages.

Sex was in the air in 1928, and its theme tune was Cole Porter's new song, the wittily suggestive 'Let's Do It' (although at the time it lacked the famous verse about birds, bees and educated fleas, which Porter inserted much later). The growing popular impact of Freud's ideas, helped along by such works as *Strange Interlude*, encouraged the modern tendency to regard any restraint upon the libido as an outmoded and unhealthy continuation of 'Victorian' repressions. Some important new books of 1928 seemed to confirm that view, if indirectly. Lytton Strachey's biographical study of Queen Elizabeth I, *Elizabeth and Essex*, his most overtly Freudian work (indeed, it was personally approved by Freud himself), accounted for many of the political instabilities of late sixteenth-century England with the hypothesis that Elizabeth's sexuality was distorted by a hysterical fear of sexual contact, resulting in her lifelong virginity and in disastrous conflicts over the succession to the throne.

Sexual inhibition, then, could be not just a private debility but a public calamity for the body politic. The opposite possibility, that of a more relaxed culture of 'free love', now seemed a more credible prospect with the appearance of *Coming of Age in Samoa* by the unknown young American anthropologist Margaret Mead. This book painted an inviting picture of Samoan village life in which teenage girls and boys, growing up in full awareness of the facts of life and death, frolic guiltlessly with one another under the palm trees, experimenting with successive lovers without pressure to marry; a charmed world in which masturbation and homosexual flirtation are accepted as normal youthful sports, and in which a man's failure to satisfy a woman makes him an object of village ridicule. Mead's book is not only a report on her fieldwork in Samoa: it clearly offers itself too as a critique of unhealthily restrictive Western sexual mores. 'Familiarity with sex,' Mead writes of Samoan culture,

> and the recognition of a need of a technique to deal with sex as an art, have produced a scheme of personal relations in which there are no neurotic pictures, no frigidity, no impotence . . . and the capacity for intercourse only once in a night is counted as senility. (Mead 2001: 105)

By contrast, young Westerners, raised in fearful ignorance of sex, and forbidden to experiment widely with its techniques and possibilities, have become emotionally damaged to the point of neurotic impotence. Mead's emphasis on the needs of girls and women chimes in with the message of the more advanced sex-manuals of the day, notably Marie Stopes's *Married Love* (1918), whose latest sequel, *Enduring Passion*, also appeared in 1928.

Beyond the realm of the senses too, 1928 was a good year for emancipated women. British women between the ages of 21 and 30 were granted the 'flapper vote' in May, bringing their suffrage rights into line with men's. Amelia Earhart became the first woman to fly across the Atlantic in June; and in the following month's Olympic Games in Amsterdam, women athletes, previously confined to the swimming and fencing contests, were for the first time permitted to take part in the track and field athletics events. At a more leisurely pace, Virginia Woolf gave two talks in October at Newnham and Girton Colleges, Cambridge, on the obstacles facing women writers, these becoming the basis for her book *A Room of One's Own* (1929), a founding work of modern feminist criticism. On the other hand, there were a few setbacks. The American comedienne Mae West was arrested in October on obscenity charges after complaints against her new show, *The Pleasure Man*. And in August the *Express* newspapers in London began a hysterical campaign to suppress Radclyffe Hall's recently published lesbian novel *The Well of Loneliness*, a campaign that resulted in a breathtakingly unjust obscenity conviction (there was no jury, and the magistrate refused to hear defence witnesses) in November. Hall's novel had been published in July to largely respectful and sympathetic reviews – although Cyril Connolly had complained of its tediously melodramatic style – until the *Sunday Express* editor James Douglas intervened with a ranting editorial headlined A BOOK THAT MUST BE SUPPRESSED, calling directly upon the Home Secretary to ban it. 'I am well aware', he wrote,

> that sexual inversion and perversion are horrors which exist among us today. They flaunt themselves in public places with increasing effrontery and more insolently provocative bravado. The decadent apostles of the most hideous and most loathsome vices no longer conceal their degeneracy and their degradation. (Souhami 1998: 176–7)

In appealing to the Conservative Home Secretary of the day, Sir William Joynson-Hicks, Douglas knew he was pushing at an opened door, for 'Jix', as he was popularly nicknamed, was a notoriously bigoted moral-purity crusader engaged in a campaign to close down most of London's nightclubs. Although he was the same man who had extended women's franchise earlier in the year (inadvertently, it was claimed), he needed no persuading of the need to stamp out degeneracy. With a cabal of like-minded prosecutors and magistrates, he speedily saw to the suppression of *The Well*, despite its obviously high-minded – indeed earnestly 'Victorian' – tone and absence of explicit eroticism. As for the year's other scandalous novel, there was to be no trial of *Lady Chatterley's Lover*, which was published privately in Italy: Lawrence knew better than even to attempt a British or American edition, and the book was simply and routinely confiscated by Customs officials on both sides of the Atlantic wherever copies (many of them pirated by pornographers) could be found or intercepted.

Allowing for his hyperbole, James Douglas was right to detect the increased visibility of the sexually unorthodox. The fast set known as the Bright Young People, with Siegfried Sassoon's flamboyant lover Stephen Tennant at their head, were at this time taking great risks with their infamous pyjama parties, and Sassoon's friends feared that he would soon be embroiled in a major scandal. In literature as well, lesbianism seemed to be in vogue: *Orlando*, although not directly sapphic in content, echoes with private jokes arising from Woolf's affair with Vita Sackville-West. Compton Mackenzie's comic novel *Extraordinary Women* (1928) gently mocks a group of wealthy lesbians based upon the circle of Romaine Brooks; and a sequence of dialogues within a lesbian group is presented in *Ladies Almanack* (privately published in Paris, 1928) by Djuna Barnes, who later won critical acclaim for her novel *Nightwood* (1936). Havelock Ellis meanwhile brought out his final volume of sexological studies, this one on *Eonism*, better known as transvestism. And hitherto unimagined perversions popped up in the advanced novels of the day: one minor character in *Point Counter Point* gets his thrills from covering his wife's naked body with the ashes of burnt newspapers.

Britain under the reign of 'Jix' was not a place hospitable to erotic experiment, and for the sexually deviant writer almost anywhere 'abroad' was preferable (except for the puritanical US, still under Prohibition). W. Somerset Maugham, for instance, emigrated to the south of France in 1928 with his male lover. The young W. H. Auden, having graduated (Third Class) from Oxford that summer, persuaded his father to subsidise his plan of travelling for a year or so before seeking employment. Most other young writers at such a point would have headed straight for Paris (Orwell and Beckett had both recently gone there); but in a significantly anti-Mandarin gesture, Auden scorned the predictably Francophile pilgrimage and set off instead for Berlin, despite knowing no German. It turned out to suit him well. He was privileged to attend one of the earliest performances of a new musical show, *Die Dreigroschenoper* (*The Threepenny Opera* by Bertolt Brecht and Kurt Weill, 1928), and he was still more delighted to discover the 'Cosy Corner', one of the city's numerous bars at which blond youths could be picked up. Writing excitedly to a friend in England, he reported that 'Berlin is the buggers [*sic*] daydream' (Carpenter 1981: 90). Early in 1929, Auden invited his friend Christopher Isherwood to come to Berlin and sample these delights for himself. The material of Isherwood's distinctive works of the Thirties, *Mr Norris Changes Trains* (1935) and *Goodbye to Berlin* (1939), had been discovered: a world of erotic daydream overshadowed by impending political nightmare.

References

Carpenter, Humphrey (1981) *W. H. Auden: A Biography*, London: George Allen and Unwin
Connolly, Cyril (1961) *Enemies of Promise*, Harmondsworth: Penguin
Mead, Margaret (2001) *Coming of Age in Samoa: A Psychological Study of Primitive Youth for Western Civilisation*, New York: HarperCollins
Sassoon, Siegfried (1961) *Collected Poems 1908–1956*, London: Faber and Faber
Souhami, Diana (1998) *The Trials of Radclyffe Hall*, London: Weidenfeld and Nicolson

Chapter 7

1936, Madrid: The Heart of the World

Cary Nelson

In that most notoriously political of all twentieth-century decades, revered by some and castigated by others – the 1930s – a singular turning point came just after the decade's mid-point, in the summer of 1936. The decade began, of course, with the worldwide depression that followed the US stockmarket crash in October 1929. As the Great Depression deepened, with a full 25 per cent of Americans unemployed and many more severely underemployed, homeless and hungry, it began to seem as if there was no end in sight to years of misery. Capitalism, it appeared to many, could not fix itself. The economic system would have to be drastically overhauled, perhaps scrapped entirely and something very new installed in its place if people were to have reliable food and shelter, a future they could believe in, and some chance of a voice in political life. In Britain, France and the United States, among other countries, the Left grew in numbers and visibility. Its discourses were partly based on revolutionary agendas elaborated since the 1917 Russian Revolution, itself underwritten by still older socialist and communist movements. In the United States, late nineteenth- and early twentieth-century movements for workers' rights and unionisation drives would prove another source for rhetoric and organisation.

The less overtly political versions of experimental modernism that define the previous two decades for many literary scholars continued to flourish. Hart Crane could publish his ambitious poem-sequence *The Bridge* in 1930 in part because it was conceived in the 1920s. Crane takes the Brooklyn Bridge as his ecstatic symbol of the potential for American unity, a vision the Great Depression would make improbable. In Britain too experimental modernism would continue to evolve. Virginia Woolf published perhaps her most radically experimental novel, or at least the one most decisively removed from ordinary speech and action, *The Waves*, in 1931. The Irish novelist (and later playwright) Samuel Beckett would depict a universal human subject in extremis in the 1938 novel *Murphy*, and his countryman James Joyce would issue the novel *Finnegans Wake*, his masterpiece of verbal play, in 1939. T. S. Eliot, whose 1922 *The Waste Land* would virtually define high modernist poetry, published 'Ash Wednesday', a poem of religious abnegation, in 1930 and 'Burnt Norton', the first of his *Four Quartets*, meditating on time and eternity, in 1936. Nonetheless, what is most distinctive and coherent about the literature of the 1930s is the outpouring of political poetry and fiction.

Yet the long-standing opposition between modernist experimentation and politically committed writing does not survive wide reading in 1930s literature. Left-wing poets such as Louis MacNeice in England, Sol Funaroff and Edwin Rolfe in the United States, adapted modernist collage to progressive themes while continuing to use traditional forms for other poems. Muriel Rukeyser's 'The Book of the Dead' (1938), one of the major long poems of modernism, mixes fragments of US congressional testimony with traditional stanzaic forms and evocative lyricism, making it one of the triumphs of a collage aesthetic. Similar impulses inform John Dos Passos's three-part radical novel *U.S.A* (1930, 1932, 1936). Meanwhile, even so apparently apolitical a poet as Wallace Stevens found himself addressing political issues in his 1930s poetry (Filreis 1994).

As the Depression deepened in the early 1930s, large numbers of Americans and Europeans, including both young and established writers, were increasingly drawn explicitly to the radical Left or to the Communist Party. Among the writers who signed a 1932 pamphlet urging Americans to vote communist were Sherwood Anderson, Malcolm Cowley, Theodore Dreiser, Granville Hicks and Edmund Wilson. In Britain, a group of young writers at Oxford – later often known as 'the Auden generation' – were drawn within the Party's cultural orbit, including W. H. Auden himself, MacNeice, Stephen Spender, C. Day Lewis and the novelist Christopher Isherwood. The widespread conviction cited above – that the old order could not be restored, and that only the most thoroughgoing social and political change could bring about social and economic justice – led many intellectuals to look for radical political solutions.

A number of active poets, novelists, and critics had already been writing from that perspective in the 1920s. For one thing, the much heralded 'roaring twenties' had not brought economic health to everyone. In the United States, not only agriculture but also the entire rural economy had remained depressed throughout the decade; moreover, several major industries were already in recession before the stockmarket crash of 1929. Especially in the South and in depressed areas in the North, working-class and labour poets and novelists, along with writers affiliated with socialism, had been writing about social and economic inequities for years. Novelists in the 1930s could look back to Jack London, Edward Bellamy and Upton Sinclair, among others, for models of socialist fiction.

Yet probably no event before the onset of the Great Depression radicalised American writers more than the trial and execution of two immigrant working-class anarchists, Nicola Sacco and Bartolomeo Vanzetti. Convinced the men were framed on the charge of robbery and murder, a number of writers, including Dos Passos, Mike Gold, Dorothy Parker, Katherine Anne Porter, Edna St Vincent Millay and Lola Ridge were among those arrested at a Massachusetts demonstration in 1927. In 1928, the year after their execution, a memorial volume of poetry included Millay's 'Justice Denied in Massachusetts'. It reads like one of the 1930s poems we will shortly encounter. We are left with 'a blighted earth', Millay wrote, 'to till/ with a broken hoe'. Sub-cultural traditions of protest literature in fact stretched back into the nineteenth century, and some of the writers in those traditions felt themselves to be not only individual voices but also participants in movements for social change. In Britain the history of radical protest in verse is still longer, beginning with Romantic poems such as Blake's 'London' and Shelley's 'Song to Men of England', and proceeding through the nineteenth century with poems like Thomas Hood's 'The Song of the Shirt' (1843) and William Morris's *Chants for Socialists* (1885).

In some cases anthologies and other collaborative work helped reinforce a sense that creative writers addressing public themes were not so much working to silence or dominate one another by competing to write the best work on a given subject but were rather contributing to a common cultural enterprise. The list would include such collections as *Anthology of Revolutionary Poetry* (1929), the three annual volumes of *Unrest* (1929–31), *We Gather Strength* (1933), *Proletarian Literature in the United States* (1935), and *The Golden*

Peacock (1939). A more successful, more eloquent, or more deeply moving work might thereby seem less a personal triumph than a victory for the cause at issue. The sense of accomplishment could thus be partly focused on literature's success at winning the moral ground in a cultural struggle, in establishing that authentic literary idealisation belonged to one side and not the other. Recognising that poetry especially had a historically constructed authority to speak with (and for) more metaphoric versions of idealisation in the culture – an authority long recognised and reinforced by both the political Right and Left – poets understood that ground to be worth the struggle.

To begin to understand what it meant to be a writer on the Left in the Depression, it is necessary to extend that recognition to the whole cultural field and accept it as a general paradox that typifies life in that period. Hand in hand with hunger and unemployment and the many difficulties of everyday life went a sense of impending revolutionary change. For those writers who participated in the mass movement of the 1930s the period combined sometimes desperate hardship with something like utopian exhilaration. Writing literature – whether a proletarian novel like Myra Page's *Moscow Yankee* (1935), which recounts the radicalisation of a young auto worker, or a revolutionary poem like Langston Hughes's 'Let America Be America Again' (1936), which calls on the country to honour its founding principles for the first time – often meant helping to articulate and dramatise both the period's suffering and its characteristic yearnings for change. To write literature was not only to comment on these cultural processes but also to help shape them. And you were not alone. Down the street, across town, and in towns and cities across the country other writers were contributing to the cultural climate in much the same way.

The part of the Romantic heritage we have chosen to remember – with its image of the writer as a solitary creative figure – was still strong, but for a time in the 1930s it gave way to something else: an image of literature as a collaborative, dialogic enterprise, an activity carried out by individuals responding to one another's work and in the service of shared but contested cultural aims. There was a chorus of assenting and dissenting voices, and none of them was heard entirely on its own. Literature became a form of social conversation and a way of participating in collaborative political action. Literature was thus in the immediate materiality of its signs dialogic – engaged in a continuing dialogue both with other texts and with the other discourses and institutions of its day. To hear that conversation is to witness texts in a constant state of disassemblage and reassemblage, as pieces of other texts are woven into any given work and pieces of every text are disseminated into related texts and discourses as we read. Part of the cultural work of reading – the semiotics of reading – was to confirm a text's participation in the mass movement of the Left by enacting it. To *read* 1930s political literature is thus in part to personify – to act out in one's person – a version of the intertextuality of that time. A proper reader of this literature comes to occupy the cultural field in somewhat the same way the literature itself did.

Such motives animate much of the progressive political literature of the 1930s, which often focuses on economic hardship and revolutionary change, on general social conditions rather than private experience. Even when individual experience is recounted, it is often recounted because of its representative character, its simultaneous enabling and determination by current history. The novel, of course, could construct much fuller narratives about individual characters. There were also conspicuous plot features shared by many of these novels, most notably the labour strike. Mary Heaton Vorse's *Strike* (1930) and Grace Lumpkin's *To Make My Bread* (1932) were the first of six novels inspired by a textile industry strike in Gastonia, North Carolina. Robert Cantwell's *Land of Plenty* (1934) follows a brutal lumber strike in the Pacific Northwest. John Steinbeck's *In Dubious Battle* (1936) chronicled activism by migratory workers in California. There were many such novels, but the most fundamental characteristic of the genre was not the strike but the recurrent treatment of a central protagonist's gradual political awakening. In these novels maturity comes not so much with self-knowledge as with social and political understanding. Heightened consciousness, moreover, typically leads to action. Its corollary was the novel of failed political consciousness, most famously exemplified by James T. Farrell's *Studs Lonigan* trilogy (1932–5) and Richard Wright's *Native Son* (1940). Some of the novels detailing a successful political awakening were largely autobiographical, among them Agnes Smedley's *Daughter of Earth* (1929), Mike Gold's *Jews Without Money* (1930), and Jack Conroy's *The Disinherited* (1933) (Foley 1993).

Some of the major subjects of 1930s poetry and prose represented not new directions but rather wider adoption and intensification of issues from the previous decade. In an unpublished fragment, Angelina Weld Grimké, well-known during the Harlem Renaissance of the 1920s, would now write with a deeper, more musical anguish about America's continuing race crisis:

> I am the woman with the black black skin
> I am the laughing woman with the black black face
> I am living in the cellars and in every crowded place
>   I am toiling just to eat
>   In the cold and in the heat
>   And I laugh
> I am the laughing woman who's forgotten how to weep
> I am the laughing woman who's afraid to go to sleep
>
> (Nelson 2000: 146)

Increasingly, white poets would take up the subject. In a poem from the 1930s published posthumously, New York radical poet Sol Funaroff wrote in dialect: 'Ah wukked mah time an overtime/ Ah wukked mah time an too much time' (Funaroff 1943: 9). A series of white poets responded to the surge in Ku Klux Klan memberships with poems about lynching, here represented with brief excerpts. As we read these passages in sequence, we can begin to see how a multiply authored text was being woven out of 1930s poems:

> Now I climb death's tree.
>
> (Ford in Nelson 2000: 706)

> The moon lies like a tombstone in the sky,
> Three black men sway upon a lonely hill.
>
> (Trent in Nelson 2000: 706)

> The bloodhounds look like sad old judges
> In a strange court. They point their noses
> At the Negro jerking in the tight noose;
> His feet spread crow-like above these
> Honorable men who laugh as he chokes.
>
> (Patchen 1968: 162)

The forest falls, the stream runs dry,
the tree rots visibly to the ground;
nothing remains but sixteen black
bodies against a blood-red sky.

(Rolfe 1993: 68)

Nine dark boys spread their breasts against Alabama,
schooled in the cells, fathered by want.

(Rukeyser 1978: 29)

They are ours; we claim them and we claim
what they have suffered, upon our backs is laid
the stone of their dark days, and we have made
their name our name.

(A. B. Magil in Hughes 1949: 63)

. . . I know that one of my hands
Is black, and one white.

(Patchen 1968: 86)

Langston Hughes, on the other hand, regularly took the Great Depression's widespread suffering as an occasion to unify all those denied access to the American dream:

I am the poor white, fooled and pushed apart,
I am the Negro bearing slavery's scars . . .
I am the farmer, bondsman to the soil.
I am the worker sold to the machine.

(Nelson 2000: 515–16)

And Sterling Brown evoked solidarity among members of those unions committed to organising both black and white sharecroppers, with a promise that white racists (brushwood) would eventually be eliminated: 'We gonna clean out dis brushwood round here soon,/ Plant de white-oak and de black-oak side by side' (Nelson 2000: 484). Just as many poets turned to the Left; some earlier associated with various aestheticisms acquired a social conscience. Here is the Imagist John Gould Fletcher suddenly addressing the black experience and anticipating revolutionary change:

And slowly rises the river,
seething, chocolate-brown;
stealthily drifts on its current,
sweeping, with many a shiver,
Over the cottonwoods, roosting on sandbanks, spectrally grey
and surprising;
Writhing their branches to the sky; –
Slowly the black tide is rising.

(Hughes 1949: 183)

Even more insistently than race, however, the omnipresence of poverty occupied Great Depression writers. Reversing thousands of years of literary tradition, the two archetypal humanised settings – the country and the city – ceased to be treated as opposing settings (one crude or innocent, the other cultured or depraved) and became two sides of the same impoverished coin. Edwin Rolfe, who had begun writing radical poetry in the 1920s, and Genevieve Taggard both adopted a kind of anguished lyricism to bring the urban poor to life:

> This is the sixth winter.
> This is the season of death
> when lungs contract and the breath of homeless men
> freezes on restaurant window-panes.
>
> (Rolfe 1993: 95)

> See the set faces hungrier than rodents. In the Ford towns
> They shrivel. Their fathers accept tear gas and blackjacks.
> When they sleep, whimper. Bad sleep for us all.
> Their mouths work, supposing food.
>
> (Taggard 1936: 18)

Brief quotations gathered together into a collective stanza suggest the common purpose at work in so many city-based poems:

> We have grown used to nervous landscapes, chimney-broken horizons,
> and the sun dying between tenements
>
> (Wright in Nelson 2000: 584)

> The hungry digging the wild roots
> From hillsides
>
> (Lechlitner 1937: 28)

> the parched young,
> The old man rooting in waste-heaps, the family rotting
> In the flat, before eviction
>
> (Benét 1936: 44)

> There are mice in the granary, rats running in the roof-beams, ants
>   Chewing at the foundations.
> Death-beetles tick under the wall-paper, punctuate the
>   evening quiet
>   Of families gathered at home.
>
> (Neugass 1953: 85)

> This is the season when rents go up.
> Men die, and their dying is casual.
>
> (Rolfe 1993: 95)

> deep in the gangrened basements
> Where Whitman's America
> Aches, to be born
>
> (Gold in Salzman and Zanderer 1978: 64)

> Out there on the ruin of Kansas . . .
> Downtown in the ruins called Denver
>
> (Lewis in Salzman and Zanderer 1978: 122)

Poems about country life typically focused on farm foreclosures, hunger amid natural bounty, looming starvation, the Dust Bowl in the Southwest, and the same grinding poverty seen in cities like Detroit and New York. The root cause, virtually all writers on the Left agreed, was the failure of capitalism, which had turned failing farm and abandoned factory into mirror images of one another:

> The mills are down
> The hundred stacks
> are shorn of their drifting fume.
> The idle tracks
> rust . . .
> Smeared red with the dust
> of millions of tons of smelted ore
> the furnaces loom –
> towering, desolate tubes –
> smokeless and stark in the sun . . .
>
> (Beecher 1974: 36)

> Flanking the freightyards: alleys, wooden shacks,
> And hovels: a grim battalion
> Of crouching rats covered down by the waters
> Of fog that trickles down their slimy backs.
> Near these: the blackened sheds
> Of foundries, smelting furnaces,
> And forges flanking the grey backs of the river
>
> (Burnshaw 1936: 48)

The barons of industry and their financiers became demonic, amoral figures. Depression era poetry, fiction, and painting issued comparable portraits:

> Under the sign of the coin and the contract,
> under the mask of the two-faced double-dealing dollar,
> under the fetish of the document, stocks and bonds,
> the parchment faces trade in securities.
>
> (Funaroff 1938: 62)

> Men of paper, robbing by paper, with paper faces.
>
> (Benét 1936: 12)

> the headsman hacks a worker's life to bone.
>
> (Funaroff 1938: 59)

Over and over again 1930s literature begins with angry protest and concludes with calls for revolutionary action:

Awake and sing, you that dwell in the dust.

(Funaroff 1938: 16)

Brothers, Comrades, pool the last strength of men
in party, in mass, boil into form, and strike.

(Taggard 1936: 57)

let the workers storm from the factories,
the peasants from the farms;
sweep the earth clean of this nightmare.

(Freeman in Salzman and Zanderer 1978: 134)

If the dispossessed should rise,
Burning anger in their eyes . . .
Oh my brothers in the mire,
Clothe with lightning, shoe with fire . . .

(Weiss 1935: 17)

Banners of rebellion, surging to the storm,
Rousing men to vision, turning cold blood warm

(Trent 1929: 14)

Fists tight-clenched around a crimson banner

(Rolfe 1993: 59)

We shall rise up, create our own new lands
Red in the sky our torches write
Resurgence over death

(Lechlitner 1937: 32)

The red train starts and nothing shall stop it

(Aragon, trans. by e. e. cummings in Kostelanetz 1998: 54)

Listen, Mary, Mother of God, wrap your new born babe in
the red flag of Revolution.

(Hughes in Nelson 2000: 1231)

Of course literature's revolutionary intertext was also in conflict with reactionary discourses, and it was in some contexts fissured from within by competing visions of social
change. In the United States the Southern Agrarians – including Donald Davidson, Allen
Tate, John Crowe Ransom and the young Robert Penn Warren – mounted a conservative
counter-reaction that continued through the 1950s. Yet they were also antagonistic to mass
culture and to industrialisation and were thus deeply involved in an alternative cultural
politics. By 1939 the critic Cleanth Brooks had added his voice to those opposing the
decade's progressive literature. Yet perhaps no American poet resisted the turn to the Left
more decisively than Ezra Pound. Already enamoured of the Italian fascist dictator Benito
Mussolini in the 1920s, Pound had written his four 'Malatesta Cantos' as a history lesson
with contemporary echoes. They concern Sigismundo Pandolfo Malatesta (1417–68),

a famous condottiere (Italian leader of mercenary soldiers), military engineer, and patron of the arts. Ruthless and brutal, he also built an impressive temple. That end, Pound decided, justified the means. Malatesta was, Pound believed, a model for Mussolini, and *The Cantos* are replete with apologies for European fascism. Pound continued to work on *The Cantos*, a book-length sequence of 116 poems through the 1930s and 1940s, leaving it unfinished but complete in 1969.

There were also major differences on the Left. But communists and Christian socialists alike nonetheless contributed to a broader revolutionary intertext whether they chose to do so or not. The surrounding intertext thus provided a figurative analogue for the common ground of an alliance politics that the Left could not really achieve in the early 1930s. Collectively, works from a variety of socialist, communist, anarchist, and liberal democratic writers offered a shared vision of human devastation, social and economic critique, and revolutionary aspiration. The intertext to a notable degree dissolved political differences while putting in their place an unstable but coalescing system of representation.

It was not until the summer and fall of 1936 that a more consciously collaborative and coherent literary discourse came into effect. At that point both utopian aspirations and practical political beliefs began to coalesce. Fearing a major threat from European and Japanese fascism – made still more real by Japan's invasion of Manchuria and Italy's invasion of Ethiopia – the Communist International (Comintern) had urged a unified Popular Front against fascism among radical and democratic parties in 1935. Writers across the world, however, were not quite ready to abandon explicitly revolutionary tropes. Despite the Communist Party's supposed control over both its members and its fellow travellers, progressive writers continued to publish poems urging the overthrow of capitalism for much of the next year.

When the Spanish military, allied with wealthy land owners and conservative clergy, rose up to overthrow the democratically elected government of Spain in July 1936, however, progressive writers recognised the fascist threat was growing. Italy had been under Mussolini's control since the 1920s, and Hitler had come to power in Germany in 1933. It could no longer be denied that fascism represented the threat both of external aggression and of upheaval from within. It was a threat still more terrible than the unprincipled exploitation and severe inequities of capitalism. Over a period of but a few months in 1936 the character of literary production across Europe and the Americas underwent a sea change. The choral poetry of revolution was transformed almost immediately into the still more coherent and more powerfully collective poetry of anti-fascism.

Suddenly, modern poetry had a distinctly international configuration. Its first subject was the heroic defence of the city of Madrid. From 1936 to 1939 there erupted something like a chorus of voices calling back and forth to each other about the besieged capital of Spain, under assault by four columns of fascist troops. In poem after poem, in country after country the name Madrid is used as a rallying cry and an incantation, sometimes with and sometimes without an exclamation mark. The poems echo one another across time and space and national or political difference, ring changes on the suffering and courage of the Madrileños, and establish in print, in voice, and in dream and nightmare the point of articulation of an anti-fascist politics for its time.

In the United States, Norman Rosten inserted a slogan between each stanza of 'The March' and ended the poem with the words 'Madrid—*Madrid*—MADRID!' (Nelson 2002: 97). In Spain, Frances Fuentes wrote 'Revolutionary Madrid'; Manuel Altolaguirre wrote 'Madrid'; José Vila wrote 'Madrid Front'. The 29 October 1936 issue of *El Mono Azul* had included Rafael Alberti's 'Defensa de Madrid', Manuel Bolin's 'Alerta los madrileños',

Luis Perez Infante's 'A Madrid', and Altologuirre's 'Arenga', which declared the city the capital of Europe. In France, Jacques Romain answered with 'Madrid', Paul Eluard with 'November 1936'. In Britain, Richard Church answered with 'The Madrid Defenders', Elisabeth Cluer with 'Analogy in Madrid'. Among Americans, Joy Davidman wrote 'Snow in Madrid', Langston Hughes wrote 'Madrid – 1937', and Ben Maddow in 'The Defenses' cried out 'Madrid, Madrid! . . . your great trenches hold/ Death back from love' (Nelson 2002: 100); Norman Rosten hailed 'Madrid!/ Burning in the night . . . but still standing' and turned the famous slogan into a command: 'Make Madrid the tomb of Fascism' (Nelson 2002: 177). 'Madrid awoke', wrote Sol Funaroff in 'The Bull in the Olive Field', a 'toreador in overalls . . . people poured like rain/ upon the face of the streets' (Nelson 2002: 139). Such poems continued to appear through 1938; that year the Catalan anthology *Poesia de Guerra* included Ernest Mateu's 'Als Defensors de Madrid' and Adriá Jori's 'Record de Madrid'.

Part of what is notable about the poetry focused on Madrid is its paradoxical mixture of sloganeering and invention. 'Greetings, Madrid, heart of the country', wrote Luis de Tapia in 'Salud' (1937); Alberti (Benardete and Humphries 1937: 22–3) called the city 'heart of Spain,/ heart of earth'; 'Madrid is the heart', Auden wrote in 'Spain' (Cunningham 1980: 99), echoing La Pasionaria, the popular name of Spain's most famous deputy, Dolores Ibarurri. 'Pasionaria speaks', wrote Rosten, 'and the silence/ is greater than the soaring of birds'; he opened 'Invocation' with this stanza:

> Spain, the body,
> and in its center
> calmly beating
> the great heart, Madrid.

(Nelson 2002: 176)

Stanley Richardson (1938) addressed Madrid as 'Life's glorious capital'. George Barker, on the other hand, said the city was 'like a live eye in the Iberian mask' (Cunningham 1980: 160), while José Moreno Villa described the besieged city in winter as 'an island tomb,/ Alone, in an asphalt sky' (Cunningham 1980: 299) and Eluard said it was a 'city as if at the base of the ocean made of only one saved drop of water'. Like the more broadly revolutionary poetry of the 1930s, this poetry is partly echolalic, with poet after poet deploying some of the same images and phrases in a choral literary project of political commitment.

Though poets would continue to write laments to Madrid in the decade that followed the war, the international outpouring of poems on the topic is mostly confined to 1936–9. Yet, like the war itself, at least one other more specific topic holds its power today and continues to be the subject of new poems, in part because it fused loss and aspiration, betrayal and solidarity, death and longing from the outset – the murder of Federico García Lorca. Lorca was not primarily a political writer in the conventional sense of addressing current events; nor did he join a political party, though he was visibly active in support of the Popular Front. The day before the national elections in Spain of 16 February 1936, the major communist newspaper *Mundo Obrero* published a manifesto titled 'The Intellectuals and the Popular Front' with 300 signatures; at the top of the list was Federico García Lorca. That spring, with rumours of a right-wing coup in the air, Lorca read his intense attack on the widely hated paramilitary police force, the Guardia Civil, his poem 'Ballad of the Spanish Civil Guard', before a mass meeting at the Madrid Workers' Club. Even if his support for the Left had not been so widely publicised, neither his lines attacking the Guardia Civil nor the church were neutral and likely to prove harmless in the fatal world of Spanish politics.

His consistent stands against social and sexual repression and his open homosexuality carried inevitable political implications in Spain. That class positioning of his work made it a rallying point for the people's aspirations. His work was known to many working people; his books were everywhere; his poems were quoted throughout the country.

The poetic memorial service for García Lorca started almost immediately after his death in August at the outset of the Spanish Civil War, continued heavily for more than a decade, and sustained itself intermittently through the rest of the century. *El Mono Azul* of 17 Sepetmber 1936 dedicated its two-page spread of poems to García Lorca and opened with Emilio Prados's elegy. The League of Revolutionary Writers and Artists in Mexico published a selection of García Lorca's poems in November 1936, within months of his death, under the title *Breve Antologia* (1936), accompanied by an astonishing preface of revolutionary solidarity by Juan Marinello. Emilio Prados's anthology *Romancero General de la Guerra de España* is dedicated to Lorca, and the July 1937 anthology *Poetas en la España Leal* opens with Antonio Machado's poem about Lorca. That same year Emilio Prados edited a 200-page collection of elegies for Lorca, *Homenaje al poeta García Lorca: contra su muerta.* By the time *Poems for Spain* was published in Britain in 1939, elegies for Lorca were among the central and inescapable categories used to construct the war's intelligibility and its continuing power in the experience and memory of the Left. Edited by Stephen Spender and John Lehmann, the *Poems for Spain* anthology is divided into six thematic categories: 'Action', 'Death', 'The Map', 'Satire', 'Romances', and finally, bringing the text full circle back to the war's opening months and to its core poetics of anguish, 'Lorca'.

Among the poets who devoted poems to García Lorca in books, magazines and broadsides are Alberti, Altolaguirre, Jacob Bronowski, Luis Cardoza Y Aragon, Oscar Castro Z., Louis Cernuda, Davidman, Funaroff, Eldon Grier, Miguel Hernández, Aaron Kramer, Raúl González Tuñón, Jorge Guillén, Nicolás Guillén, Claudia Lars, Pedro García de Lorca, Leopoldo de Luis, Hugh MacDiarmid, Antonio Machado, Martha Millet, Vincius de Moraes, Leopoldo Panero, Geoffrey Parsons, Pablo Neruda, Emilio Prados, Alfonso Reyes, Rolfe, Rosten, Héctor Suanes and Leopoldo Urrutia. Prose tributes came, among others, from Vicente Aleixandre, Pablo Neruda, and William Carlos Williams. Of these, Cardoza Y Aragon was Guatemalan; González Tuñón was Argentinian; Lars, Salvadoran; Moraes, Brazilian; Reyes, Mexican; Nicolás Guillén, Cuban; MacDiarmid, Scottish; and Castro Z., Neruda and Suanes, Chilean, though only nominally so in this context. Grier and Parsons were British. Bronowski was a Polish-born British emigré. Davidman, Funaroff, Kramer, Millet, Rolfe, Rosten, and Williams were Americans, though in this context, again, only nominally so. For several modern American and British poets, the period of the Spanish Civil War was one when they were no longer primarily *American* or *British* writers; they were part of an international political struggle and an international community of writers. Part of what is important about these poets' contributions to the dialogue about Spain, therefore, is that a number of them figuratively gave up nationhood as the ground of their being.

For some, their changing politics would take them away from the Popular Front over the next two decades. Davidman would eventually become Christian; Williams, the exemplary fellow traveller during the 1930s, would gradually drift away; MacDiarmid, a lifelong socialist and Scottish nationalist, would found the 'Scottish Renaissance' and be cast out of the Communist Party in 1938, only to rejoin in 1957. Kramer and Rolfe would abandon Party activism but remain fiercely loyal to their socialist principles. While the literary wake for Lorca was most powerfully underway, however, they were all bound together into one community.

The poems, prose poems and statements that make up this unique and extended international wake are almost impossible to think about only as discrete texts, for they make up a kind of reflexive Lorca cantata whose music is the sound of love amid war and lamentation. Among the distinctive and sometimes uncanny continuities in these elegies to García Lorca are the number of times poets address him directly by his first name and the affectionate, plaintive, and often rather childlike calls to him many poets issued. He is repeatedly 'Federico', friend, brother, comrade, lover, and lost child:

> Why is Federico not here?
> I have wonderful news for Federico!—
> news for his private ear . . .
> Federico! Federico! Too soon! . . .
> Federico, wait for me! Wait!
> I must talk with you! Look! . . .
> I have so much to tell you, Federico!
>
> (Prados in Benardete and Humphries 1937: 59–61)

> I cry in pain, 'Oh, Federico! Federico!' . . .
> where does a gypsy go to die?
> Where do his eyes change to silver frost? . . .
> Where will Federico be,
> where will he be that he won't be back?
>
> (Guillén in Davidman 1943: 253)

Nothing else in the modern elegy has quite this haunting tone or this elaborately international sixty-year history. American poets sometimes address Whitman by his first name, as Hart Crane did repeatedly in the 'Cape Hatteras' section of *The Bridge* – 'My hand/ in yours,/ Walt Whitman' (Nelson 2000: 405) – but Crane's effort is to link hands prophetically and sexually with a poet whose whole rich career invites fraternity, not to commemorate the impossibility of contact with a poet whose life and career were brutally curtailed. Largely unrecognised in literary histories, even in histories of the modern elegy, the elegies to García Lorca are nonetheless one of the hallmarks of twentieth-century poetry. As they echo common concerns and forms of address, drawing on recurrent tropes in García Lorca's own poetry, they soon form a choral response that helps define the war and haunts the century's collective memory:

> Ay, Federico García,
> How swiftly death, dagger in hand, draws nigh! . . .
> Ay, Federico García,
> Death is here, is here!
>
> (Urrutia in Spender 1939: 107)

> O this is your end, your end, your end . . .
> You joked with the dead: did you not hear
> their voices lower year by year?
>
> (Bronowski in Cunningham 1980: 208)

> Federico, do you remember
> under the ground,

do you remember my house with balconies where
the light of June was drowning flowers in your mouth

(Neruda 1973: 257)

When he burst into song
the whole of Spain sang with him.

(Castro Z. in Fitts 1942: 527)

where now there is only silence and no
darkness we can say is his, Federico's.

(Levine in Nelson 2002: 286)

They shot him and made a bonfire of his books

(MacDiarmid 1962: 182)

They heard his poem rising up, and spreading over Spain.

(Kramer in Nelson 2002: 153)

   carve a monument
out of dream stone
for the poet in the Alhambra,
over a fountain where the grieving water
shall say forever
The crime was in Granada, his Granada.

(Machado in Benardete and Humphries 1937: 63)

Lorca, you who were the morning song of Spain,
the song is on the lips of the people!

(Funaroff in Nelson 2002: 98)

More powerfully than in any single poem, this collective elegy makes García Lorca a figure for the Republic as a utopian return to a prelapsarian cultural moment. It would be a moment when difference – so often fatal in Spain and throughout the modern world – was merely polymorphous diversity, when every impulse and desire was purified of worldly corruption. Lorca's verbal resources become after his death the poetic equivalent of the Spanish harvest, a literary version of the earth's bounty. In some fundamental way, then, Lorca's death demonstrated that it was at once innocence and poetry itself the fascists sought to kill.

The war produced a small number of highly focused topics – the defence of Madrid, the murder of García Lorca, the role of the 'Internationals' who came to fight for the Republic – that were unlike anything in the poetry of the first half of the decade. No single Depression setting had the real and symbolic force of Madrid under siege. Poverty in London was readily understandable from the vantage point of poverty elsewhere, as George Orwell demonstrated in *Down and Out in Paris and London* (1933). But few could confidently have proclaimed either Paris, London or New York City the 'heart of the world'. For a few years that is exactly how people did describe Madrid. Indeed, that figure reflected the beliefs of a broad international constituency. From Paris to Edinburgh to Boston to Mexico City, every person sympathetic to the Left held Madrid in special honour. It was the focus of a Manichaean conflict that might shape not only Spain's destiny but also that of the entire West.

In echoing and counterpointing one another – even when the poets themselves are not aware of all existing parallel passages – and in accumulating a field of potential correspondences for future poems, the poems of the Spanish Civil War do something more than contribute to a growing international intertext. They hail one another – and their writers and readers – with extraordinary directness and intensity. To be hailed in that way is to be positioned as an international political subject – and to experience that cultural positioning with pathos, anguish, pride and anger. The effects of varied lines on similar subjects, then, are not simply additive, complicating our view, say, of how civilians suffered under fascist bombing, or how Madrid withstood fascist assault. A sense of strong linkage, of shared necessity, of centripetal focus on the heart of Spain, coalesces in each of the metaphors, phrases and topics that recurs in the worldwide poems about the war.

Although this poetry helped build the anti-fascist consensus that enabled the democracies to defeat Germany in the Second World War, it was not, however, enough to stand against the force of arms in Spain. The Spanish Republic fell in the opening months of 1939. In the aftermath of the war, exile elegy and loss took over the Spanish Civil War discourse, as in Orwell's *Homage to Catalonia* (1938). As these impulses coalesced into the distinctive contextualised form of *exiled witness*, a different kind of choral pattern emerged from poetry written throughout the Americas and Europe. Millay's 'Say That We Saw Spain Die' would prove one of the signature poems of this new mood in the United States. As dust settled on blasted stone, as blood soaked into the land, the parallel metaphors in different poems acquired a mutual transparency, a palimpsestic quality of shared and layered memory. Poet after poet remained haunted by Spain, and that haunting was less personal than historical and generational. It was a shared experience and those who gave witness to it in their poetry constituted a far-flung chorus amid the ruins of memory. Those modern poets of the Left who survived the modern period and retained their political convictions – among them Rolfe and Rukeyser in the United States, Neruda in Chile, MacDiarmid in Scotland, Altolaguirre in exile in Mexico – took with them this experience of international solidarity and subsequent disaster. It haunted their work for the rest of their lives.

Even those who abandoned or distanced themselves from their 1930s Left commitments and communist sympathies continued for years to rewrite and repeatedly explain their involvement in the decade's passions. Notable in this regard in Britain are the 'Auden generation' of writers who came of age in the 1930s. Auden himself, in particular, was later to revise or even repudiate many poems which had reflected his political commitments of the 1930s, including to the struggle in Spain.

Just when the decade's literary culture ended remains open to debate. When Irish poet William Butler Yeats died in 1939 – soon elegised by Auden – it seemed to some that modernism had come to an end. In retrospect it would seem that the radical pluralism of *Finnegans Wake* ushered in postmodernity. Others might be forgiven for believing that the outbreak of the Second World War the same year marked a more decisive dividing point. But for the literary culture of the Popular Front – so fully embodied in Spanish Civil War poetry and activism – one has to wait one more year for the defining death knell. That came in 1940 with the publication of Ernest Hemingway's Spanish Civil War novel *For Whom the Bell Tolls*. A fierce supporter of the Republic's cause throughout the war, Hemingway now believed the war was over and the battle lost and wrote a novel that settled accounts, even using living men and women as characters under their own names. Some of the friends of the Spanish Republic, he believed, should never wield power again. For those convinced the battle was a continuing one, this amounted to an unforgivable betrayal. They broke with Hemingway and panned the novel in print. When veterans of Spain tried to revive the Popular Front coalition in the midst of the McCarthy era in the 1950s they forbade Hemingway's participation and the effort failed. Yet the tradition and its capacity for inspiration lived on nonetheless. Thomas McGrath, among many others, would write radical poetry and produce proletarian fiction in the ensuing decades. His *Letters to an Imaginary Friend* (1962–85) amounts to a radical alternative to Pound's *Cantos*, and attests to the persistence of a tradition of political literature stretching, from the Spanish Civil War to the era of Vietnam War protests and beyond. That tradition remains a resource down to the present day.

References

Beecher, John (1974) *Collected Poems 1924–1974*, New York: Macmillan

Benét, Stephen Vincent (1936) *Burning City*, New York: Farrar and Rinehart

Benardete, M. J., and Rolfe Humphries, eds (1937) *. . . and Spain Sings: 50 Loyalist Ballads*, New York: Vanguard Press

Burnshaw, Stanley (1936) *The Iron Land*, Philadelphia: Centaur Press

Cunningham, Valentine, ed. (1980) *The Penguin Book of Spanish Civil War Verse*, Harmondsworth: Penguin

Davidman, Joy, ed. (1943) *War Poems of the United Nations*, New York: Dial

de Tapia, Louis (1937) 'Salud', *International Literature* 10–11: 191

Filreis, Alan (1994) *Modernism from Right to Left: Wallace Stevens, The Thirties, and Literary Radicalism*, New York: Cambridge University Press

Fitts, Dudley, ed. (1942) *Anthology of Contemporary Latin-American Poetry*, Norfolk, CT: New Directions

Foley, Barbara (1993) *Radical Representations: Politics and Form in U.S. Proletarian Fiction, 1929–1941*, Durham, NH: Duke University Press

Funaroff, Sol (1938) *The Spider and the Clock*, New York: International Publishers

——(1943) *Exile from a Future Time*, New York: Dynamo

Hughes, Langston, and Arna Bontemps, eds (1949) *The Poetry of the Negro*, New York: Doubleday

Kostelanetz, Richard, ed. (1998) *AnOther E. E. Cummings*, New York: Liveright

Lechlitner, Ruth (1937) *Tomorrow's Phoenix*, New York: Alcestis Press

MacDiarmid, Hugh (1962) *Collected Poems*, New York: Macmillan

Nelson, Cary, ed. (2000) *Anthology of Modern American Poetry*, New York: Oxford University Presss

—— ed. (2002) *The Wound and the Dream: Sixty Years of American Poems About the Spanish Civil War*, Urbana, IL: University of Illinois Press

Neruda, Pablo (1973) *Residence on Earth*, trans. Donald D. Walsh, New York: New Directions

Neugass, James (1953) 'The Hour of Lateness', *Alcestis: A Poetry Quarterly* 4.4, July, 26

Patchen, Kenneth (1968) *Collected Poems*, New York: New Directions

Richardson, Stanley (1938) 'To a Certain Priest', *Spain at War*, no. 3, June, 13

Rolfe, Edwin (1993) *Collected Poems*, ed. Cary Nelson and Jefferson Hendricks, Urbana, IL: University of Illinois Press

Rukeyser, Muriel (1979) *Collected Poems*, New York: McGraw Hill

Salzman, Jack, and Leo Zanderer, eds (1978) *Social Poetry of the 1930s*, Philadelphia: Burt Franklin and Co.

Spender, Stephen, and John Lehmann, eds (1939) *Poems for Spain*, London: Hogarth Press

Taggard, Genevieve (1936) *Calling Western Union*, New York: Harper

Trent, Lucia (1929) *Children of Fire and Shadow*, New York: Packard

Weiss, Henry George (1935) *Lenin Lives*, Holt, MN: B. C. Hagglund

Chapter 8

1941, London under the Blitz: Culture as Counter-History

Tyrus Miller

In his 'London Letter' to the *Partisan Review* of 3 January 1941, George Orwell recounted the bombing of London a few months earlier and described a collective feeling of watching the world in which they had grown up come to an end. But another, still stranger discovery was in store for Orwell in the nights of bombing: despite the fires, despite floodlights and flak and sirens piercing the air, much of the old world, that framework of grey everydayness in equal measure musty and reassuring, was still holding firm, as if by sheer force of habit and lack of sufficient adventurousness even to come crashing dangerously down. 'When all is said and done', Orwell wrote,

> one's main impression is the immense stolidity of ordinary people, the widespread vague consciousness that things can never be the same again, and yet, together with that, the tendency of life to slip back into the familiar pattern. On the day in September when the Germans broke through and set the docks on fire, I think few people can have watched those enormous fires without feeling that this was the end of an epoch. . . . But to an astonishing extent things have slipped back to normal. (Orwell 1968: 2: 54–5)

In his 'Ode', written in May 1940 during the disastrous rout of the British forces at Dunkirk, the anarchist poet and art critic Herbert Read similarly observed that it was –

> Human to relapse
> into the old ways, to resume
> the normality so patiently acquired
> in days of peace.
>
> (Read 1966: 159)

Whereas, however, Read saw this clinging to normality as a symptom of collective trauma, Orwell esteemed the surprising firmness of habit among the British popular classes. There was in them, he believed, a mulish inuredness to disaster, which would allow them to resist the Nazi strategy of forcing surrender through terror by air. At the same time, however, they also demonstrated an equally beast-like inability to imagine the future as very much different from how things were in the present. The British were immune to any radical fear of the future that would allow terror to shake the national spirit, but also to radical hopes that nourish wishes for a utopian future. If there were ever to be a New Jerusalem of socialism in England's green and pleasant land, it would have to arise from those already existing cities of grey little houses and neat garden plots and yeasty public houses, now being gutted by falling bombs and the fires of the Blitz.

Orwell discerned an 'anti-historical' cultural streak in the British, which he hoped had made them unsuited to become the 'truly modern men' of totalitarianism, who blended organisational science, ideology, technology within a frightening new human type. In a treatise published later that same year, *The Lion and the Unicorn: Socialism and the English Genius* (1941), Orwell would return to this argument, now in surprisingly optimistic tones. Orwell sets out a dual task for the British in the year 1941: to win the war against these truly modern enemies, thus preserving much of the mediocre, petit-bourgeois, democratic culture deeply rooted in the British populace, and at the same time, to restructure the skewed and unjust class relations that in his analysis had led the nation to the very brink of defeat by continental fascism. British socialism would come into being not through a national catastrophe and Bolshevik-like coup, nor through a utopian philosophy of history collectively realised, but rather as an organic outgrowth of the wartime spirit of community and sacrifice. It would be founded on a vague, somewhat inconsistent, but deep communal structure of feeling closely associated with nationalist sentiments and dating back centuries. Thus, the men and women of British socialism would not primarily embody an historical vision oriented towards the future, but rather modulate a history long since sedimented into culture. They would draw on ingrained habits of moderate liberty, local pride, relative egalitarianism, and hard-headed patriotism – just what Orwell thought Great Britain needed to stand firm in an age of big History of converging totalitarian regimes, against a world of concentration camps, purge trials, mass deportations, technological war, and global economic collapse.

Having already recounted the machinations of the Soviets in his 1938 memoir of the Spanish Civil War, *Homage to Catalonia*, by 1941 Orwell was thoroughly disenchanted by Stalin's compromises with Hitler and pursuit of his own imperial designs in Poland and the Baltics. Orwell thus also contributed to the *The Betrayal of the Left* (1941), a blistering polemic that Left Book Club publisher Victor Gollancz directed against the British Communist Party and its servile acceptance of the Stalin–Hitler pact. This book, along with *Homage to Catalonia* and the essay 'Inside the Whale' (1940), which attacks the boy-scoutish boosterism of the Left intelligentsia, is the negative face of the positive argument of *The Lion and the Unicorn*. One might reasonably conclude, then, that these assorted 'occasional' writings of the late 1930s and early 1940s, as much as his more accomplished novels such as *Burmese Days* (1934) and *Coming Up for Air* (1939), prepared the ground for those works that ensured Orwell's later worldwide literary fame, his post-Second World War satires of totalitarianism, *Animal Farm* (1945) and *Nineteen Eighty-Four* (1949).

In an essay entitled 'To Hell with Culture', originally published as a pamphlet in Routledge's 'Democratic Order Series' in 1941, Herbert Read quoted the artist Eric Gill, who not long before denounced 'culture' as a dope worse than Marx's opiate of the masses, religion. Soon, however, one comes to realise that Read sends to hell not 'culture' as the naturalised habitus of a people, but rather that specialised elite 'Culture' separated from popular life. The problem with 'culture' is not that there is too much of it, but rather too little, since culture can only flourish in the soil of democratic freedom, presently suffering a drought. Authentic culture will not nourish profit or mirror a philosophy of history, but rather satisfy universal human needs:

> To hell with such a culture! . . . Let us celebrate the democratic revolution creatively. Let us build cities that are not too big, but spacious, with traffic flowing freely through their leafy

avenues, with children playing safely in their green and flowery parks, with people living happily in bright efficient houses. Let us place our factories and workshops where natural conditions of supply make their location most convenient. . . . Let us balance agriculture and industry, town and country – let us do all these . . . things and *then* let us talk about our culture. (Read 1963: 30)

Projecting onto industrial, urban life the image of a pastoral idyll, Read seeks to recover the 'cold' stability of archetypal myth out of the 'hot' dynamism of modernity.

If Orwell and Read envision a naturalised cultural habitus as a bulwark against a threatening history, the elder statesman of utopian thought H. G. Wells provided his own vision of a post-historical, rationally administered culture as the solution to the violent crisis of the historical present. For decades this Edwardian novelist had offered readers witty social commentary in novels such as *Tono-Bungay* (1909), *The New Machiavelli* (1911), and *The World of William Clissold* (1926); gripping science fiction such as *The War of the Worlds* (1898) and *The First Men in the Moon* (1901); and countless edifying and educational non-fiction works in the service of his eudaemonistic faith. Returning to ground that he had already covered fictionally in *The War in the Air* (1908) and *The Shape of Things to Come* (1933), in his *Guide to the New World: A Handbook of Constructive World Revolution* (1941), Wells advanced the position that the air-war gripping Britain was a radically new event in history that needed to be confronted and brought under the control of a rational world order. His program had three main pillars: '(I) immediate world air control, extending as soon as possible to a world transport control, (II) progressive world conservation and control of world resources, and (III) the establishment of a fundamental world law of freedom and security' (Wells 1941: 16). While these ideas were not wholly implausible, though optimistic in a year of war, Wells extends them into a utopian myth in which history is neutralised:

> If sanity wins . . . we shall see . . . city planning . . . resumed with a great access of energy. Architecture will become the master art, as it was in the days of Pericles. . . . All good buildings from the past will be cherished and given air and space; the new exploits need not crowd upon them. And these centres, that we shall still call by the name of cities, will be more and more individualized. All this will be well underway by 1951. Given world peace. (Wells 1941: 97)

Even a well-known book of 1940, ostensibly a 'social history' of the period 1918–39, reveals a curiously anti-historical bias in its interpretation of those years. As its title suggests, Robert Graves's and Alan Hodge's *The Long Week-End: A Social History of Great Britain, 1918–1939*, presents its events as being outside the main action, a drama played out 'between the acts', as Virginia Woolf's final novel would have it. For Graves himself, the interwar period had been a long, strange 'weekend', which included his shedding of a Georgian trench-poet past in his cathartic war memoir *Goodbye to All That* (1929), his running of the Seizin Press in collaboration with poet Laura Riding and artist Len Lye in Mallorca until they had to flee from the Spanish Civil War, and a passionate extra-marital affair with Riding that ended only in 1940. But however personal the precipitating causes had been, in his outlook Graves captured a period mood. In his mythopoetic war memoir *In Parenthesis* (1937), Graves's fellow Welsh poet David Jones noted that 'our curious type of existence here is altogether in parenthesis' (Jones 1937: xv); while artist and novelist Wyndham Lewis remarked in his 1937 autobiography *Blasting and Bombardiering* that 'The "post-war" was in a sense a recrudescence of "the Nineties". The realities that had begun to peep out in 1914 in England were submerged for a decade' (Lewis 1982: 223). Evelyn Waugh's 1930 novel *Vile Bodies* shows young lovelies racing about in bubbleheaded distraction until the final, apocalyptic chapter, which cynically shifts to a grim battlefield. By 1941, it was possible to see Waugh's comic-book satire as having had more than a grain of prophetic truth, just as Waugh himself would treat the absurdities of the war years in the unfinished *Work Suspended* (1942), in *Put Out More Flags* (1942), and in his *Sword of Honour* trilogy (1965).

Notably, Graves's and Hodge's 1940 history is written as a summation of newspaper files, and it ironically foregrounds the juxtaposition in the popular mind of the significant and the trivial. Typical in this regard is the title of the final chapter, 'Rain Stops Play, 1939', which deals with the Munich crisis, Hitler's annexation of Czechoslovakia, and Britain's declaration of war following the invasion of Poland. The long weekend was called to a premature end by a sudden outbreak of reality, but evidently, the press carried on with the habits of the past, before things got so very serious. In fact, the book begins by reflecting on the decay of popular memory encouraged by a new mediatised mass culture, which, especially in the medium of radio, had risen to dominance in the interwar years:

> The more newspapers people read, the shorter grows their historical memory; yet most people read little else. Any sudden overwhelming public event . . . is a sponge for all that immediately preceded it. The cheapening in the price of newspapers and their immediate circulation to remote villages in the kingdom has even broken down the traditionally long memory of the countryman. And news heard on the radio is forgotten even sooner. (Graves and Hodges 1963: 11)

What Graves and Hodges attempted to write in 1940 was thus not simply a 'history' of the period, but also its 'meta-history', a month-by-month genealogy of the disintegration of the British historical sense, the displacement of historical memory by a new culture of rapidly served-up spectacles and events, forgotten with equal dispatch.

On 6 November 1941, one month before the Pearl Harbour attack, the expatriate American poet Ezra Pound went on the Italian radio to broadcast one of his rambling, pro-fascist disquisitions. He was one step shy of a long fatal slide into treason, which would carry him into captivity in a metal cage overseen by US Army guards, his composition of the *Pisan Cantos* (1948) under the threat of the death penalty, and his extended confinement in St Elizabeth's mental hospital in lieu of direct punishment of his political misdeeds. In his broadcast, Pound gallops upon credit, usury and other of his various monetarist hobby-horses; but he begins by commenting on literary publication, which has gone on apace, as if impervious to the catastrophe already befalling Europe and Asia:

> A consignment of the unpopular American magazines has reached me. . . . Thus I learned that Professor I.A. Richards, one of England's few respectable high brows in America, is lecturing: yes, naturally, lecturing.
>
> And apparently the normal effort to keep things going, goes on. Wallace Stevens, J.G. Fletcher, ole Doc Williams, and kumrad kumminkz [e. e. cummings] knowing a bit more about writing than the younger men who haven't quite made up their minds whether they want to do a real job of work, and LEARN how.
> [. . .]
> Well, that's a human touch, and a relief from the noise of the American papers. We need more communication between the five continents. (Pound 1978: 16)

This was essentially the same message that Pound had emphasised eleven months earlier in his radio eulogy for James Joyce, who had died on 13 January 1941:

> A recent American pall bearer, obviously preferring funerals to birth, tried to bury a whole generation along with our eminent Irish colleague. This wont do, even for an American lachrymose weekly book review. Mr. Lewis is still quite alive as Joyce ever was. . . . And as to possum Eliot . . . the ole possum is still goin' strong under tribulation and stuka bombardment . . . Even Ulysses can be considered the first [in a] trilogy of live books, that is the series Ulysses, cummings' EIMI and Lewis' Apes of God. This is a healthier way of reading Ulysses than that of considering it the END of double decked stories, however much it be truly the tomb and muniment of a rotten era portrayed with the pen of a master. (Reid 1967: 271–2)

Unbeknown to Pound, not Lewis and Cummings, not even Scott Fitzgerald, whose last unfinished novel was brought out in 1941 by Edmund Wilson under the title *The Last Tycoon*, or the still more junior Nathaniel West, who had died in a car crash in 1940, but other little-recognised authors would carry Joyce's legacy towards a mode that would later be christened 'postmodernism'. The Irish expatriate Samuel Beckett, whose novel *Murphy* appeared in 1938, the unsold copies of which were destroyed in the London Blitz, had begun a strange novel called *Watt* and was beginning to shift from English to French as his language of art. Another Irishman, Flann O'Brien, *aka* Brian O'Nolan, Myles na gCopaleen, the Count O'Blather, George Knowall, Peter the Painter, Brother Barnabus, John James Doe, Winnie Wedge, and An Broc, had written an uproarious metafictional novel called *At Swim-Two-Birds* (1939), drafted *The Third Policeman* the following year, and wickedly satirised Irish provincialism in his Gaelic novel *An Béal Bocht* (*The Poor Mouth*, 1941). And a surgically ironic Russian immigrant named Vladimir Nabokov had turned his back on his impressive legacy of Russian-language novels to remake himself as a master fabulist in English. But Pound, splendidly 'exiled' to the Italian Riviera, dreamed only of modernist literature, rivalries and friendships dating back to 1910, and his own authority to guide a still-living movement. All should go on as before, untouched by dive bombers, premature deaths, political regimes, and international war. What was paramount was just that 'the job' get done, the labour of good writing. Given Pound's isolation, one might dismiss this pronouncement of literary normality as the product of an alienated mind. Yet as I have suggested, it is not the evasion of reality that is most striking in this preamble to Pound's broadcast, shortly before the Pearl Harbour surprise attack. It is how much in tune he is with the mentality of his contemporaries, most of whom were constitutionally far less autistic than Pound.

*

Orwell, Read, Wells, Graves and Pound were each major literary figures, but the works of 1941 so far discussed are mostly minor: essayistic, journalistic, occasional in their focus, even vulgarly sub-literary in the case of Pound's radio broadcasts. Not so Virginia Woolf's posthumously published last novel, *Between the Acts* (1941), one of her greatest achievements, ranking alongside her innovative novels of the 1920s, *Mrs Dalloway* (1925) and *To the Lighthouse* (1927), and closing the interwar parenthesis with a modernist masterpiece. *Between the Acts* was fully drafted but not finalised at the time of Woolf's suicide by drowning on 28 March 1941. The war, the novel, and the author's suicide are intertwined in a complex way. Her husband Leonard Woolf believed that her suicide was occasioned by the strain of writing this novel, which pushed her delicate mental condition to the breaking point. One can discern her fragile balance of agitation and stoical calm in a letter written to Dr Octavia Wilberforce on New Year's Eve, 1940. It deals with a 'business proposition' that Wilberforce had made, offering a precious month's milk and cream in exchange for a copy of *Between the Acts* when it was finished. Woolf dismisses the 'proposition' with friendly modesty, yet more ominously observes: 'I've lost all power over words, cant do a thing with them' (Woolf 1980: 456). She responds to Dr Wilberforce's remarks about her Roger Fry biography and contrasts her own hand, unable to write, with that of her correspondent: 'you cant write long enough letters to *this* author – but, having been book lugging, up at our hired room, I cant, as you see, make my hand cease to tremble. Now as a doctor, your hand is firm. So you can write' (Woolf 1980: 456). All this points towards Woolf's precarious state of mind and to her struggle with her writing as the central problem with which she was grappling. As if, however, providing a sudden glimpse not inward, but outward from her psychic window, Woolf adds a hasty postscript to the letter, rematerialising the war in its most intimate dimension: 'this sheet of paper came out of our bombed house – thats the dirt on it – bombs' (Woolf 1980: 456).

Between the Acts narrates the preparation and performance of a community theatrical event in the English provinces in 1939. The emotional estrangement of a husband and wife and the looming threat of war mark the virtual boundaries of the outdoor theatre in which a clumsy historical pageant is being staged by the locals. Nature at times echoes this human drama, providing ironic counterpoint, but at other times inhumanly ignores the play's narrative, at once confirming human insignificance and proffering a potential source of solace beyond history. Woolf's 'history play' itself is a compendium of cultural clichés, and her actors make up a pantheon of local culture. The play, moreover, resonates with another instance of the popular culture of history referred to in the novel, H. G. Wells's bestselling *Outline of History* (1920), which provided generations of readers with a pageant-like succession moving in an evolutionary chain from the natural historical formation of the earth and its creatures to the present. In both cases, Woolf takes up a 'history' that has lost its contingency and been simplified into cultural myth, in desperate consolation for a violent, unpredictable actuality.

Woolf crosscuts between her characters' inner psychic states, the pageant and the outer worlds of history and nature. An underlying rhythmic pattern emerges that sums these complicated syncopations up into an almost unbearable tension, followed by a sudden release. The point of maximum tension arrives during an interval in the festival just before the act representing the present. Each character is solipsistically alone, silent, yet connected precisely by his or her imprisoning unhappiness in dispersion:

> [Giles] said (without words), 'I'm damnably unhappy.'
> 'So am I,' Dodge echoed.
> 'And I too,' Isa thought.
> They were all caught and caged; prisoners; watching a spectacle. Nothing happened.
> The tick of the machine was maddening.
>
> (Woolf 1941: 205)

A wave of release follows as the virtual reality of staged history breaks open into the emotional, real historical, and natural dimensions. A group of planes flying in formation interrupts a speaker in mid-word; this event is echoed by sudden flights of swallows and blackbirds; the play is concluded prematurely by a summer downpour that sends the guests scurrying for cover like yet another flock of birds; and at last, in the final words of the book, a reckoning between husband and wife begins, resounding beyond the fictional border of the closing passage: 'Then the curtain rose. They spoke' (Woolf 1941: 256).

In his novel *The Aerodrome*, contemporaneous with Orwell's reflections on English socialism and Woolf's confrontation of provincial myth and world history, Rex Warner similarly measured the boozy, unsophisticated world of an average English village against contemporary history in the guise of the thoroughly modern men of the nearby 'aero-drome', where a techno-military social revolution is being plotted. *The Aerodrome* is a first-person retrospective narration, told from the perspective of a young man who begins with his mental horizons restricted to the village world in which he has grown up, who then is tempted into exploring the new way of life that the aerodrome represents, and finally comes back to the village, having realised that civil freedom depends on one's accepting the messy imperfection of English culture as a relatively static whole.

The allegorical image of flight governs the novel's central conflict between traditional stasis and utopian (or dystopian) innovation. The revolutionary airmen see their task as overcoming not just a particular social order, but a whole epoch of earthbound humanity:

> it is against the souls of the people themselves that we are fighting. . . . Think of them as earth-bound, groveling from one piece of mud to another . . . tied up for ever in their miserable and unimportant histories, indeed in the whole wretched and blind history of man on earth.

Flight represents everything that is free of 'the smell of earth', hence, by metonymy, also free of those social traits characteristic of the farmer, the rural labourer, the vicar, and the village merchant (Warner 1982: 223, 224). It represents full modernity, unconstrained by tradition, against the stubborn 'backwardness' of village roots. Yet Warner, like Orwell, ultimately suggests his preference for the cultural habits of moderate liberty over the utopian aims of radical modernism, for the blunt virtue of traditional community over the headlong intensity of futurist speed.

*

In his December 1941 radio broadcast, Pound evoked a group of poets continuing the project of modernist poetry in the face of the coming storm of history. As I have noted, this pronouncement was not without its delusional element. But what were the poets really doing in 1941? Were they too setting up poetry as a dyke against the flood of a chaotic, violent historical fate? If one were to look at T. S. Eliot's long poem in progress, eventually to become the *Four Quartets*, and particularly the section that appeared in 1941, 'The Dry Salvages', one would have to answer yes – *The Waste Land*'s 'fragments shored against ruins' had reknit into a seamless mythology of place. Eliot's poem conjures forth a dark, chthonic presence, metaphorised in the strong god of the river and in the tides of the ocean, mythic forces that the modern civilisation of the city forgets, but that remain waiting and watch-ing; waiting to erupt back through the façade of civilised human order. It is impossible to imagine times that are 'oceanless', Eliot considers, alluding to the necessary limits of any attempt to assert the victory of human history over natural time, which hollows out the triumphalist pretensions of the human world and reduces its glorious cities to dust and ruins. For Eliot, poetry can only teach us a way of being traditional, which is precisely *not* existence in history as a medium of human action and self-making. Rather, it is recognis-ing one's singular relation to the place of one's undoing, the death of our person and our histories. We are called to think of where we will consign our lives to the ground, to a piece of soil which becomes significant as we nourish it in our dissolution.

Wallace Stevens still more actively elevated poetry to the role of a defensive fiction against the too-pressing flood of 'news'. As he put it in his 1941 address 'The Noble Rider and the Sound of Words', 'for more than ten years, the consciousness of the world has concentrated on events which have made the ordinary movement of life seems to be the movement of people in the intervals of a storm' (Stevens 1951: 20). The poetic imagination must push back if the human species is to survive its own history, which threatens to outstrip the ability of humanity to adapt itself. The poetic mind, Stevens writes, is part of human nature, part of its capacity to survive. It is a means of violence as much as a fang or claw, but 'it is a violence from within that protects us from a violence without. It is the imagination pressing back against the pressure of reality' (Stevens 1951: 36). Yet in his unpublished stanzas for 'Examination of the Hero in a Time of War' (1941), Stevens seems to grapple with a reality that challenged even his formidable imaginative capacity to transfigure the pressure of reality into poetic images that bear the negative imprint of that reality, registering the historical world most perfectly when abstraction conceals its explicit presence. Though one can only conjecture about the 'referent' of these stanzas, the images of mass mobilisation in the first stanza ('An immense drum rolls through a clamor of people'; the 'new, modern monsters' of 'A race that is a hero' in the second stanza; and 'the hero/ as hangman' in the third, allusively suggest the reality of Nazism (Stevens 1957: 83, 84). In the second stanza, Stevens deconstructs the equation of heroism with the military virtues of fascists and soldiers, offering a new model of heroism in the 'naked' existence of the dying. With the third stanza, though Stevens could not have known in 1941 the chilling echoes his last line would take on, the poem becomes a lament for poetry's inadequacy before the unheroic heroism of suffering, for poetry's helpless figurality before the disfigured agony of fascism's executed victims:

> What misanthrope, impugning heroica,
> Maligning his costumes and disputing
> His roles, would leave to the clouds the righting,
> The immediate and intolerable need
> Of the very body instinctively crying
> A challenge to a final solution.

(Stevens 1957: 84)

W. H. Auden, who had been the most celebrated British poet of the politically turbulent 1930s, responded to war and expatriation in the United States with two complementary works of 1941, both of which confront the problem of transcendent belief in a time all too burdened by worldly history. The operetta *Paul Bunyan* was first staged on 5 May 1941, with music by Benjamin Britten, who had previously set Auden's poem 'Our Hunting Fathers' (1936) to music and collaborated with him on documentary films such as Harry Watt's and Basil Wright's *Night Mail* (1936). *For the Time Being*, a Christmas oratorio, was begun in October 1941 and dedicated to the poet's mother, who had died that year. Both works weave mythic and religious stories together with allusions to contemporary predicaments, resulting in a complex tone ranging from elegiac to comically satirical to nearly mystical.

The operetta was broadly humorous, and one feels the campy high-spiritedness that Auden and Britten could not resist in the lumberjack motif and the kitschy folk material. The underlying theme, however, was quite serious: to what extent can American democracy, historically based on individualist self-reliance, immigrant dreams, and a dynamic of pioneer settlement, still motivate belief, now that its heroic, 'mythic' phase is over? A mystical vision of America is expressed in Paul Bunyan's gnomic closing lines, in which he bids farewell to his men:

> Where the night becomes the day,
> Where the dream becomes the fact,
> I am the Eternal Guest,
> I am Way, I am Act.

> (Auden 1993: 46)

For the Time Being further elaborates this modern American spiritual dilemma, reworking the Christmas story to explore what gives meaning to life 'for the time being' before salvation. Even more than in *Paul Bunyan*, the dual historical reference is at the surface, as in this passage from the significantly titled section 'The Massacre of the Innocents':

> On the Left are grinning dogs, peering down into a solitude too deep to fill with roses,
> On the Right are sensible sheep, gazing up at a pride where no dream can grow.
> Somewhere in these unending wastes of delirium is a lost child, speaking of Long Ago in the
>   language of wounds.

> (Auden 1991: 396)

Still more openly confronting current history than Auden is another religiously motivated poet, the American objectivist Charles Reznikoff, who shared with his fellow objectivist Louis Zukofsky the ambiguous status of being a Jewish, Left-leaning follower of Ezra Pound. Like Reznikoff unable to ignore Pound's fascist and anti-Semitic activism, other young poets such as the communist objectivist George Oppen, the anarchist and pacifist Robert Duncan, and the radical democrat Charles Olson also wrestled with Pound's troublesome paternity. Reznikoff's 1941 book, *Going To and Fro and Walking Up and Down*, like Auden's oratorio, was dedicated to the poet's recently deceased mother, an emigrant from Russia. In this book, and especially in the poem entitled 'A Short History of Israel: Notes and Glosses', Reznikoff affirms his relation to Jewish tradition and to his contemporary ethnic identity, in the very year that marked Pound's treason and the escalation of Nazi anti-Jewish violence to systematic industrialised murder. In one section of the poem, Reznikoff evokes a tradition of catastrophe that is no longer text, but visible reality:

> I have heard of this destruction –
> it is in our books.
> I have read of these rains and floods,
> but now I have only to go to the window
> and see it.

> (Reznikoff 1976: 23)

Reznikoff's implication is that poetry must learn to speak more directly, if it is to continue to bear witness in this time of deep distress. Above all, it must speak to and for 'the people of Israel', Reznikoff's own historical kin.

*

Among the literary works of 1941, however, the most radical literary response to the pressure of history belongs to a quintet of novels in which the very foundation of literary character, the imagined personhood of the central figure of a narrative work, is shaken. These include: Wyndham Lewis's *The Vulgar Streak*, Arthur Koestler's *Darkness at Noon*, Henry Miller's *The Colossus of Maroussi*, Vladimir Nabokov's *The Real Life of Sebastian Knight*, and Gertrude Stein's late novel, *Ida*. A further analogous non-literary instance in which character is hollowed out to an enigmatic cipher is Orson Welles's cinematic masterpiece *Citizen Kane*, which also appeared in 1941. In Lewis's and Koestler's novels the conditions of this disintegration of the narrative subject is manifestly political and historical. Lewis's novel focuses on his character Vincent Penhale, who, in the interest of rising out of his class, has counterfeited his whole identity: his voice, his dress, his loves, his life story. Against the backdrop of the unfolding Munich Crisis, however, his character's façades crumble. In the end, Penhale suicidally discards the body he long trained into an instrument of existential fraud. 'WHOEVER FINDS THIS BODY, MAY DO WHAT THEY LIKE WITH IT, I DON'T WANT IT. Signed. ITS FORMER INHABITANT' (Lewis 1985: 230), his suicide note reads. Lewis, however, denies his character even one final moment of authenticity, by having Penhale indulge in an ostentatiously false act of mimicking direct address in his suicide note, a situation where it is impossible for the real, living 'I' to speak.

In contrast to Lewis, Koestler makes his protagonist Rubashov seek in his final duress to recover an authentic self precisely through 'the grammatical fiction' of the 'I'. A confirmed communist caught up in the purges – unlike Koestler, who left the Communist Party in 1938 – Rubashov accepts the logic of 'historical necessity' with which his jailers urge him to confess to crimes against the Soviet Union, but also clings to a selfhood mystically revealed to him shortly before his brutal death in his cell:

> the hours which remained to him belonged to that silent partner, whose realm started just where logical thought ended. He had christened it the 'grammatical fiction' with that shame-facedness about the first person singular which the Party had inculcated in its disciples. (Koestler 1963: 254)

Koestler's novel ends in a fatal stalemate between two metaphysical visions, intractably opposed and mutually exclusive: the world of historical necessity, which is granted to Stalin and communism, and the mystical freedom of the solitary self, which is nevertheless unable to affect the historical world.

Henry Miller is best known for his gritty, obscene autobiographical novel of Paris bohemian lowlife in the 1930s, *Tropic of Cancer* (1934), which provoked a landmark censorship trial in the United States when Grove Press published it in 1961. George Orwell had reviewed the book in 1935 and again discussed Miller in his important essay of 1940, 'Inside the Whale'. Orwell viewed Miller as a more organic and clear-sighted expression of the historical present than either his high-modernist predecessors like Joyce and Eliot or his callow left-wing contemporaries such as Auden or Stephen Spender. Miller represents modernism in decline, a *late* modernism, teetering on the line dividing decreptitude and decease. His work, Orwell wrote, demonstrates 'the *impossibility* of any major literature until the world has shaken itself into its new shape' (Orwell 1968: I: 527). Until that time, Orwell believed, Miller offered a salutary tonic against utopian illusions. Recounting in *The Colossus of Maroussi* his sojourn in Greece on the verge of another European war, Miller himself evoked a peace that comes not from political or military victory, but from

sheer surrender, from relinquishing the self for the ataraxy – the freedom from passions –
of inner emptiness:

> No man could have chosen a more circumlocuitous voyage than mine. Over thirty years I had
> wandered, as if in a labyrinth. I had tasted every joy, every despair, but I had never known the
> meaning of peace. . . . I had vanquished all my enemies one by one, but the greatest enemy of
> all I had not even recognized – *myself*. . . . To be joyous is to carry the ego to its last summit
> and to deliver it triumphantly. (Miller 1941: 79–80)

It is in light of Miller's statement, however, that we can begin to grasp the *historical* significance of two other, deeply enigmatic novels of 1941, Nabokov's *The Real Life of Sebastian
Knight* and Stein's *Ida*, seeing them as experiments in thinking the impossible thought of
peace in a world of total war.

Nabokov's narrator, at the novel's opening, apparently seeks to recover the enigmatic
life of his late half-brother, the writer Sebastian Knight. He writes the itinerary of his search
up to the deathbed scene of Sebastian and has what he thinks is a special revelation
through listening to the breathing of the dying man. Unfortunately, he subsequently learns
that he had been mistaken, that he was listening to the wrong man: his half-brother had
died the night before. Yet this false connection does not undermine, but rather deepens the
narrator's perceived link to the half-brother:

> Whatever his secret was, I have learnt one secret too, and namely: that the soul is but a manner
> of being – not a constant state – is that any soul may be yours, if you find and follow its undu-
> lations. The hereafter may be the full ability of consciously living in any chosen soul, in any
> number of souls, all of them unconscious of their interchangeable burden. Thus – I am
> Sebastian Knight. (Nabokov 1996: 159)

The grammatical fiction is total, and Nabokov does not shy away from the ultimate
conclusion. If Sebastian Knight and 'I' are not 'constant states', but merely temporary undu-
lations of some soul, then the soul itself is ultimately unnamable: 'I am Sebastian, or Sebastian
is I, or perhaps we both are someone whom neither of us knows' (Nabokov 1996: 160).

Stein's *Ida*, however, unseats our sense of her character's identity even more radically
than Nabokov. For Stein constantly fractures her narrative with inconsistencies in narrative succession, spatial and temporal coherence, and grammatical reference. Her title character, whose name might be understood as a punning assertion of purely pronomial
presence (an 'I' – da!, 'I'm here!'), is born, then born again as her own twin, 'Ida-Ida'. Even
this doubling does not remain stable, however, but shifts as 'Ida' begins to write letters to
herself, or as herself in the guise of the twin 'Ida-Ida':

> Ida went on living with her great-aunt. . . . She did write letters very often
> to her twin Ida.
>   Dear Ida, she said.
>
> *Dear Ida*
>   So pleased so very pleased that you are winning, I might even call you
> Winnie because you are winning. . . . now I will call you Winnie because
> you are winning everything and I am so happy that you are my twin.
>   Your twin, Ida-Ida

And so Winnie was coming to be known as Winnie.
[. . .]
It is easy to make everybody say Winnie, yes Winnie. Sure I know
Winnie. Everybody knows who Winnie is . . . everybody did begin to notice
that Winnie is Winnie.
This quite excited Ida and she wrote more letters to Winnie.

Dear Winnie
Everybody knows who you are, and I know who you are. Dear Winnie
we are twins and your name is Winnie. Never again will I not be a twin,
Your twin
Ida
(Stein 1967: 347–8)

In a year that shook Virginia Woolf's ability to survive through writing and made George Orwell stake his claim for the future on an unchanging national character, this strangely vacant figure 'Ida' stands as Stein's own defensive 'war fiction': the fiction of a life no longer constrained by history. Ida is a pure affirmation of the present, a self unburdened of longing or regret, incapable of suffering memory or expectation, and hence at peace in every moment in her self-same absence of self. Stein's *Ida*, shadowing the death of Joyce, the treason of Pound, the retreat of Eliot into quiescent orthodoxy, also marks an end of an epoch of rebellious modernism. Pronouncing her twin names 'Ida' and 'Ida-Ida', Stein's character unknowingly quotes Eliot's *Waste Land*, repeating the sacred syllable spoken by the thunder: 'Da'. Then speaking unwittingly of the avant-garde's outrage against a Europe rotting from within, she laughs along with the bitter laughter of young artists in Zurich and Paris and Hanover and Berlin at watching things fall: 'Dada'. Still unaware of repeating the final words of Joyce's modernist masterpiece *Ulysses*, like Molly Bloom she says yes to everything that had come to pass: 'Ida never said once upon a time. These words did not mean anything to Ida. This is what Ida said. Ida said yes, and then Ida said oh yes, and then Ida said, I said yes, and then Ida said, Yes' (Stein 1967: 410).

References

Auden, W. H. (1991) *Collected Poems*, ed. Edward Mendelson, New York: Vintage Books
——, and Chester Kalman (1993) *Libretti and Other Dramatic Writings*, ed. Edward Mendelson, Princeton, NJ: Princeton University Press
Graves, Robert, and Alan Hodge (1963), *The Long Week-End: A Social History of Great Britain 1918–1939*, New York: W. W. Norton and Company, 1963
Jones, David (1937) *In Parenthesis*, New York: New York Review Books
Koestler, Arthur (1963) *Darkness at Noon,* trans. Daphne Hardy, New York: Macmillan
Lewis, Wyndham (1982) *Blasting and Bombardiering: An Autobiography (1914–1926)*, London: John Calder
——(1985) *The Vulgar Streak*, Santa Barbara, CA: Black Sparrow
Miller, Henry (1941) *The Colossus of Maroussi*, in *Tropic of Cancer. Black Spring. The Colossus of Maroussi*, New York: Quality Paperbook Book Club
Nabokov, Vladimir (1996) *The Real Life of Sebastian Knight*, in *Novels and Memoirs, 1941–1951*, New York: Library of America

Orwell, George (1968) *The Collected Essays, Journalism and Letters of George Orwell* vols 1 and 2, ed. Sonia Orwell and Ian Angus, London: Secker and Warburg

Pound, Ezra (1978) *'Ezra Pound Speaking': Radio Speeches of World War II*, ed. Leonard W. Doob, Westport, CT: Greenwood Press

Read, Herbert (1963) *To Hell with Culture and Other Essays*, New York: Schocken Books

——(1966) *Collected Poems*, New York: Horizon Press

Reid, Forrest, ed. (1967) *Pound / Joyce: The Letters of Ezra Pound to James Joyce*, New York: New Directions

Reznikoff, Charles (1976) *The Complete Poems of Charles Reznikoff*, ed. Seamus Cooney, Santa Barbara, CA: Black Sparrow Press

Stein, Gertrude (1967) *Ida*, in Patricia Meyerowitz, ed., *Look at Me Now and Here I Am: Writings and Lectures 1909–45*, Harmondsworth: Penguin, 338–423

Stevens, Wallace (1951) *The Necessary Angel*, New York: Alfred A. Knopf

——(1957) *Opus Posthumous*, New York: Vintage

Warner, Rex (1982) *The Aerodrome*, Chicago: Elephant Paperbacks

Wells, H. G. (1941) *Guide to the New World: A Handbook of Constructive World Revolution*, London: Victor Gollancz

Woolf, Virginia (1941) *Between the Acts*, San Diego: Harcourt

——(1980) *The Letters of Virginia Woolf*, vol. 6, 1936–41, ed. Nigel Nicolson and Joanne Trautmann, New York: Harcourt Brace Jovanovich

III: Cold War
and Empire's Ebb

Chapter 9

1944, Melbourne and Adelaide: The Ern Malley Hoax

Philip Mead

Back in 1944 the Australian poet 'Ern Malley' was world famous for fifteen minutes, because he was non-existent. Malley was a hoax whose life and work were purportedly created one Saturday afternoon in October the previous year, in Melbourne's Victoria Barracks, by two young Australian servicemen and former school friends, James McAuley and Harold Stewart. Their purpose was to hornswoggle Max Harris, editor of the Adelaide–Melbourne magazine of contemporary writing and art, *Angry Penguins*, into publishing the work of their dead, pseudo-avant-garde poet – which he did, in a special 'Ern Malley Commemorative' issue. The whole affair was front-page news in Australia, and even around the world, reported in the UK papers as well as in *Time* and *Newsweek* for 17 July 1944. Sixty years on, one might expect this episode to be a footnote to Australian literary history, its notoriety a thing of the past. But domestic as well as international fascination with the Malley *succès de scandale* shows no sign of diminution. In Ezra Pound's sense, the handful of Malley poems, only sixteen in all, is news that has remained news. McAuley and Stewart's counterfeit, working-class poet and his 'inauthentic compositions' seem to attract increasing critical interest, as well as rich imaginative extensions. Harold Stewart had an intimation of another long-term effect of the hoax he helped to perpetrate when he wrote in 1995, the year of his death, that 'future historians will have no difficulty in proving James McAuley and Harold Stewart never existed, but were really figments in the imagination of the real-life Ern' (Stewart 1995). With every year that passes, the Malley hoax looks more and more like the originary moment of Australian literary modernism and a unique instance of cultural modernisation (Heyward 1993: 237).

Part of the explanation for this improbable state of affairs lies in the origins of what was originally intended as an act of literary-cultural sabotage, designed to break the machinery of a nascent Anglo-Australian modernism so that it could never be repaired. It went wrong from the start. Beyond its intended aims, the Malley hoax unleashed a set of cultural forces that remained volatile for a long time. The half-life of Malley has far exceeded the feverish calculations of the poet-*savants* who dared to create him. In terms of the psychoanalysis of culture, the hoax was a surface eruption that disturbed a deeper cultural contradiction, and the libidinal forces released by its scandalous, homosocial collaboration had to be paid for, it seems, in violent anti-modernist oppression (Žižek 1994: 13). If McAuley and Stewart thought that the anti-matter of 'Ern Malley''s poems would implode, sucking *Angry Penguins* and Australian poetic modernism back into the parallel universe they had mistakenly, in their view, crossed over from, then they badly miscalculated.

Angry Penguins had begun in Adelaide in 1940, subsuming the Adelaide University magazine *Phoenix*. By the time of the Malley issue Max Harris, a talented University of Adelaide undergraduate, was editor, with the backing of the Melbourne lawyer and arts patron John Reed. Harris was attracted to the English surrealist writers of the 'New Apocalypse', including Herbert Read, Dylan Thomas and others, who were influenced by European surrealism as well as by D. H. Lawrence's idiosyncratic cultural theorising in *Apocalypse* (1931). Harris's infatuation with this strand of modernist writing was in reaction to an earlier flirtation with the 'Jindyworobaks', another Adelaide-based cultural movement characterised by extreme anti-internationalism. Under Harris, the magazine became unashamedly avant-garde and internationalist. As reported in the first tabloid outbreak of the hoax, McAuley and Stewart were motivated by outrage at the importation of a selective version of northern-hemisphere modernism into Australian literary and intellectual culture:

> Mr. Max Harris and other *Angry Penguins* writers represent an Australian outcrop of a literary fashion which has become prominent in England and America. The distinctive feature of the fashion, it seemed to us, was that it rendered its devotees insensible of absurdity and incapable of ordinary discrimination.
>
> Our feeling was that by processes of critical self-delusion and mutual admiration, the perpetrators of this humorless nonsense had managed to pass it off on would-be *intellectuals* and *Bohemians*, here and abroad, as *great poetry*. (Anon. 1944: 4)

To McAuley and Stewart, neither of whom had published a collection of poetry at this stage, the bruiting of the senseless in *Angry Penguins* writing and new visual art seemed like an offence, not so much to the poetics of Surrealism as it survived in the English Apocalypse, as to their own faith in a 'universal' reason, logic and causality, values and concepts that had themselves appeared senseless to Dada and Surrealist intellectuals in the midst of the previous European war and its aftermath. Neo-rationalists, McAuley and Stewart claimed that 'No malice was intended – it was all in the cause of *enlightenment*', but they had already decided that the results of surrealist-influenced writing, whether English, European or Australian, were decayed in meaning and form (Heyward 1993: 142; emphasis added). It was the war that brought McAuley and Stewart together in Melbourne, where they worked in a quasi-intelligence unit, and it was the war in the Pacific, with its disruptions, threats and uncertainties – including Australia's political realignment with the US and away from the old imperial power – that provided the background to the hoax.

Harris's arraignment for trial for publishing the Malley poems has some murky aspects. It's not simply that some conservative authority figures in South Australia found the material indecent. At the time the Malley issue of *Angry Penguins* was being distributed in mid-1944, Harris was being sued for libel by a prominent member of the Adelaide establishment, having written a negative review of her performance in an amateur theatrical production. The libel action was resolved with a public apology from Harris, but he had seriously offended some powerful members of Adelaide's establishment and drawn their attention to his advocacy of radical art. On 1 August 1944, Harris, twenty-three years old and still an undergraduate at Adelaide, was visited by two policemen in the *Angry Penguins* office in central Adelaide. The senior officer, Detective Jacobus Andries 'Dutchie' Vogelesang informed Harris that they had been instructed to make enquiries in 'connection with the provisions of the Police Act with respect to immoral or indecent publications' (Heyward 1993: 184). Harris was then charged.

The trial began in the Adelaide Police Court on Tuesday 5 September. Harris had entered a plea of not guilty to the alleged offence of 'Indecent Advertisements', defined in

Section 108 of the Police Act as 'printed matter of an indecent, immoral or obscene nature' (Heyward 1993: 184). The Crown's prosecution case depended, then, on proving the indecent, immoral and obscene nature of some passages of the Malley poems. This legal process turned into an adversarial contest over the meanings of literary language. The trial ran for nearly four days and involved the cross-examination of Max Harris (recalled more than once) and (briefly) his co-editor John Reed, along with the testimony of expert witnesses J. I. M. Stewart (Professor of English at Adelaide University at the time), Reg Ellery (a Melbourne psychiatrist) and Brian Elliott (Lecturer in Australian Literature at Adelaide University at the time). On Friday 20 October, Harris was convicted and fined £5 in lieu of six weeks' imprisonment.

The whole state-enforced charade of the trial discounted the spurious nature of the Malley productions in favour of prosecuting their editor-publisher for their alleged content. Suddenly, in ways unanticipated by the hoaxers McAuley and Stewart, poetry was being indicted in the criminal arena, provoking a general derogation of modernist art, or perhaps any art, in the wider Australian community. In this criminal jurisdiction, Detective Vogelesang's reading of Malley's 'Night Piece' was a belligerent indictment of figural language. Here is the text:

> The swung torch scatters seeds
> In the umbelliferous dark
> And a frog makes guttural comment
> On the naked and trespassing
> Nymph of the lake.
>
> The symbols were evident,
> Though on park-gates
> The iron birds looked disapproval
> With rusty invidious beaks.
>
> Among the water-lilies
> A splash – white foam in the dark!
> And you lay sobbing then
> Upon my trembling intuitive arm.

The policeman's deposition about this poem reads: 'I have found that people who go into parks at night go there for immoral purposes' (Reed Papers [1944]). Poetry is a threatening form of language for anyone who wants to control meaning, or readers, or literary history, or society. Being able to get the Malley texts and those who believed in them into court provided a unique opportunity to punish those who wanted to privilege the non-literal uses of language, including poetry, and who believed in the existence of spurious literary figures. Nor did Harris and his legal advisers base their defence on the inauthenticity of the Malley texts; quite the opposite. It is in fact Harris who is responsible, as much as Harold Stewart, for the initial fabrication of the artificial outsider of Australian modernism, Ern Malley (Chambers 2005: 30). As Harris wrote,

> I believed in Ern Malley. [. . .] For me Ern Malley embodies the true sorrow and pathos of our time. One had felt that somewhere in the streets of every city was an Ern Malley . . . a living person, alone, outside literary cliques, outside print, dying, outside humanity but of it . . . (Carey 2003: 278)

Harris's defence rested on the assumption that the poems were authentic productions of the Ern Malley he believed in.

Since the 1970s, the Malley poems have undergone a process of canonisation in the Australian context, but they also provide a focal point for considering preceding as well as subsequent traditions of modernist and postmodern writing in ludic and unofficial traditions. His poems can be read as the work of one of the 'outsiders' of postmodern literary culture, a worthy candidate for Jarry's College of Pataphysics. They have a strange afterlife, in this context, as a distant, ambivalent adjunct to the Franco-American 'Oulipo' (*Ouvroir de Littérature Potentielle*/Workshop of Potential Literature). Having had Malley recommended to him by John Ashbery, who had noticed the Malley issue of *Angry Penguins* in the Grolier Bookshop in Cambridge in 1944, Kenneth Koch included two of his poems, 'Boult to Marina' and 'Sybilline', in *Locus Solus II*, a magazine of experimental poetic writing he edited in Paris in 1961. The editors of *Locus Solus* included Koch, Ashbery, Harry Mathews and James Schuyler. Each issue was edited by a single member of the editorial quartet. Koch's contribution, a 'Special Collaborations Issue', included Ashbery's cento poem, 'To a Waterfowl' – a kind of multiple, posthumous collaboration – as a preface. The issue also bore an unapologetic epigraph about collaboration from Lautréamont: 'La poésie doit être faite par tous. Non par un' [Poetry must be made by everyone. Not by one person]. Far from being a dismissable production of 'inauthentic' poetry, Malley's work was, for Ashbery and Koch, a successful experiment in collaborative writing.

In his editorial note on the inclusion of the two Malley poems in *Locus Solus*, Koch is untroubled by conventional questions of authenticity and authorship:

> though [Max] Harris was wrong about who Ern Malley 'was' (if one can use that word here), I find it hard not to agree with his judgment of Malley's poetry. The following 'confession' by McAuley and Stewart may help to explain some of the profundity and charm of Malley's poetry. (Koch 1971: 203–4)

Clearly attracted to the formal-experimentalist aspects of the project, Koch goes on to quote McAuley and Stewart's own description of their procedures:

> We produced the whole of Ern Malley's tragic life-work in one afternoon, with the aid of a chance collection of books which happened to be on our desk: the Concise Oxford Dictionary, a Collected Shakespeare, Dictionary of Quotations, etc.
>
> We opened books at random choosing a word or phrase haphazardly. We made lists of these and wove them into nonsensical sentences.
>
> We misquoted and made false allusions. We deliberately perpetrated bad verse, and selected awkward rhymes from a Ripman's Rhyming Dictionary.
>
> The alleged quotation from Lenin in one of the poems, 'The emotions are not skilled workers', is quite phoney.
>
> The first three lines of the poem 'Culture as Exhibit' were lifted as a quotation straight from an American report on the drainage of breeding-grounds of mosquitoes.
>
> The three rules of composition were given as follows: –
>
> 1. There must be no coherent theme, at most, only confused and inconsistent hints at a meaning held out as a bait to the reader.
> 2. No care was taken with verse technique, except occasionally to accentuate its general sloppiness by deliberate crudities.

3. In style, the poems were to imitate not Mr. Max Harris in particular, but the whole literary fashion as we knew it from the works of Dylan Thomas, Henry Treece and others.
(Koch 1971: 203–4)

This explanation was part of a statement issued by McAuley and Stewart and published in
the Sydney *Sun*'s magazine supplement *Fact* on 5 June 1944. In the 'decay of meaning'
polemic that prefaced this description of their work, McAuley and Stewart had decried the
irresponsible formlessness of modernist verse in rhetoric not far from that of *Entartung*
(degeneracy): '[f]or some years now we have observed with distaste the gradual decay of
meaning and craftsmanship in poetry' (Heyward 1993: 137–8). Koch's sense that McAuley
and Stewart's list of practices and three rules could produce poetic texts of 'profundity and
charm' may be deliberately disingenuous but it is more likely that, like Ashbery, he was
simply attracted to the poetic outcomes of such constraints, whatever may have been the
culturally specific designs of their authors.

The *Locus Solus II* context is about collaboration, hardly an ambivalence-free tradition
in English poetry. Koch is alert to Malley as an attractive instance of 'dispersed' authorial
practice, a radical counter-model to Romantic ideology's 'solitary geniuses and unique
texts' (Ruthven 1998: 249). But it is in the articulation of their chance-driven practices
of textual production that McAuley and Stewart are at their most Dadaist. For early-
twentieth-century Dada experimentalists, 'chance was the "unconscious mind" that Freud
had discovered in 1900' (Richter 1997: 57). McAuley's and Stewart's practices, recalling
those of the Dadaists, included the arbitrary temporal parameter of 'one afternoon', a range
of source texts from which to cull words and phrases, and aleatory text-production combined with collaborative *cadavre exquis* [exquisite corpse] techniques, whereby the two
poets 'wove' random selections from their source texts into 'nonsensical sentences'. In their
newspaper statement they 'revealed' the absurdity of the first three lines of 'Culture as
Exhibit' having been lifted from an American military-scientific report. In fact this was an
example of a 'ready-made', a procedure invented by Marcel Duchamp, where an already
existing non-literary or non-artistic thing or text is excerpted from the 'limbo of unregarded objects' and 'raised' to the level of poetic, in this case hoax-poetic, discourse
(Richter 1997: 88). A comprehensive exercise in Surrealist imitation, in this sense, it also
included the 'Preface and Statement' manifesto at the beginning of 'The Darkening
Ecliptic' which sounds uncannily like André Breton describing the assemblage techniques of Picasso and Braque: 'Everything is valid when it comes to obtaining the desired
suddenness from certain associations', he wrote (Breton 1972: 41), while McAuley and
Stewart write, 'There is, at this moment, no such thing as a simple poem if what is meant
by that is a point-to-point straight line relation of images' (Malley 1993: 23–4). As well,
there were the (visual) 'mechanical' procedures – another aspect of Surrealist production,
complementary to the (written) automatic – of Harold Stewart's photo-collages, which
were meant to accompany the poems. The diabolically unruly contradictions at the source
of the collaboration, surface symptomatically in the two poets' attempts to control its
reception (in the *Fact* report):

Such a literary movement as the one we aimed at debunking – it began with the *Dadaist*
movement in France during the last war, which gave birth to the *Surrealist* movement, which
was followed in England by the *New Apocalypse* school, whose Australian counterparts are the
Angry Penguins – this cultism resembles, on a small scale, the progress of certain European
political parties.

[. . .]

For the Ern Malley 'poems' there cannot be, as a last resort, any valid *Surrealist* claim that even if they have no literary value (which it has been said they *do* possess) they are at least *psychological documents*. They are not even that.

[. . .]

And, as we have already explained conclusively, the *Writings of Ern Malley* are utterly devoid of literary merit as poetry. (Heyward 1993: 139–40)

In one obvious sense McAuley and Stewart present their construction of the Malley *oeuvre* here in classically Dadaist terms. As Raoul Hausman, one of the Berlin Dadaists, described his and Johnny Heartfield's invention of the photo-montage: '[w]e called this process photo-montage because it embodied our refusal to play the part of the artist. We regarded ourselves as engineers, and our work as construction: we *assembled* (*monter*) our work, like a fitter' (Richter 1997: 118). Like McAuley and Stewart, Hausman here is referring to a technique of construction where the 'author' pointedly refuses the name and role of 'self-expressive' 'artist'. The way McAuley and Stewart present the problem, however disingenuously, is how to 'tell' the 'real product', i.e. genuine poetry, from 'consciously and deliberately concocted nonsense?' (Heyward 1993: 138). How to tell the work of the artist from that of the mere Duchampian assembly worker? They're anxious to repress the axiomatic question of the literary value (or otherwise) of 'deliberately concocted nonsense'. For them, the equation at work in the hoax only comes out if the Malley poems are 'utterly devoid of literary merit as poetry', that is, nonsense. And they want to guarantee that result by an appeal to authorial inauthenticity, (enacted) fake authorship. What happens, though, is that the Malley hoax reinscribes within the Australian cultural context the contradictory practices and effects of Dada/Surrealist and other experimental traditions of twentieth-century writing that are predicated on producing what conventional or parochial literary cultures precisely nominate as 'consciously and deliberately concocted nonsense'. Hence Kenneth Koch's understandable attraction to Malley, and Ashbery's disappointment that there would be no more Malley poems. The Dada/Surrealist provocation to normative aesthetic ideology is that its productions are not nonsense (in McAuley and Stewart's terms) but without 'sense'. The difference is crucial. The claim that 'Dada[/Surrealism] is without meaning, as Nature is', however trickily and foolishly presented, is a serious one (Richter 1997: 37). The idea of all anti-arts is founded on one kind of belief in art, but a belief that is radically antagonistic to any 'bourgeois' or instrumentalist aesthetic. Anti-art aesthetics insist on the total *functionless*ness of art in any traditional social and critical terms.

In terms of psychobiography, we know that the collaboration also served a more complex subjective and inter-subjective purpose than either of the two men ever admitted. Despite McAuley's insistence on the 'sovereign power of the shaping intellect' and that the Malley poems 'have not even a psychological value', the fact is that, for McAuley and Stewart, collaborative writing had been a decade-long practice at school and university before the Malley joint venture (Thompson 1963: 178). Nor was Ern's 'sister' Ethel Malley, who had originally sent her dead brother's poems to Harris, the only instance of cross-gendered collaboration between the two. They had already collaborated as 'Dulcie Renshaw' in Sydney University's magazine *Honi Soit* in 1941. Literary cross-dressing, or collaboration as fictive women authors, provided an outlet for two young men, one of whom was gay, and who both suffered from a self-confessed sense of 'mental disarray', 'at times on the verge of psychological disintegration' (Ackland 2001: 49, 51, 104–5). But because they were employed in the desperately therapeutic work of producing pseudo-authentic poetry, in the Malley venture, dispersing their subjective and authorial selves via collaborative sublimation, their partnership had to be misrepresented (or rather *miss*-represented) in the framing, female persona of Ethel Malley. It is not difficult to see that it was precisely *because* it was a successful therapeutic exercise – that is, genuinely homosocial, if not homosexual – that it had to be masked as producing pseudo-authentic texts. The eruptive female inflection of the hoax is more than camp jokiness. McAuley and Stewart unconsciously expressed the deeper investments of the collaboration when they admitted that 'We gave birth to *Ern Malley*' (Anon. 1944: 4). This aspect of the hoax could only be the subject of severe repression in 1944, even criminalisation. As the trial of Max Harris in Adelaide made explicit in more ways than one, poetic experiment and what was defined by the criminal justice system as sexual deviance were conjoined in Australian public discourse. This was precisely the nexus of criminal behaviour and writing that Detective Vogelesang was evoking in his reading of 'Night Piece'. For a long time, the Malley poems were caught in this tight net of homophobic reception, subjected to the politics of resentment and even criminalised.

The delight in debunking that the hoax prompted in the philistine media of the 1940s reflected in Australian society a wider suspicion – if not antagonism – towards art, and towards modernist experiment in particular (Takolander and McCooey 2004: 55, 62). The novelist Patrick White (later a friend of the painter Sidney Nolan, a member of the Angry Penguins group) offered a complex response to Australian society of the 1940s and 1950s in a series of novels featuring isolated, spiritual, sexually aberrant outsiders, often also artists. The relations of these artistic figures to suburban or middle-class Australia is always fraught, if not tortured. For other creative artists of the postwar period – Peter Porter and the opera-singer Joan Sutherland are two examples among many – escape, or voluntary exile, was the only option. By contrast, the post-1940s careers of poets like McAuley, A. D. Hope and Judith Wright, all of them antipathetic to the experimental aesthetic of Malley and the Angry Penguins, could flourish in a cultural and social space where the innovative, internationally-minded artistic impulse had been savagely ridiculed and where the 'dialectic between the traditional-conventional and the experimental' that might have characterised other western modernisms had been interdicted by the Malley hoax (Perloff and Clippinger n.d.).

A notable aspect of the Malley trial of 1944 was the role played by Shakespeare. This was initially because McAuley and Stewart had used a *Collected Shakespeare* as one of their source texts. The most obvious 'sourcing', from *Pericles*, is in 'Boult to Marina' and 'Young Prince of Tyre', but there are also out-takes from 'The Phoenix and the Turtle' and *The Merchant of Venice*. In cross-examination, Harris himself evoked Shakespeare in his defence of Ern Malley's analogous obscurity. Harris argued that the 'difficulty' of the Malley poems was just like the difficulty of Shakespeare, both equally hard for 'the man in the street' to construe. Given the adversarial context, this defence was hardly very successful, relying as it did on a totally unacceptable reading of Shakespeare as *like* Malley. But how aware were McAuley and Stewart, in networking their spurious collaboration into the textuality of Shakespeare, of the strangely complementary inauthenticities and collaborative aspects of the huge textual world we refer to, by convention, as 'Shakespeare'? They may have known, although there is no evidence about this, of Shakespeare's entanglement in a vast discourse of authorship anxieties, the subject of serious literary scholarship, but also of multiple forgeries and hoaxes over the centuries. Apart from the debates on the 'genuine' claimants to authorship of the 'Shakespeare' plays, there are spectacular instances of the conjunction of 'official' Shakespeare scholarship and outright forgery and fakery

(Ruthven 2001: 21–3, 114–20). With the Malley hoax, there is a definite delight in forgery, as complement to fakery, on the part of Stewart, at least, who hand-wrote the Ethel Malley letters and fabricated the Malley photo-montages. That's not to mention the multiple problems in 'attribution' of the Shakespeare texts, all part of a persistently unstable canon, well established evidence of multiple co-authorship, and repeated claims for contending apocrypha, such as *Edmund Ironside* and *Arden of Faversham*, for inclusion. It may be this context that prompted John Ashbery, in one of his 'Ern Malley' poems, 'Aenobarbus', to further entangle Malley and Shakespeare: 'Must we then croak a liturgy/ Spooled from wan Caesar's flowering crutch?'

According to their *post hoc* rules of composition published in the *Fact* article, the intertextual supply raid on the Shakespeare *Collected* represented only 'confused and inconsistent hints at a meaning', 'no care with verse technique' and even 'occasional sloppiness and crudity, and the imitation of the *Angry Penguins* and Apocalyptic style'. While one can index these rules against the poems and gauge the inconsistencies, crudities and direct imitation, that's only according to the set of assumptions about poetry and poetic language that McAuley and Stewart were relying on. The Malley poems are no longer caught in the social, aesthetic and cultural matrix in which they were produced, to be endlessly convicted and defended, again and again, in the punitive jurisdictions of literary value and cultural analysis. By now, they have long been acquitted. The network of Malley and Shakespeare, for example, can now be read seriously, within a different economy of meaning and reference. Rather than having to read into the Malley poems a derogation of poetry via the unexamined or ignorant evocations of the hero of western humanism, Shakespeare, we are free to understand the Malley texts as trashy, disconcerting, precious, fake, evasive, transforming poems, a little world of new combinations of words, that continue to emit a strong resistance to the norms of poetic conformity and a continuing instance of the unwelcome anxiety of authorship in literary studies, as much as in writing culture. And Shakespeare's role in this aesthetic and cultural dimension is in fact one of profound affinity, where Malley is an extension of the 'actual' Shakespeare – a name we give to a collectivity of linguistically uneven, authorially puzzling, collaboratively produced, often plagiarised and always reconstructed textuality. Which as far as Ben Jonson was concerned, at least in the case of *Pericles*, is garbage (Jonson 1968: 387). This is the sense in which Ern Malley is a national poet, or more accurately, Australia's Shakespeare.

The fact that the Malley *oeuvre* is a fake also seems to mean, paradoxically, it is extendable. Whereas the work of a 'genuine' author has a kind of inviolable quality, one that is often heavily reinforced by copyright and/or scholarly regimes, which means it can't be legitimately added to by anyone other than the author, Malley's life and work have permitted a number of contemporary extensions and posthumous collaborations. Arguably, the work of Peter Carey, beginning with the short story collection *The Fat Man in History* (1974), has been characterised by both a thematics of self-invention, more often than not self-forgery, and formal exploitation of the possibilities of pastiche (*Illywhacker* (1985), *Jack Maggs* (1997)). It is no coincidence then that Carey, who moves easily between the national and international literary contexts, should have been drawn to the Malley hoax as a recyclable instance of literary forgery, with its contending relations to both national identity and international artistic movements.

In his 'Author's Note' to *My Life as a Fake* (2003), a free adaptation of the Malley story for metafictional purposes, Carey explains his interest in the morality of hoax creation. His starting point is Max Harris's 'belief' in Ern Malley as a tragic, representatively modern man. A postmodern *Frankenstein*, Carey's novel explores the moral questions of Christopher

Chubb's – a conflation of Stewart and McAuley – bringing into existence Bob McCorkle (Ern Malley) at the age of twenty-four. McCorkle is responsible for the accidental death of his publisher Weiss (Harris) and out of hatred for his creator/father kidnaps Chubb's daughter. Eventually Chubb himself is murdered and dismembered in a ghastly reversal of the manner in which Frankenstein's monster was constructed from various body parts. Carey shifts Shelley's myth of scientific hubris onto the ground that much of his writing is obsessed with, the value of fiction as lies and the inverted morality of the artistic field. Like Shelley's novel, Carey's is also a frame-tale, narrated by the literary editor, Sarah Wode-Douglass, who provides the dominant, albeit compromised moral perspective of the novel. Her life becomes entangled with Chubb and McCorkle and her maddening, failed pursuit of McCorkle's post-hoax works of genius. Given the occurrence of trickster figures, liars and metafictional play with narrative authenticity in Carey, its seems inevitable that he would be drawn to the historical material of the hoax and its scandalous afterlife.

As Carey's novel shows, the hoax biographical apparatus that surrounds the Malley texts has an ongoing life of its own. But it is the uniqueness and power of Malley's poetic language that have drawn poets like Kenneth Koch, John Ashbery, John Kinsella and John Tranter into other kinds of Malley extensions. John Ashbery was attracted to the poems from their first publication. Decades later, with the sense that 'Ern Malley' was speaking through him, Ashbery produced 'Two Ern Malley Poems', 'Potsdam' and 'Aenobarbus'. These poems seem to be ventriloquised by Malley's peculiarly erratic and unpredictable diction – 'Know then that the emperor is translucent, his edicts/ mere paraphs, his son a scum' – and structured around amazingly clunky rhymes like 'collapsed' and 'Pabst' (Ashbery 2002). John Kinsella, the contemporary Australian poet, is involved in a much larger 'Malley' project that has so far produced more than twenty 'Malley' poems written over nearly a decade. Kinsella has signed these channelled poems 'Ern Malley via John Kinsella' and has said they 'derive from "starting points" within Malley poems and/or the original texts that the deadly duo – McAuley and Stewart – ravaged for words/ideas, their own "starting points"' (Kinsella 2002). Another contemporary Australian poet, John Tranter, editor of the influential online literary magazine *Jacket*, has also collaborated posthumously with Malley in a ten-poem project called *The Malley Variations* (Tranter 2004). These poems have been composed from computer-generated draft texts produced by the Break Down program's crunching of the Malley poems, according to letter-frequency analysis, together with other seemingly randomly selected texts. However different these literary projects may be they are driven by the desire for more Malley poems, or to validate 'Malley' as a significant cultural figure rather than a spurious one.

In the critical register, there is the suggestion from one literary historian, for example, that since Malley was gay, or even if he was only half-gay, his work might be read most appropriately within the frame of queer theory, as a conjunction of sexuality, modernism and national culture (Saldatow 1996). In 2004, the journal *Australian Literary Studies* produced a special issue, *Who's Who* (21.4), on 'Hoaxes, Imposture and Identity Crises in Australian Literature', including an essay on Carey and Malley. Beginning with the 'Mort Standish' and Malley fakes of the 1940s, the issue covers the 'Helen Demidenko' hoax of 1995, where the Brisbane writer Helen Darville, author of the first novel *The Hand that Signed the Paper*, presented herself as a writer of Ukrainian descent; the 'Wanda Koolmatrie' hoax of 1995/6, where Leon Carmen, a white, male Sydney taxi-driver passed himself off as an Aboriginal woman writer; the fabrication of the Aboriginal artist 'Eddie Burrup' by the West Australian artist Elizabeth Durack (1997); and the 'Khouri Affair' of 2004, where Norma Khouri played out a hoax in *Forbidden Love*, a book purporting to give a non-fiction account of a Muslim woman's life in modern-day Jordan. The question arises: in comparative terms, is Australian literary culture more or less founded in imposture and inautheticity compared to other national literary traditions? As queer and fake literary studies become established as part of the mainstream analysis of cultural values, the Malley texts provide a powerfully 'canonical' focus (Ruthven 1998: 243). Further, the modernist impostor Malley has become a candidate for Australia's national poet, a claim originally made by Max Harris. This contention was easy enough for the US critic David Lehman to support in 1983. Twenty years later it is an accepted fact: for Robert Macfarlane, in his review of *My Life as a Fake* for the *Times Literary Supplement*, the Malley affair is as 'canonical to Australian literary culture as the Ossian poems or Thomas Chatterton's Rowley forgeries are to British' (Macfarlane 2003: 23). To some critics and creators of Australian literature this seems like a very bad joke. But the role of forgeries and inauthentic writings in the history and foundations of national cultures suggests that Malley in fact has a distinguished, rather than a shameful, pedigree.

It may be that a significant aspect of Malley's power to define the national tradition arises from the protean energies of his inauthenticity. Inauthenticity, in some measure, may even be a necessity for national poetic status. As Brian McHale suggests, from the time of poets of the early modern period (like Camões and Spenser), who were charged with underwriting the 'dignity and legitimacy' of forged histories of descent from ancient heroes and with 'reproducing the identity-conferring functions of the Imperial Roman *Aeneid*', to James Macpherson's forged Ossian poems of the 1760s which functioned as a carefully designed and powerful origin of Scottish national identity, to Chatterton's pseudo-medieval 'Rowley' poems, variously spurious instances of poetry have significant and sometimes influential relations to discourses of nation (McHale 2003: 240–2). The lesson of Ern Malley, as with these faux-genealogising con-artists from the northern hemisphere, is that 'fake' or 'hoax' literature 'is not so much the disreputable Other of "genuine" literature as its demystified and equally disreputable Self', perhaps especially when it is linked to formative or critical moments of national identity (Ruthven 2001: 3). Hoax poetry is implicated in 'the formation and reformation of national identities, sometimes on the side of constructing or reinforcing such identities, at other times on the side of critiquing or deconstructing them' (McHale 2003: 240). From the earliest notice of the hoax in 1943, Herbert Read – in fact the ultimate target of the Malley hoax – saw the connection between Malley and Ossian (Harris 1993: 10). Poetry, fake poetry and national identity can all be variously fabricated. The corollary is that they are only relatively and contingently 'genuine', equally unstable as discourses, and equally hard to 'authorise'.

To return to the originary moment: why were writers such as Harold Stewart, James McAuley, and their close friend A. D. Hope, another powerful figure in the resistance to radical modernism, so defensive, so full of hatred? At the time of the McAuley and Stewart hoax, Hope had devised his own hoax on Harris and *Angry Penguins*, and only held off putting it into effect at the insistence of his friends McAuley and Stewart. Hope went on to become a dominant figure in Australian literary life. Hope and McAuley, both later to become professors of English and 'academic' practitioners of traditional poetic form – interested in classical myth, and upholders of old-fashioned humanist values – were easily targeted as leading anti-avant-garde figures by the Malley-loving young poets of the 'Generation of '68' like Robert Adamson, Michael Dransfield and John Tranter. For all their genuine learning, there was no possibility that writers like McAuley, Stewart and Hope would be excitedly, promiscuously open to innovative, foreign influences of any and every kind. They all seemed, in the 1940s at least, to be full of what Breton in the first Manifesto of Surrealism

(1924) called 'hate of the marvellous' (Breton 1972: 14). One can't help but compare the neurotic, cramped world of literary Australia in the 1940s with the same moment in the US as described, for example, by Brad Gooch in his biography of Frank O'Hara, *City Poet: the Life and Times of Frank O'Hara* (1993). That also was a hyperactive, predominantly young male scene, often gay, a mixture of servicemen and ex-servicemen (like O'Hara) and those who seemed utterly unaffected by the war. But the 'climate of openness' to French surrealism, and whatever else seemed non-traditional, non-academic, zany, seemed, for all its underguateness, exhilaratingly unfettered: 'Oh! kangaroos, sequins, chocolate sodas!' (O'Hara 1979: 15). The interface with the same European literary materials produces in Australia the impulse to debunk, to censor and even, to prosecute. In America, at precisely the same time, it provides, in Ashbery's words, 'la grande permission', the permission to experiment, to goof off (Caws 2004: 1313). The artist Sidney Nolan, like many visual artists of the postwar period, more internationalist and experimentally modernist than their writer contemporaries, is the lone figure in the Malley narrative who shines through the scorn and defensiveness of the time. As one of the inner circle of Angry Penguins he was obviously seduced and delighted by both the Malley oeuvre's powerful unreason and its trashiness. He believed in Malley as much as Harris did. Malley prompted in Detective Vogelesang and the South Australian criminal justice system a punitive raid on obscenity and indecency, but for Sidney Nolan he represented a welcome intrusion of the erotic (Thompson 1963: 178–9). Sidestepping the cultural combat, Nolan could greet in Malley the kind of gentleness and unrestraint he was desperately in search of – after all, he did go AWOL from the army at the time of the hoax.

It couldn't simply have been that Australian intellectuals like Hope, McAuley and Stewart felt relegated to a remote periphery of twentieth-century history and culture, and were thus defensively scornful of metropolitan avant-gardes that had no idea of their existence, practising an inverted way of expressing their sense of cultural powerlessness – though perhaps that's part of it. The horrifying backfire of the Malley experiment meant that McAuley and Stewart introduced into Australian culture the possibility of amorality, deriving from the Surrealist tenet of 'absence of all control exercised by reason, and outside all aesthetic or moral preoccupations', with its roots in the method of spiritualism (Breton 1972: 37). This provokes the representatives of structures of social control, as well as exposing the incipient Arnoldian religiosity of what Stewart referred to as the Sydney 'combine' (Hope, McAuley and Stewart), with their profound subjective and libidinal (phallocratic) investments in humanism (Ackland 2001: 236). The official, xenophobic anti-avant-gardeism of 1940s Australia was certainly a response to the further accommodation of modernity and its attendant anti-humanism and its rejection of the belief in linguistic reference. Despite their rationalist training and influences, Hope, McAuley and Stewart were in fact driven by deeply religious assumptions about culture, value and language. For them, the antitheses of these values were exemplified in the scandal of surrealism and Dada, and its recrudescence in the English Apocalyptic school.

Harris, McAuley and Stewart weren't simply involved in a contest about the importation of modernism; they were involved in an uncontrollable political drama of psychic projection and textual production that had little to do with the publicly expressed aetiologies and defences of either side. When McAuley and Stewart generated Malley, they generated a 'new [Australian] mode of pure expression': in other words, an instance of surrealist writing as psychic (collaborative) automatism, 'exempt from aesthetic or moral concern' (Breton 1972: 24, 26). They generated a small, unlawful body of writing where the eruption of the unconscious was explosively coupled to the conscious deception of a fake, outsider, sexually ambivalent poet: all offensive and provocative structures. And this volatile body of sixteen poems immediately encountered a cultural context of 1940s normative morality and above all, judgement, both cultural and juridical (Breton 1972: 44). This is why the Malley affair provides such an intense focal point for the history of morality, censorship and the politics of art. As the advent of a radical modernism, it throws into the usually dormant networks of poetic and socio-political discourse the scandalous possibility that art is as irresponsible as it is possible to be – or worse, an unrepentant and catastrophic dissolution of all previous aesthetic and social values (Sass 1992: 28). To adapt Virginia Woolf's famous assertion about modernity and 1910: on or about June 1944 human nature in Australia changed.

References

Ackland, Michael (2001) *Damaged Men: The Precarious Lives of James McAuley and Harold Stewart*, Sydney: Allen and Unwin

Anon. (1944) 'Ern Malley, Poet of Debunk: full story from the two authors', *Fact* Supplement to the *Sunday Sun* and *Guardian*, 25 June, 4

Ashbery, John (2002) 'Two Ern Malley Poems', *Jacket* 17, June, http://jacketmagazine. com/17/ashb-kins.html

Breton, André (1972) *Manifestoes of Surrealism*, trans. Richard Seaver and Helen R. Lane, Ann Arbor, MI: University of Michigan Press

Carey, Peter (2003) *My Life as a Fake*, Milsons Point, NSW: Random House

Caws, Mary Ann (2004) 'Looking: Literature's Other', *PMLA* 119.5, October, 1293–1314

Chambers, Ross (2005) 'Adventures in Malley Country: Concerning Peter Carey's *My Life as a Fake*', *Cultural Studies Review* 11.1, 27–51

Gooch, Brad (1993) *City Poet: The Life and Times of Frank O'Hara*, New York: Knopf

Harris, Max (1993) 'The Hoax', in *Ern Malley: Collected Poems*, with Commentary by Albert Tucker, Colin Wilson, Max Harris, John Reed, Sydney: Angus and Robertson

Heyward, Michael (1993) *The Ern Malley Affair*, St Lucia: University of Queensland Press

Jonson, Ben (1968) 'Ode to Himselfe', in William B. Hunter, ed., *The Complete Poetry of Ben Jonson*, New York: W. W. Norton, 387

Kinsella, John (2002) 'Introduction', *Jacket* 17, June, http://jacketmagazine.com/17/ ashbkins.html

Koch, Kenneth (1971) *Locus Solus II*, New York: Kraus Reprint

Lehman, David (1983) 'The Ern Malley Hoax: Australia's "National Poet"', *Shenandoah* 34.4, 47–73

McHale, Brian (2003) '"A Poet May Not Exist": Mock-Hoaxes and the Construction of National Identity', in *The Faces of Anonymity: Anonymous and Pseudonymous Publication from the Sixteenth to the Twentieth Century*, ed. Robert Griffin, New York: Palgrave Macmillan, 233–52

Macfarlane, Robert (2003) 'Dangerous Inventions: Peter Carey's Charismatic Con-artists', *Times Literary Supplement* 5241, 12 September, 23–4

Malley, Ern (1993) 'Preface', in *Ern Malley: Collected Poems*, with Commentary by Albert Tucker, Colin Wilson, Max Harris, John Reed, Sydney: Angus and Robertson

O'Hara, Frank (1979) 'Today', in *Collected Poems of Frank O'Hara*, ed. Donald Hall, New York: Alfred A. Knopf, 15

Perloff, Marjorie, and David Clippinger (n.d.) 'Marjorie Perloff Interview', *The Argotist Online* http://www.argotistonline.co.uk/Perloff%20interview.htm

Reed, John, and Sunday *Papers*, Australian Manuscripts Collection, La Trobe Library, State Library of Victoria, MS 13186 [formerly PA1168], Box 10/18, file 4 (b), 10

Richter, Hans (1997) *Dada: Art and Anti-Art* (1964), trans. David Britt, London: Thames and Hudson

Ruthven, K. K. (1998) 'Spuriosities of Literature: Literary "Forgery" and the Institution of Literature', in John Bigelow, ed., *Our Cultural Heritage. Occasional Paper 20, Papers from the 1997 Symposium of the Australian Academy of the Humanities*, Canberra: Australian Academy of the Humanities, 240–55

——(2001) *Faking Literature*, Cambridge: Cambridge University Press

Saldatow, Sasha (1996) 'Where Are the Phrases of Yesteryear', *The UTS Review* 2.1, 191–9

Sass, Louis A. (1992) *Madness and Modernism: Insanity in the Light of Modern Art, Literature, and Thought*, New York: Basic Books

Stewart, Harold (1995) Letter to Paul Kane, 15 May 1995, 'Harold Stewart Papers', National Library of Australia (MS8973/1/1)

Takolander, Maria, and David McCooey (2004) 'Fakes, Literary Identity and Public Culture', *Journal of the Association for the Study of Australian Literature* 3, 57–65

Thompson, John (1963) 'The Ern Malley Story: An Australian Broadcasting Commission Feature', in Clement Semmler, *For the Uncanny Man: Essays, Mainly Literary*, Melbourne: F. W. Cheshire

Tranter, John (2004) *The Malley Variations: Ten Poems*, Sydney: privately printed

Žižek, Slavoj (1994) *The Metastases of Enjoyment: Six Essays on Woman and Causality*, London: Verso

Chapter 10

1955, Disneyland: 'The Happiest Place on Earth' and the Fiction of Cold War Culture

Alan Nadel

On 17 July 1955 the Disneyland amusement park, self-billed as 'the Happiest Place on Earth', had its grand opening. In many ways, this was as much a culmination as a commencement. The hit television show, *Disneyland,* which had premièred the preceding October, was a year-long advertisement, aimed at using the power of television to sell the park to the American public, a prescient strategy, in that in the 1954–5 television season the number of American households with television sets would pass the 50 per cent mark. The power of television to affect every aspect of American life, moreover, had already been demonstrated by the *Disneyland* television show in December 1954, when the broadcast of the first of three Davy Crockett episodes created a national craze previously unequalled in speed and scope. With Davy Crockett Disney provided for the nation a Western hero at the height of the Cold War at the same time he proved television could dictate national consumerism. Even more important, the Davy Crockett craze demonstrated that a nation initially composed of disparate colonies and subsequently covering a vast cultural and geographical landscape could share a nationally homogeneous vision. Television, Disney conclusively demonstrated, was the nation's public space, the site of images shared simultaneously by a majority of all Americans, and Disneyland – the show and the park – had become that nation's town hall.

The park and television show shared not only the same name but also the same visual structure, one that divided 'The Happiest Place on Earth' into four 'lands'. These lands spatialised and temporalised national identity according to the principles of cinematic representation, creating a form of verisimilitude that powerfully combined cinema's capacity for illusion with early television's reputation for veracity. Thus the park's opening, a live televised event watched by an estimated audience of 90 million, certified television's coming of age as the matrix of narrative, commerce, and citizenship, by showing that national identity was profoundly cinematic.

So tenacious was Disney's insistence on the reality of Disneyland that when Billy Graham, after visiting the park, referred to it as a nice fantasy, Disney replied:

> You know the fantasy isn't here. This is very real . . . The park is reality. The people are natural here; they're having a good time; they're communicating. This is what people really are. The fantasy is – out there, outside the gates of Disneyland, where people have hatreds and people have prejudices. It's not really real! (Findlay 1992: 70)

Using the language of utopian idealism, however peculiar, to define reality was not inconsistent with American Cold War ideology that presented the American way of life as a visible refutation of Communism's utopian claims. Disneyland, in other words, was not just the culmination of a year-long television campaign – in the form of a hit television show – but of a national narrative that equated the American dream with the benign plots that the Hollywood and television codes mandated. Consequently, in an era obsessed with normality, Disneyland set, oxymoronically, the ideal norm.

In many ways, therefore, Disneyland was the figurative home of Tom Rath, the hero of *The Man in the Gray Flannel Suit*, Sloane Wilson's bestseller published the same month that Disneyland opened. Like Disneyland, which features rides providing constant motion in a fixed location, Rath is concerned equally with mobility and stability. A veteran of Second World War action in both the European and Pacific theatres, he wants to forget about the seventeen men he killed and the woman in Italy with whom he had briefly lived, and to devote himself to making enough money to raise his three children in a stable suburban community. Rath is exactly the kind of American, in other words, who in 1955 would be saving to take his family to Disneyland, a goal facilitated by his getting a job working for the head of a major television broadcasting company (located in Rockefeller Center). As his grey flannel suit indicates, Rath understands the value of uniform and of uniformity. Like the hero of many Frank Capra movies, such as *It's a Wonderful Life*, *Mr. Deeds Goes to Town* and *Mr. Smith Goes to Washington*, Rath, despite pressures to be a 'yes-man', is served well by his Capraesque belief in honesty, both in landing the job at the broadcasting company and, ulti-mately, in removing himself from the high-pressure fast track, so that he can work closer to home and family. In this regard, Rath contrasts sharply with the president of United Broadcasting, who has sacrificed his family life for wealth, power and celebrity.

A novel firmly in the realist tradition, full of accurate details about middleclassdom, from suburban commutes to business meetings, from drafting corporate memos to dealing with chickenpox, *The Man in the Gray Flannel Suit*, nevertheless, has a fairytale quality. This is not surprising, in that Disneyland, a world built upon faith in the fantastic, is also the apotheosis of postwar suburban family life, a place that rewards adults for devoting them-selves to their children. For Rath, succeeding according to Disneyland values means ending up with a good salary running an altruistic organisation – devoted to mental health – near his suburban home, where the town votes to build a new school and the zoning board will allow him to subdivide his property according to a plan that promises to make him very wealthy. With his wife's blessing, moreover, he will make monthly payments to the Italian child he discovers he has fathered, a kind of personal Marshall Plan in aid, not of war-torn Europe, but of one needy child.

John Cheever's characters of the 1950s inhabit the same physical and social world as the Raths. Some live in upscale suburban Connecticut or Westchester County, like Rath, while others reside in Manhattan rather than commute. As the Raths' income increases, they will encounter Cheever's characters on vacations and sit next to them on commuter trains. Like Tom Rath, Cheever's Wapshots represent wealth lost and regained. They encapsulate, in other words, a trajectory of WASP fortune over the course of the twentieth century. The life that seems for the Raths to be ideal, however, acquires for many of Cheever's charac-ters a surreal quality that highlights the way that the illusion of success is purchased – as it is in Disneyland and on television – at the price of imagination. This is hinted at, even in Cheever's early short stories such as 'The Enormous Radio' (1953) in which the purchase of a new radio – a precursor to the television sets that will arrive in the same home a few years later – allows Jim and Irene Westcott, 'the kind of people who seem to strike that satisfactory average of income, endeavor, and respectability that is reached by the statistical reports in college alumni bulletins' (Cheever 1981: 33), to tune in to the lives of the other occupants of their upscale, high-rise Manhattan apartment building. This conceit evokes not only the surveillance state mentality associated with the Red scare of the period in which the story was written but also allows the Wescotts to penetrate the patina of normality that would be so obsessively promoted by television and obsessively perfected by Disneyland. Cheever's stories and novels of the 1950s return again and again to the displacement of imagination, manifest as an inordinate longing, not satisfied by, in fact exacerbated by, the kind of normal material comfort the Raths desire and achieve.

In a middle month of the middle year of the middle decade of the twentieth century, men in grey flannel suits, benefiting from the new television industry at exactly the midpoint of its rise to national universality, converted Second World War heroes – and to some extent those of the Korean War (1950–3) – into icons of middle-class success. Unquestionably, via the television set, middle-class family members were becoming citizens of Disneyland, engaging in a citizenship that took many new forms. The children watched *Disneyland*, saw Disney features in theatrical release, and dressed as Disney creatures at Halloween. They joined the Mickey Mouse Club and owned an infinite array of paraphernalia bearing the Disney trademark, most of which they learned about from television. They shared, in other words, a set of narratives and images simultaneously with a national peer group, as marked by Mouseketeer ears and coonskin caps, that codified their identities as precisely as did their fathers' grey flannel suits. Their national public space, in becoming televisual, moreover, started to blend with their private space, as the two domains increasingly came to share a common consumerism.

This point is central to Allen Ginsberg's poem, 'A Supermarket in California', written in northern California at the same time that Disneyland was being built in southern California. The poem's speaker, addressing Walt Whitman, states 'In my hungry fatigue, and shopping for images, I went into the neon fruit supermarket, dreaming of your enumerations' (Ginsberg 1984: 136). This poem can be read as an attempt to engage the Hollywood television image empire of which Disney and his mouse were creatures and to confront the mid-century values that Disney and his land exemplified and proliferated. The supermarket, like Disneyland, sells not sustenance but images, well displayed by carefully placed artificial light, light that illuminates both the items for sale and the consumers – 'whole families shopping at night!' – such that shopping becomes a family activity and the supermarket a mini-Fantasy Land.

In contrast to fantasies reliant upon artificial light, Ginsberg posits a form of imagination that escapes the planned normality of televisual amusements and that might not be suitable for family entertainment: 'I saw you, Walt Whitman, childless, lonely old grubber, poking among the meats in the refrigerator and eyeing the grocery boys'. Highlighted by Whitman's childlessness, this trip to the supermarket juxtaposes the consumerist reality posited by Disney's imagination with one antithetical to consumerism, in which, 'in our solitary fancy' they can stroll 'possessing every frozen delicacy, and never passing the cashier'. If in this poem Ginsberg satirises the co-optation of the imagination that defines media-accepted fantasy in the mid-1950s, in the same volume, *Howl and Other Poems* (1956), the poem 'America' critiques, with equal effectiveness, the jingoism that turns language into a commodity, such that it is impossible to distinguish patriotism from conformity and conformity from consumerism. As in Disneyland, in Ginsberg's America, fantasy is at odds with deviance and spontaneity. (An executive order instructed Disneyland employees 'any ad libs must be approved before use' (Findlay 1992: 77).) In this context, it is important to place the fury of the poem 'Howl' not just against the background of the 1950's mind-crushing mental institutions, repressive sexual mores, and dehumanising schools and corporations, but equally against the tacit benignity – epitomised by Disneyland and by television – that sanitised imagination.

As such, it became one of the foundational works in the Beat movement of the 1950s, which championed spontaneity over stylistic formalism. Allying themselves with abstract art and improvisational jazz, Beat writers sought to create a radical aesthetic in diametric opposition to the social, political, sexual repression that normalised post-Second World War America. This general objective united countercultural writers, grouped generically under the rubric the 'Beat Generation'. In addition to Ginsberg, they included William Burroughs, Gregory Corso, Jack Kerouac, Lawrence Ferlinghetti, Gary Snyder, Diane di Prima, Kenneth Rexroth and, arguably, comedians Lenny Bruce, Lord Buckley and Brother Theodore.

If Ginsberg in *Howl* rallied against the repression of Disneyfied America, fellow Beat poet Lawrence Ferlinghetti in the same year created an alternative Disneyland, *A Coney Island of the Mind*. The twenty-nine-part title poem, culminating in a homage to the conclusion of James Joyce's *Ulysses* (1922), is indeed the return of Disneyland's repressed. The 'mind', as Ferlinghetti constructs it, is the repository of art, literature, lust, lunacy and desire:

> The poet's eye obscenely seeing
> Sees the surface of the round world
> with its drunk rooftops
> and wooden oiseaux on clotheslines
> and its clay males and females
> with hot legs and rosebud breasts
> in rollaway beds
>
> (Ferlinghetti 1968: 13)

The mind (unlike Disneyland) is not surrounded by a 25-foot earthen wall, and its reality does not depend on regulation and cinematic illusion. Nor does *A Coney Island of the Mind* require expensive admission tickets, a planned vacation, or the use of controlled-access highways. It is a place where anything in the world may enter as an object of desire, very much, in other words, an amusement park for the immigrant sensibility, one that is as postwar-American as Disneyland and every bit as dependent on a televisual assemblage of imagery. While the experience of Disneyland was supposed to replicate the orderliness of television programming, the experience of *A Coney Island of the Mind* comes closer to replicating the flow that Raymond Williams found in *Television: Technology and Cultural Form* (1974) to be endemic to television-watching, with its stream of imagery from a variety of commercial, informational, dramatic, and comedic realms. If Disney intended to create an essentialised, ideal America, Ferlinghetti, in the Whitman tradition, projected an America open to infinite possibilities, resembling in his poem the juxtapositions portended by the possibilities of channel-surfing, even before the age of cable and the remote control.

Thus, Disneyland's alternative is a surreal landscape, 'of/ mindless prairies/ supermarket suburbs/ steamheated cemeteries/ Cinerama holy days/ and protesting cathedrals/ a kissproof world of plastic toiletseats tampax and taxis' (Ferlinghetti 1968: 13). Ferlinghetti's amusement park is also full of rides that, like Disney's, are named after famous narratives: Kafka's castle, Dante's Paradiso, 'Goya's greatest scenes' (Ferlinghetti 1968: 9). In that sense, *A Coney Island of the Mind* shares with Disneyland the interest in taking rides. One of the favourite attractions of Disneyland was the 'Autopia' ride, where visitors traversed a simulated freeway in miniature cars: the park itself would have been impractical without the construction of the Santa Ana freeway linking it to Los Angeles and, more generally, without the interstate highway system that made it possible for millions of families to visit the Mecca of American family values. For Ferlinghetti, these pilgrims are the contemporary equivalent of Goya's suffering humanity, not roaming the aisles of Ginsberg's supermarket in California, but found instead 'on freeways fifty lanes wide/ on a concrete continent/ spaced with bland billboards/ illustrating imbecile illusions of happiness' (ibid.).

Ferlinghetti is describing, simultaneously, the potential patrons of Disneyland and Sal Paradise, Jack Kerouac's alter ego in *On the Road* (1957). Kerouac's novel of transcontinental travel in some ways could be read as turning all of America into a Disneyland full of wondrous rides. At the heart of *On the Road* is the very postwar sense of America as a transcontinental space, no doubt in part prompted by the massive troop movements during the Second World War, when, for the first time, a vast, heterogeneous regional population became a uniformed mass, assembled and deployed nationally, evoking a sense of solidarity among the even broader population that watched or facilitated their movements. If this wartime activity identified America chiefly as a nation united by rail and radio, in the 1950s, national unity owed more to highway and the television set, creating a unique Cold War sense of America as a vision of a shared space, imagery and ideology.

Although *On the Road* presents the counter-culture version of Disney's Autotopia – one in which the flow of traffic and narrative is continually aborted and disrupted – it nevertheless links national ethos to transcontinental access. In Sal's first attempt to hitchhike to Denver, he mistakenly plans his trip not based on traffic flow but on an idealised version of a national space: 'it was my dream that screwed up, the stupid hearthside idea that it would be wonderful to follow one great red line across America instead of trying various lines and routes' (Kerouac 1959: 13). The process of restarting, necessitated by Sal's screwed up dream, unites in the novel a series of transcontinental trips over several years, and affiliates *On the Road* with the narrative of starting over that certainly informed, for more than three centuries, the American pioneer spirit and several waves of immigration. That narrative was particularly cogent during the Cold War when technology, prosperity, and the 'baby boom' created a national shift in demographics and logistics.

Equally cogent was the idea implicit in *On the Road* that an American dream could be fulfilled by geographical means. In some senses, this is another version of the Coney Island of the Mind, the place where the id and ego shared exciting, thematised rides. Thus Sal's search for the dream of America turns the nation into an amusement park presenting rides, restaurants, souvenirs, and activities as a continuous array of consumer options. *On the Road*, in other words, shows how the highway system manifested postwar American identity as equated, ever increasingly, with consumerism of the sort epitomised by television. Thus the novel blurs the distinction between America as a consumer option, as a road trip, and as a set of television programmes. Leaving New Orleans, for example, Sal's description of friends left behind resembles the fadeout that marks the end of one television show and thus portends the next entertainment in a network's lineup: 'what is that feeling when you're driving away from people and they recede on the plain till you see their specks dispersing? – it's the too huge world vaulting us, and it's good-bye. But we lean forward to the next crazy venture beneath the skies' (Kerouac 1959: 130). Near the end of the novel, when Sal in Mexico is sick with dysentery, it is almost as though the hyperconsumption of America, as vision and as narrative, had found its logical conclusion, a fervid expulsion of the nation consumed so rapidly that it remained barely digested.

In some ways, Kerouac's road could be said to end at John Barth's *The End of the Road*, in the stultifying malaise of consumerism, minus the triumphalism of *The Man in the Gray Flannel Suit*. Published in 1958, *The End of the Road* presents a first-person narrative being written in October 1955. Barth's narrator, Jacob Horner is recounting (shortly after the opening of Disneyland) events set in motion in June of 1953, exactly the same month that Tom Rath decided to apply for the job at United Broadcasting. Horner, however, rejects not only upward mobility but any form of mobility at all. He is suffering from psychic paralysis for which he is being treated at an unconventional facility called the Remobilization Farm, having found himself on his twenty-eighth birthday sitting at a train terminal incapable of finding any choice worth making, any action worth taking.

As part of his therapy, Jacob takes a job teaching grammar at a community college in Wicomico, Maryland. In order to give order to his life, he is supposed to teach grammar exclusively as proscriptive, rather than descriptive, because Jacob sees all decisions as arbitrary and therefore decision-making, itself, as impossible. After securing the job, Jacob moves on, in his next quarterly visit to the Remobilization Farm, to what his anonymous doctor calls Mythotherapy, an important tenet of which is that we all 'are the heroes of our own life stories' (Barth 1967: 89). This cinematic notion of life, of course, is also the rationale for the theme park, in which every visitor can imagine merging his or her life with that of the hero of an established narrative, simply by taking a ride. Like visiting the theme park and watching television, moreover, Mythotherapy requires constantly changing roles: 'since no man's life story as a rule is ever one story with a coherent plot, we're always reconceiving just the sort of hero we are, and consequently just the sort of minor roles that other people are supposed to play' (ibid.). In defining Mythotherapy as 'this kind of role assigning. . . . for the purpose of aggrandising or protecting your ego' (ibid.), the doctor is providing the rationale for the fabulation – that is, the delight in the design and play of imaginative construction – that would characterise Barth's subsequent fiction (most notably, *The Sot-Weed Factor* [1960], *Giles Goat-Boy* [1966], *Lost in the Funhouse* [1968], *Chimera* [1972], and *LETTERS* [1979]). This notion of fabulation, certainly already prominent in the work of Vladimir Nabokov and Jorge Luis Borges, would figure strongly in the work of many other writers who gained prominence in the 1960s and 1970s, including Donald Barthelme, Richard Brautigan, Robert Coover, Kurt Vonnegut, Ishmael Reed and Thomas Pynchon.

Believing that Jacob was too unstable and too unimaginative to play one part all of the time, the doctor recommended he meet crises 'by changing scripts as often as necessary' (Barth 1967: 90). This advice epitomises the principle of television programming as the curative for the irreconcilable impetus toward, on the one hand, mobility and, on the other hand, stability, in both their social and geographical senses. The end of that road, however, is not an amusement park (although the amusement park does portend the funhouse in which Barth's characters will lose themselves a decade later), but the destruction of the nuclear family whose values parks such as Disneyland are supposed to epitomise. Jacob becomes involved in a complicated love triangle facilitated as much by philosophy as desire, involving Jacob's colleague, Joe Morgan, and Joe's wife Rennie. The relationship ends with Rennie's death during an abortion arranged by Jacob, performed at the Remobilization Farm (itself on the verge of relocating), followed by Joe's being fired from the college and Jacob's quitting. The arbitrary testing of roles and scripts, reduced to the novel's last word, 'terminal', thus signifies both the end of the road and the train depot whence departure initiates.

These dark implications of Mythotherapy give us a vision of Disneyland seen through the unforgiving lens of grotesquery. Viewed through this lens, the celebration of the nuclear family waits indeed at the end of the interstate. But the Disneyland one finds there looks less like a Mecca and operates in a horrifying place full of giant, anthropomorphic rodents, rides that spin children until they vomit, food that costs more than the patrons can afford, and entertainment so relentlessly clichéd and perspectives so relentlessly regular as to make any 'deviant' thought look evil.

This is the mythotherapeutic version of 1950s America found in the work of Flannery O'Connor. Lodged in rural Georgia, her characters are violently torn between forces of mobility and intransigence that find expression most powerfully in moments of travel, even on local conveyances such as streetcars, and that often focus on automobiles, those powerful engines of physical and social mobility. In her first novel, *Wise Blood* (1952), the fetishised Essex automobile becomes the vehicle through which religious fanaticism finds its logical culmination as a murder weapon. Her story title 'The Life You Save May Be Your Own' (1953) alludes to the highway safety slogan ('Drive carefully. The life you save may be your own.') deployed prolifically on 1950s billboards and in television public interest promos, merging the idea of driving a car with the concept of salvation. In that story, a woman pays off a one-armed day labourer to marry her retarded daughter by giving him the car he craves. Immediately after the wedding, he abandons the girl (who has no ability to communicate) in a roadside diner, a hundred miles from her home. This story of courtship and marriage that makes the love-object a car rather than a person is a fractured fairytale in which everything valuable in life is lost, rather than saved.

Thus, although quite different from *The Coney Island of the Mind*, O'Connor's world also represents the return of Disneyland's repressed, a point suggested by the proliferation of clichés that permeate the thoughts and speech of O'Connor's characters. Mrs Hopewell, in 'Good Country People' (1955) for example, enjoys a vision of the world, not unlike Walt Disney's, so saturated by clichés that she easily mistakes a corrupt, perverted itinerant Bible salesman, Manley Pointer, as exemplifying 'good country people'. And perhaps he does, in the same way that Disneyland exemplifies reality. In an attempt to expose the folly of her mother's clichés, Mrs Hopewell's daughter, Joy, a 'large blonde [32-year-old] girl who had an artificial leg' (O'Connor 1971: 271), and had renamed herself Hulga, decides to seduce Pointer and thereby corrupt him. When she takes him to the loft of an old barn, a distance from her home, she discovers that he is less interested in sex than in stealing her glasses and her prosthetic leg. This fascination with the unique, this fetishising of the artificial, stands in sharp juxtaposition to the predictability of clichéd expression that rigorously asserts normality.

The title story of her first collection of short stories, *A Good Man Is Hard to Find* (1955), is another road trip/end-of-the-road story that grotesquely parodies theme-park attractions that lure families on vacations. The family in 'A Good Man Is Hard to Find' is seduced, as millions of families were by Disneyland (which opened one month after the publication of the collection), by the allure of a special place that draws on historical themes described by the grandmother, whose relentless nagging makes life unbearable in the congested car during the short vacation. Once the grandmother's suggestion of a plantation house with 'a secret panel' – enhanced by her fictions connecting it to the Civil War and hidden silver – enters their brains, the children are relentless (like the ideal audience of children who had spent the preceding year watching the television show *Disneyland*): ' "Let's go see it! We'll find it!" . . . "Let's go to the house with the secret panel!" ' (O'Connor 1971: 123).

The secret panel that the family finds is death. In the shock of her realisation that she is mistaken about the house's location, the grandmother causes an accident that ends up tumbling the family car into a ditch. Here they are found by an escaped murderer known as the Misfit, whose henchmen execute her son, daughter-in-law, and three grandchildren while the grandmother attempts to convince the Misfit himself to pray to Jesus. The Misfit tells her that Jesus 'thrown everything off balance. It was the same case with Him as with me, except He hadn't committed any crime and they could prove I had . . .' (O'Connor

1971: 131). Having brought the ride to its conclusion, the celebrity criminal, a disfiguration of Jesus, enacts the nightmare logic that suggests that if Jesus died for other people's sins, then some people will die for Jesus' virtues. The grandmother claims that the Misfit is a 'good man'; after he kills her, he retorts that she would have been a good woman 'if it had been somebody there to shoot her every minute of her life' (O'Connor 1971: 133).

The 'good woman', like the 'good man' of the story's title, is thus a cliché hiding the truth of the Misfit's pronouncement that concludes the story: 'It's no real pleasure in life' (O'Connor 1971: 133). From this perspective, what Disney proclaimed 'the happiest place on Earth' is, by implication, no different from any other place. The conclusion to this story of coincidence and bad luck gone haywire makes it not just a metaphor for the dubious pleasures of the theme park and the nuclear family but also an indication of the violence undergirding the homiletic, sermonising universe of 1950s normality.

Deeply steeped in the psychological and physical world of bad-luck-gone-haywire, O'Connor typifies what has been called the 'Southern Gothic' tradition, of which the most famous member is William Faulkner, whose most significant works were written in the 1920s and 1930s, but who continued to write about the South until a few years before O'Connor's death in 1964. Other major Southern Gothic writers include Truman Capote, Carson McCullers, Eudora Welty and playwright Tennessee Williams. For all these writers, the powerful sense of place as the embodiment of decaying traditions, rotting estates and bankrupt values turns their characters into extreme manifestations of their own environments. This manifestation inextricably links Southern family honour to the dishonour of racial patriarchy, a dishonour through which the family traces its lineage and from which it derives its prestige (however faded), pride (however fractured), and values (however compromised).

O'Connor's world presents us with families tilted horribly askew from their obsession with normality. Because their tenacious grasping for stability is all the more radically destabilised by the commercial mechanisms of mid-century America, they become, like the dysfunctional family in 'A Good Man Is Hard to Find', propelled on a horrifying journey in search of unattainable rewards at a place where they believe stability and adventure merge. This they share metaphorically with Eugene O'Neill's Tyrones, the tragic family that takes a long day's journey into night. Although *Long Day's Journey into Night* was completed in 1940 and takes place early in the twentieth century, its posthumous première in 1958 resonates profoundly with the destructive angst characteristic of the Cold War culture of containment. That culture merged the global strategy of containing Communism with the domestic demand to live happier, more visibly normal and more normally fulfilling lives than America's Communist counterparts, so as to make Western capitalism more attractive to non-aligned states than the political economy of the rival Soviets.

Americans were thus heavily invested in projecting an aura of satisfaction that complies with the Disneyfied image of family values. The Tyrones, combining the stable parameters of one day with the unfolding adventure of a lifelong journey, give their suppressed drives and unfulfilled desires the oxymoronic condition of suspended animation, echoing in the darkest ways possible the informing principle of Disneyland's timelessness. ('"In Disneyland," publicists explained, "clocks and watches will lose all meaning, for there is no present. There are only yesterday, tomorrow, and the timeless land of fantasy"' (Findlay 1992: 54–5).) In this way, *Long Day's Journey into Night* provides the response to Disney's claim that in Disneyland, Americans were really free to be themselves (Findlay 1992: 320).

That belief, of course, was not meant to be as inclusive as Disney suggested in that he was only referring to white Americans. (The park employed no blacks until 1963 – and then only under pressure (Lipsitz 1990: 191) – and allowed none in visible roles until the late 1960s.)

By the park's own admission, it recruited 'people specialists' who possessed the 'Disney Look', accepted the 'Disney way', and presented the 1950s patron with standardised appearance and demeanour (Findlay 1992: 74). In this context – one that distinguishes what Disneyland *excluded* from what it *repressed* – the alternative family drama to *Long Day's Journey into Night* (1959) was Lorraine Hansberry's *A Raisin in the Sun* (1959). Whereas O'Neill's Tyrones re-enact the repressive forces of society, culture, and religion as they produce an irresolvable tangle of denials, anxieties, and resentments, Hansberry's Youngers internalise the network of exclusionary practices that make impossible admission to everything that Disneyland represents. If the Tyrones bear the scars of living the American dream, the Youngers, three generations – five people in all – living in a rat-infested, three-and-a-half-room Chicago apartment, act out the frustration of the dream deferred.

They are, like the unnamed protagonist of Ralph Ellison's 1952 novel, *Invisible Man*, forced 'to continue in the direction of that promise which, like the horizon, recedes ever brightly and distantly beyond the hopeful traveler' (Ellison 1990: 191). That statement is contained in a letter to a New York trustee of the southern college for Negroes where the invisible man has lost his scholarship. Written by the black president of that college, it is one of many variations in the novel of the letter – 'an engraved document containing a short message in letters of gold' – that appears at the end of the invisible man's dream in the first chapter. The dream-letter reads: '"To Whom It May Concern, . . . Keep This Nigger-Boy Running"' (Ellison 1990: 33). The running, of course, is a running in place, a way of guaranteeing that the Disney version of America, like the upward mobility of the men in the grey flannel suits, will remain homogeneously white. Ellison's novel symbolically traces the history of black Americans as they moved from the nineteenth century to the twentieth and from the South to the North, representing that history as a surreal series of encounters with the illusion of progress. Those encounters not only convert the American dream into the American nightmare, but also mark, for what Ellison has called a 'conscious' nation, the betrayal of the convictions and principles that justified that nation's creation. From the perspective of the invisible man, the enforcement of white homogeneity as synonymous with normal, happy American life – an attitude shared by Disneyland and Cold War television – becomes an act of pathological denial that haunts the American psyche.

James Baldwin, in *Notes of a Native Son*, essays published as a collection the same year that Disneyland opened, makes a similar point repeatedly, focusing on sites that stand in vivid counterpoise to the kind of American dream projected by Disneyland. The title essay stands in juxtaposition to Richard Wright's bestselling 1940 novel, *Native Son*, and the novel's powerful protagonist, Bigger Thomas, who, in murdering a rich white young woman, behaves with the instinctive fear and violence of a trapped tenement rat. If Wright's novel described in naturalistic detail the violence fostered by racism and alienation, the inaccessible limits of inarticulate rage, Baldwin's incisively articulate voice, in identifying with Wright's native son, belies Bigger Thomas's bewildered speechlessness while confirming the conditions that produced it. In the same way, Baldwin complicates Wright's construction of black alienation by speaking on behalf not only of Bigger Thomas but also of the American nation from which Bigger Thomas was an internal exile.

In an essay on 'The Harlem Ghetto', Baldwin underscores the truism presented by Disneyland: 'The American ideal, after all, is that everyone should be as much alike as possible' (Baldwin 1984: 65). It is out of that mandate for Cold War homogeneity that Baldwin forges many of his most powerful arguments, not just for the acceptance of black Americans but also for black and white acceptance of the interiorised Other who constitutes an inalienable aspect of American identity. 'It must be remembered', he points out, 'that the oppressed and the oppressor are bound together within the same society; they accept the same criteria, they share the same beliefs, they both alike depend on the same reality' (Baldwin 1984: 21). Thus the exteriority of racial difference typifies a generic version of the American character: 'We (Americans in general, that is) like to point to Negroes and to most of their activities with a kind of tolerant scorn; but it is ourselves we are watching, ourselves we are damning, or – condescendingly – bending to save' (Baldwin 1984: 64).

If Baldwin and Ellison identify America in terms of everything that Disneyland excludes and denies, Vladimir Nabokov, in *Lolita*, embraced everything the amusement park represented about mid-century American values and priorities by taking the Disney ethos to its extreme limits. Not surprisingly, the publication history of the novel is full of ironies typical of its historical moment. Because the novel of a man in his late thirties obsessed with barely pubescent girls – and one thirteen-year-old in particular – was too scandalous, especially for prudish American Cold War *mores*, the novel was first published in France, two months after the opening of Disneyland. After the English novelist Graham Greene listed *Lolita* as one of the best books of 1955, it gathered much favourable (and some very unfavourable) critical attention, which made possible its 1958 American publication. In the United States, its earnest readers then made it a bestseller by reading it straightforwardly. It was, after all, hardly less perverse than the 'charming' film musical, *Gigi*, that swept the Oscars the following year. That film, which features the song 'Thank Heaven for Little Girls', delighted audiences with the happy ending in which a mature adult man successfully proposes to a sixteen-year-old girl.

The American audience poised to laud *Gigi* was certainly ill equipped to recognise *Lolita* as a savage satire of postwar American culture. Everything about America is meat for Nabokov's skewer, from motels to comic books, from the prosperous nation's 'progressive education' to its obsession with movies, from its penchant for home-improvement projects and the kitsch sensibility of its interior decorating schemes to its countless publications catering to unskilled do-it-yourselfers and offering hints for homemakers who think good taste can be purchased from a magazine rack. Disneyland's evocation of Old World structures made quaint and charming in their American reincarnation as the sites for fairytales suggests how much America views Europe as a pleasing way to decorate American myth. Barth's ultimate Mythotherapy, viewed through Nabokov's lens, suggests that America is a nation emulating Disneyland, in the sense that the park is a paradise-for-paedophiles. Nabokov's European humbug, Humbert Humbert, by his own admission the pathetic shadow of an intellectual, is thus returning to America its own mock European fantasy, as produced by Edgar Allan Poe's poem, 'Annabel Lee' (1850). This tale of eternal love, born and lost in childhood ('she was a child and I was a child in the Kingdom by the Sea') becomes the romantic rationalisation of a pederast, in a country where his desires are so in sync with the nation's values that his shortcomings, like his transgressions, go unnoticed, and he is taken as a paragon of sophistication. To put it another way, only in America, Nabokov suggests, could Walt Disney in fact construct Humbert Humbert's Kingdom by the Sea.

But Humbert's fantasy is Nabokov's joke. Consider his description of Lolita's mother, 'one of those women whose polished words may reflect a book club or bridge club, or any other deadly conventionality' (Nabokov 1989: 37), or her household décor, 'with bedraggled magazines on every chair and a kind of horrible hybridisation between the comedy of so-called "functional modern furniture" and the tragedy of decrepit rockers and rickety lamp tables with dead lamps' (Nabokov 1989: 37–8). As for Lolita, the object of Humbert's obsession: she reads comic books almost exclusively, chews bubble gum relentlessly, and speaks sporadically, but always in expressions of brief, slangy vacuity. She is, nevertheless, evaluated by every educational system she enters as an exceptional child.

Taking Lolita on a year-long tour of America, Humbert discovers that, tainted by larger-than-life cinematic representations, she 'had no eye for scenery' (Nabokov 1989: 152). The promised allure of tourist attractions, catalogued by Humbert in scathing detail, yields no more pleasure than the second-rate motels with enticing names that seemed consistently to echo one another to the point of becoming a genre. The true allure, for Lolita, comes from the opportunities to enact the role of tasteless consumer: 'If a roadside sign said: VISIT OUR GIFT SHOP – we *had* to visit it, *had* to buy its Indian curios, dolls, copper jewelry, cactus candy. The words "novelties and souvenirs" simply entranced her by their trochaic lilt' (Nabokov 1989: 148). In thus attempting to aestheticise Lolita's vulgar taste, Humbert satirises American mid-century values by taking them to their logical limit: if one can find nothing attractive in the tangibles of a gift shop's cornucopia, its merit *must* be elsewhere, perhaps in the poetic metre of its signs. What is meaningful about travel, scenery, special attractions, according to Lolita's desires, with which Humbert is so compliant, is that they can be reduced to cheap consumable replicas of themselves. As a result, Humbert concludes,

> We had been everywhere. We had really seen nothing. And I catch myself thinking today that our long journey had only defiled with a sinuous trail of slime the lovely, trustful, dreamy, enormous country that by then, in retrospect, was no more to us than a collection of dog-eared maps, ruined tour books, old tires, and her sobs in the night – every night, every night – the moment I feigned sleep. (Nabokov 1989: 176)

The pursuit of pleasure through the simultaneous obsession with pleasing and with molesting young people thus becomes Nabokov's metaphor for national adulation of children at the height of the baby boom. Equally important, in this model of pleasure, the nation is not a space but an advertisement for what that space has to show and to sell, and, in this ultimate road novel, the automobile is the crucial device for mediating the illusory space and acquiring its consumables. Thus, no doubt, before he reached the end of the road, Humbert passed more than one billboard explaining, as it did to Flannery O'Connor's misfits, 'The life you save may be your own'.

References

Baldwin, James (1984) *Notes of a Native Son*, Boston, MA: Beacon
Barth, John (1967) *The End of the Road*, New York: Bantam
Cheever, John (1981) *The Stories of John Cheever*, New York: Vintage
Ellison, Ralph (1990) *Invisible Man*, New York: Vintage International
Ferlinghetti, Lawrence (1968) *The Coney Island of the Mind*, New York: New Directions
Findlay, John M. (1992) *Magic Lands: Western Cityscapes and American Culture after 1940*, Berkeley: University of California Press
Ginsberg, Allen (1984) *Collected Poems, 1947–1980*, New York: Harper and Row
Kerouac, Jack (1959) *On the Road*, New York: New American Library
Lipsitz, George (1990) *Time Passages: Collective Memory and American Popular Culture*, Minneapolis, MN: University of Minnesota Press
Nabokov, Vladimir (1989) *Lolita*, New York: Vintage International
O'Connor, Flannery (1971) *The Complete Stories of Flannery O'Connor*, New York: Farrar, Straus, and Giroux
Williams, Raymond (1974) *Television: Technology and Cultural Form*, New York: Schocken

Chapter 11

1956, Suez and Sloane Square: Empire's Ebb and Flow

Rick Rylance

Few texts adhere so tenaciously to the moment of their first production as John Osborne's *Look Back in Anger*. First performed by the English Stage Company (ESC) at the Royal Court Theatre, Sloane Square, London on 8 May 1956, it is anchored to its moment in three ways. First, the title invites a reassessment and suggests, albeit equivocally, a break from the past. Second, 1956 was a year of political and cultural tumult and, for many, the play seemed to articulate feelings of enraged but helpless frustration over events that included Britain's 'Suez Crisis' and the Soviet invasion of Hungary. The first of these was a major episode in Britain's imperial endgame, while the second was a significant moment in the struggle for sovereignty between new superpowers. As one empire ebbed, others flowed. Third, literary history itself has rapidly co-opted *Look Back in Anger*, and the year of its production, as a watershed in postwar sensibility. In the history of dramatic writing especially, 1956 is the year in which new attitudes, and new kinds of cultural awareness, reshaped literary practice.

This essay will explore these themes. Resuming Osborne's optical metaphor, the play will be explored as a kaleidoscope: turned this way and that to look back at some of the period's significant configurations. For it contains reflections of many of the geopolitical, social, cultural and sexual tensions that shaped postwar writing. To consider *Look Back in Anger* in this way is not new, but this is the point. That the play seemed so inaugural and representative to Osborne's contemporaries is an important fact. There has rarely been a literary work so quickly turned into history, or which was taken so speedily to define its own epoch. What was it in May of 1956 that people wanted so much that a first play by an unknown and undistinguished 27-year-old actor could deliver?

Although *Look Back in Anger* was a rapid success, its triumph was not instantaneous. On opening, reviews were largely negative. Some thought it well acted, and several admired its vivid language. However the majority thought it technically incompetent, and took a strong dislike to what they saw as Osborne's peevish, ranting, provincial anti-hero, Jimmy Porter (Elsom 1981; Lloyd Evans 1985; Page 1988; Taylor 1968). Porter's tirades against the withered manifestations of Britain in decline are directed onstage at his wife and friends. But they found their targets in a West End audience identified with 'The Establishment', a phrase coined before the war, but succinctly redefined by the journalist Henry Fairlie in the *Spectator* in 1955: 'By "The Establishment" I do not mean only the centres of official power – though they are certainly a part of it – but rather the whole matrix of official and social relations within which power is exercised' (Ayto 1999: 138). Thus *Look Back in Anger* starts with an attack on pretentious, obfuscating highbrows reviewing for the Sunday papers – 'I've just read three whole columns on the English

Novel. Half of it's in French. Do the Sunday papers make *you* feel ignorant?' (Osborne 1957: 10–11) – and elaborates a catalogue of classic 'Establishment' targets. The Church is represented by its dreary clanging bells and 'the Bishop of Bromley' appealing 'to all Christians to do all they can to assist in the manufacture of the H-Bomb' (Osborne 1957: 13). Porter's MP brother-in-law Nigel represents the ruling class: 'The Platitude from Outer Space . . . he and his pals have been plundering and fooling everybody for generations' (Osborne 1957: 21). His wife's detested parents stand for Empire: Colonel Redfern had been a military man in India. Her cultural circle are 'a romantic lot. They spend their time mostly looking forward to the past' (Osborne 1957: 56). And so on.

In the event, it was ironically those same Sunday papers that turned the play's fortunes. After a week of negative reviews in the dailies, Harold Hobson, the doyen of theatre journalists, wrote positively in the *Sunday Times*. But more significant was the enthusiasm of Kenneth Tynan, the young opinion-former at the *Observer*. Tynan's review conceded weaknesses, but hailed *Look Back in Anger* as 'the best young play of its decade'. Tynan admired its originality and energy ('Jimmy is simply and abundantly alive'), and the topical way it presented subjects 'one had despaired of ever seeing on the stage', including 'post-war youth as it really is'. This was his key theme: the play was 'likely to remain a minority taste. What matters, however, is the size of the minority. I estimate it at roughly 6,733,000, which is the number of people in this country between the ages of twenty and thirty'. The friction between polite culture and the emerging generation gave the play its power, Tynan believed, and, responding in kind to its urgent emotional voltage, he doubted he 'could love anyone who did not wish to see [it]' (Taylor 1968: 49–51).

Yet still the play was not a commercial success. Despite its eventual celebrity, the box-office return from its first run was only 59.8 per cent (Browne 1975: 112). What saved it was a new phenomenon in the cultural life of the nation: television. Two months after its first night, Osborne was interviewed on the BBC's *Panorama*, on 9 July 1956, the subject being the younger generation. The print media followed the trail, and both up- and down-market newspapers carried related features (Ritchie 1988: Chapter 2). On 16 October, the BBC transmitted a 25-minute excerpt from *Look Back*, again framed by commentary on the 'youth' issue, and watched by nearly 5 million. Despite some misplaced managerial anxiety at the Royal Court that the new medium would ruin the old, ticket sales leapt forward. On 5 November the play transferred to the larger and more mainstream Lyric theatre, to the fledgling ESC's considerable financial advantage. On 28 November Granada television transmitted it in full, warning viewers about 'very direct language'. Thus *Look Back in Anger* left the stage and entered popular culture. Osborne himself became a much-photographed celebrity. 'This is the Year of the Angry Young Men', declared the *Daily Mail* on 13 December. The following March, *Look Back* transferred back to the Royal Court. In April, Osborne's second play *The Entertainer* opened at the Court with Laurence Olivier, the most eminent actor of his day, playing the lead. In October, *Look Back* was revived in a new production. It then became a Broadway success. In 1958, the New York Critics Circle chose it as the best foreign play of the season. By 1959 it was a film starring Richard Burton. Looking back was not what Osborne's career was doing.

Emotional energy, integrity, youth and originality were the keynotes in Tynan's enthusiastic review. New technology and a new form of relationship between literature and the media secured success. In addition, the ESC at the Royal Court was itself a new kind of institution. Founded in 1955 by the director and actor George Devine (who personally discovered Osborne), 'the Court' – the Company was quickly assimilated into the venue – broke decisively from mainstream London theatre. It was committed to enlarging the range and potential audience by attracting non-traditional theatregoers, especially the young. It gave opportunity and authority to fresh, radically-minded directors like Lindsay Anderson and William Gaskill. It took an abrasive attitude towards controversy at a time when the British theatre still worked under the censorship of the Lord Chamberlain's office, only abolished in 1968, a development in which productions at the Court played a strategic role. Osborne's work was regularly harassed by the censor and sometimes reduced to 'private' performance as the Court turned itself into a theatre 'club' where unlicensed performances were lawful, though they always incurred substantial financial loss. Edward Bond, another of the new generation of young writers, attracted particular ire. The furore over his *Saved* (1965), a play about cultural and emotional deprivation amid London's urban wastelands which features the stoning of a baby in its pram, was a key, publicity-generating crisis as policemen once again tramped the Court's narrow stairways.

The company also innovated in design and stage setting. Devine cleared out the clutter and fussy ornamentation of the Edwardian auditorium. He introduced new, clean sightlines and stage spaces with bold lighting. He encouraged innovative designers such as Jocelyn Herbert to construct sets of startling simplicity and metaphoric power using new materials such as unpainted wood, fibreglass, polystyrene and metal whose symbolic modernity was as important as their aesthetic refreshment. But above all, the Court was significant in its eagerness to promote and sustain new writing: John Arden, Ann Jellicoe and David Storey, as well as Osborne and Bond, got their start. They brought new forms, new themes, and an enlarged social and intellectual range. New international work also found a home, including plays by Bertolt Brecht, Luigi Pirandello and Jean-Paul Sartre, and, from the United States, Arthur Miller (for whom *Look Back in Anger* was 'the only modern English play' [Innes 2002: 86]). The Court staged, in French, the world première of Samuel Beckett's *Endgame* (*Fin de Partie*) in 1957, and openly encouraged the new styles of European drama appearing in London for the first time in the mid-1950s: the 'absurdist' expressionism of Eugène Ionesco and Beckett (*Waiting for Godot* was first performed in London in 1955), and the searching, dialectical Marxism of Brecht, whose company the Berliner Ensemble astounded the London avant-garde in a season at the Palace Theatre in 1956. Later, Osborne – in what became for him a settled 'Little Englander' manner – dismissed Devine's Europhilia contemptuously ('French was almost obligatory [in his house], and German encouraged' [Osborne 1991: 14]). Nevertheless, the influence of international work was powerful. Complementing and amplifying the new developments at the Court, it decisively ended an insular and quiescent period in British theatre, lasting at least since the 1930s, during which innovation had seemed confined to modest redevelopments of verse drama by W. H. Auden and Christopher Isherwood, and later T. S. Eliot and Christopher Fry. The impact of Beckett was soon evident, from 1957, in the work of Harold Pinter, who also explored the 'absurd', claustrophobic predicaments of people trapped in shabby rooms and junk-filled basements. In a more comic idiom, it continued to appear in the next decade in Tom Stoppard's plays – particularly his first success, *Rosencrantz and Guildenstern Are Dead* (1967), a rewriting of *Hamlet* closely modelled on *Waiting for Godot* in vision and idiom. (Similar 'absurdist' developments in the wake of Beckett can be traced in American theatre beginning with Edward Albee's *The Zoo Story* [1959].)

The renovations in British theatre achieved at the Royal Court were constitutive, but they were enabled by major changes in the cultural infrastructure. As it made its commercially risky innovations, the Court was sustained by the newly expanding Arts Council, founded in 1946. Under successive governments, the Arts Council distributed increasing amounts of money to sustain excellence and encourage innovation: funds rose nearly ten-fold between

1956 and 1968. This was enhanced by contributions from local authorities empowered by the Local Government Act of 1948 to raise up to a sixpenny rate to support culture and the arts, which some did. Not all of this money went to drama, of course, and there was virtually nothing to support non-dramatic literature, but by 1956 the Arts Council and local authorities between them provided about £1 million for theatre. By 1970, that had risen to £10.5 million, spent on 106 projects nationwide (Elsom 1971: 76). The ESC was one of a handful of prominent companies singled out for consistent support on grounds of quality and innovation, but it had its counterparts in the regions. Between 1938 and 1958 no new theatres had been built in the UK. Between 1958 and 1970, by contrast, there were two major renovations and twenty new buildings completed, with twelve more underway, all outside London (Elsom 1971: 11, 132–3). They included civic theatres developed as part of urban regeneration programmes, like the Belgrade Theatre in bomb-blitzed Coventry. Opening in 1958, it was named after Coventry's twin city, which supplied free timber. Independent regional arts associations were established from 1956, the Southwest being the first, followed by the Midlands (1958) and the Northeast (1961).

So *Look Back in Anger*'s challenging innovations in theme, language and subject matter accompanied major structural redevelopment. Jimmy Porter's pushy, self-conscious provincialism anticipated a changing relationship between metropolitan culture and that of the regions, aided by new cultural institutions, national television and revived regional theatre. Expanding education provided a similar, enlarging development (Jimmy Porter has been to university, though 'it's not even red brick, but white tile' [Osborne 1957: 42]). In non-dramatic literature, the growth of the paperback trade increased the book-buying public and diminished the prestige of an elite literature. This was unsettling for some. Just as Jimmy Porter's attacks on the Establishment bruised theatrical sensibilities, the paperback appeared to some to alter cultural relations and insult standards. For the critic George Steiner, a champion of high culture in its traditional mode, the paperback represented 'both the triumphs and illusions of the new, post-bourgeois literacy'. It made quality writing accessible, but Steiner feared its 'low cost, visual attractiveness, and ease of acquisition'. Paperback access was 'pre-packaged'; the challenge of great, difficult writing was being lost to artless populism (Steiner 1969: 107). In fact, it is arguable that Penguin Books, especially, played a major role in the extension of the serious reading public and the spread of education. They also played a prominent role in the liberalisation of literary attitudes and in the reduction of the state's direct interference in culture, especially following the famous 'Lady Chatterley' trial of 1960, in which Penguin defeated a prosecution for the publication of D. H. Lawrence's novel under the Obscene Publications Act.

Issues of access, and the abrasion between older and more recent cultural forms, became a regular theme in cultural debate and in this, too, *Look Back in Anger* pinpoints a trend. Such themes featured in the work of a new generation of influential critics raised in working-class homes, such as Richard Hoggart and Raymond Williams, whose *The Uses of Literacy* (1957) and *Culture and Society* (1958) respectively, paperbacked by Penguin, became surprise bestsellers. It featured too in work by writers of working-class or regional origins such as the novelists John Braine from Bradford (*Room at the Top*, 1957) and Alan Sillitoe from Nottingham (*Saturday Night and Sunday Morning*, 1958), both of whose careers were promoted, like Osborne's, by the new professional engines of paperbacks, media celebrity and the successful film version. 'Makes ROOM AT THE TOP look like a vicarage tea-party' was prominently quoted from the *Daily Telegraph* on the cover of the Pan paperback of Sillitoe's novel, alongside a drawing of an aggressively-posed Albert Finney in the lead role from the film version that John Osborne's new company, Woodfall

Productions, had made. Arnold Wesker from the Jewish East End presented a different but parallel case, indicating the spread of the new sensibility. His play *Roots* was first performed at Coventry's Belgrade Theatre in 1959, and includes characters from London's East End. But it centres on Beatie Bryant, a farm labourer's daughter, and is set in Norfolk. The plot turns on the romantic betrayal of Beatie by her East End boyfriend. But the play ends affirmatively as Beatie, abandoned, discovers her own articulate voice, which resonated from Norfolk to Coventry.

More restive than *Roots* in its conclusions was the long-running BBC television comedy *Steptoe and Son*, featuring two south London scrap dealers, first transmitted in 1962. Typically, the abrasion between new and old is explored between generations, and the father, an old-style rag-and-bone man, and his culturally aspiring son are poignantly in conflict week by week. Desperate for scrounged books ('my library'), out-of-date fashion, and wannabe Establishment habits, including golf (pronounced 'gawf'), the son aspires to a different form of cultural belonging. The comedy, painful at times, observes the slow, sometimes crunchingly destructive process of change. Unease about this was everywhere. In 1955, on the eve of *Look Back in Anger*, the novelist Nancy Mitford teased readers of *Encounter* magazine with a famous article on 'U and non-U' (socially acceptable and unacceptable) use of words for concepts such as toilet or luncheon. The magazine hurriedly produced a thousand offprints of her piece for separate sale and, amplified through the press, what started as a sport tapped, in 1956, into people's nervous need for literal reassurance on how to articulate cultural and class transition.

In the theatre, commentators and practitioners wondered about the impact of new audiences. While some feared an era of Porter-ish oafishness – one reviewer thought Jimmy ought to be 'ducked in a horse pond or sentenced to a lifetime of cleaning latrines' (a National Service punishment) to teach him manners – the new venues looked eagerly for a new kind of theatregoer (Taylor 1968: 43). Regional theatres developed community outreach and education programmes, and more militant directors searched for a new, politicised populism. Stephen Joseph, founder of the celebrated Victoria Theatre in Stoke-on-Trent in 1962, could see no reason why theatre, as it had been in earlier times, 'should not be as popular as football, why it should not provide social activity as free and easy as that we find everyday in the pub, why it should not be as accessible as fish and chips, and much more enjoyable' (Joseph 1967: 9). Joan Littlewood and her colleagues founded Theatre Workshop in Manchester in 1945 from the remnants of prewar left-wing groups. It played in temporary billets, or was taken precariously on tour, before settling in London in 1953 at the Theatre Royal in Stratford, very much east of the West End.

Littlewood was more directly politicised than most. Her inspiration came from socialist agit-prop theatre of the 1930s and early experience as a radio journalist recording daily lives in the northwest. This fruitful marriage of continental avant-garde politics and the documentation of ordinary resilience and vitality produced a theatre committed to the international and the local simultaneously. Enjoying a huge reputation abroad (larger, it was often pointed out, than at home), Littlewood's work nonetheless remained committed to her theatre's immediate community. Best known for shows such as *Oh What a Lovely War* (1963), an anti-war play based on the Edwardian seaside Pierrot show, she also introduced London audiences to the work of the Irish dramatist Brendan Behan – *The Quare Fellow* (1956), *The Hostage* (1959) – and to *A Taste of Honey* (1958), written by a Salford teenager, Shelagh Delaney. This work appeared alongside an innovative repertoire of continental and British classics (Shakespeare, Jonson, Molière) and popular, locally based 'Cockney' shows such as Frank Norman's *Fings Ain't Wot They Used T'Be* (1959), with lyrics by Lionel

Bart, and Stephen Lewis's *Sparrers Can't Sing* (1960). For Littlewood, this canon-crossing mix questioned accepted cultural levels, documented unknown lives and, most importantly, produced a distinctive theatrical energy. Though *A Taste of Honey* is usually understood as a piece of 'gritty' northern naturalism, partly because that is how it was filmed (again by Osborne's Woodfall Productions, in 1962), in the theatre it is rather different, featuring an onstage jazz band, songs and routines, percolating into dialogue sometimes modelled on comedians' patter.

To a certain extent, there is a similar tension between grit and greasepaint in *Look Back in Anger*, which is largely a naturalistic piece (for discussion see below). But Act 3 features a music-hall routine improvised by Jimmy and Cliff, appearing as 'T. S. Eliot and Pam': 'Now there's a certain little lady, and you all know who I mean,/ She may have been to Roedean, but to me she's still a queen' (Osborne 1957: 81). As the name of their 'act' suggests, the routine collides high and low culture for comic effect, but it also introduces a theatrical animation into the static, drab and imprisoning environment, something developed further in Osborne's next play, *The Entertainer*, which explicitly uses the decline of the music hall as a metaphor for the nation. Critics were troubled by *Look Back in Anger*'s supposed flaws in construction, but these are partly attributable to a deliberate effort to collide cultural registers and theatrical forms, including gross sentiment, in the same way that the play's content confronts Establishment culture with the reckless cynicism of provincial youth. However, the fact that the dying form of the music hall was a 'looking back' in terms of popular culture is some measure of the play's ambivalent contemporaneity and uncertainty about the future. In the film version of *Look Back*, this is played down. Much more is made of Jimmy's interest in jazz.

The Royal Court deliberately sought a young audience. George Devine was quoted in the *London Evening Standard* in 1960:

> I deliberately set out to create a disturbing, exciting sort of theatre. I want to appeal to a vast, new, untouched audience. They are the LP record public, the serious jazz public. They think of the London theatre as a weird, tiara world. To appeal to them I will broaden my technique, use music and dancing . . . (Roberts 1986: 9).

But while there is clear convergence between this aspiration and some aspects of *Look Back in Anger*, Devine's hopes were unfulfilled. The Arts Council report for 1961–2 commended the Court's 'outstanding' contribution, but noted that 'there is no reliable audience to ensure a reasonable amount of financial stability' (Roberts 1986: 14). Devine privately conceded to Neville Blond, the chairman of the ESC, that 'the "new movement" except through the rapidly reforming cinema does not reach the "new public" ' (Roberts 1999: 82). For William Gaskill, who succeeded Devine as Artistic Director after the latter's untimely death in 1965, 'the younger audience which will take a risk on a new play is still very small, though devoted' (Roberts 1986: 47). Ticket price reductions had some impact, but were financially doubtful. Consistently the Court sold largish numbers of seats but returned significantly reduced box-office receipts, as student and other concessions swelled the first and diminished the second, as was the case with *Look Back in Anger* (Browne 1975: 21, 121). Meanwhile, the reputation of the theatre as a 'weird, tiara world', as Devine put it, continued to deter. The director Peter Brook, in an article in 1959, mockingly yearned 'Oh for Empty Seats', and drama uninhibited by 'tiara' dress codes, expectations and discouraging prices (Marowitz, Milne and Hale 1965: 68–74). For Stephen Joseph, exulting in his fastness in Stoke, mainstream theatre was 'too stupid a ritual to allow of a new audience' (Joseph 1968: 127). For him, Arts Council subsidy only shored-up privilege. Joan Littlewood remained bitter at the Arts Council's refusal to support her kind of popular theatre.

These are difficult arguments, but they are at the heart of a good deal of cultural and literary debate in the period. They focus on the relationship between 'high' cultural forms and new styles, audiences and expectations. Some, like Stephen Joseph, came to see the Court as an extension of, rather than an alternative to, Establishment culture. Others, such as Arnold Wesker and Peter Brook, sought alternative venues or new theatrical opportunities abroad. Joan Littlewood, who had never worked in the mainstream, began in the early 1960s to dream of building a people's 'Fun Palace' in London's docklands as an alternative institution that would be a 'university of the streets' and 'lift the heavy stone laid on the theatre by the Puritans' (Littlewood 1995: 704, 639). Disappointed, she too went to work abroad. The equally politicised John Arden left to live in Ireland, disgusted by the theatrical and political Establishment alike. Younger dramatists briefly associated with the Royal Court in the later 1960s, such as David Hare and John McGrath, also sought alternatives through touring companies that took them away from the metropolis. With Howard Brenton, Hare founded Portable Theatre in 1968, while McGrath famously declared he would 'rather have a bad night in Bootle' than a season in London (McGrath 1975: 54). In a more sustained way than Hare, he abandoned mainstream English theatre in favour of work in Scotland, or in smaller venues in England, with the politically and theatrically radical company, 7:84, which he helped to found in 1971. For Hare at least, the Royal Court style had, by the late 1960s, become the theatrical convention to be defied. Through its very success, Hare argued, it had become 'the dominant staging cliché of the day' (Findlater 1981: 139).

Yet if one dynamic was, in the parlance of the subsequent decade, to force a decision between 'getting out' and 'selling out', another story tells of the absorption of the changing cultural moment in new literary work. 1956 saw Elvis Presley's first hit record, 'Heartbreak Hotel', quickly followed by 'Hound Dog' and 'Love Me Tender'. It was the year in which blue jeans were first sold in the UK as fashion and not work-wear. It was the year in which James Dean's film *Rebel Without a Cause* was made poignant by the star's death in a car smash. Parallels between Dean's film and Jimmy Porter's slogan 'There aren't any good, brave causes left' (Osborne 1957: 84) were quickly identified, as were those with another pouting, rebellious American, Marlon Brando in the 1954 biker film *The Wild One* (Taylor 1968: 44). Asked 'What are you rebelling against, Johnny?', Brando's character replies 'Whaddya got?'. In 1956, too, *Rock Around the Clock* arrived in a film of its own, the song having previously featured in the more serious 'disaffected youth' film *The Blackboard Jungle* in 1955. In 1956, drainpipe-trousered, brothel-creeper-shod youths, and big-skirted girls, were expelled from cinemas in Britain for jiving in the aisles to Bill Haley and the Comets. Out in the street they jived some more until police moved them on, or arrested them for 'insulting behaviour', all photographed by the attendant media. It is 'intense, angry, feverish, undisciplined. It is even crazy. But it is young, young, young', wrote one early critic in the *Daily Express*, not of rock'n'roll but of *Look Back in Anger* (Elsom 1981: 79). Another American arrival in these years had a more righteous purpose. The Christian evangelist Billy Graham made the first of his annual UK 'crusades' in 1954 – 180,000 packed his closing rally. This too finds its echo in *Look Back in Anger*'s persistent topicality. Jimmy mocks a woman

> who went to the mass meeting of a certain American evangelist at Earls Court. She went
> forward to declare herself for love or whatever it is, and, in the rush of converts to get to the

front, she broke four ribs and got kicked in the head. She was yelling her head off in agony, but with 50,000 people putting their all into 'Onward Christian Soldiers', nobody even knew she was there (Osborne 1957: 14).

We live, according to Jimmy, in 'the American Age' (Osborne 1957: 17). In the various tensions that criss-cross *Look Back in Anger* – young and old, provincial and metropolitan, high and low culture – the American contribution is profound. The Australian Colin MacInnes was perhaps the most perceptive writer to document London's changing cultural hinterland in this period. His trilogy of 'youth' novels *City of Spades* (1957), *Absolute Beginners* (1959) and *Mr Love and Justice* (1960) broke ground in terms of subject, though others, like Lynne Reid Banks's *The L-Shaped Room* (1960), covered similar terrain. In 'Young England, Half English', a piece on the British rock'n'roller Tommy Steele for the American-backed *Encounter* magazine in 1957, MacInnes described how Steele inhabited two cultural worlds simultaneously:

> This strange ambivalence is very apparent in Tommy's art. In his film or when, on the stage, he speaks to his admirers between the songs, his voice takes on the flat, wise, dryly comical tones of purest Bermondsey. When he sings, the words (where intelligible) are intoned in the shrill international American-style drone. With this odd duality, his teenage fans seem quite at ease: they prefer him to be one of them in his unbuttoned moments, but expect him to sing in a near foreign tongue: rather as a congregation might wish the sermon to be delivered in the vernacular, and the plainsong chanted in mysterious Latin. (MacInnes 1966: 18)

The 'American' issue and the 'youth' issue were enmeshed, and their convergence challenged cultural norms. In *The Uses of Literacy*, Richard Hoggart fulminated against the 'shiny barbarism' of American youth culture invading traditional working-class life (Hoggart 1958: 193). There was growing bewilderment about where values lay in this 'strangely ambivalent' world (as MacInnes has it), and a sense that, in 'the American age', Britain's position was becoming bafflingly peripheral.

The recognition of a profound alteration in the global balance of power was probably the most significant aspect of the 'Suez Crisis' of 1956, when British troops, in league with the French and Israelis, invaded Egypt to reverse the nationalisation of the Suez Canal Company. The Americans, who were kept in the dark about British designs, and the Russians, who supplied the Egyptians and threatened escalation, opposed the invasion. Unable to resist militarily, Egypt's President Nasser skilfully played the powers against each other. Sinking block-ships in the Canal, he starved Europe of oil. Widespread fuel shortages were only one symptom of a mounting monetary crisis, staved off temporarily by panic selling of British currency reserves. The Americans vetoed International Monetary Fund aid and, in November 1956, suitably humbled, France and Britain capitulated, both moving towards an accelerated, if increasingly messy, programme of decolonisation.

Powerlessness and incompetence (not to say mendacity) were what Suez demonstrated about Britain for many. While the episode was underway, Russian troops invaded Hungary, suppressing liberal, anti-Soviet dissent beneath distracting smoke from Middle-Eastern fires. The fact that, despite this, the American President Eisenhower, on the eve of an election, chose to reinforce Russian threats and strong-arm Britain towards yielding, merely confirmed what clearer-sighted commentators had already noticed about the emerging geopolitics of the Cold War. As the British Empire ebbed, the country was caught in the cross-currents of a new global tide. Relative powerlessness and an atmosphere of resentful decline emerged as a dominant structure of feeling.

Look Back in Anger is only incidentally a 'Suez' play, though it is often associated with the crisis. The Suez invasion began in October, nearly six months after the play opened, though, as its run extended, its full-throated protests against a debilitated Establishment seemed to strike an appropriate note. (Osborne's next play *The Entertainer* was much more explicitly about Suez: Mick Rice, soldier son of the main character, dies in the invasion, while his brother Frank is a conscientious objector and his sister Jean a war protester.) Geopolitical events starkly demonstrated a new world order; at home, there was rampant confusion about appropriate values. Jimmy Porter's cruel tale of the woman injured at the Earls Court evangelist's rally appears cynical about American religion, and about Christianity itself. But it is also a tale of helplessness, of a voice shouting in pain but unable to be heard. Like so much in the play, it is, in effect, Jimmy's self-projection, ranting and hurting in a heedless world. Perhaps it is also not too far-fetched to say that the episode is symbolic of Britain damaged and threatened in 'the American age', not least because, as both *Look Back* and *The Entertainer* insist, the nuclear Bomb hangs ominously over events.

Look Back opened eleven days after the first H-bomb test. 'There aren't any good, brave causes left', Jimmy famously declared. But the context of the rest of his speech is noted less often:

> if the big bang does come, and we all get killed off, it won't be in aid of the old-fashioned, grand design. It'll just be for the Brave New-nothing-very-much-thank-you. About as inglorious and pointless as stepping in front of a bus. (Osborne 1957: 84–5)

The relationship between being powerful and being meaningful – or, more directly, between impotence and futility – is made very clear. The literature of ethical and political paralysis, made sharp and urgent by the Bomb, became common in Britain in the late 1950s. In his poem 'A Woman Unconscious' from *Lupercal* (1960), Ted Hughes juxtaposes a woman dying in hospital against the sense of helpless, imminent Armageddon as 'Russia and America circle one another'. In the poem, the anguish of the individual death, and the imagined 'world-cancelling black' of the nuclear threat, conspire in a long 'malingering of now' (Hughes 1970: 15). In much of Hughes' celebrated 'nature' poetry the violence he depicts in the natural world is criss-crossed by parallels, analogies and allusions to an aggressive and increasingly threatening human story.

The new, Americanising culture of the period produced radical uncertainty. A poem in Thom Gunn's *A Sense of Movement* (1957), 'Elvis Presley', shows admiration for the rock'n'roller's spidery energy ('his gangling finery/ and crawling sideburns, wielding a guitar'), but also a more unconvinced sense of its transience, insubstantiality and inauthenticity. Gunn wonders to what degree revolt, for the Jimmy Porter generation, is mere posture:

> Distorting hackneyed words in hackneyed songs
> He turns revolt into style, prolongs
> The impulse to a habit of the time.
>
> Whether he poses or is real, no cat
> Bothers to say: the pose held is a stance . . .

(Gunn 1968: 31)

What Gunn calls Presley's 'posture for combat', like his 'revolt into style', is not unlike Jimmy Porter's, and in both there is ambivalence about substance. Nonetheless Gunn moved to the US in 1954, eventually settling permanently.

The recognition that changed times need to bring changed values, but a corresponding doubt about what these values might be, was widely explored. Gunn's complex 'A Kind of Ethics' is a key poem in his first collection *Fighting Terms* (1954), whose title suggests both the Cold War and a necessary renegotiation of categories. The poem begins with the invocation of old trees and the 'simple religion' of nature they represent. These are 'forced into the cold', and into disregard, because 'The past that they have led/ Makes unapproachable and hidden sin'. This is Porter-ish territory: Gunn's 'Dry tangled twigs lie dead' in the 'foul confusion of their thicket' might be Jimmy sounding off about the Establishment. But the poem struggles with this modern dilemma. Finding no solace in religion, or in nature where 'Wild animals give birth to sharp toothed young', Gunn asserts that, nevertheless, 'an undeniable good' may emerge from 'a possibly bad' (Gunn 1970: 32). One can be hopeful, but values are nonetheless haphazard, partial, contingently discovered and unsupported by tradition. They cannot be described, articulated or inculcated; they can only be desired.

It is a commonplace of the history of twentieth-century ethical thought that, under the scrutiny of forensic 'logical positivism', it became impossible to make 'foundationalist' claims about ethical positions. (A 'foundationalist' position is one that claims that values are founded in nature or metaphysics, rather than actual human behaviour. 'Logical positivism' scrutinised the verbal forms of ethical statements to demonstrate that they were, in a strictly logical sense, merely assertions and therefore valueless in any absolute way.) By the 1950s the most influential version of this argument was known as 'emotivism'. It derived from the work of A. J. Ayer and the American C. L. Stevenson. 'Emotivist' views of ethics were that ethical positions ('x is good') were not statements of fact or even reason but merely of emotional preference. Insofar as they had impact, it was only as an effort to persuade others that 'x was indeed good'. They were meaningful only to the degree that they did so persuade, but this did not imbue them with absolute value. Even the most persuasive position, for example 'killing is bad', is, for the 'emotivists', no more foundationally valuable than any other emotionally-derived preference, even though most beings on the planet assent to it.

So beliefs, values and causes are, in this version, entirely rhetorically derived. Thom Gunn's poem tackles this issue. It contends that, although traditional ethical foundations – religions and nature – cannot be relied upon, there may still be 'an undeniable good' which, whatever its origins, we can recognise if not explain. This is a strong counter to the 'emotivist' position in that it implies that there is a 'good' out there independent of articulation or emotional preference. Related challenges to 'emotivist' theory were made by existentialist thinkers, whose work was busily translated into English from the late 1940s and influenced some literary writers a good deal, not least Gunn. The existentialists emphasised that ethical choices were primarily based upon the integrity and good faith of the chooser who, in making his or her choices, recognises the validity of others choosing to act in the same way. Thus choosing selfishness is, they argued, self-defeating because others will behave selfishly towards the chooser. This gave substance to Gunn's 'kind of ethics'.

It is unlikely that John Osborne engaged much with 'emotivist' theory, though he read earnestly in existentialist thought at one stage (Osborne 1982: 164–71). Nonetheless, the world described by 'emotivism' is bleakly recognisable in *Look Back in Anger*, where Jimmy Porter's thought might be described as a stream of emotionally supercharged assertions linked to anti-foundational statements such as 'There aren't any good, brave causes left'. This is a world without surety or confidence in foundational principles, in which persuasion is not a rational process but a rhetorical and emotional battering, and in which Jimmy's self-asserted honesty and integrity are gained through the blows he aims at the integrity of others, particularly his wife. If, in 1956, Jimmy yelled credibly and with stimulating frankness at Establishment pieties, in his personal relations he gains advantage by rhetorical and emotional bullying. *Look Back in Anger* represents an extreme version of the consequences of the dwindling of foundational values in a world of notional, but only very partial, social mobility and declining national authority. This is why rhetorical power is so important in the play. No substantial transformation is possible. It ends where it begins. Some commentators make comparisons with Chekhov in this respect: both dramatists imagine an inert, talkative condition and no action. But it is a condition echoed more widely in the literature of the late 1950s: a world of partiality, modest deprivation, limited access, insubstantiality and insecure or frustrated achievement. All of these are registered in the titles of its characteristic work. In these books, we are asked to look back (not forward) in anger (not pride); have only a taste of honey; experience a kind of ethics, or 'a kind of loving' (the title of Stan Barstow's novel of 1960); have time itself abridged to Saturday nights and Sunday mornings; and find space condensed to limited room at the top, Pinteresque basements, L-shaped attics, or (in *Look Back in Anger*) a 'one-room flat in a large Midland town'.

Of course the most painful and shocking aspect of this unrestrained emotivism is the play's misogyny, and Jimmy's treatment of Alison, his wife. On every page Jimmy blames women for his predicament and this has, understandably, offended many. The trouble with 'emotivism', writes the moral philosopher Alasdair MacIntyre, is that it 'entails the obliteration of any genuine distinction between manipulative and non-manipulative social relations' (MacIntyre 1981: 22). But the finally unanswerable question in this and similar cases in literature is always 'is this a misogynist work, or a work about misogyny?' The play's sexism is so powerful and omnipresent it cannot be avoided. But the degree to which it indulges, diagnoses, endorses, displays or sanctions misogyny remains an open question. And it is one that runs powerfully and unignorably through the male literature of the period where frustration, and angrily-voiced aggression towards women, is a feature of, for example, powerful novels by David Storey, Alan Sillitoe and John Braine in a way that appears to be different from the more straightforward and carelessly indulged male chauvinism of Ian Fleming (the James Bond novels appeared from 1953) or Kingsley Amis, whose comic novel *Lucky Jim* was a huge success in 1954. To call this behaviour 'historical', in the sense that it was a particular condition of the period, is important for the historian. But, like discussion of racism in *Othello* or anti-Semitism in *The Merchant of Venice*, it is probably inadequate in a different kind of argument.

Look Back in Anger is a 'naturalist' play. This means that it aims to depict, sometimes in a revelatory way, characters, events and environments that are replicated from the mundane world. Looking at the opening of the play-text brings home what this naturalism means. It consists of nearly two pages of close, stage-direction description of the flat, its furniture and those who inhabit it. This is in part an effort to get things right, to tell metropolitan designers, directors and audiences what 'a one-room flat in a large Midland town' looks like. But these directions extend beyond visual description to character insight and psychological nuance. Actors, too, are to get things right. The set is heavy, specific and static. It cannot be moved and isn't designed to be. Its pedestrian ordinariness authenticates its naturalism and startles an audience used to 'tiara' elegance. (Osborne joked that the famous ironing board at which Alison labours was the first celebrity in a cast all bound for fame.) But, in its shabby, impassive weight, the immoveable set represents the imprisoning condition that great naturalist drama from Henrik Ibsen onwards had been committed to exploring, as

Raymond Williams argued in his *Drama from Ibsen to Eliot* (1952). The single, solid, unchanging rooms of these plays manifest the force of ensnaring circumstance in which dilemmas, actions and lives are fought out. The act of leaving – as, famously, when Nora leaves her husband at the end of Ibsen's *A Doll's House* (1879) – is always supercharged with significance. In *Look Back in Anger*, Jimmy never leaves, and Alison comes back. In this too the play stands full square in the majority forms of writing in the 1950s by men, in which protagonists feel themselves trapped by mean circumstances, lack of opportunity, social discrimination and – they often claimed – the snares of women. (Often the narratives figure these predicaments in the persons of dreadful mothers-in-law, pregnant girlfriends or blameable marriages.) As the decade came to a close, and writers entered the 1960s, this voice of entrapment in single rooms persists, only it came to be re-described very differently by women writers like Sylvia Plath, Doris Lessing, Nell Dunn, Lynne Reid Banks and others. But in these works too, protest and frustration, new beginnings and absolute ends, real change and real obstruction summon in their unstable paradoxes equal and opposite affiliations to their particular literary and cultural moment.

References

Ayto, John (1999) *Twentieth-Century Words*, Oxford: Oxford University Press

Browne, Terry W. (1975) *Playwright's Theatre: The English Stage Company at the Royal Court Theatre*, London: Pitman

Elsom, John (1971) *Theatre Outside London*, London: Macmillan

——(1981) *Post-war British Theatre Criticism*, London: Routledge and Kegan Paul

Findlater, Richard, ed. (1981) *At the Royal Court: 25 Years of the English Stage Company*, Ambergate, Derbyshire: Amber Lane Press

Gunn, Thom (1968) *The Sense of Movement*, London: Faber and Faber

——(1970) *Fighting Terms*, London: Faber and Faber

Hoggart, Richard (1958) *The Uses of Literacy: Aspects of Working-Class Life*, Harmondsworth: Penguin

Hughes, Ted (1970) *Lupercal*, London: Faber and Faber

Innes, Christopher (2002) *Modern British Drama: The Twentieth Century*, Cambridge: Cambridge University Press

Joseph, Stephen (1967) *Theatre in the Round*, London: Barrie and Rockcliff

——(1968) *New Theatre Forms*, London: Pitman

Littlewood, Joan (1995) *Joan's Book: Joan Littlewood's Peculiar History as She Tells It*, London: Minerva

Lloyd Evans, Gareth, and Barbara Lloyd Evans, eds (1985) *Plays in Review 1956–1980: British Drama and the Critics*, London: Batsford

MacIntyre, Alasdair (1981) *After Virtue: A Study in Moral Theory*, London: Duckworth

Marowitz, Charles, Tom Milne and Owen Hale, eds (1965) *The Encore Reader: A Chronicle of the New Drama*, London: Methuen

McGrath, John (1975), 'Better a Bad Night in Bootle . . .', *Theatre Quarterly* 5, no. 19, 39–54

MacInnes, Colin (1966) *England, Half English: A Polyphoto of the Fifties*, Harmondsworth: Penguin

Osborne, John (1957) *Look Back in Anger: A Play in Three Acts*, London: Faber and Faber

——(1982) *A Better Class of Person: An Autobiography*, vol. I: *1929–1956*, Harmondsworth: Penguin

——(1991) *Almost a Gentleman: An Autobiography*, vol. II: *1955–1966*, London: Faber and Faber.

Page, Malcolm, ed. (1988) *File on Osborne*, London: Methuen

Ritchie, Harry (1988) *Success Stories: Literature and the Media in England, 1950–1959*, London: Faber and Faber

Roberts, Philip (1986) *The Royal Court Theatre 1965–72*, London: Routledge and Kegan Paul

——(1999) *The Royal Court Theatre and the Modern Stage*, Cambridge: Cambridge University Press

Steiner, George (1969) 'The Pythagorean Genre' (1965), in *Language and Silence: Essays 1958–1966*, Harmondsworth: Penguin, 102–16

Taylor, John Russell, ed. (1968) *John Osborne 'Look Back in Anger': A Casebook*, London: Macmillan

Chapter 12

1960, Lagos and Nairobi: 'Things Fall Apart' and 'the Empire Writes Back'

Patrick Williams

The 1960s are popularly remembered as going out on a wave of radicalism, international in extent, and often student-led: May '68; the Italian 'hot autumn' of '69; protests against the Vietnam War; Black Power in the United States. The decade came in, however, on something more resembling a global tidal surge of decolonisation, but one whose events, because they occurred on the peripheries of Empire rather than in its heartlands, figure less in the memories both of the period and of its significant protests. Although Eldridge Cleaver of the Black Panthers could claim at the end of the 1960s that Fanon's *The Wretched of the Earth* (1961) was the Bible of the Black Power movement, it was on another continent, at the other end of the decade, and in another kind of struggle that Fanon was writing and fighting: in the first place against French colonialism, but beyond that, against the global reach of the capitalist system. As the Caribbean critic C. L. R. James noted, writing of the French Revolution and the great slave rebellion in Haiti, rather than history consisting of Europe affecting ('educating', 'civilising') Africa or Asia, there was, at the very least, a reciprocal effect. One example of this in our period is the way in which Third World anti-colonial struggles (including their cultural dimension) affected politics and culture in the West, variously radicalising and internationalising them.

'Things fall apart'; 'the Empire writes back': these phrases from W. B. Yeats and Salman Rushdie, are, in their different ways, so much part of the common currency – even, in the latter case, the clichés – of the field of postcolonial literature and theory. From a certain traditionalist perspective, the fact of the latter, the emergence of writing from the formerly colonised areas of the world, in the shape of novels, poetry, plays and essays, was not merely a sign of things falling apart – the edifice of literary culture crumbling along with the greater structure of Empire itself – but also a significant contributory factor in the catastrophe. It is one of the many important achievements of postcolonial studies that it has been able to overturn that perspective, and see the emergence of anti-colonial and postcolonial texts as an unquestionably positive phenomenon. This chapter will examine a (necessarily small) representative sample of postcolonial authors and the way their various modes and strategies of resistant textuality – their different forms of 'writing back' – relate to the larger historical process of the 'falling apart' of the colonial empires. The writers discussed are principally of African and Caribbean origin, partly because the Indian subcontinent did its writing back both earlier and later than the period under examination here.

'Writing back' may indeed have become something of a cliché, but it is not simply to be discarded on that basis. The different histories and political agendas involved in writing back, the varying aesthetic and cultural modes adopted and adapted, mean that it is more than straightforwardly resistant or revolutionary writing – even if that is its principal form – and therefore that its complexities need to be unravelled, even though a fully detailed unravelling is beyond the scope of a chapter such as this. Also, while it is true that many things were falling apart in this period, not least the colonial empires, it is equally true that many things were coming together. One of the inevitable legacies of Empire – and often in spite of the efforts of the imperialists – was cultural mixing. This hybridisation of culture is represented in a remarkable variety of ways by the authors discussed in this chapter, but before we approach them some further contextualisation is necessary.

'*They cannot represent themselves; they must be represented.*' For Edward Said in *Orientalism* (1978) Karl Marx's ironic comment on the European peasantry – suitably applied and exemplified – provides one of the keys to understanding the attitude of colonial rulers to the peoples they governed. On the one hand, the latter were deemed incapable of representing themselves politically, of governing themselves effectively and independently. On the other, they were supposedly incapable of representing themselves textually or discursively: writing their own histories, telling their own stories. The result of this was the strange, but also common, occurrence during the colonial period of Europeans explaining Indian culture to Indians, or informing Africans about African history. As Said points out, the fact that the ways in which Europeans represented themselves as civilised, expert, moral or dynamic – and colonial peoples as in various ways the opposite of all of these – was a central aspect of the continuing power relations of colonialism.

As a result of this, the 'long' decade of the 1960s (running roughly from 1956 to 1973) is marked by struggles to overturn both these regimes of representation: to achieve political independence, and to produce indigenous cultural forms both valid and valuable. To some, the idea that the production of essays, novels or poems might somehow be as important as the political, or armed, struggle for independence can seem like the self-serving, self-aggrandising ploys of artists and intellectuals. It did not, however, seem that way to those involved in the struggles, and two of the mid-century's most important activist intellectuals in the context of the liberation movements – Amilcar Cabral and Frantz Fanon – both stressed the importance of culture in the broader fight for freedom. For Cabral,

> The experience of colonial domination shows that, in the effort to perpetuate exploitation, the colonizer not only creates a system to repress the cultural life of the colonized people, he also provokes and develops the cultural alienation of a part of the population, either by so-called assimilation of indigenous people, or by creating a gap between the indigenous elites and the popular masses . . . Thus, it may be seen that if imperialist domination has the vital need to practice cultural oppression, national liberation is necessarily an act of *culture*. (Cabral 1993: 56, 57)

For Fanon, not only are the political and cultural dimensions both important, they are inseparable:

> To fight for national culture means in the first place to fight for the liberation of the nation, that material keystone which makes the building of a culture possible. There is no other fight for culture which can develop apart from the popular struggle. (Fanon 1983: 187)

Clearly, 'writing back' is an integral part of fighting back.

However, although the 1960s represented a particularly important and visible conjuncture, 'writing back' by colonised people was not a new thing. In a manner reminiscent of Caliban's use of Prospero's language to curse his colonial master, colonial subjects had been 'writing back' for as long as they had been able to write in English, and we can briefly mention here two very different but nonetheless representative moments: the late eighteenth century and the 1930s. In the first of these, the narratives of former slaves, most notably Olaudah Equiano (1789), deploy their newly acquired, hard-won skills of literacy and literary style to attack the practice of slavery. Here, the essence of the process of writing back is to use the concepts and ideals of the West – in this case civilisation, decency and Christianity – to expose its hypocrisies and shortcomings. The relation between slavery and the Enlightenment ideals of Europe also surfaces in one of the paradigmatic examples of resistant writing from the 1930s, C. L. R. James's *The Black Jacobins* (1938), a radical analysis of the first successful revolt by black slaves inspired by the ideals of the French Revolution, and betrayed by the Revolution's leaders. If *The Black Jacobins* was an attempt to write back to the discipline of history and its received notions of slave resistance, then Jomo Kenyatta's *Facing Mount Kenya* (1938) was an equivalent attempt to confront ethnography's stance on 'primitive' peoples, as it produced a very different form of knowledge about African culture (in this case Gikuyu) as complex, developed, ethical – in other words, all the things it was supposed not to be. James and Kenyatta were among the many intellectuals, activists and future independence leaders who came together in the context of the Pan-African Congresses and the associated wider movement. Others included George Padmore, Eric Williams, Kwame Nkrumah, W. E. B. Du Bois, and the diffusion of radical ideas which this process enabled was one of the forces feeding into the resistant writing of subsequent decades.

The tension between Western forms, Western discourses and ideologies, and non-Western authors exemplified in *The Black Jacobins* and *Facing Mount Kenya* has remained a feature of the kind of texts produced a generation later. For a writer such as the Nigerian novelist Chinua Achebe, Western representations of Africa, both fictional and historiographical, were the direct motivation for his own choice of career: 'at university, I read some appalling novels about Africa (including Joyce Cary's much-praised *Mister Johnson*) and decided that the story we had to tell could not be told for us by anyone else, no matter how gifted or well-intentioned' (Achebe 1988: 25). In many ways, worse than the representations offered by colonialist novels such as *Mister Johnson* was the effect of a writer as talented as Conrad, and a narrative as powerful as *Heart of Darkness* (1899). What is at stake is not the truth, accuracy or otherwise of the representations. It is the fact that they have, over a number of generations, provided the basis and legitimation for colonial domination, racial oppression and economic exploitation, as Achebe argues:

> I am talking about a book which parades in the most vulgar fashion prejudices and insults from which a section of mankind has suffered untold agonies and atrocities in the past and continues to do so in many ways and many places today. I am talking about a story in which the very humanity of black people is called in question. (Achebe 1988: 10)

Achebe's comments on Conrad have remained controversial for many – though they are perhaps no more than a particularly blunt restatement of the kind of general argument Said makes. A different order of insult, however, is offered by historiography. Achebe notes Hugh Trevor-Roper, Professor of History at Cambridge – parasitic upon, but not acknowledging,

Hegel – denying that Africa had any history. This image of Africa also requires to be opposed, and Achebe says:

> Here then is an adequate revolution for me to espouse – to help my society regain belief in itself and put away the complexes of the years of denigration and self-abasement. And it is a question of education in the best sense of that word. . . . I would be quite satisfied if my novels (especially the ones I set in the past) did no more than teach my readers that their past – with all its imperfections – was not one long night of savagery from which the first Europeans, acting on God's behalf, delivered them. (Achebe 1988: 30)

The pedagogic revolution is necessary to counteract the typical, traditional power of the European as 'expert', claiming to know Africa better than the Africans (and no doubt believing that he does). More than this, however, the recovery of the past Achebe refers to is one of the essential elements in the forging of a properly *post*colonial identity. Fanon was aware of how much the erasure of the history of colonised peoples was a deliberate colonial strategy:

> Perhaps we have not sufficiently demonstrated that colonialism is not simply content to impose its rule upon the present and the future of a dominated country. Colonialism is not satisfied merely with hiding a people in its grip and emptying the native's brain of all form and content. By a kind of perverted logic, it turns to the past of the oppressed people, and distorts, disfigures and destroys it. This work of devaluing pre-colonial history takes on a dialectical significance today. (Fanon 1983: 169)

The process of historical reclamation and reconstruction is not simply a case of knowing more about the past for its own sake. Especially in a situation of conflict or resistance, the past can carry a particular political power, as writers in other contexts, and analysing the prospects of other oppressed groups, were aware:

> Social Democracy thought fit to assign to the working class the role of the redeemer of future generations, in this way cutting the sinews of its greatest strength. This training made the working class forget both its hatred and its spirit of sacrifice, for both are nourished by the image of enslaved ancestors rather than that of liberated grandchildren. (Benjamin 1973: 262)

Achebe's first novel, *Things Fall Apart*, was published in 1958, at the start of 'the long 1960s' and hard on the heels of the declaration of independence for Ghana, inaugurating the decade in which most of Africa, by various means, removed the formal shackles of colonialism. Nigeria's own independence came in the *annus mirabilis* of 1960, in which something like a quarter of the countries of Africa gained their freedom, and the perceptive British Prime Minister Harold Macmillan noticed that 'a wind of change' was blowing through Africa. (At the same time, the Sharpeville massacre in South Africa that year was a powerful reminder that change was not occurring everywhere.) Although *Things Fall Apart* does not exactly offer detailed images of 'enslaved ancestors', it chronicles the pressures on Ibo society in the late nineteenth century from the encroaching power – political and religious – of European colonialism, and examines the way in which one particular, inflexibly traditionalist, way of life, embodied in the figure of Okonkwo, falls apart, ending with the moment of the British takeover. It is a text which is quietly resistant at all levels in its assertion of the value of African peoples and cultures. The first of these affirmations of worth is at the level of form and genre, as its deceptively simple narrative voice takes the reader into a novel which is in fact a close approximation of an African oral narrative.

Achebe's subtle and skilful incorporation of an African narrative mode into a European one highlights the persistent dilemma of anti-colonial or postcolonial writers: in what languages, what cultural forms, or what intellectual or conceptual frameworks should they couch their opposition? How *do* you effectively resist your oppressor, if not in terms which he can understand? On the other hand, do you lose the purity of your protest if you articulate it in the language of your enemy? Still worse, is that protest somehow vitiated, even defused, if it draws upon terminology and conceptual categories which originate in the culture that dominates you, and are therefore willy-nilly imbued with the ideologies of that culture? As Edward Said remarks: 'that is the partial tragedy of resistance, that it must to a certain degree work to recover forms already established or at least influenced or infiltrated by the culture of empire' (Said 1993: 253). This shared terrain is part of the 'overlapping territories, intertwined histories' which for Said constitute colonial and postcolonial relations, rather than any simple or straightforward dichotomy. For some writers and critics, this hybrid, politically and ideologically tainted state is profoundly disempowering; for others, it is something of an irrelevance: denouncing the abuses of colonialism can as well be done – or even is best done – in the language and forms of the culture of colonialism. In this perspective, neither the language nor the concepts nor the cultural forms have any inherent dominatory 'colonial' essence: it is all a question of how they are inflected and appropriated – and that can be for resistant or oppositional purposes as much as to indoctrinate or assimilate. As Achebe says: 'let no one be fooled by the fact that we may write in English, for we intend to do unheard-of things with it' (Achebe 1988: 50). Many would feel that his prediction has been borne out.

The poetry of Christopher Okigbo, Achebe's fellow Ibo, killed in the tragic Biafra war of 1967–70, perhaps represents some of these 'unheard-of things'. These are profoundly intellectual poems (influenced by Eliot and Yeats, Virgil and the *Epic of Gilgamesh*) but also sensual, and political, inspired by contemporary African problems. Many were conceived as interactions of the spoken word and music – something which occurs in the work of other writers later in this chapter – but given Okigbo's propensity for cultural mixing, the music could as easily be European modernist as traditional African, or both. Although the poems' resistance as far as readers are concerned is most obvious in their forms of difficulty – formal or grammatical fragmentation, obscure vocabulary, enormous range of cultural reference – Okigbo's 'writing back' is most powerfully directed to the traditionalists and cultural purists, in his repeated affirmation that cultures not only can mix, but absolutely must.

Although the Biafra war reduced Achebe to silence for over a decade, his first four novels (*Things Fall Apart, No Longer at Ease* [1960], *Arrow of God* [1964], *A Man of the People* [1966]) were all published during the 'long 1960s', pre-dating that catastrophe for his people. Chronologically, they span the period from the British incursions of the late nineteenth century to the contemporary moment, and in part they chart the rise of what Achebe called 'the messenger class' – the black middle class which began literally as messengers for the British. We see their ascendancy from a somewhat risible British-affiliated servant class to the kind of black bourgeoisie, rulers of the newly independent nation, which Fanon warned against in *The Wretched of the Earth*. Regardless of whatever power it may wield domestically, this class remains ideologically affiliated to and serving the needs of the West: according to Fanon, 'the national bourgeoisie turns its back more and more on the interior and on the real facts of its underdeveloped country, and tends to look towards the former mother country and the foreign capitalists who count on its obliging compliance' (Fanon 1983: 133).

A novelist from the opposite side of the continent whose work has involved, even more than Achebe, a continuous historical survey of his country and a ferocious opposition both to Western imperialism and to its associated black bourgeoisie – ever more servile and corrupt – is the Kenyan Ngugi wa Thiong'o. One of the touchstones of Ngugi's oppositional stance is the Mau Mau War of the 1950s, as an example of ordinary people's resistance to colonial military power; as an index of the importance of history and historical memory; as well as of the failures of the indigenous ruling class in the post-independence period. Like *Things Fall Apart*, Ngugi's *The River Between* (1965) deals with the early European incursions and the clashes these provoke. Here, the particular focus is the power struggle involving African spirituality and Christianity, centred on the issue of female genital mutilation in the 1930s. Ngugi's other two novels of the 1960s, *Weep Not Child* (1964) and *A Grain of* Wheat (1967) both deal with Mau Mau, and, in the latter, the moment of Uhuru (independence) in 1963. *A Grain of Wheat* is a complex examination of questions of commitment and resistance, betrayal and forgiveness in the Mau Mau years, and though written so soon after independence, the novel intimates how the black bourgeoisie immediately set about betraying the ideals of the struggle.

If at the level of narrative mode, through the 1960s and beyond, Achebe is content to keep to linear or sequential realism (though one which, as we have seen, will allow for the incorporation of African narrative styles), Ngugi appears engaged on a restless search for the relevant form and style to fit the particular content: *A Grain of Wheat* is structurally much more complex than the first two novels, using flashbacks and multiple perspectives. *Petals of Blood* (1977) further extends this complexity, *Devil on the Cross* (1981) moves beyond ordinary realism towards symbolic modes, and *Matigari* (1987) incorporates fully allegorical ones. The formal changes are also related both to the question of writing back and to one of the central thematic and political relations in Ngugi's novels: the individual and/versus the community. In particular, there is cultural opposition here: traditional African society (not least Ngugi's own Gikuyu people) gives precedence to the community over the individual; Western society, or the other hand, is ever more individualistic. Therefore, for Ngugi, to be a more properly African writer involves downplaying the individualistic focus of his earliest works, and the later novels do this in a variety of ways. In all of this, there is opposition to what the West, insofar as it is neocolonialist or capitalist, is doing to Africa, but Ngugi is also 'writing back' to his own corrupt ruling class. Indeed, the very act of writing *Matigari* is one of opposition to the regime of Daniel Arap Moi – an opposition recognised by the regime's subsequent farcical attempts to arrest the individual called Matigari reportedly roaming the countryside fomenting anti-government unrest.

At the same time, Ngugi exemplifies a resistant indigenisation of cultural production. Beginning in the 1960s, and increasingly since the 1980s, he has been a vociferous champion of the use of African languages to produce appropriately African literature. His novels *Devil on the Cross* and *Matigari* and his plays *I Will Marry When I Want* (1980) and *Mother, Sing for Me* (1982) were written in Gikuyu (and other Kenyan languages in the case of the second play). His collection of essays *Decolonising the Mind* (1986) announced a 'farewell to English as a vehicle for any of my writings. From now on it is Gikuyu and Swahili all the way' (Ngugi wa Thiong'o 1986: xiv). His declared strategy is both to develop Gikuyu as a language for written literature, and to force the West, via the medium of translation, to confront the world embodied in an African language, and to give it due recognition.

The politics of recognition is, of course, an important component of colonial and postcolonial relations. Fanon writes in *Black Skin, White Masks* (1952) of the way in which the Hegelian master–slave dialectic, the classic philosophical model for the constitution of identity through reciprocal recognition, maps onto colonial and racial formations – or not. Fanon argues that where proper recognition is absent, as in the (post)colonial situation, the attempt to force it from the Other remains an almost obsessional preoccupation. That would be one explanation for a certain repetitiveness in some writing back: the continuing struggle to achieve appropriate recognition seen to be continually withheld. Repetitive or not, the emphasis on appropriate recognition is justified, since inappropriate recognition – belittling, condescending, grudging or hypocritical – by the culturally dominant group is an all too common occurrence.

As well as the politics of recognition, there is also a deliberate politics of reception in Ngugi's approach. Although literacy levels in Gikuyu may not be especially high, and surplus income for the purchase of novels not readily available, there is evidence of a collective consumption of *Matigari* in Kenya, with chapters being read aloud in bars or workplaces in a kind of updated version of traditional oral narrative. The political potential in this writing to (if not back to) his own people – as with Ngugi's work in the 1970s with rural communities collectively devising plays using African languages – is completely unacceptable to the postcolonial regime. The plays resulted in his imprisonment without trial and subsequent exile; the novel might have been even more dangerous for him had he still been in the country. Although Ngugi has been criticised for supposedly putting African literature into a linguistic ghetto, his approach can be regarded as the logical continuation of the position he adopted when, as a lecturer at the University of Nairobi in the 1960s, he called for the abolition of the English department and the replacement of its Eurocentric curriculum with one more relevant to the lives and culture of African students, concentrating first on Africa and other developing world literature before turning to English. It certainly represents as much as one writer could do, not only to protect his language and culture from denigration or even obliteration by the West, but perhaps to reverse the trend.

In another part of the declining Empire, a very different process was underway. Numbers of Caribbean writers and intellectuals – more than from Africa or the Indian subcontinent – were making what Edward Said called 'the Voyage In' to the metropolitan heartland. Rather than writing to the Mother Country they were travelling to it, as part of what the poet Louise Bennett famously called 'colonisation in reverse'. Sam Selvon, George Lamming, C. L. R. James, Una Marson, V. S. Naipaul, Louise Bennett, Wilson Harris, James Berry, E. K. Brathwaite and Linton Kwesi Johnson were among many who came to Britain on a temporary or permanent basis. The 'voyage in' is a timely reminder of the importance of the 'centre' in what we have been discussing, as the fuller versions of the Yeats/Achebe and Rushdie quotations make clear: 'Things fall apart; the centre cannot hold'; 'the Empire writes back to the centre'. The 'voyage in' was so much the case that by the 1960s a majority of the best-known Caribbean writers were based in Britain, producing another aspect of hybridisation to add to the formal, generic and thematic ones already mentioned. the question of naming or defining writers. Were they now Caribbean, British, or black British writers? Or some kind of mixture of all of these? Or, as some would claim, just 'writers'?

For Said, the 'voyage in' which Lamming and the others made represents 'a still unresolved contradiction or discrepancy within metropolitan culture, which through co-optation, dilution and avoidance partly acknowledges and partly refuses the effort' (Said 1993: 295). Whatever the response of the imperial centre, the different voyages in are the sign of something important:

> The Voyage In, then, constitutes an especially interesting variety of hybrid cultural work. And
> that it exists at all is a sign of adversarial internationalisation in an age of continued imperial

structures. No longer does the *logos* dwell exclusively, as it were, in London and Paris. No longer does history run unilaterally, as Hegel believed, from east to west . . . becoming more sophisticated and developed, less primitive and backward, as it goes. (Said 1993: 295)

Unusually here, Said, normally so judicious, even cautious, in his assessments, seems to over-estimate the necessary presence of the 'adversarial' in the international. How, for example, could we see V. S. Naipaul as adversarial, other than in his opposition to the 'backward' cultures of India or Africa, or to the 'primitive' adherents of Islam? To some, Naipaul is simply telling the unfortunate unpalatable truth of the postcolonial world; to others, he is flattering the sensibilities of the West, which in turn rewards him with literary prizes, honours and titles.

> It is part of Naipaul's general (and with liberal Western readers, popular) indictment of the Third World that lumps together the corrupt viciousness of a few grotesque rulers, the end of European colonialism, and postcolonial efforts at rebuilding native societies as instances of an overall intellectual failure in Africa and Asia. (Said 1978: 8)

Drawing up a typology of postcolonialism, Vijay Mishra and Bob Hodge identify two major forms: the oppositional and the complicit. The former includes the kind of writing we have been concerned with in the chapter so far. The latter, 'an always present "underside" within colonisation itself', aligns itself, as the name suggests, with Western values and ideologies, and finds its most celebrated representative in Naipaul (Mishra and Hodge 1993: 284). Naipaul is a particular example of a process which Fanon analyses in *Black Skin, White Masks*, where being a product of the colonial periphery (the Caribbean) and lengthily schooled in the cultural superiority of the metropolis produces an especially intense identification with metropolitan values. To be sure, Naipaul also criticises what he regards as the failings of the West, but it is his scorn for non-White/non-western peoples which so many find objectionable in novels such as *The Mimic Men* (1967), *Guerrillas* (1975) and *A Bend in the River* (1979), and travel narratives like *An Area of Darkness* (1964) and *Among the Believers* (1981). Although he has made the 'voyage in' and has taken up permanent residence in Britain, there remains a sense in which Naipaul does 'write back to the centre', since he travels to many areas of the formerly colonised world and produces essays and narratives which have the air of dispatches home from frontier outposts. In addition, he adopts a classically Orientalist pose: the expert observer/recorder of the native Other. As various critics have pointed out, however, Naipaul's knowledge or understanding of other cultures is often very limited (not to mention biased) and his would-be analytical summations are frequently based on very flimsy evidence – which, the sceptical commentator would say, precisely continues the tradition of colonial 'knowledge' of the Other.

While Homi Bhabha (1994) theorises mimicry as a (post)colonial strategy of resistance or subversion, for Naipaul, mimicry marks the inability of (post)colonial individuals or societies to be anything other than bad copies of a western original, and their inability to escape from their parasitic relation – condemned, in Naipaul's infamous phrase, to be the people who can use the telephone, but could never invent it – is the essence of the postcolonial condition in Naipaul's view. Even when, as a young man, Naipaul comes to London and finds the supposed centre of his world is not what he expected – that in a sense there is no 'centre' – his ideological affiliations remain unchanged. London may even resemble the postcolonial world in being somehow counterfeit – a mimicry of its supposed real self – but the civilisational values of the West retain their hold on Naipaul.

If fewer Caribbean authors show the same degree of opposition noted in relation to Africa, there are, nevertheless, more surreptitious methods of writing back which are still highly effective. Sam Selvon's *The Lonely Londoners* (1956), for example, lies somewhere between the positions of Achebe and Ngugi in rejecting both standard English and traditional narrative styles. Written in a version of Trinidadian creole, its informal manner and episodic structure approximate to the 'liming' or storytelling of Caribbean culture, while something of its rhythmic qualities, as well as its humour, are linked to calypso. *The Lonely Londoners* is one of the first novels to deal with the experience of postcolonial migrants to Britain, and certainly the first to do this from their perspective and in their language. Naipaul's not finding the centre is replicated here in the altogether typical experience of disappointment that the reality of England does not match the image propagated abroad. Nevertheless, while the novel (gently) criticises the generally unwelcoming, variously racist side to British society, it also celebrates both the vitality of Caribbean culture and the opportunities which life in Britain offers. As such, it is very much part of the double movement which Paul Gilroy later identified in the phrase: 'black expressive cultures affirm while they protest' (Gilroy 1987: 155). Although Gilroy subsequently expressed some doubts about the potentially overgeneralising nature of his description, it continues to provide a useful perspective, an important awareness of culture's ability to criticise and celebrate simultaneously or in the same work. Clearly, there is no reason why this dual potential should be the sole preserve of black culture. Equally clearly, there are important historical reasons why black culture might need to do both of these more – more overtly, and more repeatedly – than white culture.

In a manner similar to Ngugi (who later became his friend), poet and historian E. K. Brathwaite is concerned to establish the value of 'non-standard' Caribbean English, coining the term 'nation language' – a response in part, no doubt, to the kind of question in 'The Emigrants':

> Once when we went to Europe a rich old lady asked:
> Have you no language of your own
> no way of doing things
> did you spend all those holidays
> at England's apron strings?
>
> (Brathwaite 1973: 55)

In his trilogy *The Arrivants* (1967–9), Brathwaite reminds us that beyond the 'facts' of history and geography, questions of representation and the (ideological/cultural) construction of perception remain all-important:

> So looking through a map
> of the islands, you see
> rocks, history's hot
> lies, rot-
> ting hulls, cannon
> wheels, the sun's
> slums – if you hate
> us. Jewels
> if there is delight
> in your eyes.
> The light

shimmers on water,
the cunning
coral keeps it
blue.

(Brathwaite 1973: 204)

A different kind of writing back is at work in *The Arrivants*, in addition to linguistic, formal or stylistic strategies already encountered. Although he includes themes of diaspora and dispossession, slavery and contemporary migration, and criticises their negative aspects, Brathwaite's protest seems a larger, almost metaphysical one, against the state of a world ruined by greed and materialism. In the face of that loss, literature, and especially poetry, in Brathwaite's view, has a lofty mission – not only to write back but to claim back: reclaiming, rescuing and restoring a different condition of community, culture and at its broadest, humanity.

The currents of radicalism which we have been examining in this chapter – textual and political, hybridising and oppositional – come together at the end of 'the long 1960s' in the work of black British writers like Linton Kwesi Johnson. Local events such as the police siege of the Mangrove restaurant in London, and international ones like the race riots in the US combined to further radicalise black writers in Britain, and with a youthful background in the Black Panthers and Marxist politics, Johnson pushes formal and linguistic 'non-standard' strategies even further, while tackling subjects including unemployment, poverty, daily racism, police harassment, black resistance, and international working-class politics. For Selvon, the musical form to be appropriated into literature was calypso; for Brathwaite it was jazz and calypso; in Johnson's case it is the Caribbean's most enduring musical legacy – reggae – which forms the musical underpinning to his work, and his poems are performed to the 'dub' backing of a reggae band.

This is perhaps as far as one can get from the canonical idea of English poetry. There is a similar sense, not only of distance travelled but also of progress made, in the content of Johnson's poetry. Its oppositional stance is clear from the title of one of his best-known poems, 'Inglan is a bitch'. The nature of its affirmation and celebration is particularly significant, however, in the context of Fanon's argument that one of the aims, and dialectically, one of the effects, of resistance was to move the colonised peoples from a position of being the objects of history to becoming its subjects; from being those to whom history happened (usually catastrophically), to those who were the creators of their history. After the events of 'the long 1960s', it seems altogether appropriate to find a black poet writing:

it is noh mistri
wi mekkin histri
it is noh mistri
wi winnin victri

(Johnson 1991: 45)

and for it not to seem a hollow boast.

References

Achebe, Chinua (1988) *Hopes and Impediments: Selected Essays 1965–87*, London: Heinemann

Benjamin, Walter (1973) 'Theses on the Philosophy of History', in *Illuminations*, London: Collins, 253–64

Bhabha, Homi (1994) *The Location of Culture*, London: Routledge

Brathwaite, Edward Kamau (1973) *The Arrivants*, Oxford: Oxford University Press

Cabral, Amilcar (1993) 'National Liberation and Culture', in Williams and Chrisman 1993, 53–65

Equiano, Olaudah (1969) *The Interesting Narrative of the Life of Olaudah Equiano*, London: Heinemann

Fanon, Frantz (1983) *The Wretched of the Earth*, Harmondsworth: Penguin

——(1986) *Black Skin, White Masks*, London: Pluto

Gilroy, Paul (1987) *There Ain't No Black in the Union Jack*, London: Hutchinson

James, C. L. R. (1980) *The Black Jacobins*, London: Allison and Busby

Johnson, Linton Kwesi (1991) *Tings an Times: Selected Poems*, Newcastle: Bloodaxe

Kenyatta, Jomo (1938) *Facing Mount Kenya*, London: Secker and Warburg

Mishra, Vijay, and Bob Hodge (1993) 'What is Post(-)colonialism?', in Williams and Chrisman 1993, 276–90

Ngugi wa Thiong'o (1986) *Decolonising the Mind*, London: James Currey/Heinemann

Said, Edward W. (1978) *Orientalism*, London: Routledge and Kegan Paul

——(1981) *Covering Islam*, London: Routledge and Kegan Paul

——(1993) *Culture and Imperialism*, London: Chatto and Windus

Selvon, Sam (1956) *The Lonely Londoners*, London: Longman

Williams, Patrick, and Laura Chrisman, eds (1993) *Colonial Discourse and Post-Colonial Theory*, Hemel Hempstead: Harvester Wheatsheaf

Chapter 13

1961, Jerusalem: Eichmann and the Aesthetic of Complicity

R. Clifton Spargo

The trial of Adolf Eichmann was a threshold moment of Holocaust memory, ushering in an era of widespread knowledge about the Holocaust as a historical event, distinct from the events of the Second World War. Especially in Israel and the United States, the trial served as a means for retrieving a history that had occurred in a far away place and what in 1961 seemed already, in an ever-renewable and erasable modern world, a far-away time. As Sidra DeKoven Ezrahi has provocatively intimated, the trial may have especially resonated with the Israeli and American publics because of what Eichmann represented – which was in large part a capacity to keep atrocity, even when one is systemically responsible for it, at an imaginative distance from the ordinary workings of the psyche or conscience. In short, Eichmann's imaginative distance from his own crimes, whether honest or merely self-justifying, connoted for much of the non-European world a distance from the events of the Nazi genocide that had informed their own original reception of such horrible news.

Israeli Prime Minister David Ben-Gurion's hope for the trial – in refusing proposals to conduct it elsewhere under international jurisdiction, and in wanting the world to see justice executed against Eichmann under Israeli sovereignty – had been unapologetically propagandistic, and Hannah Arendt famously termed the entire affair, with provocative analogy to the Moscow Trials of 1937, a 'show trial'. In the overreaching tendentiousness of the arguments of the prosecution, Arendt perceived a distorting effect on the very possibilities of criminal jurisprudence. Her arguments about the nationalistic function of the trial, about the enigmatically ordinary aspect of the defendant's nevertheless spectacular criminality, and about the complicity of the Jewish councils in Nazi deportations of Jews would become every bit as culturally significant as the trial itself. However one understands the value of Arendt's famous book *Eichmann in Jerusalem: A Report on the Banality of Evil* (1963), originally published as a series of articles for *The New Yorker*, her most basic objection pertained to the tremendous gap between what the Israeli prosecution wished to demonstrate and what a trial concentrating on Eichmann's criminality ought to entail. She did not worry that Eichmann was not getting a fair trial, and she certainly did not portray him, as critics such as Lionel Abel charged, as more sympathetic than his victims. Nevertheless, Arendt's arguments about the prosecution's inability to stay focused on legal matters pertaining to Eichmann's criminality were almost immediately misunderstood as extenuating arguments, of the moral or political if not legal kind, on the defence's behalf. She famously objected to the prosecution's overstatement of Eichmann's monstrosity, believing that Eichmann's criminality needed to be expressed within the normalising idiom of his culture. Yet Arendt had hardly invented this line of objection. It was commonplace in the press and among the American general public to react with varying degrees of surprise to Eichmann's less than monstrous appear-ance. What Arendt did was to refine the superficial response to Eichmann's purported ordin-ariness so that he might be more accurately perceived – not as based on appearances but as constructed through the historical parameters of his actions – as relatively typical of Nazi political culture. Eichmann, she believed, was as an ideologue neither passionate nor eloquent. His motives pertained largely to professional advancement and were propped up by an instinct for obedience and conformity that became tantamount to the character of citizenship under Nazified totalitarianism, and, as Arendt repeatedly emphasised, even Eichmann's claim to representativeness teetered on the edge of ideological cliché.

Arendt's scepticism about the legal proceedings led to certain categorical misinterpre-tations of her characterisation of Eichmann – perhaps most enduring among them, the notion that Eichmann's so-called ordinariness could be taken as a figure for humanity in its everyday function within society. This influential misreading of Arendt's book ran par-allel to a line of literary interpretation concerning the Eichmann trial, and eventually came to serve as the means for not only legitimating but canonising a view of Eichmann as an everyman figure. This line of cultural interpretation preceded Arendt, and yet as the mis-reading of *Eichmann in Jerusalem* became, as viewed by detractors and supporters, the ortho-dox reading of the text, Arendt's Eichmann seemingly helped to refine it. Over the course of the decade of the 1960s, Eichmann became an occasion for recollecting the Holocaust and also for figuring the average person's complicity with or obedience to unjust political structures. Since this construct of complicity was fundamentally in tension with Arendt's own argument, we might well conjecture that a vein of American literature figuring Eichmann in these terms would have emerged without Arendt. Nevertheless, the contro-versy over Arendt's portrait of Eichmann illustrates much of what was at stake in repre-senting Eichmann and how firmly a part of a Western (and especially American) cultural lexicon this aesthetic of complicity was quickly to become.

It is important to note that literature featuring Eichmann constitutes a mere subset of a vast canon of Holocaust literature, and perhaps a peculiar subset at that. Nevertheless the literary works discussed in this chapter, written mostly during the decade of the 1960s or shortly thereafter, recapitulate and recast some of the most fundamental questions pertain-ing to the moral and historical obligations of literature written about the Holocaust. According to the Holocaust survivor Elie Wiesel, for example, the ordinary workings of imaginative literature were supposed to be entirely inadequate to the task of representing such large-scale slaughter. In a certain sense, the most significant international literary event of the decade following the war proved this very point. The phenomenon of *The Diary of Anne Frank* (English translation, 1952) – with its immediate rise to bestseller status in the United States, succeeded by an adaptation of the diary as an acclaimed Broadway play that eventually toured internationally, and a slightly less successful Hollywood movie based on the play – may be taken as indicative of the general public's proclivity for literary treat-ments of the Holocaust that buffered or perhaps altogether evaded the gruesome reality of genocide (Bettelheim 1979; Rosenfeld 1991; Spargo 2001). Arguably, such an ideological orientation, prominent throughout the 1950s, corresponded with the universalising ten-dency in many representations of the Holocaust, in which the basic facts of the predomi-nantly Jewish identity of Holocaust victims was typically muted. The literature that arose in response to the Eichmann trial draws many of these issues to the fore, specifically since the trial maintained a dual, sometimes inconsistent emphasis on the universal standards by which Eichmann's crimes were to be judged and an increasingly nationalistic sense of the victims as martyrs to their Jewish identity. The aesthetic of complicity that emerges in the literature dependent on the trial and on the figure of Eichmann undertakes a revision in the construct of the universal, potentially founding a global construct of humanity upon each reader's recognition of his or her implication in bad political culture. It does so, however, perhaps only by wresting specific historical context and the specific victims of the Nazi genocide into an ever shifting, and imperfectly analogous, contemporary context.

Eichmann without Arendt

If by the mid-1960s it became difficult to imagine the figure of Eichmann without the mediation of Arendt's thesis or the popular misunderstanding of it, Arendt's *New Yorker* articles and book were nevertheless belated in their commentary on a trial that had already generated a tremendous amount of interest. Although the manifold voices of the victims, in excess of any real evidentiary need for their testimony, marked the trial as unique in the annals of jurisprudence, the figure of Eichmann compelled the popular imagination at least as much. A structure of identification markedly visual in emphasis was encouraged as though it marked a moral response to the events, on one occasion functioning as the hook to an advertisement placed by WABC-TV in New York papers to get people to tune in to the trial: 'let us now watch the judgment of Eichmann by sitting in judgment of ourselves'. The years immediately following the appearance of *Eichmann in Jerusalem* yielded such works as the Canadian poet Leonard Cohen's 'All there is to know about Adolf Eichmann' (1964) and the British novelist Muriel Spark's *The Mandelbaum Gate* (1965), but among literary responses to the trial that precede Arendt's mediation, Denise Levertov's poem 'During the Eichmann Trial' (1961) and Sylvia Plath's poem 'Lady Lazarus' ([1962] 1965) are perhaps the best known.

Denise Levertov, who was born in England and emigrated to the United States in 1948, becoming a naturalised citizen in 1956, emerged in the 1960s as an activist and feminist poet, who lectured and wrote against the Vietnam War. Although Levertov's own ancestral syncretism – her father was raised a Hasidic Jew and became an Anglican priest, and her mother's family were Congregationalists – may have contributed to her inclination to embrace a universalising reading of the Holocaust, Levertov's poetic assertion of identification is significantly mediated by the figure of Eichmann, oddly at the point in the poem after she recalls Eichmann's recollection of visiting a mass grave in Lwow and seeing there that 'A spring of blood gushed from the earth':

> Pity this man who saw it
> whose obedience continued –
>
> he, you, I, which shall I say?
> He stands
>
> isolate in a bulletproof
> witness-stand of glass,
>
> a cage, where we may view
> ourselves, an apparition
>
> telling us something he
> does not know: we are members
>
> one of another.

(Levertov 1961: 63)

According to Levertov's use of the aesthetic properties of the glass cage, which might well have reflected images of the audience and others members of the court, Eichmann mirrors a potential in each person in the court and by extension the viewing world, his complicity a confusing, oddly promiscuous sign of ethics. With strategic irony the poet argues for the merits of a universally ethical fact Eichmann himself failed to recognise – namely, that he was socially implicated in the lives of those he persecuted, just as they were similarly bound to him. By thus eroding the difference between those who committed atrocities and those who have not but could potentially do such things, Levertov's mode of moral consciousness is predicated upon an identification with perpetrators, who seem only exaggerated versions of our own complicity in political injustice.

It is especially the failure to make distinctions based on historical and political context that promotes in Levertov's poetry an easy rather than a rigorous universalism. In a similar vein, the Holocaust poetry of Sylvia Plath has been a lightning-rod for critical arguments about the dangers of appropriating the Holocaust in a falsely universalistic manner. Plath, an American-born poet who lived her professional life in England and committed suicide there in 1963, was celebrated as one of the champions of the Confessional School of poetry upon the posthumous publication of the book *Ariel* (1965), in which her most famous Holocaust poems appear. While some critics have begun to defend her poetic responses as culturally symptomatic of their moment or as morally complex utterances, the prevailing critical opinion has been that Plath blithely maps the experiences of Holocaust victims onto her own pained domestic life (Young 1988; Rose 1991; Spargo 2004). Yet it is possible to read Plath's rhetorical sensationalism as historically inspired. For example, the extravagant theatricality of her poem 'Lady Lazarus' may well have been modelled on the staged event of the Eichmann trial, which put the atrocities of the Holocaust and some of the victims who had suffered them spectacularly on display for the world's prurience.

Given the relative absence of the Holocaust from Plath's 1950s poetry, her frequent invocation of Holocaust images and themes in the poetry she wrote in London in 1962 may well have been inspired by the Eichmann trial, which was covered regularly by the British press. In the same year, in *The New Poetry*, A. Alvarez demanded 'a new seriousness' of British poetry generally, specifically in response to 'forces of disintegration which destroy the old standards of civilization', 'mass extermination', and 'concentration camps'; Plath would be posthumously included in the second edition of his anthology, in 1966 (Alvarez 1962: 24, 22). It is not a great stretch to imagine the courtroom audience of press and survivors in Jerusalem or all those audiences virtually present through the technology of television as the 'peanut-crunching crowd' of Plath's poem, who relish the resurrection of Lady Lazarus as if it were a circus routine. Several newspapers explicitly described the trial, according to a summary review of press coverage published by The American Jewish Committee, as 'the worst stage-managed circus in modern history'. Not only does the emphasis on staged spectacle elicit connotations of the trial as performance but it suggests the viewers' uncomfortably complicitous relation to the spectacle of suffering. In witnessing this staged recapitulation of the Holocaust, Plath's poem may be asking, is an audience consenting to its recurrence?

Such concern about recurrence would follow from the traumatic behaviours of several survivor-witnesses at the trial. Perhaps Plath's most direct allusion to the trial occurs through use of the narrating persona, Lady Lazarus, who can be seen as a version of one of the trial's most dramatic witnesses, the survivor Rivka Yoselewksa. Many of the survivors who testified before the court were obviously reluctant to do so, none more so than Yoselewska. Yehiel De-Nur, who wrote as a novelist under the name Ka-Tzetnik 135663, had earlier collapsed while on the witness stand. Rivka Yoselewska's dramatic trauma, however, preceded her testimony, which had to be delayed when, in stressful anticipation of the event, she suffered a heart attack on the very day she was to present her story in court. A few days later, on 8 May 1961, she appeared before the court with what the *New York Times* described the next day as a 'gaunt and tragic face' (p. 16), visibly shaken as she imparted her story of surviving a mass grave. Especially in light of this witness's recent cardiac event, it is not hard to imagine that those central lines from Plath's poem, 'There is a charge/ For the eyeing of my scars, there is a charge/ For the hearing of my heart', allude specifically to the psychic consequences of Yoselewska's testimony (Plath 1966: 8). It is as though Plath were asking a question Arendt would soon raise – whether it had truly been necessary to subject the survivors to such public remembrance when their testimony was not necessary, in the legal sense, to establish Eichmann's guilt.

During her time on the stand, Yoselewska's voice betrayed the trauma she experienced in being called upon to revisit the occasion of her near-death. Indeed, the aura of Yoselewska's testimony, in which she describes the suffocating force of the bodies above her and the desperation with which she struggled to climb through countless corpses in order to return herself to the land of living, gave the impression that she was speaking posthumously. At one point in her account of how she was shot and then buried alive in the mass grave, Yoselewska emphasised her more than metaphoric death: 'I thought I was dead, but that I could feel something even though I was dead' (*Trial of Adolf Eichmann* 1: 517). She wandered around the mass grave after that, ignored by soldiers engaged in killing children, almost as though she were invisible to them, and subsequently tried to dig herself back into the grave with her bare hands. Prosecutor Gideon Hausner, in his summary argument, explicitly deployed Yoselewska's story as an allegory for 'all that happened to the Jewish people', transforming her into the figure of collective resurrection in *Ezekiel*, an example of 'dry bones [that] have been given sinews' (*Trial of Adolf Eichmann* 5: 2004). In this sense, Plath's imaginative appropriation – as she constructs a persona who is alternately a repeat suicide and a murdered Holocaust victim, but in either case someone miraculously resurrected before the marvelling, voyeuristic crowd – is hardly original, however brazen its revisions of the victim's perspective may sound:

> It's the theatrical
> Comeback in broad day
> To the same place, the same face, the same brute
> Amused shout:
>
> 'A miracle!'
> That knocks me out.

> (Plath 1966: 7–8)

Plath's mock-triumphant victim adopts an attitude Yoselewska could no more claim for herself than she could lay hold of the redemptive meaning the prosecution had imposed upon her story.

Lest Plath's seem too obviously ahistorical an appropriation of Yoselewska's testimony, there should be no mistaking the fact that the exhibitionism of Plath's persona exists in proportion to the audience's prurient and rapacious curiosity, her bravado an expression of a public demand placed upon her. There is, as some of Plath's critics have charged, an ahistorical trajectory to her poetic language, especially with its ascent into prophetic rhetoric, as the mythicised Lady Lazarus becomes a vengeful goddess, exacting her punishment on the poem's Nazified but categorically male villains. The poem generalises an opposition between a besieged, yet resilient woman and her persecutors in order to read her as a metonymy for the burdens of women under patriarchy, with its characteristic sexual and medical oppressions of female bodies. It thus makes Nazism metaphorical of patriarchal oppression, and again renders the social question of complicity as an inherent function of established – and not specifically fascistic – modes of sociality.

Most ingenious of all the poem's rhetorical manoeuvres is the way Plath deploys the thematics of complicity. Explicitly representing neither Eichmann nor an Eichmann-influenced portrait of an ordinary perpetrator, she instead deploys a strategic displacement of Eichmann (who may be vestigially present in the poem as the fantastically addressed interlocutor) for the prominent cultural idea of complicity with which he was almost immediately associated. Thus in 'Lady Lazarus' the emphasis on complicity pertains especially to the crowd's taking pleasure in the show of the persona's repeated deaths and resurrections. In Plath's rendering, the complicitous crowd, joyful at another performed miracle, prepares the way for the poem's addressing of no-longer-so-metaphoric perpetrators. By this tactic the poem encourages a confusion, dependent partly on a metaphoric slippage in Plath's use of the term 'charge', whereby the persona seems first to imply that she will charge admission for the eyeing of her scars and hearing of her heart; next interprets the charge as part of the exacting of sacrificial blood mystified by Christianity until the woman imagines herself ironically as both saintly martyr and relic ('And there is a charge, a very large charge/ For a word or a touch/ Or a bit of blood/ Or a piece of my hair or my clothes' [Plath 1966: 9]); and only then makes the transition to charging her persecutors (who moments ago were understood to be an amalgamation of the general public and the historical Christian Church) as bona fide Nazis. According to this quick slide from an audience demanding either justice or just a good show to the hateful men who have committed atrocities against an allegorically female body, the persona's accusation is every bit as defiantly aimed at the audience as at her real-life persecutors, who might well be real or metaphorical Nazis. In standard readings of the poem the accused perpetrators are never supposed to be historical Nazis so much as metaphoric misnomers for conventionally patriarchal oppressors. I am suggesting instead that the confusion of reference Plath here encourages is a symptom of an emergent aesthetic of complicity through which Eichmann's meaning for later, non-fascist societies was assessed.

Beginning a New Era of Remembrance?

Although the prosecution maintained clear moral distinctions between the victims and the on-trial perpetrator, one of the more perplexing results of the trial was that Eichmann's apparent ordinariness resulted in sometimes conflated sympathies for victims and perpetrator alike. Eichmann was tried under an Israeli law originally aimed – since the newly founded state entertained little hope, while drafting the law, of apprehending primary agents of the Nazi genocide (let alone bringing them to trial under Israel's sovereignty) – at Jewish collaborators with Nazism. Knowledge of this fact may have emboldened British actor and author Robert Shaw to write the novel *The Man in the Glass Booth* (1967), subsequently adapted by him for the stage and made into a 1975 Hollywood movie, in which a Jewish man is accused of being a Nazi war criminal. As the title suggests, the scenario of Shaw's fictional trial was inspired by the conceit of visual sympathy for Eichmann that resulted from his caged presentation in the Israeli courtroom. Such complex identification with both the testifying survivors and the perpetrator was also evident in Norma Rosen's

Touching Evil (1969), which, by featuring the Eichmann trial as it was televised on a local New York channel, emphasised the spectacle of the trial itself. Rosen, a Jewish-American novelist who became well known also as a feminist author, deploys the televised trial as an opportunity for remembrance in the Freudian sense of working through the unresolved past. According to her novel, the trial serves doubly to introduce a new generation to such awful history and to force the wartime generation not to forget what Jews suffered in their recent European past. Rosen assumes that a recent generation's memory of such events will depend on the previous generation's cultural knowledge in complex ways. For Rosen any notion (such as the hypothesis argued by Peter Novick [1999]) that Holocaust memory had lain dormant for many years and was suddenly awakened around the time of the Eichmann trial would grossly underestimate the historical significance given to the event by the wartime generation. As she imagines the historical significance of the Holocaust to be already constituted as the paradigmatic example of socially manifested evil, she also represents the Holocaust in the light of the cultural context of the novel's setting (during the trial) and the novel's authorship (during the late 1960s, as the Holocaust became increasingly central to Jewish-American identity). Thus, the re-emergence of the Holocaust in the narrator-protagonist Jean's life depends upon her contingent solidarity with Hattie, a young pregnant mother obsessed by the Eichmann trial, whose identification with the victims might potentially, as her husband fears, endanger her unborn child.

Rosen's novel implicitly recalls a former era of Holocaust representation from 1944 to 1961, in the US and elsewhere, when these events were not so much absent from political discourse as enfolded within the wider, more universalistic concerns of other political, cultural, philosophical and psychological idioms, such as human rights, genocide and crimes against humanity. In the novel's view, the former era of Holocaust remembrance had been governed by a horror inspiring a desire to forget or avoid the subject. Yet even if such memory is oblique, inactive or even suppressed, it is not without influence. Photographs from the liberation of the camps, which Susan Sontag would identify in *On Photography* (1977) as archetypal images of atrocity, and which would later be deployed by Joyce Carol Oates in the opening of *You Must Remember This* (1987), and by the British novelist Maureen Duffy in *Change*, published in the same year, also figure crucially in *Touching Evil*. When recounting Hattie's encounter with the 1944 photographs, Rosen declares that they were 'destined to become one of the classic sights of the world', comparing them to world-famous architectural ruins (Rosen 1969: 73). Jean proves so susceptible to their power as to allow herself to be seduced on a laboratory floor by a professor who is also reacting to the photographs, searching for some sort of ordinary pleasure after witnessing scenes that belong more properly, he declares, in films about mad scientists. As the postwar era of Holocaust memory is interpreted through Jean's experiences, society divides according to its willingness to access the memory of atrocity, so that there are 'only two kinds of people' for Jean – 'those who knew and those who didn't know' (Rosen 1969: 77).

Though Rosen posits an intergenerational continuity, she also allows for an upsurge in cultural memory after 1961, and some of the evidence for this is in her own belated encounter with the Holocaust after her marriage to a survivor of the *Kindertransport* (an effort that rescued thousands of refugee Jewish children from Nazi Germany, 1938–40) and her subsequent witnessing of the genocide through the Eichmann trial. As a secularised American Jew, Rosen has accused herself of a diasporic failure to integrate Judaism into her life, and as such she is symptomatic of a generation of Jews whose Jewish identity was honed belatedly on the Holocaust. In the light of this, it is somewhat remarkable that her novel adopts none of the emergent nationalistic interpretation of the Holocaust advocated by the Israeli prosecution in the courtroom, which drew so much of Arendt's attention and ire. Indeed, *Touching Evil* does not present a single significant Jewish character. Despite Rosen's own subsequent protests to the contrary, the novel adheres to a universalistic sense of the Holocaust as a negative meaning – specifically, the human capacity for evil – within Western culture. The two complementary yet antinomous main characters, Jean and Hattie, function as a split self-representation of the author. The figure of Jean represents an ideal construction of an authorial self that would have at least hypothetically been more affected by the Holocaust had the author fully considered it earlier – which is to say, she is in this sense a hypothesis of self-accusation. The figure of Hattie represents, by contrast, the sudden incursion of Holocaust consciousness into Rosen's life, albeit belatedly. Like Hattie, Rosen watched the Eichmann trial while pregnant, and Hattie's extraordinary naivety recalls a knowledge Rosen and Americans in general formerly possessed without having incorporated it into their lives. Jean, then, is an idealised vehicle of the author's own responsiveness in that former era of Holocaust memory, and as a vicariously righteous gentile she responds with a kind of compensatory excess for all those, including Rosen herself, in America or beyond, who have not known the significance of these events as they were supposed to. And yet according to the novel's vision of intergenerational transmission of Holocaust history and its appreciation of the pedagogical value of the Eichmann trial, Jean has all but relinquished her Holocaust consciousness until she subjects herself rather unhappily to the ordeal of watching the Eichmann trial with Hattie. As the American public is similarly forced to revisit that history in greater depth, the upshot of such knowledge seems to be a heightened awareness of collective complicity in dehumanising structures that are mitigated at novel's end only by Hattie's pregnancy-inspired and hallucinatory – in short, hardly historical – vision of redemption through her maternal womb.

Eichmann as an Everyman?

A year after Rosen's novel, the Eichmann trial and the popular understanding of Arendt's infamous book again figured prominently in an American novel about the Holocaust. Although the Canadian-born, Jewish-American novelist Saul Bellow, who would subsequently win a Nobel Prize, had treated the Nazi genocide on the periphery of such earlier works as *The Victim* (1947) and *Herzog* (1964), he did not treat the central historical catastrophe of Western Europe in the twentieth century at any length until *Mr. Sammler's Planet* (1970). As James Atlas has emphasised, the novel takes the 'form of a polemic' – especially railing against the radical politics of the student anti-war movement, women's liberation, and the revolutionary struggle of the black counter-culture (Atlas 2000: 386). Offering his own caricatured version of Arendt's thesis through the fictionalised survivor Artur Sammler, Bellow proceeds as though Arendt had put forward an apology for Eichmann's misunderstanding of his own behaviour:

> But do you think the Nazis didn't know what murder was? Everybody (except certain bluestockings) knows what murder is. That is very old human knowledge. The best and purest human beings, from the beginning of time, have understood that life is sacred. To defy that old understanding is not banality. (Bellow 1970: 18)

Even apart from the clearly misogynistic tactic of calling Arendt a 'bluestocking', Sammler's misunderstanding of one of the most prominent late twentieth-century intellectuals must be understood as either deliberate or so deeply influenced by the mael-strom of criticism brought against the book that he entirely misconstrues Arendt's point about the legal question of murder. It is clear throughout *Eichmann in Jerusalem* that Arendt rejects, ironically and fiercely, almost all of Eichmann's self-apologetics, even as she also complains that the trial continually misses the mark on the prosecutable dimension of Eichmann's guilt and the meaning of his criminality, and much of her complaint is in the service of seeing the Holocaust as a historical event far surpassing the ordinary criteria of murder. Sammler's solution, which I think it is fair to attribute to Bellow himself, is to suppose that morality is not contingent and that the use of violence is not ideologically constructed. Such a criticism would seem to advocate a rejection of the phenomenon often associated with Arendt's book – namely, the tendency to identify with Eichmann as a sign of one's own complicity in structurally determined political injustices.

It is perhaps curious that only two months after the publication of a novel implicitly charging Arendt with sympathy for Eichmann, Bellow interpreted his own difficulties with student audiences through the figure of Eichmann. Expressing his anxiety about the anticipated audience size for an upcoming lecture in April 1970 at Purdue University in Indiana, which seemed to evoke memories of a disastrous public lecture given at San Francisco State University in 1968, Bellow lamented, 'I'm not being *punished* for some-thing. I shouldn't be put on display like Eichmann in Jerusalem' (Atlas 2000: 398). That Bellow should fancy himself to be even falsely equated with Eichmann shows just how widely disseminated and imaginatively forceful the image of a caged Eichmann was. In *Mr. Sammler's Planet*, the cultural attention paid to Eichmann as a vehicle for consider-ing the systemic dimensions of genocide is, at least by Bellow's account, a diversion from an honest focus on the murderousness characterising the crimes of the Holocaust. The novel's answer is to overlook Eichmann rhetorically so as to clear space for Bellow's own Sammlerian worldview, in which there persists a nostalgia for old European culture and its immemorial codes of individualistic honour. And in such a worldview, complicity in bad political culture – even in the systemic determinations contributing to the perpetra-tion of genocide – remains an immediately, indeed personally discernible act. In this sense, the Holocaust survivor Sammler's nostalgia for a political culture premised on clearly per-ceptible lines of individual responsibility testifies to the trenchant, conservative dimen-sion of liberal culture in America.

Eichmann, I am suggesting, denoted a crisis in the meaning of moral responsibility, as the social meanings attached to his mode of murderousness were transmuted – by Arendt but also more broadly in the public view – into a sign of complicity with collectivist ideology that heralded the loss of individualist political agency. Allowing the general notion of banal-ity to stand implicitly for the more complex philosophical notion of complicity, in which the individual's agency is necessarily a function of structural determinations refracted through ideological and cultural commitments, Bellow's Sammler supposes that to refuse such an analogy in advance – not to see yourself as an Eichmann, which is to say as someone who might commit murder as though it were banal – would be to disallow the possibility of such an action. Although Sammler rejects Arendt's banality precisely because it renders the Nazis' extreme criminality a possibility in the everyday world, by putting their actions into implicit analogy with ordinary psychological and moral motives, the novel cannot sustain its note of protest against analogy. Indeed, the effect of intermingling Sammler's Holocaust remem-brances with his complaints against late 1960s' America is to make criminality a ruling conceit for interpreting the moral licence and violently anarchist tendencies of contempor-ary America. In the name of rejecting the universalising tendencies of analogy, the novel reifies the very term it would strive to preserve as extraordinary – namely, criminality. And insofar as culturally licensed criminality and an almost inevitable complicity with it seem to typify an entire generation, *Mr. Sammler's Planet* offers a bleak portrait of the currents of political change, hopelessly longing for a status quo with which it cannot honestly be said to be any more enchanted. Taken together, Bellow's and Rosen's novels force us to ask – in neither case as a direct consequence, apparently, of the author's own inquiry – whether the recognition of one's complicity in political structures of oppression corresponds to critical consciousness or merely to resignation.

On the other side of Rosen's fantastically, maternally staged redemption of humanity from complicity in *Touching Evil* is Erica Jong's *Fear of Flying* (1973), a novel that extends the canon of feminist-minded responses to the Holocaust in its own peculiar direction. Remembered for the notoriety of its story of a woman's sexual liberation, in which the protagonist Isadora Wing seems a female counterpart of the notoriously sex-obsessed male protagonist of Philip Roth's *Portnoy's Complaint* (1969), *Fear of Flying* is an unlikely medium for Holocaust consciousness. Yet again Jong's point seems to be that Holocaust consciousness is as inescapable for contemporary Jews as the actual historical genocide was for its Jewish victims. The novel opens with Isadora travelling as a journalist to report on the return of the psychoanalysts to Vienna: 'the people who invented *scmaltz* [sic] (and crematoria) were going to show the analysts how welcome back they were' (Jong 1973: 5). Already Jong's irony permits a connotation of foreboding, in which a contemporary tourist-industry welcome, tainted always by memory of the deceptive hospitality of the concentration camps, might revert to violence. Isadora's fear of flying is coupled with her fear of arriving upon the scene of genocide as though it were still the era of Nazism, and she cannot keep herself from conjecturing that if her parents had been German, despite her Aryan looks, she would have ended in a concentration camp. Once in Vienna her Holocaust consciousness borders on paranoia, as she picks a fight with a female security person who denies her entrance to the convention. The guard has not been authorised to admit the press, but as Isadora's persecutorial fancies increase, she thinks to herself, 'the Nazi bitch . . . the goddamned Kraut', and when the woman says, 'I haff instructions to obey', Isadora quips, 'You and Eichmann' (Jong 1973: 25, 26).

According to Isadora's morbid witticism Eichmann stands for blind obedience to authority in such a way that a security guard's unreflective adherence to professional duty seems interchangeable, even perhaps indistinguishable, from the political culture of fascism. Eichmann is expressly not a figure of identification here, as he was for Levertov or even Rosen, but then again – to emphasise what should be only too obvious – this isn't Eichmann or even someone much like him. Alluding to the late 1960s' cultural lexicon in which Eichmann figures complicity, Jong's scenario permits Isadora to set herself apart from such complicity as a vicarious victim and to stand in the role of righteous accuser. The novel portrays Holocaust consciousness as a mode of aesthetic perception in which the present not only devolves from the past but becomes, in a fundamental sense, interchangeable with it. Isadora's paranoia has at least a hypothetical plausibility behind it: how do we really know, she asks, that anything has changed in Germany or Austria or more generally in the Teutonic mind since 1945?

What Isadora wants from the Germans is an honest reckoning with the historical past. On an earlier visit to Germany, some twenty years before, the owner of a local bookstore had spoken frankly with Isadora, admitting that at some level all Germans admired the Nazis and that most people knew about the deportations, but did nothing because most people 'are not heroes and most people are not honest' (Jong 1973: 67). The result of this exchange is that Isadora suddenly finds common ground with this man who has been so honest about his ideological and ethical complicity, as she wonders – with some relief – 'would I have been more heroic than he?' (Jong 1973: 67). Jong's representation of the German citizen's confession of complicity fits with the Freudian definition of remembrance, in which what is unpleasant and therefore repressed by consciousness can be elicited from the recesses of the psyche and, after being brought to light, exorcised as unconscious motivation. *Fear of Flying* emphasises the twofold dimension of complicity – as both a descriptive social and psychological category and also an interpretive tool for critique – so as to make the critical mechanism entirely dependent on a recognition of the pervasiveness of complicity as a social phenomenon. In her paranoid state of mind more than twenty years later in Austria, Isadora seems to expect such confessions to be repeated even where they are not especially relevant. In other words, the guard at the convention is another Eichmann insofar as she, by following orders, fails to recognise the analogy between her present conduct and the Nazi past, remaining entirely unreflective about her dutiful obedience as a potential mode of complicity with bad political culture. In discovering the symptoms of Nazified complicity in someone carrying out truly banal duties, Isadora's suspicion of complicity functions as sociological hypothesis rather than historical indictment. There is no direct continuity, or at least none is presented, between the guard's present behaviour and Nazism; one might as well say that the mere existence of law enforcement officials inclines a society toward the police state. And yet Isadora's Holocaust consciousness is all about perceiving such false continuities. The confession of complicity she would require, rather than increasing genuine knowledge of the Holocaust, functionally belittles the history with which she has professed concern.

Much of *Fear of Flying*, insofar as it is about the Holocaust, seems a portrait of misremembrance, and it is difficult to determine just how self-reflexive the novel is about its patterns of misremembrance. Insofar as the novel pushes for confessions of complicity detached from genuine, historically realised political actions, it provokes the question of whether such a cultural discourse facilitates effective political critique. Throughout the novel Isadora demands confessions of complicity from everyone but herself, and if her structure of thought exposes the self-exonerative tendency in all critique (the one who identifies the cultural workings of complicity is, hypothetically, exempted from their influence), it does not seem to be intended to serve that purpose by Jong. There is certainly some ironic commentary evident in the fact that Jong's heroine searches Europe – first postwar Germany, and then Austria in the early 1970s – for the afterlife of Nazism and then subjects herself to a mode of fantasy straight out of Sylvia Plath's conflation in 'Daddy' of fascists and oppressive, yet sexually compelling men. Citing those infamous lines, 'Every woman adores a Fascist,/ The boot in the face'– which in Plath's poem are still metaphorical for the woman's quasi-masochistic wrestling with patriarchal legacies – Jong describes a heroine who really does fall in love with a man not just for his metaphoric fascism, but for his honest anti-Semitism and his professionally expert belief that women really want to be dominated (Plath 1966: 5). Jong's overt allusion to Plath's mildly feminist exposé of women's complicity with patriarchal desire means that Isadora, like Plath's persona, has taken the imaginative possibility of vicarious victimisation as a course of action, or perhaps we should say as an unconsciously reactive response to the ubiquitous signs of complicity. In short, we are left to wonder whether *Fear of Flying* superficially elaborates the persecution fantasies of Holocaust consciousness in order to construct a critical space, apart from fantasy, that might encourage the recognition of complicity, or whether such a recognition of complicity only predicts cooperation with its rules.

All of the literary texts I have discussed here offer a version of this dilemma. For as the Eichmann trial occasioned a recognition of complicity with bad political culture that was perhaps more aesthetic than political, the question of dissent was repeatedly de-emphasised by this literature in order to stress the deep psychological and sociological forces reifying the citizen's obedient, complicitous relation to political oppression. In the verdict Hannah Arendt would like to have heard pronounced against Eichmann, she imagined refuting his claim that it was accident more than intention that had brought him to do what he had done and that there was 'a potentiality of equal guilt on the part of all' who lived in the Nazi state, and insisting against such obviously self-justifying logic that there is 'an abyss between the actuality of what you did and the potentiality of what others might have done' (Arendt 1964: 278). Justice perceives the abyss and insists upon the distinction. To the extent that fictional fantasies such as Jong's – or Levertov's, Rosen's, or Bellow's – dissolve the distinction between perpetrators and the rest of us and propose constructing a *realpolitik* upon the common ground of criminal potentiality, they must become profoundly banal or at least unoriginally complicitous with the political structures they might otherwise lament.

References

Alvarez, A. (1962) *The New Poetry*, Harmondsworth: Penguin

Arendt, Hannah (1964 [1963]) *Eichmann in Jerusalem: A Report on the Banality of Evil*, New York: Viking

Atlas, James (2000) *Bellow: A Biography*, New York: Random House

Bellow, Saul (1970) *Mr. Sammler's Planet*, New York: Viking

Bettelheim, Bruno (1979) 'The Ignored Lesson of Anne Frank', in *Surviving, and Other Essays*, New York: Knopf, 246–57

Ezrahi, Sidra DeKoven (1980) *By Words Alone: The Holocaust in Literature*, Chicago: University of Chicago Press

Jong, Erica (1973) *Fear of Flying*, New York: Holt

Levertov, Denise (1961) *The Jacob's Ladder*, New York: New Directions

Novick, Peter (1999) *The Holocaust in American Life*, Boston, MA: Houghton Mifflin

Plath, Sylvia (1966 [1965]) *Ariel*, New York: Harper and Row

Rose, Jacqueline (1991) *The Haunting of Sylvia Plath*, Cambridge, MA: Harvard University Press

Rosen, Norma (1969) *Touching Evil*, New York: Harcourt, Brace

Rosenfeld, Alvin (1991) 'Popularization and Memory: The Case of Anne Frank', in *Lessons and Legacies: The Meaning of the Holocaust in a Changing World*, ed. Peter Hayes, Evanston, IL: Northwestern University Press, 243–78

Spargo, R. Clifton (2001) 'To Invent as Presumptuously as Real Life: Parody and the Cultural Memory of Anne Frank in Roth's *The Ghost Writer*', *Representations* 76 (Fall), 88–119

——(2004) *The Ethics of Mourning: Grief and Responsibility in Elegiac Literature*, Baltimore, MD: Johns Hopkins University Press

The Trial of Adolf Eichmann: Record of the Proceedings in the District Court of Jerusalem (1992–5), 6 vols Jerusalem: Ministry of Justice, State of Israel

Young, James E. (1988) *Writing and Rewriting the Holocaust: Narrative and the Consequences of Interpretation*, Bloomington, IN: Indiana University Press

Chapter 14

1963, London: The Myth of the Artist and the Woman Writer

Patricia Waugh

Sex

Sexual intercourse began
In nineteen sixty-three
(Which was rather late for me) –

(Philip Larkin, 'Annus Mirabilis')

1963: the worst of years and the best of years. As the impact of the revelations about the concentration camps was felt, following the trial of Adolf Eichmann in 1961, George Steiner would write that 'the house of classic humanism, the dream of reason which animated western society, have largely broken down . . . We come after' (Steiner 1969: 15). Yet Martin Luther King would announce, in his 'I have a Dream' speech, delivered on the steps of the Lincoln memorial in Washington DC in August, that 'nineteen sixty-three is not an end but a beginning. The whirlwind of revolt will come to shake the foundations of our nation until the bright day of justice emerges' (King 1985: 95).

In London, despite the popular myths of the sixties, the city would not be 'swinging' for another two or three years, at least until *Time* magazine officially announced the birth of 'Swinging London' in April 1966. 'Top of the Pops' made its first appearance (on BBC television) in 1963, but so had Mary Whitehouse's 'clean-up TV' campaign. Britain was recovering from the Cuban Missile Crisis of 1962, with its unignorable demonstration of Britain's loss of world power to the US, just as its relations with Europe were also taking a downward turn with refusal of entry into the Common Market. However, in the popular imagination, at least, 1963 will probably always be commemorated as 'nineteen sixty-three', the 'Annus Mirabilis' of youth culture, new sexual freedoms, and of Philip Larkin's middle-aged sense of having just missed the boat. Identified with the very myths of the moment it sought to explode, Larkin's poem became a receptacle for the projected desires and mythologies of posterity: 1963 now stands as the year when 'sexual intercourse began', with the Larkinesque ambivalence and the vocally intricate play of poetic irony most often wilfully ignored.

By 1964, the Beatles' first LP had grossed £6 million: in the US and in Britain, censorship had eased – particularly, in the latter, since Penguin Books celebrated legal defence of their edition of D. H. Lawrence's *Lady Chatterley's Lover* (1928) in 1960. David Storey's novel *Radcliffe* treated openly the theme of homosexual desire, and Margaret Drabble an extra-marital affair in *A Summer Bird-Cage*. Other contemporary novels – Iris Murdoch's *The Unicorn*, and, in the US, William Burroughs' *The Naked Lunch* and John Updike's *The Centaur* – explicitly represented a heady Gothic brew of sex and death. In *Honest to God*, John Robinson, Bishop of Woolwich, defended sex as sacred. Early in the year, Charles Marowitz began to rehearse the Royal Shakespeare Company's Theatre of Cruelty season, responding to the horrors of the concentration camps with the kind of return to the body and to ritual recommended by the theatre theorist Antonin Artaud. The sense of language struck dumb and of reason collapsed might be negotiated by opening the self physically to the cosmic terror of the erotic and the thanatic: to total sensation, reviving the Dionysian source of theatre in the fundamental drives. Unforgettable images in Peter Weiss's *Marat/Sade* (part of the Theatre of Cruelty season) suggested that the failure of rationalism as a viable source of political will might produce an acceptance of those elemental forces whose repression had produced violence, sadism and genocide.

Sexuality in Larkin's poem is likewise considered as liberated, but not as an unproblematic or polymorphously joyous force. The heavily ironised reference to '*sexual intercourse*', rather than plain *sex*, captures wonderfully the prim legalese of the *Lady Chatterley* trial, where defence and prosecution alike blended vocabularies of Lawrentian physical passion with those of an often prim or medicalised moral hygiene (Larkin 1988: 167). But 'nineteen sixty-three' functions primarily as a vehicle for Larkin to address the issue of love in an age of consumer values: love freed up from the necessity of emotional bargaining ('the wrangle for a ring'), or indeed from any other higher commitment. This is sex, welfare-capitalist-style. Everyone can share this 'brilliant breaking of the bank' – another line which mixes allusions to gambling, sexual defloration, and perhaps even to the Great Train Robbery in August 1963, the robbers escaping to be lionised by the popular press as romantic adventurers. In the new age of consumer liberation and the contraceptive pill, widely available in Britain from 1962, no one loses and 'everyone felt the same'. However, Larkin sees that without even a residually sacramental sense of marriage or a lively fear of unwanted pregnancy, the profanity of sexual transgression also dies. The Lawrentian myth of sex as the profound source of selfhood similarly finds its days numbered. The Romantic gleam, ever in thrall to the exchange of the marriage economy, is now further endangered by the brave new commodified world Larkin lamented as 'going, going, gone': a world of money, the cool store, and the new leisure and entertainment industries. From henceforth, the Frankfurt School theorist Herbert Marcuse would claim, the music of the soul will only be heard as the music of salesmanship, and sexual explicitness, according to A. Alvarez, literary editor of the *Observer*, as 'almost a form of conservatism', rather than the proclaimed and heady road to freedom (Marcuse 1964: 57; Alvarez 1974: 282).

Women writers were certainly beginning to arrive at a similar conclusion. Betty Friedan's *The Feminine Mystique*, also published in 1963, exposed the shortcomings of the sexual revolution viewed from the perspective of women. Noting the increasing obsession with sex, its commodification, and its medicalisation in the two Kinsey reports of 1948 and 1953, she observed that although 'sex is the only frontier open to women who have always lived within the confines of the feminine mystique', it is also absolutely central to the construction of that mystique (Friedan 1965: 228). The educated housewife, queen in her suburban palace with its array of labour-saving devices, enters what Friedan contentiously referred to as 'the comfortable concentration camp' (245) of middle-class home-making, via myths of romantic love and domestic bliss. Escape into extra-marital affairs and consumer fantasies is simply more of the same.

Although Sylvia Plath committed suicide before the appearance of Friedan's book, several of her last poems subvert the feminine mystique through a cartoonish but violent animation of domestic commodities, in kitchens where the 'potatoes hiss' and the 'smog of cooking' is the 'smog of hell', or where the 'smile' of iceboxes is annihilating (Plath 1965: 34). In her novel *The Bell Jar* (1963), the 'motherly breath' of the suburbs seems 'a large but escape-proof cage' (Plath 1963: 120). The shining white kitchens of *Ladies' Day* magazine serve up the 'dressed' crabmeat which poisons her and, throughout the novel, women are subjected to a variety of machines which subdue, restrain or kill – ECT, birth-stirrups, the electric chair.

Sex, Confession and the Woman Writer

> At their worst, women are low, sloppy beasts.
>
> (Norman Mailer, *The Presidential Papers*)

Featuring the sexual shenanigans of the Profumo affair, downfall of Harold Macmillan's Conservative government, the July 1963 issue of *Encounter* bore the sombre headline, 'Suicide of a Nation'. If not always associated with suicide, sex in Britain in 1963 was more likely to be associated with demise and political corruption than with liberation. Even across the Atlantic, John Berryman introduced the Profumo affair into Song 66 of his *77 Dream Songs* (1964), linking it with a Buddhist priest who burns himself in protest against American interference in Vietnam. Both Berryman's cosmopolitan theatre of darkly absurd vice in high places, and Larkin's invocation of parochial lower-middle-class English *mores*, explode the myth of sexual liberation and deliberately blur the boundary between truth and fiction and private and public history. Perhaps the only writer who seems to buy into the myth wholeheartedly is Norman Mailer, whose *The Presidential Papers* was also published in 1963, invoking the erotic energies of Dionysus or 'the psychic outlaw' as the antidote to the machine and 'theoretic man'.

Yet these are culturally sanctioned positions of poetic authority. If Larkin appropriates the poetic persona of a man talking to men, of the Poet as Common Man, Berryman's *Dream Songs* are a (deliberately chaotic) rendition of the Growth of the Poet's Mind in the mode of the Holy Fool, as a precarious order is ripped cosmically out of the chaos of a personal and collective unconscious. Like Larkin's persona, Berryman's Henry is also at odds with a world that is meaningless, absurd, 'a place/ where I do not care to be any more' (Berryman 1990: 593), and in both cases it is hard to separate the persona from the poet. The confessional turn in contemporary poetry was stimulated by the publication of Robert Lowell's *Life Studies* in 1959 and then associated particularly with Lowell's circle and with Norman Mailer (Sylvia Plath and Anne Sexton had also both attended Lowell's poetry seminars in 1959). Throughout *The Presidential Papers*, Mailer insists that 'the first work of art in an artist is the shaping of his own personality' (Mailer 1968: 284). But he was also concerned with the failure of language and of the textual representation of reality, and invents a personal style, a mixed mode of the documentary and the mythopoeic, that deliberately breaks down distinctions between fiction and documentary, invention and biographical fact, author and persona. Much like Berryman, with his complex and shifting voices, his appropriation of black-faced minstrelsy, and identifications with the Negro and the Jew, he insisted that 'I became a quick-change artist, as if I believe that I can trap the Prince of Truth in the act of switching a style' (Mailer 1992: 18).

Lowell also observed that,

> I feel it is extreme (and perhaps unique even) about the U.S., that the artist's existence becomes his art. He is re-born in it, and he hardly exists without it . . . that would seem embarrassing to an Englishman, and inhuman probably, to be that 'all out' about it. (Lowell 1965: 43)

Less obviously than the Lowell circle, Larkin follows Eliot's dictum that the poet should write out of his nervous system, and his digestive tract, and not simply the cerebral cortex. Yet, like them, he also rejects the fiction of impersonality. His authorial voice of the Common Man, like Berryman's crazy and unstable Henry or Mailer's device of shifting from the first person to references in the third person to a theatricalised 'hipster' figure called Mailer, plays equally with autobiographical identifications. It is impossible to say whether these are antic masks or authentic voices. The reader is teased with the kind of conundrums concerning the relations between biographical and authorial selves that the Argentinian short-story writer, Jorge Luis Borges, made explicit in 'Borges and I', published in *Labyrinths* in 1962.

Nevertheless, each of these male writers is able to occupy a secure, well-established authorial position. Each establishes himself at an appropriate tangent to myths of 'liberation' and as a figure at odds with the age, exiled or dispossessed or marginalised. But each of these positions had an honourable and ultimately socially inclusive lineage which was either unavailable to or problematic for the woman writer: there is no equivalent female position to the Poet as Common Man, or Holy Fool, Aristocratic Hero, or Sexual Adventurer. For the woman writer, confession, anger and revolt are construed simply as expressions of private hysteria or insufficient aesthetic distance, and this double standard ensured that while Mailer could celebrate sexual liberation it was often in misogynistic terms and well before writers such as Erica Jong, Kate Millett and Lisa Adler would dare to try (and fail) to reverse these gender positions. Though Lowell's 'Skunk Hour' is read both as a private poem about his mental illness and as a commentary on the alienation of the age; or Mailer's performative self-fashioning is seen as an assertion of the individual spirit against an age of conformism and the machine; few, if any, critics read Plath's *The Bell Jar* in such terms, or as anything other than a semi-autobiographical account of her nervous breakdown of 1953. The confessional mode for women writers is problematic because it tends to be read as exclusively concerned with the private life, and this is certainly not the case for male writers of the times. Appropriated without a full awareness of their gender implications, these constructions of authorial modes would either prove enormously destructive for women writers such as Sylvia Plath and Anne Sexton, or function as catalysts for contestation and challenge to raise the consciousness and awareness of gender difference in the writing of Doris Lessing, Muriel Spark, Iris Murdoch and Denise Levertov.

Marcuse's critique of repressive desublimation and the commercialisation of human relations was beginning to influence the New Left, but movements for women's and gay liberation, growing out of Civil Rights and the demand for racial equality in the US, would not begin to gather force until later in the 1960s. *Sexual* liberation may have begun in 1963, but women's liberation was not officially underway until some five or six years later. Friedan's *The Feminine Mystique*, published in that year, came too late for many women writers who began to publish in the late 1950s. Numerous novels published in 1963 – Mary McCarthy's *The Group* and Penelope Mortimer's *The Pumpkin Eater*, as well as *The Bell Jar* – rehearse the themes of Friedan's book but reveal their authors, as well as their heroines, still caught up in aspects of the feminine mystique. Margaret Drabble was at Cambridge at the same time as Plath, but studying under F. R. Leavis, and had read de Beauvoir's

The Second Sex. The allusion to John Webster's seventeenth-century play *The White Devil* in the title of her first novel, *A Summer Bird-Cage*, is there presumably to reinforce the novel's theme of the domestic imprisonment of accomplished young women, fresh out of Cambridge, but with marriage or vocational celibacy as mutually exclusive options because 'you can't be a sexy don' (Drabble 1967: 183). Yet sympathetic as Drabble is to Sarah's plight, and to her attempt to avoid a Jane Austen marriage plot without falling into the deathly, thanatopic endings of earlier novels such as Woolf's *The Voyage Out* (1915), she seems also to endorse Sarah's view of her progressive friend Simone, described as 'sad, gaunt Simone with her dark face and her muddled heritage, her sexless passions and her ancient clothes, gathered from all the attics of Europe' (Drabble 1967: 70). Simone begins to sound less like a feminist icon and more like the sadistic and misogynistic portrayal of Hermione, the over-educated and hysterically aggressive intellectual aristocrat whom Lawrence based on Lady Ottoline Morell, in *Women in Love* (1921).

Drabble's portrayal of Simone seems to echo a passage from Plath's *Journal*, describing Cambridge women dons as 'grotesques'. Though 'very brilliant or learned', their experience is for Plath 'secondary . . . tantamount to a kind of living death'. Instead, she seeks to 'move into the world of growth and suffering where the real books are people's minds and souls' (Plath 2000: 198). Plath finished the passage by insisting that she wants a husband and a home. Yet if the confessional male writer blurs the distinction between life and art, public and private, then surely the turn to the confessional mode and the new explicitness about sex would eventually offer to women writers the chance to resolve the dilemma voiced by Plath – the seemingly mutually exclusive choice between the public role of author and the private and domestic space of marriage and child-bearing. Certainly, retrospectively, one can view the enormous emphasis on confession in 1963 as offering women an opportunity. But without an organised women's movement, the strategy was risky and without the later recognition that 'the private is the public' – the most important slogan of the early women's movement – confession seemed already to be so much a part of the 'feminine mystique' and of the perceived emotionality and submissiveness of women, that many politically aware writers, such as Doris Lessing, were extremely reluctant to be explicitly construed in this fashion. In an interview in October 1963, Lessing voiced her anger over the reviews of *The Golden Notebook*, published the year before, insisting that the formal and analytic qualities of the novel had been ignored because 'they tried to turn it into The Confessions of Doris Lessing' (Lessing 1972: 51).

Yet in the same essay, Lessing names her favourite American writer as Norman Mailer. I think that what she had already perceived was that Mailer's experimental confessionalism was a mode of writing which, in destabilising essentialist concepts of selfhood and identity, not only expressed a sense of the existential uncertainty of the times, but also offered a liberatory mode of writing for women which was far removed from any old-style 'Confessions of . . . '. Indeed with the publication of Roland Barthes' seminal essay, 'The Death of the Author' within a few years, the concept of authorship and its underpinning by a liberal humanist concept of the unified subject would come under the critical spotlight, but writers in 1963 were already ahead of literary critics and theorists. Lessing's fiction was already playing with such concepts from the publication of *The Golden Notebook* in 1962. Like *The Bell Jar* and *A Summer Bird-Cage*, with their alter-ego writer-protagonists, her work might be regarded as the prototype for a new genre of metafictional *Kunstlerromane*; a fiction of personal and artistic development concerned specifically with the conflictual positioning of the female author and the instability of the 'I' who writes and the 'I' who is written.

Viewed in this light, novels of the early 1960s that seem indifferent to feminist politics can be seen to engage with such issues. Like her first novel, *The Comforters* (1957), Muriel Spark's *The Prime of Miss Jean Brodie* (1961), for example, offers an early self-reflection on the problem of female authorship. Spark's Brodie is condemned for her romantic and (politically) dangerous confusion of art and life; but in the context of the puritanical and 'correct' culture of her own time (middle class, 'respectable', narrowly Presbyterian Edinburgh in the 1930s), she is also curiously sympathetic and genuinely charismatic. Spark rightly condemns Brodie's ethical blindness, yet also presents her stubborn way-wardness in a proto-feminist light, as a meditation on the problems and dangers of avail-able constructions of authorship for the woman writer.

Surely, one of the reasons for the immense significance for later feminists of *The Golden Notebook* is that its main theme concerns the problems of female authorship. The novel's self-begetting structure ends with Anna overcoming her writer's block to begin writing the novel that we are reading. In the preface to the novel, Lessing justifies her commitment to humanist character and to the writing of fiction as a means of exploring contingent experi-ence, the 'raw feel' of being a woman or a man living in the late twentieth century, in terms which illustrate her concern to identify a new mode of the 'confessional'. She states that

> the way to deal with the problem of 'subjectivity', that shocking business of being preoccupied
> with the tiny individual who is at the same time caught up in such an explosion of terrible and
> marvellous possibilities, is to see him as a microcosm and in this way to break through the per-
> sonal, the subjective, making the personal general, as indeed life always does, transforming a
> private experience . . . into something larger. (Lessing 1973: 7)

But she also voiced her unease with the capacity of expressive realism to articulate the complex fragmentariness of late modernity in terms that neither reduce social experience to particularised flashes of insular personal emotion, nor subsume the particular into the generalised impersonality of the rationalised discourses of social science and political theory. Initially, Anna Wulf, the writer, tries to work her way through the problem and overcome her writer's block by separating herself out into distinct voices, one for each of the four notebooks, convinced that if the essence of neurosis is conflict, then dividing up, separating out the voices, is the way to stay sane. But in the final, golden notebook, she begins to break down and to experience a complete dissolution of the voices into each other and into those of other characters. For Lessing, only *immersion* in the cacophonous vocal chorus which is the 'small personal voice' of the late twentieth century, offers a way of breaking through to new political identities. Lessing drew on R. D. Laing's ideas about madness as an expression of the psychosis of the times and also as a potential route back to health, and her irritation at the way in which critics ignored her broader political engage-ment and attended only to the personally confessional in the novel is understandable. Women writers could usefully appropriate the new confessionalism, but all too often the ironies, parodies and subversiveness would be ignored and the work read as a straightfor-ward *cri de coeur*, another version of 'women's talk'.

Almost all women writers of 1963 show an acute if sometimes veiled awareness that sexual liberation is by no means the democracy where 'everyone felt the same', of Larkin's poem. Perhaps though the most shockingly explicit counterpart to 'Annus Mirabilis' was Denise Levertov's angry poem 'Hypocrite Women', collected in the volume *O Taste and See* of 1964, which, as if in answer to Woolf's famous injunction to women to refuse to serve as invisible mirrors for the gratification of the male ego, counsels that if 'a white sweating bull

of a poet told us/ Our cunts are ugly – why didn't we/ admit we have thought so too?'
(Levertov 1986: 57). Levertov deals with the same theme of internalised self-hatred projected onto the body as that of the black homosexual writer James Baldwin who drew on W.
E. B. Du Bois' concept of double-consciousness as 'this sense of always looking at one's self
through the eyes of others, of measuring one's soul by the tape of a world that looks on in
amused contempt and pity' (Du Bois 1994: 2). Although the women's movement would not
begin for another four or five years, women writers were drawing on the insights of male
black writers who were at the centre of the Civil Rights movement. Baldwin's *The Fire Next
Time* was an immensely successful publication of 1963. Taking its title from an old slave
song, it advises resistance to humiliation and to the internalisation of the white man's image
of the Negro, and, like Friedan – and in a way Plath and Sexton – draws on a problematic
identification with the figure of the Jew as concentration camp victim.

Madness and the 'Myth of the Artist'

> Madness and booze, madness and booze.
> Which'll can tell who preceded whose?
>
> >   (John Berryman, 'Pereant qui ante nos nostra dixerunt')

If there is one authorial construct that perhaps subsumes all others and proves most problematic, and most crucial, for women writers in 1963, it is what Alvarez would later refer
to as 'the myth of the artist'. Alvarez defines it as a 'general belief – by the public as well as
the artists – that the work and the life are not only inextricable but also virtually indistinguishable' (Alvarez 2005: 196). The myth took sustenance from the enormous influence
of Freud, particularly in the US, in the 1950s and early 1960s. Many of the writers mentioned were in analysis or drew explicitly on the Freudian grand narrative of the family
romance: Friedan, for example, saw Freud as the most important single source of the feminine mystique. Edmund Wilson's influential essay, 'Philoctetes: The Wound and the Bow'
(1941) had explicitly married the Greek tale of the wounded artist to the Freudian account
of the grounding of art in neurosis, pain and suffering. The Freudian account of art also
offers in this way a parable of creation: of the emergence of order out of the chaos of sensation and the biological drives. This idea of artistic creativity gives to the Freudian
account the transferred resonance of the Greek and Judeo-Christian theodicy, for art, creativity, is the place in this life where, in the end, we find our happiness or not at all. In the
absence of an operative deity, the biological drives which are the origin of the unconscious
now become the source and bedrock of our cultural redemption, our modern version of
divine inspiration.

The myth was also revived by R. D. Laing at the beginning of the 1960s and almost immediately taken up by a number of writers, including Doris Lessing and Norman Mailer, who
were searching for a justification of art as an antidote to an instrumentally rationalist culture
of mediocrity and conformism. In Laing's account, all madness, including the frenzy of the
creative artist, is a refusal of the slave morality whose violence destroys those ascetic fictions
which compel our conformity through internalised guilt and shame. His work is pervaded
with the metaphor of the Dionysian as daybreak, of madness as breakthrough. The main
source for 'the myth of the artist', however, was Nietzsche's reworking of the Dionysian
legacy of German Romantic thinkers, for whom Dionysus stood as a symbol of the poetic
imagination, into a fully-fledged aesthetic anti-rationalism. In Nietzsche's writings,

Dionysus comes to stand as a symbol of psychic renewal through a self-dissolution involving an ecstatic release of the instincts in primordial ritual.

The writer who most closely appropriates the myth in its full Nietzschean form in 1963 is Norman Mailer, who draws together the myth of the Fisher King – of the US as both waste land and wounded body, diseased and carcinogenic – together with the myth of Dionysus as a mode of 'disease as cure', of art as an outgrowth of the wounded psyche yet also as a means of cultural redemption even at the expense of the artist's own sanity. Mailer too calls to the original fantasy of the re-incorporation of the savage god, or the stranger within, who must be acknowledged as a prerequisite for psychic renewal in a world controlled by scientific rationality, technology and the 'stultifying techniques' of mass culture. In *The Presidential Papers*, he argues of the US that

> our history has moved on two rivers, one visible, the other underground; there has been the history of politics which is concrete, practical . . . and there is the subterranean river of untapped, ferocious, lonely and romantic desires, that concentration of ecstasy and violence which is the dream life of the nation. (Mailer 1968: 57, 51)

Mailer draws on the myth of Dionysus as a way of integrating the two and breaking down boundaries between the public and the private, the mythopoeic and the documentary. As described in A. Alvarez's study *The Savage God* (1971), the revival of the myth in relation to art is largely understood as an activity of the Few in response to the Many, of the artist as a wounded God attempting to redeem the consumer-driven herd or, as Plath would describe them in 'Lady Lazarus', 'the peanut-crunching crowd'. Similar views appear in John Fowles's *The Aristos* and *The Collector* and in David Storey's *Radcliffe*, each published in 1963–4 and portraying wounded artists and the Dioysian sources of the poetic.

Part of Alvarez's argument, though, is that having created myths of themselves 'as a by-product of creating art, they finished by sacrificing themselves to those essentially trivial myths' (Alvarez 2005: 201). This is his reading of both Plath's suicide and her final poems. It would stand alongside a number of alternative myths, including that of Ted Hughes himself who draws on the myth of the White Goddess to read (and rearrange) the final poems so that they reflect what he tries to argue was an elemental emergence of Plath's voice out of the dumbness of the 'primitive . . . female', with the birth of her first child in April 1959. But in formulating the concept of 'the myth of the artist', Alvarez was later anxious to deny that he wrote *The Savage God* in 1971 to endorse the myth as the idea that extreme art may only be justified by an extreme life, pain, suffering, madness and suicide. He is at pains to argue that his position had always been that madness is no substitute or necessary prelude to creativity. But the myth certainly flourished in both Britain and the US: Berryman cursed a 'god who has wrecked this generation' and talks of poetry as an operation 'of great delicacy' that he performs upon himself (Berryman 1990: 74); Theodore Roethke wrote about a quest for self-induced Dionysian poetic inspiration and then died of drink-related illness towards the end of the year. Lowell, in interview, talked of a generic disease of madness afflicting the artists of his time; Sexton wrote poems of suicide-envy and referred to the way in which she and Plath had 'sucked' on death. The poet B. S. Johnson published his first experimental novel, *Travelling People*, in 1963, inventing a mode of mixed metafiction and confession which for Jonathan Coe, his biographer, launched him as 'Britain's one-man literary avant-garde of the 1960s' (Coe 2004: 3). He too saw writing as a mode of confession, of removing 'from myself, from my mind, the burden of having to bear some pain, the hurt of some experience' (Johnson 1973: 18). He too committed suicide a few years later.

So why does Alvarez insist that the myth was based on and grew out of the 'terrible precedent set by Sylvia Plath'? (Alvarez 2005: 196). Why has this most aristocratic and masculine of myths become so identified with a thirty-year-old middle-class American woman poet? Plath certainly talked of art as something which might 'heal her bloody private wounds' (Plath 2004: 188), but as we have seen, she was hardly alone in this in the early years of the 1960s, and unlike Berryman, for example, she never wrote explicitly of the need to sacrifice one's self for one's art. Almost every writer who publishes in 1963 plays with the myth of the artist, identifying with it one moment and subverting it the next, caught between a desire to locate the sources of the self in some foundational version of an unconscious or the body, or to construct the self openly as an aesthetic project, a performance or play with words. This is as true for the Lowell circle in the US as for Larkin in Britain; for Mailer, Burroughs, Thomas Pynchon, Kurt Vonnegut in the US as for Fowles, B. S. Johnson, Spark, Lessing, Storey and Drabble in Britain. Plath is no exception and, if anything, the Gothic play with the Freudian grand narrative in 'Daddy' or the parody of feminine stereotypes in 'Lady Lazarus' are explicit warnings against naïve expressive realist readings. Did Plath, the artist, 'play tag with death' in her poems, as Philip Larkin suggested, until the art overwhelmed the life, or did the circumstances of the life and the instability in her personality finally destroy both? (Larkin 1983: 201). How should we read the construction of Plath as author, and what light does this throw on the situation of the woman writer in general in the early 1960s?

Death

> Dying
> Is an art, like everything else.
> I do it exceptionally well.
>
> (Sylvia Plath, 'Lady Lazarus')

London, 1963: 'an unspeakable winter, the worst, they said, in 150 years. The snow began just after Christmas and would not let up. By New Year the whole country had ground to a halt . . . Nerves failed and marriages crumbled. Finally the heart failed. It seemed the cold would never end' (Alvarez 1974: 48). On 11 February, 1963, the body of Sylvia Plath was discovered by an Australian *au pair*, arriving new that morning to help take care of Plath's children after the separation from Ted Hughes a few months earlier. The first full account of what she found appeared in Alvarez's *The Savage God* in a passage which seems to echo the opening of Dickens's *Bleak House* (1853) with its references to implacable weather. It has something also of the tone of Virginia Woolf's *Orlando* (1928) in the famous and whimsical description of the Great Frost of London in the early seventeenth century. For Plath, writing in her journal in 1957, England had begun as a dream, a hope for the future, and for escape from the contradictions of the feminine mystique. For Alvarez, however, this is England, dominated by the 'gentility' described in his influential Introduction to *The New Poetry* in 1962: a place where people and poets alike had failed to respond to the apocalyptic realities of the times.

Plath was different, one who had lived the 'myth of the artist' and now, as in a costume drama, here is her body and there on the table is a black spring binder containing the forty last poems which would be edited and rearranged by Hughes for publication as *Ariel* (1965). In theatricalised language, Alvarez himself describes the discovery of the body thoroughly in the performative terms of the 'myth of the artist'. And since then, Plath has been read again and again as both the dramatist and the tragic heroine of her own Gothic plot, as Muse to her own autopoetic voice, whose suicidal drive is motivated by a desire to hone her body into the cold perfection of words. Elizabeth Hardwick, for example, would write: 'Orestes rages, but Aeschylus lives to be almost seventy. Sylvia Plath, however, is both heroine and author; when the curtain goes down, it is her own dead body there on the stage, sacrificed to her own plot' (Hardwick 1974: 107). But Plath's was not the only sacrifice that year to the 'myth of the artist'. Berryman would later express his sense of belonging to a doomed generation in Song 153 of *The Dream Songs*, with some interesting additions to the list of fatalities: 'I'm cross with god who has wrecked this generation./ First he seized Ted, then Richard, Randall, and now Delmore./ In between he gorged on Sylvia Plath' (Berryman 1993: 172). Berryman, Sexton and Lowell all wrote obituaries of Plath in the form of poems which play out a complex identification with the lure of death and sacrifice, and also express a thanatopic envy about what Sexton, for example, refers to as 'the death I wanted so badly and for so long' (Sexton 1981: 126).

Plath is read then by her contemporaries as fodder to the God who must be paid his due (though he is often converted in the poems themselves to a sinister Muse, gendered female, and associated with the moon). Anne Stevenson, in her controversial biography of Plath tried to dismiss the 'myth of the artist' as 'akin to the beliefs of fundamental religious fanatics', an offence against the canons of good sense and reason. Yet, like Alvarez, who is regarded as an arch-enemy, she too blames Plath *herself* for the myth:

> no art, no 'great' poem is worth that much human suffering . . . I believe Sylvia, encouraged perhaps by her Freudian and well-meaning therapist, Ruth Beutscher, found her own psychodrama (a word I prefer to 'mythology') so intoxicating . . . that she lost all perspective. (Malcolm 2005: 80)

Again then, Plath is effectively read as instigator of a myth that it was virtually impossible not to be caught up in at the time she is writing. I am not suggesting that she did not at some level, and in spite of the antic play, the teasing and *danse macabre* of identifications and stage performances, finally buy into the myth, but she certainly did not spin it fresh out of her own entrails. This is to read her without taking account of the historical and cultural context in which she was writing. Her last poems would inevitably be construed as a series of suicide notes leading to that final eradication of the body and purification of an artistic legacy where, 'this is a case without a body./ The body does not come into it at all' (Plath 2004: 31). The 1965 edition of *Ariel* finished with the self-reflexivity of 'Words' where the words of the poem, 'dry and riderless' (writerless?), are juxtaposed against the 'bottom of the pool' where 'fixed stars/ Govern a life'. Or in the penultimate poem, 'Edge', where the body of the woman is finally eradicated altogether. Wearing the 'smile of accomplishment/ The illusion of a Greek necessity', she is perfected ekphrastically in marble, but actually of course in the Grecian urn, the burial urn, the well-wrought urn, which is the poem itself. 'Edge' seems to enact the transformation of corpse into corpus as the Muse (the moon) reclaims her daughter, 'staring from her hood of bone' with the final Gothic line, 'her blacks crackle and drag' suggesting a kind of electric current, a dark Barbarella of artistic inspiration (Plath 1965: 85–6). Plath is both poet and Muse to herself.

The body as waste, fodder for the god Dionysus, is of course part of the myth of the artist – but it must have been especially alluring for a woman writer like Plath, caught up in the contradictions of the feminine mystique. From this gendered perspective, the body was not simply a sacrifice to the Muse, but also perceived as the source of that debarment from 'transcendence' which de Beauvoir had read as the heart of the myth of immanence of the Eternal Feminine. In turning herself into words, Plath escaped one myth, only to fall willing victim perhaps, to the other. Throughout her *Journals*, Plath is anxious to separate talk, speech (implicitly associated with the feminine, and the physical), from writing as a stern – and properly artistic – vocation. Again, we are back to the problem of confession and its gendered associations: talk, chat, is endlessly associated with women – women come and go in rooms, talking of Michelangelo – and when Woolf famously invoked her image of the Angel in the House in 'Professions for Women', she metonymically represented her as a voice, slipping behind the woman poised with her pen, whispering and assuaging, supplicatory, ever soft and low, advising flattery and submissiveness. She might be killed with an inkpot, but dies hard. A blank page remains, rather like David Hume's famous image of the newborn consciousness, a blank slate awaiting the impress of experience and with no innate content of its own. In her very earliest journal, written while still a teenager, Plath repeatedly refers to a sense of not possessing her own experiences until she had *written them down*, 'my happiness streams from having wrenched a piece out of my life, a piece of hurt and beauty, and transformed it to typewritten words on paper' (Plath 2004: 22). Almost the last words she would write: 'riderless words'.

Resisting Myths of the Artist and of the Angel

1963: the best of years and the worst of years. 1963 stands poised between the failed rationalist utopias of modernity, those visions of the Good which had led to pogroms and genocide, and the postmodern utopianism of the counter-culture, with its identity politics and anti-rationalisms. In this situation, in essays published that year as *The Dyer's Hand*, W. H. Auden discusses the responsibilities of the writer in contemporary mass society, warning against abuses of the magical in art, and the potential ethical dangers of unrestrained aestheticism. His views were close to those of his friend, the philosopher Hannah Arendt, whose controversial *Eichmann in Jerusalem* also appeared in 1963. Ostensibly a report on the Eichmann trial of 1961, it was also a continuation of Arendt's preoccupation with the human craving for meaning. Arendt sees this expressed in the need to tell stories, but sees also its dangerous possibilities when mythopoeic craving finds release in the construction of world-historical logics and utopian thinking which project perfect aesthetic orders onto the contingency and muddle of history.

The theme became central to the ethically motivated metafictions of Thomas Pynchon's *V.*, Kurt Vonnegut's, *Cat's Cradle* and John Fowles' *The Collector*, all published in 1963, and to John Updike's examination of the 'myth of the artist' in *The Centaur*. There are similarities, too, between Updike's half-realist, half-mythic novel and two others published in Britain that year, Iris Murdoch's *The Unicorn* and Muriel Spark's *The Girls of Slender Means*, which interrogate the myth through concepts of truth provided, respectively, by Platonic philosophy and by Catholic theology. Iris Murdoch's novel exposes fiction-makers as fantasists and locates its vision of the good in the only character who refuses both the contemporary gratifications of the 'myth of the artist' and the compensatory fictions it generates. Escaping the world-absorbing egomania of male artist-narrators and enchanters, goodness in Murdoch's fiction is more often discovered in the muted responses of women characters or 'feminised' males who accept the contingent, the brute materiality of the world. In all three novels, the strenuous attempt to live the Good Life leads to suffering or death, and the 'myth of the artist' is presented as a potentially dangerous fantasy, harming the other as well as the self.

Again, however, even these three philosophically subtle writers are only partially aware of the gender implications of their critique. For surely part of the lure of the myth of the artist for women writers in 1963 was its promise of escape from the gender-specific myth of the 'Angel in the House'. Though Murdoch, for example, seems to associate the Good with feminisation or femininity, the myth of the Angel as pure altruism had placed the role of authorship almost entirely out of bounds for women, by identifying writing with egotism and selfishness. The gradual and full exposure of these complex and buried aspects of the 'feminine mystique' would take years of feminist effort. What women writers had begun to discover in 1963, however, was that if the constructions of art and the artist are never gender-neutral, neither are those of the Good and Goodness; nor can they be entirely separated.

References

Alvarez, A. (1974) *The Savage God: A Study of Suicide*, Harmondsworth: Penguin
——(2005) 'The Myth of the Artist', in Corinne Saunders and Jane Macnaughton, eds, *Madness and Creativity in Literature and Culture*, Basingstoke and New York: Palgrave, 194–201
Baldwin, James (1964) *The Fire Next Time*, Harmondsworth: Penguin
Berryman, John (1990) *The Dream Songs*, London: Faber and Faber
Coe, Jonathan (2004) *Like a Fiery Elephant: the Story of B.S. Johnson*, London: Picador
Drabble, Margaret (1967) *A Summer Bird-Cage*, Harmondsworth: Penguin
Du Bois, W. E. B. (1994) *The Souls of Black Folk*, London: Dover
Friedan, Betty (1965) *The Feminine Mystique*, Harmondsworth: Penguin
Hardwick, Elizabeth (1974) *Seduction and Betrayal: Women and Literature*, London: J. M. Dent and Sons
Johnson, B. S. (1973) *Aren't You Rather Young to Be Writing Your Memoirs?*, London: Hutchinson
King, Martin Luther (1985) 'I Have a Dream', *The Words of Martin Luther King*, selected by Coretta Scott King, London: Fount, 95–8
Larkin, Philip (1983) *Required Writing: Miscellaneous Pieces 1955–1982*, London: Faber and Faber
——(1988) *Collected Poems*, London: Faber and Faber
Lessing, Doris (1972) *A Small Personal Voice*, ed. Paul Schleuter, New York: Vintage
——(1973) *The Golden Notebook*, St Albans: Panther
Levertov, Denise (1986) *Selected Poems*, Newcastle: Bloodaxe
Lowell, Robert (1965) 'A Talk with Robert Lowell' (interview with A. Alvarez), *Encounter*, XXIV, February, 39–43
Mailer, Norman (1968) *The Presidential Papers*, Harmondsworth: Penguin
——(1992) *Advertisements for Myself*, Cambridge, MA, and London: Harvard University Press
Malcolm, Janet (2005) *The Silent Woman: Sylvia Plath and Ted Hughes*, London: Granta

Marcuse, Herbert (1964) *One-Dimensional Man*, London: Routledge

Plath, Sylvia (1963) *The Bell Jar*, London: Faber and Faber

——(1965) *Ariel*, London: Faber and Faber

——(2000) *The Journals of Sylvia Plath 1950–62*, ed. Karen V. Kukil, London: Faber and Faber

——(2004) *Ariel; the Restored Edition*, London: Faber and Faber

Sexton, Anne (1981) *The Complete Poems*, Boston, MA: Houghton Mifflin

Steiner, George (1969) *Language and Silence*, Harmondsworth: Penguin

IV: Millennium Approaches

Chapter 15

1967, Liverpool, London, San Francisco, Vietnam: 'We Hope You Will Enjoy the Show'

John Hellmann

In the August 1967 issue of *Atlantic* magazine, John Barth argued in his 'Literature of Exhaustion' that forms and modes of art can be used up. Speaking years later, Barth pointed out, 'I wrote the essay in 1967 . . . in the middle of a very apocalyptic time in the history of our republic . . . a time when people could be forgiven for wondering whether a lot of institutions were falling apart' (Reilly 1981: 7). Barth cited the disturbances on university campuses and Marshall McLuhan's claims in his *The Medium is the Massage* (1967) that the age of print was over.

The sense that history as well as the forms and functions of art and literature were on the verge of epoch-making transformation was strong in 1967. The most-discussed and most popular artwork of that year was a rock album, a form that only a few years earlier was not taken seriously even within the hit-singles world of pop music. The Beatles' *Sgt. Pepper's Lonely Hearts Club Band* was released two months before the publication of Barth's essay. The album contains references to different aspects of the time and points to new developments in art and literature. *Sgt. Pepper* is an expression of major currents intersecting among Liverpool, London, San Francisco and Vietnam that reached a pivotal moment in 1967. That intersection produced an emphasis on fantasy, theatre and performance to break through the Cold War ideological 'consensus' and imagine new artistic possibilities beyond the premises of modernism.

The conceit of the album is that the Beatles are inviting their audience to join them in a theatrical pretence. As Paul McCartney has explained,

> We would be Sgt. Pepper's band, and for the whole of the album we'd pretend to be someone else. So, when John walked up to the microphone to sing, it wouldn't be the new John Lennon vocal, it would be whoever he was in this *new* group, his fantasy character. It liberated you – you could do anything when you got to the mike or on your guitar, because it wasn't *you*. (*Beatles Anthology* 2000: 241)

The Beatles wanted to transcend the limits of their image as mass-entertainers of adolescents and of pop music as determined by audience expectations. After initial sounds of a pit orchestra tuning up and an audience stirring in their seats, in the guise of the Sgt. Pepper band the Beatles open the album with the title song, in which they parody old-time music-hall performers who in turn pretend to their audience that 'we'd like to take you home with us', a line then repeated with an ambiguous play on the destination meant by 'home' – 'we'd love to take you home' – suggesting in the fantasy-songs to come a more fundamental return to primal consciousness and community. A similar double-meaning is present in their music-hall assurance that 'We hope you will enjoy the show'. Before introducing the first real song of the pretended revue, McCartney steps forward to caution that, while 'I don't really want to stop the show', he wants them to know that the singer is about to 'sing a song' and that he 'wants you all to sing along'. As this introduction segues into the first song of the fictional performance, the fictional audience is heard to shriek in excitement, perhaps an allusion to the screaming fans of Beatlemania that they have left behind with their decision to stop touring. In inviting their fictional audience to join with their fictional alter egos in turning away from their previous 'reality' in favour of a self-conscious performance or 'show', a playful inhabiting of a fantasy self and a fantasy communal relation, the Beatles were adopting a strategy that was emerging as a major tendency of the 1960s. In his novels Barth had already moved away from realistic representation toward an exuberant performance of his powers of parody, self-reference and fantasy in *The Sot-Weed Factor* (1960) and *Giles Goat-Boy* (1966). In his 'Literature of Exhaustion' essay Barth characterised these two works as 'novels which imitate the form of the Novel, by an author who imitates the role of author' (Barth 1967: 33). In *Giles Goat-Boy* George reflects that 'I looked upon my life and the lives of others as a kind of theatrical impromptu, self-knowledge as a kind of improvisation, and moral injunctions . . . whether high-minded or wicked, as so many stage directions' (Barth 1966: 81). In the literature and art of the 1960s parody served as a means of calling attention to the artifice of established forms and relations, thus opening artist and audience to the imagining of a new 'show'.

The suspicion that a monolithic 'reality' might simply be a fantasy contrived by a person or persons with greater power catalysed intimations of the absurd. By 1967 laughter had become a major way of refusing to play straight man. The Beatles' readiness to satirise and subvert had been much on display in 1964 when they stepped off the plane for the first time in the United States, a strategy for holding at bay the absurdities and pressures of their career. At the airport press conference they responded to reporters' questions:

> 'Will you sing something for us?'
> 'We need money first', said John.
> 'How do you account for your success?'
> 'We have a press agent'.
> 'What is your ambition?'
> 'To come to America'.
> 'Do you hope to get haircuts?'
> 'We had one yesterday'.
> 'Do you hope to take anything home with you?'
> 'The Rockefeller Center'.
> 'Are you part of a social rebellion against the older generation?'
> 'It's a dirty lie'.
> 'What about the movement in Detroit to stamp out Beatles?'
> 'We have a campaign to stamp out Detroit'.
> 'What do you think of Beethoven?'
> 'I love him', said Ringo. 'Especially his poems'.

(Davies 1968: 220)

With their origins in the grimy port city of Liverpool, the Beatles had grown up in a working-class culture in which a cheeky mockery and flip rudeness were a favoured form of confrontation. When *Sgt. Pepper* reaches its apocalyptic conclusion with a solemn chord that sustains for nearly a full minute, a brief coda answers it with mocking laughter and a maniacally chanted 'it never could be any other way'. Such absurdist laughter reflected and influenced a broader artistic and literary response of their age. At the middle of the decade Bruce Jay Friedman assembled a collection of contemporary authors' work entitled *Black Humor* (1965). He described the movement as novelists determined 'to take a preposterous world by the throat and say okay, be preposterous, but also make damned sure you explain yourself' (Friedman 1965: xi).

Joseph Heller's *Catch-22* (1961) was the first and most famous of the many novels during the decade that adopted this stance. Heller's novel refuses to accept the rationalist premises of the military-industrial complex, using comic exaggeration and shocking juxtaposition to human pain and death to make visible the ridiculous effects produced by remote and abstract power. The title phrase is Heller's name for the ability of bureaucratic power to always invoke a supposed 'rule' that justifies its other rules, however absurd. For instance, when Doc Daneeka rejects Yossarian's request to stop flying bombing missions on the grounds that he is insane, Daneeka invokes Catch-22 as the rule that says that if a man shows a concern for his own safety he is demonstrating a rational mind and therefore he is not insane. As Charles B. Harris observes, while Heller set the novel in the American military in the Second World War, his target was 'bureaucratic power' (Harris 1971: 35), and his satire echoed the complaints about the postwar United States of sociologist C. Wright Mills in *The Power Elite* (1956) and psychologist Paul Goodman in *Growing Up Absurd* (1960). Heller's perception so resonated in the social awareness of the 1960s that 'catch-22' entered the language as a common lament concerning the power of bureaucracy to disguise its absurdity in 'rational' discourse with which it was useless to argue. Similar protests emanated from other writers. Kurt Vonnegut wrote a send-up of the reverence for science and religious piety during the Cold War in *Cat's Cradle* (1963). The shipwrecked Lionel Boyd Johnson, who has become the 'prophet' Bokonon, voices a black-humourist view of the supreme virtue urged by the liberal ideological consensus during the Cold War: 'Maturity is a bitter disappointment for which no remedy exists, unless laughter can be said to remedy anything' (Vonnegut 1963:134). Terry Southern brought the black-humour approach to the 1964 screenplay about the possibility of nuclear war that he co-wrote with director Stanley Kubrick. The film was an adaptation of Peter George's novel *Red Alert*, first published in Britain as *Two Hours to Doom* (1958). Deciding to alter the melodramatic and jingoistic tone, Kubrick hired the author of *The Magic Christian* (1959). Southern brought his talent for absurdist comedy to the screenplay, 'beginning with', as Kubrick's biographer reports, 'its retitling as *Dr. Strangelove or How I Learned to Stop Worrying and Love the Bomb*' (Baxter 1997: 177). 'Dr. Strangelove' would join 'Catch-22' as part of the vernacular of the 1960s.

Disaffection from social 'reality' led from comic absurdity to dreams of escape. One of the finest songs on *Sgt. Pepper* is 'Lucy in the Sky with Diamonds'. Taking up another meaning of the album's 'show' frame, Lennon begins the song with an imperative to 'Picture yourself in a boat on a river'. The suggestion is that the singer is to sit back and watch images flow by from the unconscious. A childlike vision of Eden is presented, consisting of such surreal images as 'tangerine trees and marmalade skies', complete with a dazzling feminine archetype, the 'girl with kaleidoscope eyes' that in an interview Lennon identified as 'the image of the female who would someday come save me' (*Beatles Anthology*

2000: 242). The Beatles insisted that the 'drug song' with its initials LSD was actually inspired by a drawing Lennon's son had brought home and that the images were drawn from *Alice in Wonderland* (*Beatles Anthology* 2000: 242). Their explanation points to the broad role of fantasy in the 1960s, whether achieved through hallucinogens, conscious imitation of childlike innocence, or literature's return to fable.

During 1967 critic Robert Scholes published *The Fabulators* (1967), later reissued in expanded form under a new name. Scholes' influential book drew an analogy between British and American fiction during the decade and dream, asserting that both provide 'an imaginative experience which is necessary to our imaginative well-being' (Scholes 1979: 24). In Britain Iris Murdoch took her protagonists and readers on a self-conscious and allegorical journey back to the Gothic romance in *The Unicorn* (1963). In her *The Sea, the Sea* (1978) Murdoch uses a self-doubting Prospero-like narrator who worries about the morality of imposing either his 'reality' on other people or his words on 'reality' in his journal. In *The Magus* (1965) John Fowles revisits *The Tempest* in a parallel way. His 'angry young man' travels to a Greek island where he finds life re-enchanted by a series of fantastic and erotic adventures orchestrated by a mysterious figure suggestively named Conchis. In his subsequent *The French Lieutenant's Woman* (1969) Fowles dramatises himself as author figure. He self-consciously imitates the voice and manner of the Victorian novelist in this tale of nineteenth-century love, while at the same time positioning his narrative persona in the twentieth century. At a climactic moment, with self-displaying bravado, he enters his created world as a character who manipulates it at will. Emerging in the 1960s as a recoil from realism's attempts to imitate the surfaces of social life, as well as modernism's plumbing of the interior depths of consciousness, this new mode of fiction would only in the next decade acquire the periodising label associated with it down to the present: postmodern fiction.

Fiction writers returned to fable to break free of the forms of a 'fiction' within which white male upper-class ideology had sealed itself, closing off too many possibilities. This fiction ran parallel to a social dislocation underway in Britain and America. In both countries the 1960s witnessed an extraordinary move away from conventional behaviour, giving new meaning to perennial forms of internal migration: toward the capital, in Britain, westward in the United States. On *Sgt. Pepper* the Beatles include an aching tale called 'She's Leaving Home' of a young woman leaving her parents in search of something that had been missing: 'stepping outside she is free'. In Britain youth gravitated to London to make their mark in fashion, photography, art and music while creating the world of mini-skirts and drugs known as 'swinging London'. In addition to the youthful artistic and social revolution in Britain, by the mid-1960s a counter-culture of disaffected youth was revolting against the values, morals and norms of American society. In the United States a conspicuous minority followed the 'on the road' impulse of the 1950s Beats to run away from home to the bohemian Haight-Ashbury district of San Francisco. During the 'summer of love' of 1967, as Terry H. Anderson points out, the '75,000 who visited the Haight that summer returned home or to their campuses with different values' (Anderson 2004: 99). Communes began springing up that abandoned the nuclear family and practised various forms of drug use and free love, an impulse celebrated on *Sgt. Pepper* with the song 'A Little Help from My Friends'. According to historian James T. Patterson, between 1965 and 1975 'some 10,000 such experiments blossomed in the country' (Patterson 1996: 447). In a move analogous to psychedelic-drug guru Timothy Leary's exhortation to 'tune in, turn on, and drop out', fiction authors were offering their readers alternative visions of what could be real. With the issues of black Civil Rights and the Vietnam War, the move away from the familiar became for many in the United States also a move toward radical politics. In *The*

Crying of Lot 49 (1966) Thomas Pynchon's conventional housewife Oedipa Maas has already experimented with adultery early in the novel in attempting to liberate herself from an empty marriage. Pursuing mysterious 'signs' of an underground communication system known by the acronym WASTE, she goes to the Berkeley campus of the University of California to find

> a plaza teeming with corduroy, denim, bare legs, blonde hair, hornrims, bicycle spokes in the sun, bookbags, swaying card tables, long paper petitions dangling to earth, posters for undecipherable FSMs, YAFs, VDCs, suds in the fountain, students in nose-to-nose dialogue. (Pynchon 1999: 82–3)

Oedipa, a member of the 1950s' 'silent generation', has come upon the campus ferment of the 1960s. The 'undecipherable' signs proclaim the 1964 Free Speech Movement (FSM), in which activists, returned from the Civil Rights struggle during Freedom Summer in the South, revolted against the repression of a university administration that saw itself as wielding parental authority; the Young Americans for Freedom (YAF), a conservative organisation that questioned the liberal ideological consensus from the right; and the 1965 Vietnam Day Committee (VDC), which early opposed the bombing of North Vietnam and the massive intervention of regular American troops in South Vietnam.

'Preposterous' news, and the unfamiliar spectacles offered by radicals and hippies, pressured the methods of journalists as well as writers of realistic fiction. The Beatles begin the song that closes *Sgt. Pepper* with Lennon's telling the listener that 'I read the news today oh boy' about a man who 'blew his mind out in a car'. The singer relates that he had to 'laugh' when he saw the 'photograph'. McCartney has said that the lines were intended as a commentary on history:

> Malcolm Muggeridge said that all history is a lie, because every fact that gets reported gets distorted. Even in the Battle of Hastings, King Harold didn't die with an arrow in his eye; that's just what the Bayeux tapestry says – they put it in because it looked better. (*Beatles Anthology* 2000: 247)

The power of representation, with its inevitable distortions of actual events and persons, emerged as a major concern. As Patterson observes, 'it was in the 1960s that TV came into its own as a major force in American life, promoting a more national culture while at the same time casting its eye on profound internal divisions' (Patterson 1996: 446–7). Television brought urban riots and Black Panthers, hippies and happenings, assassinations and mass murderers directly into suburban living rooms, but it did little to explain them or even to provide the context by which to try to understand them. Newspapers and the weekly news magazines looked through the prism of a limited ideological consensus and conventional formulas. In response writers such as Tom Wolfe, Joan Didion and Norman Mailer produced a 'new journalism' in which the topic was the subjective, interior experience of persons and events beyond the 'norms' of the middle range of experience explored by realism and modernism. In January 1967 the counter-culture presented itself to the mass media in San Francisco's Golden Gate Park when disaffected youth showed themselves with a demonstration of clothes, art and rituals called the Human Be-In, or Gathering of Tribes. Wolfe approached this material with the journalistic contract promising adherence to observation, either his own or that of his subjects, and a readiness to use the whole range of resources developed in fiction for the expressionistic depiction of extreme states of consciousness. In *The Electric Kool-Aid Acid Test* (1968) he constructs a comprehensible history of the success of Ken Kesey and his Merry Pranksters in creating 'this new San Francisco-L.A. LSD thing, with wacked-out kids and delirious rock'n'roll' (Wolfe 1999: 283–4).

In *The Armies of the Night: History as a Novel/The Novel as History* (1968) Mailer sets up *Time* magazine as his major antagonist among a media creating a 'forest of inaccuracy' (Mailer 1994: 219) in their portrayal of the October 1967 march on the Pentagon in protest against the Vietnam war. Reflecting in tranquillity upon his experience as one of the protesters arrested that day, Mailer casts his participating self as 'our comic hero' and uses him as 'the narrative vehicle for the March on the Pentagon' (Mailer 1994: 54). Mailer has thus brought Barth's strategy of writing 'novels which imitate the form of the Novel, by an author who imitates the role of author' to a journalistic representation that acknowledges its own necessary artifice. It was left to Hunter S. Thompson to take this approach to the point where the 'performing selves' of the fabulist Barth and new journalist Mailer could logically meet. In 1967 he published his account of riding with the notorious San Francisco-area outlaw motorcycle gang, *Hell's Angels: A Strange and Terrible Saga* (1967). By the end of the 1960s he had created a schizophrenic persona, divided playfully into the two characters Dr Hunter S. Thompson and Raoul Duke (both names appeared on the masthead of the counter-culture music magazine *Rolling Stone*, first published in 1967). In *Fear and Loathing in Las Vegas: A Savage Journey to the Heart of the American Dream* (1971) Thompson presents his journalistic report as the fabulist product of a wildly unreliable narrator who might be a uniquely American seer, 'Horatio Alger gone mad on drugs in Las Vegas' (Thompson 1971: 12).

In 1967 the new journalists were participating in yet another 'confusion of realms', the breaking down of the modernist distinction between high and low culture. *Sgt. Pepper* presented itself as mass entertainment as high art. The tinted-collage cover took Andy Warhol and other 1960s Pop artists at their word, returning the mass-market form that they had re-framed for the elite museum and re-framing it for the consumer bin. The cover was designed by Peter Blake, an accomplished and conspicuous British Pop artist. The collage asserts the breakdown of distinctions by gathering together a crowd of famous images from philosophy (Karl Marx), literature (Edgar Allan Poe), movies (Marilyn Monroe), and history/movies/fantasy (Peter O'Toole as T. E. Lawrence as Lawrence of Arabia). The Beatles appear as both the Fab Four in the waxwork figures preserved at Madame Tussaud's museum and in their vibrant new fantasy as Sgt. Pepper's band; all belong simply because they are characters the Beatles 'liked' (*Beatles Anthology* 2000: 248). The music within likewise alludes to whatever sources the Beatles found in their culture, from the noises of Saturday morning cartoon animals ('Good Morning, Good Morning') to themes and imagery echoing W. B. Yeats and T. S. Eliot ('A Day in the Life').

Hovering to the right and slightly elevated above the rest of the crowd is the face of Bob Dylan. Dylan first won an audience within the folk music community, which in the early years of the decade had sought to achieve a purity by refusing the bread and circuses of mass entertainment. Observing the energy catalysed by the Beatles, Dylan had by 1965 begun putting aside folk-based melodies and acoustic instrumentation for electrified rock'n'roll. Dylan insisted that art and literature should not be confined to museums, to the stage or to shelves but rather be present 'where people hang out' (Ephron 2004: 68). Dylan's success in transforming pop music into a realm for an individualistic, romantic and avant-garde sensibility dismayed purists' concept of a folk community untainted by mass commerce. Theodor Adorno held that popular music was actually mass culture, forced to conform to the dictates from corporate elites, but, as Mike Marqusee observes in his *Chimes of Freedom: The Politics of Bob Dylan's Art* (2003), Adorno 'discounted the complex impact of the new popular access to traditional music' (Marqusee 2003: 184). Dylan and the Beatles, along with the Rolling Stones, were able to select from and critically reconfigure a diverse range of sources to address contemporary concerns in new aesthetic forms. Dylan drew upon both white and black American folk sources from different regions of the country that had been widely made available by Harry Smith in his multiple-LP *Anthology of American Folk Music*. Growing up in a conventional middle-class home in London, Mick Jagger of the Rolling Stones listened to African-American blues records; he agreed with his father's description of it as 'jungle music' but found it 'the most real thing I'd ever known' ('Mick Jagger' 1971: 45). The Beatles' George Harrison vastly expanded the sources of rock music to include Indian classical music. The Beatles, Rolling Stones and Dylan influenced each other in fulfilling McLuhan's global village while defying Adorno's view of a strictly top-down culture. All three of these musical artists wrote original songs that spoke so compellingly to the new youth audience of consumers that they wrested creative control from musical companies who could not reject such successful 'product'.

In San Francisco, the folk-rock bands that developed in response to the British bands and Dylan soon brought together their own experiences in the local drug culture and their own folk roots in bluegrass and country to create psychedelic music. They in turn influenced the Beatles. McCartney visited America and came back to London with the idea of parodying the long and deliberately anachronistic names of such San Francisco bands as Big Brother and the Holding Company and Country Joe and the Fish with the fictional alter egos of Sgt. Pepper's Lonely Hearts Club Band (*Beatles Anthology* 2000: 241). Leonard Cohen, having established himself as a poet and novelist in Canada, debuted as a singer-songwriter at the Newport Folk Festival during the summer of 1967, and before the year was over the crooner Noel Harrison (son of the musical-comedy star Rex Harrison) took Cohen's 'Suzanne' onto the pop charts. Two other Canadian singer-songwriters became part of the burgeoning rock scene in 1967. Neil Young joined the California band Buffalo Springfield, while Joni Mitchell signed her first record contract. Both would prove to be relentless experimenters, with Mitchell moving from her early confessional folk songs to forays into the world music that would become so pervasive by the end of the century. As Barth and other elite fiction writers played upon the narrowing confines of an 'exhausted' white male upper-class ideology and experience, young rock performers were drawing on a diverse range of energy from its borderlines: the blues of African-American victims of slavery and Jim Crow, the high-art and religious music of Indians formerly subjects of the British Raj, the music hall of the British working class, combining them with chamber music and avant-garde European movements.

The 'swinging London' of the Beatles, Rolling Stones, Mary Quant's mini-fashions and David Bailey's photography was the creation of youthful members of the working and lower middle classes of the port city of Liverpool and other margins of the old class structure. In 1965 the International Poetry Incarnation at the Albert Hall drew 7,000 people, many of whom sat in boxes sharing wine, marijuana and conversation. American Beat poet Allen Ginsberg, in town to meet with the touring Dylan and the Beatles, read a new poem with the title 'Who Be Kind To' celebrating 'The Liverpool Minstrels of Cavernsink . . . in electric Africa hurrah' (Marqusee 2003: 130). During his stay in London, Ginsberg made a trip to Liverpool, which he proclaimed to be 'at the present time the center of consciousness of the human universe' (Miles 2004: 79). Brian Patten, Adrian Henri and Roger McGough became known as the Liverpool Poets as they followed the ebullient spirit of their town's famed musicians. In 1967 Penguin devoted a volume to the Liverpool Poets entitled *The Mersey Sound* (1967). In 'Tonight at Noon' Henri combined the visionary catalogues of Ginsberg and Dylan, announcing a world in which 'Girls in bikinis are moonbathing' and 'Poets get their poems in the Top 20' (Henri, McGough and Patten 1967: 11). *The Mersey Sound* eventually sold a quarter of a million copies, was still in print at the end of the century, and was a key success for the Penguin Modern Poets series, which in 1963 had also published a volume of Ginsberg, Lawrence Ferlinghetti and Gregory Corso.

If poetry was being drawn out of the quiet lecture hall toward the festival, it was also being drawn by Vietnam toward the demonstration. Poets were moving away from the conscious technique of modernism toward methods that sought a greater role for the unconscious of both poet and audience. At the Albert Hall gathering, expressing his discomfort at watching a 'murderous world' on television, Adrian Mitchell read his poem 'To Whom It May Concern', in which he recited stanzas about 'being run over with the truth' and 'every time I shut my eyes all I see is flames' to conclude each time with the insistent demand 'tell me lies about Vietnam' (Mitchell 1991: 48). In the United States 1967 saw the publication of the anthology *Where Is Vietnam?* (1967). In the preface Walter Lowenfels linked the poets in the volume to Dylan and other songwriters while extolling the 'divine average' constituted by the audience now 'becoming part of the creative scene', for 'when the poem enters somebody else's eye or ear, it . . . enters a new existence in the life of others' (Lowenfels 1967: xii). He also quoted approvingly Denise Levertov's account of 'two mysterious, soulful, non-political dream poems . . . that . . . released, at last, the Vietnam poem' (Lowenfels 1967: xi).

Robert Bly's *The Light Around the Body* (1967) includes 'Counting Small-Boned Bodies'. Secretary of Defense Robert S. McNamara measured achievement in his strategy of attrition through a weekly body count. Bly's body-counter muses that if the bodies could be made 'smaller', perhaps a 'whole year's kill' could be placed 'on a desk!' (Bly 1967: 32). Bly's theme resonates with the Beatles' final image on *Sgt. Pepper* of 'Four thousand holes in Blackburn, Lancashire' that, while 'small', when counted provide the information of how many 'holes' are needed to 'fill the Albert Hall'. The 'four thousand holes' refer to a mining disaster, but the massive job of counting, combined with the calculation that the data can be useful in planning a capacity audience for a spectacle, offers a surreal vision of the connection between victims and spectators conceived only as quantified, useful data in a technocratic corporate capitalism.

Developing the overall 'show' frame, specific songs on *Sgt. Pepper* assert the theatricality of society. In 'Being for the Benefit of Mr. Kite!' Lennon recites the promises of an old circus poster for the night's performance. A fifteen-year-old girl interpreted the song, shortly after its release, as a vision of 'life as an eerie perverted circus' (Christgau 2000: 45). In 1967 this vision was compelling to alternative theatre groups who had been inspired by the 'happenings' of the art world to challenge audiences to wake up from the theatre of their lives. The year before John Cage wrote that 'theatre takes place all the time wherever one is and art simply facilitates persuading one this is the case' (Cage 1966: 174). Influenced by the experimental Polish director Jerzy Grotowski and the 'Theatre of Cruelty' of Antonin Artaud, Peter Brook developed a theatre in London that emphasised the 'power of gesture, mime, movement, and physicality' – powers increasingly deployed by contemporary mainstream playwrights such as Peter Schaffer in *The Royal Hunt of the Sun* (1964) and *Equus* (1970) (Stevenson 2004: 368). Brook directed the show *US* (1966), which included songs with lyrics by Adrian Mitchell protesting the war in Vietnam. The ambiguity of the title sought to break down the distinction between performers and audience, for it simultaneously pointed to the televised carnage perpetrated on the television news by the US and to the viewing audience formed by the British audience, or 'us'.

In this spirit The Living Theatre in the United States was committed to a political activism determined to erase the boundaries separating audience and performers. Led by Julian Beck and his wife Judith Malina, they formed what was in essence a commune of actors. In such plays as *Paradise Now* (1968) its members walked among the audience, complaining of restrictions on their lives and stripping off their own clothes in a model of transformation for the spectator. They sought to create ecstatic experiences consisting of rites, visions and actions that ended with cast and audience members spilling into the street, sometimes in a state approaching nudity that invited arrest by a waiting audience of police. As C. W. E. Bigsby has observed, the premise of these performances was 'that change has to operate internally on the self and externally on society . . . this is the justification for a structure which tries to pull together the private and the public' (Bigsby 1985: 89). The Open Theater, which spun off from the Living Theatre, also entered the public stage of politics. In 1967 they staged Megan Terry's *Viet Rock* (1966), which was developed by the company in workshops and improvisations, countering the media's presentation of the Vietnam War with black humour. Protesters against the war had been using street theatre, with such companies as the San Francisco Mime Troupe involved in demonstrations in the Haight. In 1967 they adapted the European street theatre of the 1500s, *commedia dell'arte*, to the Vietnam War in *L'Amant Militaire* (1967). The musical *Hair* (1967) premièred near Greenwich Village in New York in October 1967, and in 1968 would bring celebration of the counter-culture and onstage nudity to mainstream success on Broadway.

When Michael Herr arrived in Vietnam in late 1967, he detected that the war as much as Haight-Ashbury was serving as a stage for a culture's projections. In his new-journalistic memoir *Dispatches* (1977) Herr observes of a soldier about to go into the jungle that 'his face was all painted up for night walking now like a bad hallucination, not like the painted faces I'd seen in San Francisco only a few weeks before, the other extreme of the same theater' (Herr 1977: 6). The sentence plays on the military and dramatic meanings of 'theater', a special zone in which license exists to put on a mask and perform a role. In 1967 nearly 500,000 American troops were mired in what the American news magazines *Time*, *Newsweek* and *U.S. News and World Report* were now telling their educated readers was a 'stalemate', and in October for the first time Americans answering 'yes' to the question of whether the United States had made a mistake sending troops to Vietnam outnumbered those who replied 'no'. American dead often exceeded 200 a week, the draft was taking 20,000 young men per month, and President Johnson had asked Congress for a Vietnam War income tax surcharge of 6 per cent (Landers 2004: 182). US policy elites were worried as the Cold War ideological consensus that had reigned for twenty years was cracking apart. Disillusioned, McNamara secretly commissioned what would be known as the Pentagon Papers to identify how the United States had reached this impasse. Herr's book and also his work on the screenplays for the films *Apocalypse Now* (1978) and *Full Metal Jacket* (1986) articulate the challenge Vietnam presented in 1967 for cultural myths celebrating white American masculinity, 'from the lowest John Wayne wetdream to the most aggravated soldier-poet fantasy' (Herr 1977: 20). Two of the most resonant texts to be subsequently produced, Maya Lin's Vietnam Veterans Memorial on the mall in Washington DC and the title story of Tim O'Brien's *The Things They Carried* (1990), are structured as mere lists. Taking the place of the French who had failed to hold onto their colony in Vietnam, Americans found themselves unable to enact their own cultural narrative of a westward-moving 'progress'.

The formerly colonised East is a voice on *Sgt. Pepper*. Harrison's composition 'Within You Without You' resulted from his study of Indian classical music and religion. In the *London Evening Standard* article in 1966 in which Lennon had made his notorious observation that the Beatles were 'more popular than Jesus now', he had also extolled the civilisation of India and attacked colonial arrogance: 'This music is thousands of years old; it makes me laugh, the British going over there and telling them what to do' (Cleave 2004: 160). In the 1960s the assault on a peasant Asian nation by the technological might of the United States elicited identification with the Vietnamese by liberation movements within and without the United States. In 1967 heavyweight boxing champion Muhammad Ali resisted conscription, asking 'why . . . so-called Negro people' should 'put on a uniform and go ten thousand miles from home and drop bombs and bullets on brown people in Vietnam' (Charters 2003: xxxiv). 1967 was the peak year of the violent riots of 1964–8 as black power escalated from rhetoric to rebellions in the impoverished areas of many American cities. In Detroit forty-three people were killed and 1,300 buildings were burned. Order was restored only after 'forty-seven hundred U.S. Army paratroopers occupied the flaming ghetto along with eight thousand National Guardsmen' (Gitlin 1989: 244).

As an ally of the black power concept of the mid-1960s, the Black Arts Movement emphasised an aggressive performance of self-consciously black expression that would have a political and social impact. In his poem 'Black Art' (1966), LeRoi Jones wrote that 'we want poems that will wrestle cops into alleys' (Jones 1969: 116). During 1967 Harold Cruse published *The Crisis of the Negro Intellectual* (1967). Cruse insisted that black intellectuals must be 'spokesmen on behalf of their ethnic group, the Negro masses' (Cruse 1967: 10). It was also in 1967 that poet and dramatist LeRoi Jones changed his name to Amiri Baraka, an African 'blessed prince' (Lacey 1997: 50). During the 1967 uprising in Newark he was arrested on a charge of gun possession. Proclaiming a black aesthetic, writers of the Black Arts Movement such as Don L. Lee wrote in his *Think Black* (1967), 'We must destroy Faulkner, dick, jane and other perpetuators of evil' (Lee 1967: 6); the preeminent American modernist author and the little white boy and girl of American first-grade primers were identified alike as a trio of cultural hegemony. Nikki Giovanni's *Black Feeling* (1967) found a large audience among black readers.

The turn to multicultural perspectives began during this moment in 1967. Native American, Asian, Latino and other oppressed ethnic groups in the United States would soon step forward in the assumed character of their own suppressed cultural identities. The nascent feminist movement was about to announce gender as an identity molded through performance as well. On *Sgt. Pepper* the Beatles acknowledge women who bend the gender norms, as McCartney sings in 'Lovely Rita' of his attraction to the meter maid whose uniform and bearing make her 'look a little like a military man'. Earlier in the decade Doris Lessing's *The Golden Notebook* (1962) and Betty Friedan's *The Feminine Mystique* (1963) had suggested an unease with traditional roles, but it was in 1967 that Sue Kaufman's bestselling *Diary of a Mad Housewife* (1967) signalled the gathering dissatisfaction of women.

In *Magic Circles: The Beatles in Dream and History* (2003), Devin McKinney concludes that *Sgt. Pepper* 'offered not the depths its time demanded, but only the escape its moment desired' (McKinney 2003: 1920). Yet *Sgt. Pepper's Lonely Hearts Club Band*, like the year 1967, stands as a reference point of a unique time, culminating in the May events in Paris in 1968, when so many dared to act on their fantasies of achieving individual and communal liberation. 'We hope you have enjoyed the show', the Beatles sing as they return together as Sgt. Pepper's band in the frame song before leaving us the chilling 'A Day in the Life'. That encore segues into news of mass death, routine life as somnolence, and finally the echoing dream-wish 'I'd love to turn you on' as the violins build to an impossible crescendo, ending in a crashing chord.

That wish continues to reverberate, but so does the counter-wish that 1967, and all that it stood for, had never happened. The backlash against 1960s culture began almost immediately after the close of the era, culminating in the repudiation of the decade's ethos during the Reagan/Thatcher years of the 1980s. Conservative revisionists sought to stigmatise and undo the 1960s, an effort that peaked again in the neo-conservative loathing of America's first 'baby-boomer' president, Bill Clinton. Controversy over what the 1960s accomplished and over whether those accomplishments were positive or negative was accompanied by the apostasy of some former radicals and counter-culture figures and the erosion of the reputation of others. The bold experiments of 1967 have continued to exert their spell, whether beneficent or baneful, down to the present.

References

Anderson, Terry H. (2004) *The Sixties*, New York: Longman

Barth, John (1966) *Giles Goat-Boy*, New York: Doubleday

——(1967) 'The Literature of Exhaustion', *Atlantic*, August, 29–34

Baxter, John (1997) *Stanley Kubrick: A Biography*, New York: Carroll and Graf

The Beatles Anthology (2000), San Francisco: Chronicle

Bigsby, C. W. E. (1985) *Beyond Broadway*, Cambridge: Cambridge University Press

Bly, Robert (1967) *The Light Around the Body*, New York: Harper and Row

Cage, John (1966) *Silence*, Cambridge: Cambridge University Press

Charters, Ann, ed. (2003) *The Portable Sixties Reader*, New York: Penguin

Christgau, Robert (2000) *Any Old Way You Choose It: Rock and Other Pop Music, 1967–1973*, New York: Cooper Square

Cleave, Maureen (2004) 'How Does a Beatle Live? John Lennon Lives Like This', in Mike Evans, ed., *The Beatles Literary Anthology*, London: Plexus, 159–63

Cruse, Harold (1967) *The Crisis of the Negro Intellectual*, New York: Morrow

Davies, Hunter (1968) *The Beatles*, New York: Dell

Ephron, Nora, and Susan Edmiston (2004) 'Bob Dylan Interview', in *Younger Than That Now*, New York: Thunder's Mouth, 59–69

Friedman, Bruce Jay, ed. (1965) *Black Humor*, New York: Bantam

Gitlin, Todd (1989) *The Sixties: Years of Hope/Days of Rage*, Toronto: Bantam

Harris, Charles B. (1971) *Contemporary American Novelists of the Absurd*, New Haven, CT: College and University Press

Henri, Adrian, Roger McGough and Brian Patten (1967) *Penguin Modern Poets 10: The Mersey Sound*, Harmondsworth: Penguin

Herr, Michael (1977) *Dispatches*, New York: Vintage

Jones, LeRoi (1969) *Black Magic: Poetry 1961–1967*, Indianapolis, IN: Bobbs-Merrill

Lacey, Henry C. (1997) 'Amiri, Baraka', in William L. Andrews, Frances Smith Foster and Trudier Harris, eds, *The Oxford Companion to African American Literature*, New York: Oxford University Press, 49–51

Landers, James (2004) *The Weekly War: Newsmagazines and Vietnam*, Columbia, MO: University of Missouri Press

Lee, Don L. (1967) *Think Black!*, Detroit, MI: Broadside

Lowenfels, Walter, ed. (1967) *Where Is Vietnam? American Poets Respond*, Garden City, NY: Doubleday

Mailer, Norman (1994) *The Armies of the Night: History as a Novel/The Novel as History*, Harmondsworth: Penguin

Marqusee, Mike (2003) *Chimes of Freedom: The Politics of Bob Dylan's Art*, New York: New Press

McKinney, Devin (2003) *Magic Circles: The Beatles in Dream and History*, Cambridge, MA: Harvard University Press

'Mick Jagger and the Future of Rock' (1971), *Newsweek*, 4 January, 44–8

Miles, Barry (2004) *Hippie*, New York: Sterling

Mitchell, Adrian (1991) *Adrian Mitchell's Greatest Hits*, Newcastle upon Tyne: Bloodaxe

Patterson, James T. (1996) *Grand Expectations: The United States, 1945–1974*, New York: Oxford University Press

Pynchon, Thomas (1999) *The Crying of Lot 49*, New York: HarperPerennial

Reilly, John (1981) 'An Interview with John Barth', *Contemporary Literature*, 1–23

Scholes, Robert (1979) *Fabulation and Metafiction*, Urbana, IL: University of Illinois Press

Stevenson, Randall (2004) *Oxford English Literary History*, vol. 12, 1960–2000: The Last of England?, Oxford: Oxford University Press

Thompson, Hunter S. (1971) *Fear and Loathing in Las Vegas: A Savage Journey to the Heart of the American Dream*, New York: Popular Library

Vonnegut, Jr, Kurt (1963) *Cat's Cradle*, New York: Dell

Wolfe, Tom (1999) *The Electric Kool-Aid Acid Test*, New York: Bantam

Chapter 16

1970, Planet Earth: The Imagination of the Global

Ursula K. Heise

Satellite View

The launch of the Soviet satellite Sputnik-1 on 4 October 1957 changed not only the history of twentieth-century technology, but also politics, philosophy and aesthetics. It marked the start of a space race between the two Cold-War superpowers, with satellites put into orbit and the first humans, Yuri Gagarin and Gherman Titov in 1961, and John Glenn in 1962, undertaking orbital flights. Satellites and cosmonauts sent back photographs of Earth taken from space that enabled humankind, for the first time in history, to look at its planet as a whole. This new perspective galvanised the public as the planet's beauty, its systemic interconnectedness and its limits all visibly emerged in photographs of the earth rising above the moon that were sent back by the Apollo 8 mission in 1968, and culminated in the 'Blue Planet' image generated by Apollo 17 in 1972 (Figure 16.1). 'No Science Fiction expected this Globe-Eye Consciousness/ Simultaneous with opening a hatch on Heaven', the Beat poet Allen Ginsberg comments in a poem on the occasion of the first moon-landing (Ginsberg 1984: 528). The emergent environmentalist movement seized on the symbol of Earth in space as an expression of the need for a new holistic consciousness, and featured it prominently at the celebration of the first Earth Day in 1970. In ecology as well as technology, the image of the 'Blue Planet' prompted new ways of thinking about the globe as a unitary system.

The utopian hopes that were sometimes connected with this icon undoubtedly arose in part because it seemed to offer an alternative view of a world bitterly divided between superpowers that fought proxy wars around the globe and kept each other in check with the threat of nuclear annihilation. But they also emerged because individuals were in fact becoming more connected with the rest of the globe through advances in communications and transportation technologies during the 1960s. The still relatively new medium of television broadcast images of remote places and cultures into the average family's living-room even as the development of the jet airliner put distant areas of the globe within reach of tourist travel. These trends toward technological integration accelerated in subsequent decades, with the introduction of the personal computer and the Internet. At the same time, the collapse of the Berlin Wall in 1989, the disintegration of the Soviet Union in 1991 and the gradual transformation of China set the signal for the worldwide spread of capitalist economic structures that many consider the core of what we have come to call 'globalisation'. Perhaps unsurprisingly, finance capital reappropriated the image of the Blue

Figure 16.1.   The Blue Planet (TopFoto.co.uk)

Planet for its own vision of global connectedness when Mastercard began to engrave it on credit cards together with the slogan, 'the world in your hands'. (See Sachs 1992, and 1999: 110–28, for a history of the 'Blue Planet' image.)

But greater connectedness, in contrast to the images of world unity and peace that the 1960s counter-culture dreamed of, often increased disparities in political power between different regions, accentuated socio-economic and cultural differences and provoked more intense political and military conflicts. As the ideological differences between the capital-ist West and the communist East waned, the economic chasm between the 'global North' of developed nations and the 'global South' of developing ones widened. At the same time, stark contrasts arose between countries that successfully embarked on economic develop-ment, such as South Korea or Taiwan, and those that were unable to make the leap ahead, such as Haiti and much of sub-Saharan Africa. Greater connectedness also meant that local conflicts and crises resonated more deeply around the world: movements for independence in Chechnya or Taiwan, ethnic confrontations in Rwanda or Yugoslavia, and economic crises in Asia or Latin America as they occurred during the 1990s took place in the media presence of the entire world and often involved agents and institutions from around the globe.

This tension between awareness of the planetary whole and sharpened perception of differences also marks the imagination of the global in literature and culture. Writers, thinkers and social movements that focus primarily on the implications of global connectedness have tended to rely on allegorical representations such as the 'global village', 'Gaia' or 'Spaceship Earth', while those most interested in the accentuation of differences have more often relied on modernist and postmodernist techniques of collage, fragmentation, paradox and self-reflexivity. Some writers celebrate the opening up of new domains beyond the nation as a utopian transformation of the human mind and body, while others comment with alarm on the uprootings and dislocations that global mobility entails. Some portray globalisation, especially in its economic and corporate dimensions, as the rise of a sinister new world order that fosters control, homogenisation and exploitation, while others welcome the multiple cultural encounters, hybridisations and reinventions of identity that global connectedness enables. (For a good survey of the hopes and fears surrounding internationalism and globalisation, see Tomlinson 1999.) Indeed, the question whether 'globalisation' is a process that obeys a single underlying logic or consists of a range of differently oriented processes is a matter of intense debate in the humanities and social sciences. (See Giddens 1990, Beck 1992, Albrow 1996, Wallerstein 1974, Sklair 1991, and particularly Appadurai 1996: 27–47, who insists that globalisation consists of a variety of processes that are not homologous and synchronous with each other.)

From this range of perspectives, several distinct sets of images and stories about the global crystallised between the 1960s and the turn of the millennium. One of the most influential image clusters revolves around the networks that advances in information and communications technologies have created, from Marshall McLuhan's 'global village' in the 1960s to the 'cyberspace' of 1980s and current concepts of the 'Internet'. The second set arose from the burgeoning environmentalist movement, including James Lovelock's metaphorisation of the earth as Gaia, Buckminster Fuller and Kenneth Boulding's image of 'Spaceship Earth' and Garrett Hardin's notion of a 'global commons' – allegorical concepts that foreground the connectedness of the Earth's natural systems as well as their limited resources. A related but distinct set of stories revolved around the way in which the threat of nuclear annihilation, an ever-present danger during the Cold War decades, unifies all inhabitants of the planet in a shared danger. In conjunction with concerns about an array of other technological and environmental hazards, this threat transmuted into the idea of a global 'risk society', proposed by German sociologist Ulrich Beck in 1986. Focusing more on the economic and political than the technological reconfiguration of the planet, a fourth group of stories foregrounds the role of transnational corporations and the way in which they shift power away from nation-states. Sometimes paranoid in their fear of corporate conspiracy, sometimes hard-headed in their analysis of economic transactions, these narratives range from writers such as William Burroughs and Thomas Pynchon to the anti-globalisation movement of the 1990s. In more optimistic fashion, the fifth set of stories foregrounds global migrations and displacements that bring about unforeseen hybridisations and reveal the fundamentally dynamic and impure nature of cultural traditions. Such 'traveling cultures', as anthropologist James Clifford calls them (Clifford 1997: 17–46), manifest themselves particularly in postmodern metropolises, around which another set of global stories revolves.

McLuhan's global village, Pynchon's corporate conspiracies, and stories of transnational and cross-cultural migration have left the most lasting mark on anglophone literature. But these visions of the global have also particularly challenged literary form. In fiction, neither nineteenth-century narratives that portrayed the evolution of nations, social classes and families nor high-modernist investigations of individuals' minds and memories can be unproblematically deployed in the representation of global networks, and the traditional Western emphasis on the expression of subjectivity in lyrical form poses similar obstacles. In response to such challenges, contemporary novelists and poets have revived older forms such as epic and allegory, and have quite often blended them with modernist strategies such as collage or the fragmentary structures of the urban novel so as to create works of literature that defy conventional genre categories in their attempt to grasp an elusive planetary totality.

Whole Earth Utopias

'After three thousand years of explosion, by means of fragmentary and mechanical technologies, the Western world is imploding . . . after more than a century of electric technology, we have extended our central nervous system itself in a global embrace, abolishing both space and time as far as our planet is concerned', Marshall McLuhan boldly declared in 1964, at the beginning of *Understanding Media* (McLuhan 1994: 3). His prophetic vision of the dawning of an electric age that connects the entire world in a 'global village', doing away with divisions of the print age such as nationalism and individualism, provided one of the most important templates for the imagination of a new global media space – from its first publication in 1964 to the emergence of Internet and cellphone culture in the 1990s. While this vision relied on the centrality of information and communications to postulate an entirely artificial, technologically mediated global sphere, the emergent environmental movement celebrated a new awareness of Earth's *natural* wholeness with similar enthusiasm. Atmospheric scientist James Lovelock, taking his cue like McLuhan from the newly available images of Earth from space, postulated that the entire planet functions as a single cybernetic feedback system or super-organism that he named Gaia, in reminiscence of the Greek Earth goddess. The scientific details of his theory were soon forgotten by the general public, but the Gaia image could be easily connected to age-old images of Mother Nature and became one of the most popular symbols of a new earth consciousness not only for environmentalists, but also for the feminist movement in the 1970s and the New Age movement in the 1980s.

McLuhan's and Lovelock's allegories of planetary unity undoubtedly owed part of their popularity to their emergence during one of the darkest decades of the Cold War, when the Cuban Missile Crisis had brought the world to the brink of nuclear destruction and war was raging in Vietnam. The lethal dangers of atomic war left a deep mark on literature, from the complete extinction of humankind described in the Australian novelist Nevil Shute's *On the Beach* (1957) to the perhaps even more nightmarish idea – that successive civilisations on Earth will again and again reach the point of technological self-destruction – at the core of Walter Miller's science fiction novel *A Canticle for Leibowitz* (1959), as well as the American poet James Merrill's epic sequence of poems *The Changing Light at Sandover* (1976–82). Against such visions of a planet divided and destroyed, Gaia and the global village held out images of unity, freedom and peace. In different ways, both the return to nature and the advent of a new kind of technology promised a different, less destructive type of social order.

The impact of both whole-earth visions surfaces in the work of two quite different American poets, Gary Snyder and John Cage. Both were associated with the Beat movement in the 1950s and 1960s and derived from it a sustained interest in how the very different worldviews of the Christian West and Buddhist East might be brought into dialogue. Snyder later became a prominent environmentalist much of whose poetry rooted itself in particular places and landscapes. When his poems, mostly written in fairly conventional free verse, reach toward the global, they do so by means of metaphor and allegory. New York City, for example, which Snyder describes as a giant living ecosystem in one of his poems, turns out to form part of economic and communication flows constituting a global 'Sea of Information'. One of the most compelling ways of translating this unbounded unity of the planet into artistic form is, in Snyder's view, the continuous Chinese scroll painting. One such painting appears at the beginning of his aptly titled poetry collection *Mountains and Rivers without End*. But it is of necessity broken down into successive pages – not just a constraint of the Western printed book, but perhaps also Snyder's hint at the inherent difficulties of realising such an unbounded vision.

Cage's more playful and avant-gardiste verse foregrounds such tensions between whole and part, global and local, more forcefully. In many of his experimental poems and lectures, Cage describes himself, his collaborators, or fictional characters travelling around the world, constantly facing cultural and linguistic differences along the way. Yet Cage's collage technique juxtaposes the familiar and the exotic, the industrial and the pre-modern in such a way that distinctions fade: the travelling troupe eats Japanese meals in the US and in Japan as well as Indian dinners in Paris; a Japanese abbot in a remote monastery turns out not only to speak perfect English, but to be well informed about the Hollywood celebrity market; and Japanese composer Tohru Takemitsu's three-year-old daughter Maki, when asked what she thinks of the US, answers that it is another part of Japan. Cage comments drily: 'we live in a global village . . . Maki is right' (Cage 1969: 33). Even more pointedly, in a long poem called 'Diary: How to Improve the World (You Will Only Make Matters Worse)' that Cage wrote serially in the 1960s and 1970s, the protagonist searches for the total number of 'global services'. The quest leads him to articulate a utopian vision of electronic connectedness, freedom from material ownership and benevolent anarchy that is indebted to the counter-culture as much as to McLuhan; but while the allegory of the global village undergirds all of the poem, its fragmentary, anarchic structure resists any neat summing up of the details into a total image.

Not entirely by coincidence, Japan plays an important role in both Snyder's and Cage's imaginations of the global. It also did for other writers concerned with the fate of nature and the evolution of technology. 'The sky above the port was the color of television, tuned to a dead channel', the famous first sentence of William Gibson's classic cyberpunk novel *Neuromancer* (1984), refers to Chiba City, east of Tokyo. With its mixture of ancient cultural traditions and cutting-edge technologies, its national uniqueness and capacity of assimilation, Japan seemed like a paradigm of globalisation to many writers. In cyberpunk fiction (a mode that grafts futuristic cybernetic technology onto the aggressively low-life style of the punk music sub-culture), Japan often serves as the geographical counterpart to the post-geographical realm of what Gibson famously termed 'cyberspace', the network of international computer connections and databases. While McLuhan himself had mainly based his reflections on media such as telephone, telegraphy and television, the emergence of the personal computer in the 1970s and the advent of the Internet in the early 1990s made them seem all the more prophetic. In striking visual descriptions of the new computerised environment, Gibson expands McLuhan's idea of a global village to a virtual city that encompasses the entire planet. When the protagonist of *Neuromancer*, the 'console cowboy' Case, connects to this network through his digitally adapted nervous system, he perceives an 'unfolding of his distanceless home, his country, transparent 3-D chessboard extending to infinity' (Gibson 1984: 52).

This abstract geometric landscape, 'horizonless fields' of an 'endless neon cityscape' (Gibson 1984: 256), becomes the principal way of representing the new global realm of information not only in Gibson's, but also other cyberpunk novelists' work. Whether it is referred to as the 'net'(in Bruce Sterling's *Islands in the Net* [1988]), the 'Dataline' (in Pat Cadigan's *Synners* [1991]), or the 'Metaverse' (in Neal Stephenson's *Snow Crash* [1992]), digital connectedness envisioned as an alternative space becomes the ground zero for the experience of the global. At the same time, the protagonists of many of these novels travel incessantly around in real space, mostly through landscapes and cities scarred by political and economic repression, social inequality, crime, poverty, environmental pollution and uncontrollable urban sprawl. Cyberspace, against this background, functions sometimes as a parodic double, sometimes as an escapist idealisation, and sometimes as a utopian alternative, but it is always presented as an inescapable part of the experience of the real in the twenty-first century, and often celebrated as the next step in the evolution of humankind. In a particularly interesting return to the dual utopian images of Gaia and the global village, David Brin's novel *Earth* (1990) envisions this step as a merger of geological with informational structures that gives rise to a global eco-mind.

Typically, cyberpunk combines a measure of McLuhanesque techno-utopianism with a dystopian portrayal of the physical and social world. Transnational corporations dominate the world in many cyberpunk texts, sometimes to the point where they take over functions formerly fulfilled by nation-states. Such powerful corporate nations are absent from McLuhan's panorama of an electronic age of tribal dispersal, anarchy, dehierarchisation and emancipation; instead, cyberpunks derive this dimension of their future visions from a different source, the paranoid views of the global in the fictions of Philip K. Dick and Thomas Pynchon.

Technology, Paranoia and the Global Corporation

If visions of world unification through technology held undeniable appeal during the decades of the Cold War, the idea of global connectedness also took on a more sinister aspect. As the threat of nuclear conflict persisted, not a few thinkers, writers and especially young people came to suspect that ideological divides were really just part of an overarching system designed to perpetuate outdated social structures by hemming in creativity, sexuality and nature. While many of the counter-cultural movements of the time in France, Germany, Japan, Mexico and the US associated this oppressive regime with the particular features and history of their own nations, some came to see it as a worldwide problem with different surface manifestations. 'The Man', 'The Firm' or 'The System' became ways of referring to a hidden global conspiracy designed to control individuals' bodies and minds and to hold them in check through political and economic structures. The belief in political and economic conspiracies has a long history in the culture of the United States (see Hofstadter 1996), and found rich new material during the 1960s with the assassinations of President John F. Kennedy, his brother Robert Kennedy, and civil rights leaders Malcolm X and Martin Luther King. But the portrayal of social systems controlling individuals' minds and bodies, often through corporate operations, had already evolved into a familiar theme in the science fiction of Alfred Bester, Cyril Kornbluth, Frederick Pohl, and Philip K. Dick. It also found forceful expression in the literature of the Beat Generation, especially the poetry of Allen Ginsberg and the fiction of William Burroughs. But its most influential articulation appeared in the works of Thomas Pynchon, who drew on both genres.

Possible networks of conspiracy and the attempt to track them down already play an important role in two novels Pynchon published in the 1960s, *V.* (1963) and *The Crying of Lot 49* (1966), but these conspiracies assume truly global shape in his classic *Gravity's Rainbow* (1973). Set in the German 'zone' around the end of the Second World War, it explores the nature and origins of the global geopolitical order that was to dominate the following fifty years. Pynchon's narrative idiom oscillates between the 1940s and the counter-cultural and Cold War discourses of the 1960s: starting out as a spy novel or perhaps a detective story with a psychoanalytical twist, *Gravity's Rainbow* traces the encounter of an American G. I., Tyrone Slothrop, with the forces that trigger war and peace, and which shape social structures and technological development in modern societies. As Slothrop investigates the nature of these forces, he begins to suspect that ideological oppositions might conceal a deeper coherence: world wars might just be manoeuvres orchestrated by an international conglomerate of corporations to spur countries on in the development of crucial technologies that will ultimately benefit corporate interests.

Disturbing as this may be, an even more sinister suspicion gradually grips Slothrop and other figures in *Gravity's Rainbow*: even this international business cartel might no longer be the principal agent of history, but rather the propulsive force of technological development itself. Certain types of technologies might no longer be controlled by humans at all, but might be evolving according to a logic of their own. This anti-McLuhanite perspective is never fully substantiated in *Gravity's Rainbow*, however. Slothrop and others attempt to track down the scattered clues that might shed light on the global structures in which they are caught up, but while hints and suggestions proliferate, none of them ever leads to any definitive conclusion. The spy and mystery plots peter out amid a welter of accumulating narrative fragments, and notions of coherence and conspiracy themselves become elusive: 'if there is something comforting – religious, if you want – about paranoia, there is still also anti-paranoia, where nothing is connected to nothing, a condition not many of us can bear for long' (Pynchon 1973: 434). Increasingly anti-paranoid, Slothrop loses coherence as a character, fizzles out and disappears from the narrative:

> There is also the story about Tyrone Slothrop, who was sent into the Zone to be present at his own assembly – perhaps, heavily paranoid voices have whispered, *his time's assembly* – and there ought to be a punch line to it, but there isn't. The plan went wrong. He is being broken down instead, and scattered. (Pynchon 1973: 738)

As character, plot and visions of conspiracy all break down, Pynchon replaces them with a different kind of narrative architecture. Many critics have pointed out the bewildering profusion of characters, stories and historical as well as scientific detail in the novel's 750 pages, which has led them to call it an 'encyclopedia', a 'data bank', or a 'cosmic web' (Mendelson 1976: passim; Weisenburger 1981: 141; Hayles 1984: 168–9). In its own way, an encyclopedia or data bank is as totalising a structure as a corporate conspiracy, though it lacks the intentionality, agency and plotting associated with such a network. The importance of *Gravity's Rainbow* as a matrix for the cultural imagination of the global, therefore, lies not only in its visions of worldwide conspiracy, but rather in the way in which the conspiratorial imagination breaks down in the form of the novel and gives way to a 'database imaginary' that may well be aesthetically the most significant translation of global connectedness into textual and visual form in the last half-century.

What later writers took from *Gravity's Rainbow*, however, was mainly its portrayal of corporations with power beyond that of nations. This vision gained credibility in the 1980s and 1990s with the spread of capitalist economic patterns to formerly Communist countries and to developing nations, some of which began to overtake developed countries in their economic growth rates. With transnational corporations spearheading the capitalist conquest of the planet, nation-states and national boundaries seemed to recede in importance as flows of economic exchange gained relevance in public awareness. While much of this economic transformation was dominated by US corporations – with ubiquitous McDonald's restaurants and Starbuck's coffee-shops as icons of Americanisation – Americans noted with unease the simultaneous take-over of such quintessentially American institutions as the Rockefeller Center and Columbia Pictures Studios by Japanese corporations in the late 1980s. It became less easy to identify products, places and institutions in national or even regional terms when a famous British department store such as Harrod's was in fact owned by an Egyptian and a well-known American publisher such as Random House by the German multinational Bertelsmann. Growing awareness of the scope and power of transnational corporations led to anti-corporate backlashes in the 1990s, sometimes from the political right and frequently from the left, culminating in the running battles of the anti-globalisation movement against riot police and the National Guard during the World Trade Organization meeting in Seattle in 1999. Accompanied by such books as Naomi Klein's popular *No Logo*, the anti-globalisation movement portrayed transnational corporations as sinister Pynchonesque forces in a new world order engineered for the benefit of global capital. These conflicts resonate in the minutely detailed account of a wealthy corporate executive's limousine trip across Manhattan in Don DeLillo's novel *Cosmopolis* (2003). In the limousine's encounter with urban crowds of different sorts, signs of resistance to the global monetary order symbolised by the young multimillionaire surge up again and again, suggesting violence and revolution to come.

The mistrust of big business and its impact on social and cultural life was not, of course, entirely new: the dehumanising effects of excessive commercialism are a staple topic of twentieth-century literature. But Pynchon's view of business as not only a national but a global force differs markedly from these earlier critiques, and influenced a range of quite different works. Edward Abbey's *The Monkey Wrench Gang* (1975) records the struggle of an environmentalist band of saboteurs against what they see as a 'megalomaniacal megamachine', a 'whole conglomerated cartel spread out upon half the planet Earth like a global kraken, pan-tentacled, wall-eyed and parrot-beaked, its brain a bank of computer data centers, its blood the flow of money, its heart a radioactive dynamo' (Abbey 1975: 139, 142). Eschewing such explicit paranoia for a more historical and analytical approach, Richard Powers' novel *Gain* (1998) nevertheless delivers an equally disturbing portrait of corporate growth and the harm it inflicts on individuals and communities. In his account of how a family-run soap-and-candle-making business in 1830s' Boston develops into a multinational chemical and pharmaceutical corporation by the 1990s, corporate growth appears as a force that is in practice if not in principle beyond human control, constantly generating more of itself: not conspiracy but cancer is Powers' basic metaphor for this planetary force.

Speculative novels about the near future, developing Pynchon's vision further, tend to take it for granted that corporations will replace nations as the crucial agents in global geopolitics. From Gibson's *Neuromancer* and Bruce Sterling's *Islands in the Net* to Stephenson's *Snow Crash* and Alexander Besher's *Rim* (1994), such novels describe the world as carved up into corporate rather than national territories: companies shape cultures and lifestyles, create and enforce laws and policies, and punish disloyalty in much the way nations used to penalise high treason. In these visions of the future corporate rule is no longer secret but openly displayed, and the characters accept it as part of a generally dystopian social landscape in much the same way in which they take for granted urban dysfunction and environmental destruction. While some literary critics have chastised this portrayal of the future as complacent and politically conformist (cf. Ross 1991: 145–56), it can also be read as an implicit warning about the kind of society current economic structures might produce. Whether conformist or resistant, this type of speculative fiction has crystallised into narrative reality what was perhaps only paranoid delusion in earlier works – a global society ruled by transnational corporations with little regard for either culture or nature.

Travelling Cultures and the Global City

The question of who holds power in the global order and how it is used also informs a very different set of literary works. In analyses of the transformations that transport and communications technologies have triggered in our experience of space, it is common to represent the Earth as a sphere steadily shrinking in size (Figure 16.2). At first sight, this image seems to imply that the globe has become more accessible and transparent to all. It shows neither how differences in power and affluence might limit individuals' access to global services and spaces, nor how even the privileged might experience the closeness of other cultures as a disempowering panorama of confusion rather than a broadening of horizons. As one character in Don DeLillo's novel *The Names* (1982) reflects,

> modern communications don't shrink the world, they make it bigger. Faster planes make it bigger. They . . . connect more things. . . . The world is so big and complicated we don't trust ourselves to figure out anything on our own. No wonder people read books that tell them how to run, walk and sit. We're trying to keep up with the world, the size of it, the complications. (DeLillo 1982: 322–3).

This tension between the sense that the entire world has come within the individual's reach in an entirely new way, and anxiety over the bewildering multiplicity such connectedness might bring, runs deep in much recent literature.

The struggle to understand an increasingly complex world lies at the core of many stories about the cultural transfers, fusions, hybridisations and clashes that arise from various forms of travel and migration. Many British and American novels of the last three decades tell the stories of immigrant families, political exiles, economic refugees and migrant workers that took citizens of Asia, Africa and Latin America to Europe and North America. These fictional explorations are often framed by probing re-examinations of what it means to be 'British' or 'American', and how non-European or non-white populations have been excluded from concepts of nationhood in the developed world even when they played a crucial role in shaping economic and cultural life. Such narratives reveal how the life of cities, nations and regions is embedded in a global network of relations that particular social groups tend to highlight or conceal for reasons of their own political, economic or cultural interest. In tracing the lines of connection that link what seem at first sight like distant and distinct places, and in revealing how cultural elements from far-away regions inform what seem to be the purely local customs of a particular community, such novels

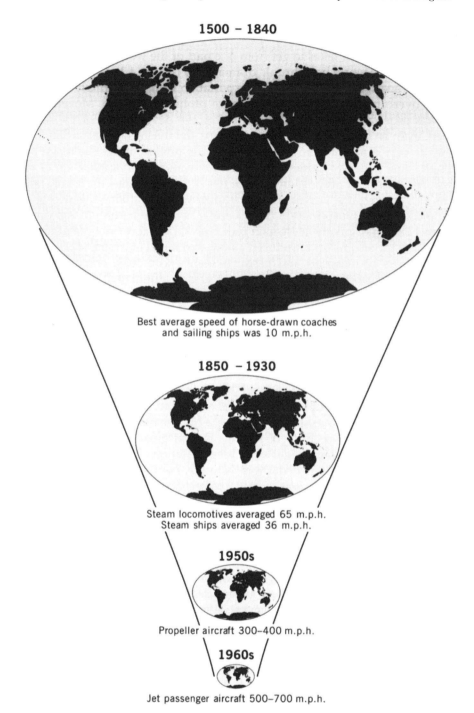

Figure 16.2.   The Shrinking Globe (Source: Based on diagram in J. McHale, *The Future of the Future*, New York: George Braziller, 1969. As used in P. Dicken, *Global Shift: Reshaping the Global Economic Map in the 21st Century* (4th edn), Sage Publications, 2003. Reproduced with permission.)

portray a global society fundamentally shaped by unequal distributions of power and wealth, but also in constant dynamic transformation at the hands of both rich and poor.

While migration and exile are literary themes with a long tradition in anglophone literature, the more recent fiction draws on a much broader range of cultural movements and encounters. In the US, novels such as Bharati Mukherjee's *Wife* (1975) and *Jasmine* (1989), Maxine Hong Kingston's *The Woman Warrior: Memories of a Childhood among Ghosts* (1976) and *China Men* (1980), Amy Tan's *The Joy Luck Club* (1989) and *The Kitchen God's Wife* (1991), or Chang-rae Lee's *Native Speaker* (1995) address the deep conflicts of identity that immigrants from Asia and, in many cases, their American-born offspring encounter in their travel around the world, from the homeland to the new country – and sometimes back again to a 'native' culture that has itself become 'alien' with distance and time. In Britain, Hanif Kureishi's play *Borderline* (1981) and his novel *The Buddha of Suburbia* (1990), as well as his very successful film *My Beautiful Laundrette* (1985), touch on similar topics involving the lives of Pakistani immigrants to London, while Timothy Mo's *Sour Sweet* (1982) focuses on a Chinese immigrant family's experience. At the same time, the internationally acclaimed novels of Indian-born Salman Rushdie, Japanese-born Kazuo Ishiguro, and V. S. Naipaul, born in Trinidad from an Indian family, frequently address issues of cultural clashes and transitions (with less explicit focus on the immigrant experience) that have repeatedly triggered heated debates about the nature of Britishness and British literary expression in the new global context.

Some of these works are at least partially autobiographical in the materials they draw on, and quite a few resort to realist and high-modernist modes of narration that had been rejected by experimentalists of the 1960s and 1970s. Yet even the more conventional texts convey a sense that older models of individual and collective identity, with their connotations of authenticity, continuity and integrity, will not hold up in a world of global flows. Characters' individual selves tend to be permanently suspended in the ambiguous borderlands between different cultural spaces, and ethnic and national images of identity are shown to rest on partial, shifting and thoroughly artificial grounds rather than any 'natural' differences. As Rushdie argues in one of his essays,

> The effect of mass migrations has been the creation of radically new types of human being: people who root themselves in ideas rather than places . . . people in whose deepest selves strange fusions occur . . . between what they were and where they find themselves. The migrant suspects reality: having experienced several ways of being, he understands their illusory nature (Rushdie 1991: 124–5).

These shifts, uncertainties and ambiguities in the definition of one's social and geographical corner of the globe also insinuate themselves into linguistic and narrative structures. Most obviously, the use of different languages in a single text conveys such shifts: minimally, the appearance of foreign words in an English text signals the presence of another cultural space, such as the use of Spanish in Gloria Anzaldúa's *Borderlands/La Frontera: The New Mestiza* (1987), or Theresa Hak Kyung Cha's insertion of French and Chinese into *Dictée* (1982). More radically, some authors write entire sections of text in different languages. British novelist Christine Brooke-Rose's *Between* (1968), the story of a simultaneous interpreter travelling to international conferences, includes extended passages in French and German; Karen Tei Yamashita's more recent *Circle K Cycles* (2001) contains sections in English, Portuguese and Japanese that reflect the story's triangulation between Japan, Brazil and the US. More subtly, contemporary authors also introduce narrative materials and strategies from non-English cultural traditions into their texts. Maxine Hong Kingston links her story of a girl growing up in San Francisco's Chinatown with materials from Chinese mythology, just as Chinese-American playwright Henry Hwang blends Western and Chinese theatrical techniques in plays such as *F.O.B.* (1978) and *The Dance and the Railroad* (1981); and Ana Castillo, in a novel that describes the visit of a young Chicana woman to Mexico, *The Mixquiahuala Letters* (1986), models the narrative architecture on Argentinian novelist Julio Cortázar's classic *Rayuela* [Hopscotch] (1963). In all of these cases, cultural transfers and hybridisations are inscribed not only into the stories the texts tell, but into their linguistic and narrative texture itself.

In many of these novels, the global manifests itself in the memories and experience of an individual or family displaced from the home country. Some recent fictions go one step further by interweaving the stories of various migrant groups, typically against the background of a metropolis that turns into a zone of encounter for different cultures and languages. Zadie Smith's *White Teeth* (2000), for example, traces the entanglements of Jamaican and Bangladeshi immigrants with the British working and middle classes in lovingly detailed descriptions of the changing social geography of London neighbourhoods, transformed into patchworks of immigrant communities from different parts of the globe. In both scenarios, the local becomes a miniature replica of the boundaries and alliances that structure the global.

Japanese American novelist Karen Tei Yamashita similarly frames Los Angeles as a 'global city' in her novel *Tropic of Orange* (1997).[1] Chicanos and Mexican immigrants, Japanese Americans born in the suburbs of L.A., and a Chinese immigrant who passes himself off as Vietnamese, all rub shoulders in this thoroughly international city. At the same time, L.A. functions as a nodal point for all kinds of legal and illegal exchanges of international goods, as well as for the information circuits operating through newspapers, radio, television and the Internet. In the novel's most striking metaphor, the northward journey of an ancient man with wings toward the US border – a character lifted straight out of one of Colombian novelist Gabriel García Márquez's short stories – distorts time and space as he quite literally pulls the Tropic of Cancer with him. Under the name of El Mojado ('The Wetback'), he goes on to confront his opponent 'Super-NAFTA' in an allegorical wrestling match that pitches the economic interests of the global South against those of the global North. Urban space and time become literally unmappable as the characters move about in a text that draws on the varied literary traditions of the *noir* detective story and the multicultural literatures of the United States, the magical realism of Latin American fiction, and the techno-postmodernism of Japanese novelist Haruki Murakami. Like Cage, Brin or Rushdie, Yamashita fuses allegory and narrative montage in her attempt to show both the unity and the disjunctions of daily lives lived in the context of globalisation.

While allegorical concepts such as the global village, the Blue Planet, Gaia, Spaceship Earth or The Firm try to understand the workings of worldwide systems as subject to a unitary overarching logic, montage techniques have typically represented the world as a patchwork of different processes, practices and developmental patterns that cannot easily be added up into a coherent whole. At its extreme, this literary procedure generates the 'encyclopedic novel' whose profusion of characters, plots and specialised discourses can no

---

[1] The notion of the 'global city' derives from Saskia Sassen's analysis of cities such as New York, London, Tokyo or Frankfurt which, in an increasingly decentralised economic and technological landscape, take on the centralised management functions that this decentralisation structurally requires (Sassen 2001).

longer be contained in forms that are easily recognisable as 'narrative'. *Tropic of Orange* gestures toward such an inventory or database form with an alternative table of contents entitled 'HyperContexts' (Figure 16.3). Structured like a calendar or TV programme guide, this map of narrative time and space alludes to the non-linear structure and infinite links of hypertext. Idiosyncratic as this device may seem, it suggests that one of the more important forms the imagination of the global in literature is currently taking is that of the electronic database with its infinite possibilities for reordering and linking.

World Literature

Many of the writers who focus on experiences of travel, migration and exile in the increasingly globalised world of the late twentieth century have achieved international renown. Novelists such as Salman Rushdie, Kazuo Ishiguro, Amy Tan and Maxine Hong Kingston have seen their works translated into dozens of languages and sold around the world, and V.S. Naipaul was awarded the Nobel Prize in 2001. The international attention their fictions have attracted forms part of a broader pattern: in the last few decades, publishing has become an increasingly globalised branch of business that circulates literary works in quantities and over geographical reaches that writers could only dream of in the first half of the twentieth century. The number of literary translations worldwide has increased dramatically, though much of this cross-cultural transfer takes place from English to other languages and only to a lesser degree in the other direction. Nevertheless, the global circulation of literary texts has led to the emergence of a new international canon that has come to replace the older canon of mostly European classics: authors such as Gabriel García Márquez, Carlos Fuentes and Isabel Allende from Latin America, Derek Walcott from the Caribbean, Nadine Gordimer, Chinua Achebe, Wole Soyinka and Naguib Mahfouz from Africa, and Asian writers such as Bei Dao or Haruki Murakami are familiar to readers around the world. Many of them have been awarded Nobel Prizes or other prestigious literary awards that tended to be reserved for writers of European extraction earlier.

The imagination of the global, therefore, takes place not only within literary texts, but also shapes the framework in which they are currently produced, circulated, and read. The force of this globalised publishing industry has increased to the point where

> [i]n recent decades a growing proportion of works has been produced for foreign consumption . . . This is a fundamentally new literary development: for the first time in history, authors of highly successful works can hope to have them translated into twenty or thirty languages within a few years of publication, and foreign countries may even provide the primary readership for writers who have small audiences at home or who are censored by their governments. (Damrosch 2003: 18)

Whether the international circulation of literary works encourages an affirmation of shared values or the conversion of literature into yet another consumer commodity (cf. Damrosch ibid.), whether it enhances creativity or merely fosters the most easily sellable genres, and whether it helps to make a greater diversity of authors available to readers or definitively erases the visibility of those that do not enter the global canon are matters of intense debate among comparatists. Similarly, some critics worry that the increasing worldwide consolidation of publishing houses into mega-conglomerates will negatively affect the distribution of literary works that do not sell millions in their first years of publication, while others

HyperContexts

	Monday Summer Solstice	**Tuesday** Diamond Lane.	**Wednesday** Cultural Diversity
Rafaela Cortes	**Midday-**Not Too Far from Mazatlán chapter 1	**Morning** -En México chapter 10	**Daylight** -The Cornfield chapter 18
Bobby Ngu	**Benefits** -Koreatown chapter 2	**Car Payment Due** -Tijuana via Singapore chapter 12	**Second Mortgage** -Chinatown chapter 15
Emi	**Weather Report** -Westside chapter 3	**NewsNow** -Hollywood South chapter 9	**Disaster Movie Week** -Hiro's Sushi chapter 20
Buzzworm	**Station ID** -Jefferson & Normandie chapter 4	**Oldies** -This Old Hood chapter 13	**LA X** -Margarita's Corner chapter 16
Manzanar Murakami	**Traffic Window** -Harbor Freeway chapter 5	**Rideshare** -Downtown Interchange chapter 8	**The Hour of the Trucks** -The Freeway Canyon chapter 19
Gabriel Balboa	**Coffee Break** -Downtown chapter 6	**Budgets** -Skirting Downtown chapter 14	**The Interview** -Manzanar chapter 17
Arcangel	**To Wake** -Marketplace chapter 7	**To Wash** -On the Tropic chapter 11	**To Eat** -La Cantina de Miseria y Hambre chapter 21

Figure 16.3.   HyperContexts from *Tropic of Orange*, © 2001 by Karen Tei Yamashita, published by Coffee House Press. Used by permission of the author and publisher.

hope that the ease of electronic publishing will on the contrary make texts oriented toward small audiences more accessible.

However these issues may be settled, the fact remains that the creation and dissemination of literary texts at the turn of the millennium takes place in a global context that writers cannot ignore. As they offer up visions of the global that range from images of unity to panoramas of anarchy, from utopianism to paranoia, and from allegory to collage, the texts that articulate these visions are destined to become themselves entangled in worldwide

Thursday	Friday	Saturday	Sunday
The Eternal Buzz	Artificial Intelligence	Queen of Angels	Pacific Rim

Dusk	**Dawn**	**Nightfall**	**Midnight**
-To the Border	-The Other Side	-Aztlán	-The Line
chapter 24	chapter 30	chapter 38	chapter 45

Life Insurance	**Visa Card**	**Social Security**	**American Express**
-L.A./T.J.	-Final Destination	-I-5	-Mi Casa/Su Casa
chapter 26	chapter 34	chapter 40	chapter 49

Live on Air	**Promos**	**Prime Time**	**Commercial Break**
-El A	-World Wide Web	-Last Stop	-The Big Sleep
chapter 27	chapter 29	chapter 41	chapter 44

You Give Us 22	**AM/FM**	**The Car Show**	**Hour 25**
Minutes-The World	-FreeZone	-Front Line	-Into the Boxes
chapter 22	chapter 31	chapter 37	chapter 48

Lane Change	**Jam**	**Drive-By**	**SigAlert**
-Avoiding the Harbor	-Greater L.A.	-Virtually Everywhere	-The Rim
chapter 28	chapter 35	chapter 42	chapter 46

Time & a Half	**Overtime**	**Working Weekend**	**Deadline**
-Limousine Way	-El Zócalo	-Dirt Shoulder	-Over the Net
chapter 25	chapter 32	chapter 39	chapter 43

To Labor	**To Dream**	**To Perform**	**To Die**
-East & West Forever	-America	-Angel's Flight	-Pacific Rim Auditorium
chapter 23	chapter 33	chapter 36	chapter 47

networks of exchange. In their trajectory across different cultures, media and audiences, the readings that these works receive trace an image of the global that may in the end be as important as the one they spell out in their substance and form.

References

Abbey, Edward (1975) *The Monkey Wrench Gang*, New York: Avon

Albrow, Martin (1996) *The Global Age: State and Society beyond Modernity*, Cambridge: Polity Press

Appadurai, Arjun (1996) *Modernity at Large: Cultural Dimensions of Globalization*, Minneapolis, MN: University of Minnesota Press

Beck, Ulrich (1992) *Risk Society: Toward a New Modernity*, trans. Mark Ritter, London: Sage

Cage, John (1969) *A Year from Monday*, Hanover, NH: Wesleyan University Press

Clifford, James (1997) *Routes: Travel and Translation in the Late Twentieth Century*, Cambridge, MA: Harvard University Press

Damrosch, David (2003) *What Is World Literature?* Princeton, NJ: Princeton University Press

DeLillo, Don (1982) *The Names*, New York: Knopf

Gibson, William (1984) *Neuromancer*, New York: Ace

Giddens, Anthony (1990) *The Consequences of Modernity*, Cambridge: Polity Press

Ginsberg, Allen (1984) *Collected Poems 1947–1980*, New York: Harper and Row

Hayles, N. Katherine (1984) *The Cosmic Web: Scientific Field Models & Literary Strategies in the 20th Century*, Ithaca, NY: Cornell University Press

Hofstadter, Richard (1996 [1964]) *The Paranoid Style in American Politics and Other Essays*, Cambridge, MA: Harvard University Press

Klein, Naomi (2000) *No Logo: Taking Aim at the Brand Bullies*, New York: Picador

McLuhan, Marshall (1994) *Understanding Media: The Extensions of Man*, Cambridge, MA: MIT Press

Mendelson, Edward (1976) 'Gravity's Encyclopedia', in George Levine and David Leverenz, eds, *Mindful Pleasures: Essays on Thomas Pynchon*, Boston, MA: Little, Brown, 161–95

Pynchon, Thomas (1973) *Gravity's Rainbow*, New York: Viking

Ross, Andrew (1991) *Strange Weather: Culture, Science, and Technology in the Age of Limits*, London: Verso

Rushdie, Salman (1991) *Imaginary Homelands: Essays and Criticism 1981–1991*, London: Granta

Sachs, Wolfgang (1992) *Satellitenblick: Die Visualisierung der Erde im Zuge der Weltraumfahrt*, Berlin: Wissenschaftszentrum Berlin für Sozialforschung

——(1999) *Planet Dialectics: Explorations in Environment and Development*, Halifax, CA: Fernwood Publishing.

Sassen, Saskia (2001) *The Global City*, 2nd edn, Princeton, NJ: Princeton University Press

Sklair, Leslie (1991) *Sociology of the Global System*, Hemel Hempstead: Harvester Wheatsheaf

Tomlinson, John (1999) *Globalization and Culture*, Chicago: University of Chicago Press

Wallerstein, Immanuel (1974) *The Modern World System*, New York: Academic Press

Weisenburger, Steven (1981) 'The End of History? Thomas Pynchon and the Uses of the Past', in Richard Pearce, ed., *Critical Essays on Thomas Pynchon*, Boston, MA: Hall, 140 56

Yamashita, Karen Tei (1997) *Tropic of Orange*, Minneapolis, MN: Coffee House Press

Chapter 17

1979, Edinburgh and Glasgow: Devolution Deferred

Cairns Craig

On 1 March 1979, the Labour Government of the United Kingdom held a referendum in Scotland on proposals to establish a devolved Scottish parliament that would take responsibility for those local issues which, since the Union of Scotland and England in 1707, had been the responsibility of the Westminster parliament in London. The proposals were the Labour Party's response to the success, since the late 1960s, of the Scottish National Party, which campaigned for the dissolution of the Union and the re-establishment of an independent Scottish state. The referendum outcome, however, was indecisive: although a small majority voted in favour, the total vote was split in almost equal proportions between 'yes', 'no' and 'didn't vote'. Labour refused to proceed with its proposals; the Scottish Nationalists withdrew their support for the Labour government, forcing a general election; and Margaret Thatcher's Conservative Party swept to power, dismissing all issues of separate Scottish political representation as irrelevant to the creation of an 'enterprise' economy that would re-establish Britain's world importance. With each of her following election victories cultural activists in Scotland predicted a 'doomsday scenario' – a massive Conservative victory in England, a massive Conservative defeat in Scotland – which would culminate not only in the destruction of Scotland's industrial infrastructure but in the elimination of Scottish cultural identity.

Devolution's failure posed fundamental questions about the nature and history of Scotland. If it failed to vote for even limited self-government was it really a nation at all? Had Scotland, divided as it was between the three languages of Gaelic, English and Scots, and divided between Highland and Lowland, ever fulfilled the minimum requirements of a *national* culture? Had the Union induced a culture of *deferral* to English values that made the Scots incapable of taking responsibility for their own future? Or had Scottish culture succeeded, as some argued, only in periods when it had adopted and accepted English cultural norms? In the 1920s and 1930s there had been a Scottish cultural revival, based on the revitalisation of the traditions of writing in Scots (as in the work of Hugh MacDiarmid and Lewis Grassic Gibbon) and on a return to the Celtic roots of Scottish tradition (in the novels, for instance, of Neil Gunn, in the art of J. D. Fergusson and in the Gaelic poetry of Sorley Maclean), but this so-called 'Scottish Renaissance' had neither the political impact of the Irish Revival movement, nor the international impact of Irish writers such as W. B. Yeats and James Joyce. Its weaknesses underlined, it was suggested, fundamental problems about Scotland that meant devolution had not just been *deferred* – it was a cultural and political impossibility.

Such questions, together with the intense economic depression of the early 1980s, provoked a state of despair that was captured in the most important literary work published in the aftermath of the Referendum, Alasdair Gray's *Lanark* (1981). Though Gray had been working on his novel since the 1950s, the failed career of its artist-hero, Duncan Thaw, seemed to offer an image of – and an explanation for – the failures of Scotland itself. Thaw muses, in a now famous passage, that the problem with Glasgow is that 'nobody imagines living here' because, 'if a city hasn't been used by an artist not even the inhabitants live there imaginatively'. Scotland is a place where the imagination has failed so that 'the only imaginable future was a repetition of a present which had shrunk to a tiny painful act' (Gray 1981: 243, 184). The impact of Gray's novel derived in part from the fact that the condition it described was so familiar: it represented a restatement of Edwin Muir's analysis of the failure of Scottish culture – and of the Scottish Renaissance movement – in *Scott and Scotland*, first published in 1936 but reissued in 1982, as though Scotland, like Duncan Thaw, had been trapped in the intervening years in 'a repetitive cycle of improvement and deterioration' (Muir 1936: 311). For Muir, the failure of Walter Scott as a writer and the failure of Scotland as a nation were two sides of the same coin: Scott's art was maimed by the fact that 'he spent most of his days in a hiatus, in a country, that is to say which was neither a nation nor a province' (Muir 1936: 1–12). His legacy, as Muir wrote in the *Free Man* in 1931, is 'an emptiness and unreality quite peculiar to Scotland', so that 'into this semi-vacuum the population of Scotland are born, imaginary citizens of an imaginary country' (Noble 1982: 106) – imaginary but nonetheless resolutely hostile to the artistic imagination which might redeem it.

The continuing significance of Muir's analysis – or the unchanging nature of the Scotland which it described – was confirmed by the most influential account of Scottish culture in the 1980s, Tom Nairn's *The Break-up of Britain* (1979). For Nairn, Scotland's modern nationalism represented the country's 'belated' arrival at a developmental stage typical of the rest of Europe in the nineteenth century. Ironically, Walter Scott had been one of the major inspirations of that European upsurge, but while Scotland might inspire nationalist revolt elsewhere what mattered to Scott was to render nationalist sentiment in Scotland '*politically* null – to make certain that it would not be felt that contemporary Scotland should be the independent continuation of the auld sang' (Nairn 1981: 150). As a consequence, Scotland's cultural identity became delusional, its potential for political action endlessly postponed. The deferral of devolution was, in effect, not a singular event but a re-enactment of the very nature of Scotland as a culture whose deferral to its neighbour ensured that an independent identity would always be beyond its reach.

In such a context it is hardly surprising that 'deferral' became a dominant theme in Scottish writing in the aftermath of 1979. In *Lanark*, Duncan Thaw's is a life deferred: his experiences in the 'real' world of Glasgow in the 1940s and 1950s are suspended (by suicide or madness) for an alternative, fantasy continuation of that life in the character of Lanark, a continuation, however, which moves forward in time without ever moving forward in achievement: 'My life is moving in circles. Will I always come back to this point?' (Gray 1981: 529). Equally, the protagonist of James Kelman's *The Busconductor Hines* (1984) is forever on the point of transforming his life by giving up his job but always deferring the moment of decision:

> I want to jack it I'm telling you come on.
> Right then you can jack it, I don't have to stop the bus but.

> Aye you do, I need to jack it; I want to have jacked it.
>
> Well you've jacked it.
>
> How can I have fucking jacked it if I'm still standing here in the scabby bastarn transport green with machine and cashbag for christ's sake! (Kelman 1984: 65)

The desire to *have already* achieved transformation is defeated by the fact of being still where he ought to be if had not 'jacked it'. And in Janice Galloway's *The Trick Is to Keep Breathing* (1989), the narrative recounts Joy Stone's refusal to recover from her partner's death: 'This is of the essence. The defendant is afraid of health. There is a certain power in illness she is reluctant to relinquish for the precise reason it lets folk off the hook' (Galloway 1989: 200). Like the Scotland she inhabits, Joy Stone wishes to defer her return to the 'real' world, while in A. L. Kennedy's *So I Am Glad* (1995), Jennifer lives in a state of constant deferral because, 'when the hoped-for future finally appears, I would rather not see what it brings because hope has already robbed it, mortgaged it to the bone. Hope ruins the future, fills it with clumsily balanced disappointments, every one ready to fall' (Kennedy 1989: 83). As Frank Kuppner summarised it in *A Concussed History of Scotland* (1990),

> I have always had the keen suspicion throughout my life that I was the hidden person sleeping on the other side of a locked door. Of course, I often wake up – but frequently only because of the noise which someone leaving makes in slamming it shut. (Kuppner 1990: 124)

For the Scottish novel in the 1980s and 1990s, it is always, as James Kelman puts it in *The Busconductor Hines*, 'too late it is too late, too fucking late' (Kelman 1984: 98); or, as Iain Banks's central character broods in *The Bridge* (1986): 'By the time we were ready to play our part it was already too late; we were always too soon or too late' (Banks 1986: 261). Scotland, at the forefront of world development in the eighteenth century, the workshop of Empire in the nineteenth, had become, by the late twentieth century, 'an emptiness and unreality' – a nation deferred.

*

In the traumatic aftermath of the devolution referendum – and in the years of de-industrialisation that followed – Scotland was a nation painfully turned in upon itself. However, the fact that Wales had also – and much more decisively, by a proportion of 4 to 1 – rejected the Labour government's proposals for a devolved government in Cardiff underlined how far the United Kingdom was from reaching the condition prophetically invoked by the title of Tom Nairn's, *The Break-up of Britain*. It was an irony underscored by the fact that in the one part of the United Kingdom which had had devolved government since the 1920s – Northern Ireland – the local parliament had been suspended as a result of the 'Troubles' that began in 1968, and then by the defeat of the 'power sharing' proposals of 1974 when the Ulster Protestant working class refused to cooperate with its largely nationalist Catholic minority. What seemed in Scotland to be a unique experience of the failure of national spirit was actually part of a complex readjustment in the relations between the four nations that had once formed the United Kingdom, a readjustment temporarily obscured by the neo-imperial grandeur of Mrs Thatcher's challenge to the dictators of Argentina, in the Falklands Crisis of 1982, but dramatically illustrated in literary terms when Seamus Heaney challenged the role attributed to him in the introduction to

Blake Morrison and Andrew Motion's *The Penguin Book of Contemporary British Poetry* (1982). Despite the fact that so many of his most famous poems were rooted in an Ulster childhood, he refused to be located within their conception of 'British' – 'Be advised! My passport's green' (Heaney 1983). On the other hand, the significance of that passport radically changed in 1988 when Britain and Ireland, as members of the European Community, both signed to the Single European Act, which effectively brought to an end their history as *independent* and *sovereign* states. From a European, if not from a British perspective, it became increasingly possible to envisage a Europe in which former nations, like Scotland, or claimant nations, like the Basque country, could co-exist in a federated power-structure which would make the old centralised nations of Europe largely redundant – at least in terms of the traditional conception of *sovereignty*.

It was a vision given credence by the analysis of postmodernism offered by Jean-François Lyotard in *The Postmodern Condition*, originally published in French in 1979 and in English in 1984. Lyotard's conception of postmodernism as the collapse of the 'grand narratives' that have characterised Western culture since the Renaissance was taken to undermine, in particular, the value of the nation and of the structures which underpinned it:

> what is new in all of this is that the old poles of attraction represented by nation-states, parties, professions, institutions, and historical traditions are losing their attraction. And it does not look as though they will be replaced . . . (Lyotard 1984: 14)

Lyotard's report was originally written for the 'Conseil des Universités' of the government of Quebec and it could be seen as a justification for the kind of decentralised, provincialised political structure characteristic of Canada as a state which had never had a 'grand narrative', and therefore had none of the typical features of European nationalisms. It was a point of view taken up in relation to Ireland by Richard Kearney, who argued in *Postnationalist Ireland* (1997) that Lyotard's analysis allowed us to reach beyond nationalism because 'the ultimate reference of postmodern narrative is not some totalising centre of meaning – Party, King, Nation-State – but other narratives' which deconstruct the 'Official Story' of 'modern imperialism and modern nationalism' in favour of an 'open plurality' of narratives (Kearney 1997: 63–4).

Lyotard's analysis was published, however, at the very moment when the Parti Québécois was pressing for a dissolution of the existing structure of the Canadian federation in favour of a new relationship based on 'sovereignty association', *i.e.* one in which Quebec would be accorded all the rights and status of an independent and sovereign nation on the basis of that most traditional of nationalist claims, its distinctive language and culture. In the referendum on this proposal, held in May of 1980, the 'sovereignty-association' proposal was defeated by 59 per cent to 40 per cent but to many in the Parti Québécois it represented only deferral – a prologue rather than conclusion to the search for recognition of Quebec's special status. Ironically, Quebec's assertion of its separate cultural history had developed through the 1960s and 1970s at the same time as, and in tandem with, the rise of a more general Canadian nationalism, which sought to distinguish Canada's cultural ethos from that of its far more powerful neighbour to the south. This was marked and to an extent facilitated by the foundation of the Canada Council in 1957, and, in its literary aspects, by the establishment two years later of *Canadian Literature*, the first journal entirely devoted to discussion of Canadian writing. Another significant expression was Margaret Atwood's account, in *Survival* (1972), of the particular themes and qualities that distinguished specifically *Canadian* writing from the other national literatures of North America.

As in Scotland, the dynamism of a resistant cultural nationalism produced a creative upsurge which carried Canadian writers to international success. Previously marginalised in Canada itself until the 1960s, much as Scottish literature had been in Scotland – and known abroad, if at all, mostly in the fiction of Robertson Davies – Canadian literature achieved a level of world recognition by the end of the century that was confirmed by the many awards to its leading writers. Carol Shields's *The Stone Diaries* (1993) won the Pulitzer Prize for fiction, and Alistair MacLeod's *No Great Mischief* (2000) the Dublin Literary Award, while the Booker Prize went to Michael Ondaatje for *The English Patient* (1996), and to Margaret Atwood – late in her highly influential career – for *The Blind Assassin* (2000). Atwood's prolific writing as poet, novelist and feminist critic showed how the very lack of definition in Canada's literary tradition could provide opportunities for those marginalised elsewhere, as was evidenced by the successes of Alice Munro and Margaret Laurence in exploring women's roles and identities.

While Scottish writers were becoming increasingly confident in their use of material intensely local both in setting and in language, the powerful, decentralising upsurge of Canadian fiction in the latter decades of the twentieth century was marked not only by a similar regionalism – for example in Laurence's *Manawaka* sequence and in Alice Munro's vividly fictionalised rural Southern Ontario – but by a reaffirmation of Scottish connections among writers of Scottish descent. In the prize-winning short stories of Alistair MacLeod on the lives of Cape Breton miners, fishermen and loggers, for instance, Canadian regionalism was often connected directly with a sense of continuing Scottish identity in Canada. MacLeod's writing systematically inserts an increasingly distant Scottish past into the Nova Scotian present of his first-person narratives, and Margaret Laurence's *The Diviners* (1974) hinges on a return to ancestral Scotland in order to stabilise an emergent, and specifically Canadian, cultural identity, while Scottish names and historical fields of reference significantly animate a number of Munro's stories.

Whatever the pluralism of its multicultural strands, this upsurge in Canadian writing represented the assertion of both residual *national* self-consciousnesses within the Canadian polity – French, Scottish, Caribbean – and of a self-consciously *Canadian* national identity which was defined by the interaction of these residual nationalisms. The establishment of legal status for the French language throughout the entire territory of Canada confirmed Canadian national identity not as somehow *beyond nationalism* but as an identity asserted in and through the enduring cultural and regional nationalisms which had originally been brought into the Canadian Federation at its inception, or which had been brought into the country by subsequent immigrants. These displaced nationalisms became the vehicles by which Canadians asserted their shared resistance to the proximity of what was, after 1989, the world's only cultural superpower. Paradoxically, therefore, local resistance to the Canadian centre – effectively to Toronto and Ontario – became the very marker of a shared Canadian identity. The constant threat of the dismemberment of the Federation – expressed for instance, in secessionist claims by Newfoundland, the last province to join the Canadian Federation in 1949 – was the very basis for its survival, since only by the constant arousal and then deferral of further devolution could the globalising force of American culture – and Toronto's participation in its role as the 'little apple' to New York's 'big apple' – be resisted. In the 'little narratives' of the Canadian regions and ethnic communities was enacted a shared resistance to Americanisation which constituted in itself a Canadian nationalism: not a 'grand narrative' in Lyotard's sense but exactly the kind of composite national narrative which had been characteristic of nationalist *nation* building – as opposed to nationalist *empire* building – throughout the development of the nation. If

Canada was taken to be representative of the postmodern condition, it appeared to be a condition offering an opportunity for the reassertion of cultural and political nationalism rather than a prophecy of its demise.

*

In 1979, the implications of the work of Jacques Derrida were beginning to impact on British critical theory, and for Derrida 'deferral' is of the very nature of language: all signs are 'deferred presence', so that 'whether we are concerned with the verbal or written sign, with the monetary sign, or with electoral delegation or political representation, the circulation of signs defers the moment in which we can encounter the thing itself' (Kamuf 1991: 61). A nation deferred is thus, paradoxically, the very definition of the nation: all nations exist in a continuous state of deferral – always incapable of reaching a 'presence' that would confirm their ultimate meaning. This revision of the conception of the nation found support in two enormously influential works of the early 1980s, Benedict Anderson's *Imagined Communities* (1983) and Hobsbawm and Ranger's *The Invention of Tradition* (1983). Anderson's argument that nations are, of their very nature, imaginary, and that the unity to which they appeal is a fictional construction, was supported by Hugh Trevor-Roper's contribution to *The Invention of Tradition*, a detailed analysis of how Walter Scott had imposed on Scotland a 'bizarre travesty of Scottish history, Scottish reality. Imprisoned by his fanatical Celtic friends, carried away by his own romantic Celtic fantasies, Scott was determined to forget historic Scotland, his own Lowland Scotland, altogether' (Hobsbawm and Ranger 1983: 29–30). In the aftermath of 1979, Scotland, which had become a *political* irrelevance in the UK, became significant in nation theory precisely because, in its inability to *achieve* nationhood, it epitomised the impossible search of all nationalist movements for the fulfilment of their imaginary identities. Scotland came, in the words of its leading sociologist, David McCrone, to stand 'at the forefront of sociological concerns in the late twentieth century' because, 'rather than being an awkward, ill-fitting case, it is at the centre of the discipline's postmodern dilemma' (McCrone 1992: 1), a dilemma inaugurated by the dissolution of the traditional unities that had defined the nation.

In Scotland after 1979, however, deferral led not to acceptance of the 'emptiness and unreality' of its 'imaginary' status but rather to a search for the *difference* by which deferral could be overturned. Scottish thinkers set out to recollect and to reconstruct their national traditions: to insist on the nation's previously unacknowledged difference from English – and, indeed, British – cultural norms. Publishing ventures such as Canongate Classics made available lost masterpieces of Scottish writing, including the almost entirely forgotten works of major women writers like Nan Shepherd and Willa Muir; interventions such as Beveridge and Turnbull's *The Eclipse of Scottish Culture* (1989) and Murray Pittock's *The Invention of Scotland* (1991) challenged the historiography on which Scotland's failed national identity was premised; studies such as Alexander Broadie's *The Tradition of Scottish Philosophy* (1990), Duncan Macmillan's *Scottish Art 1460–1990* (1990), John Purser's *Scotland's Music* (1992), Michael Lynch's *Scotland: A New History* (1991), together with the four-volume, multi-author *History of Scottish Literature* (1987–9) presented Scottish culture as a continuous and autonomous development, unbroken by Reformation, Enlightenment or industrialisation. Lindsay Paterson's *The Autonomy of Modern Scotland* (1994) insisted on Scotland's *de facto* independence within the Union while the very title of Tom Devine's *The Scottish Nation, 1700–2000* (1999) represented an assertion of national cultural continuity that defied earlier accounts of Scotland as a nation divided and fragmented by the consequences of the Union. Scotland, symbol of the nation as endless deferral, began to assert with ever greater confidence the specific differences on which its national identity was based – an assertion accompanied by an unmatched outpouring of artistic creativity. The experimentalism of the music of James MacMillan, poetry by Edwin Morgan, and the art of Steven Campbell, Alison Watt or Calum Colvin was matched by the international success of popular genre writers such as Ian Rankin (not to mention, J. K. Rowling, Scottish-based and supported by the Scottish Arts Council in the writing of the first Harry Potter book), as well as the assertively *Scottish* popular music of The Proclaimers and Runrig. In television drama (such as John Byrne's *Tutti Frutti* [1987] and *Your Cheatin' Heart* [1990]) and in film (*Shallow Grave* [1995] and *Trainspotting* [1996], for instance), Scotland achieved a level of international recognition defying expectations that it would be reduced to a cultural desert. Indeed, so rich were the cultural achievements of the twenty years after 1979 that many came to describe it as a second Scottish Renaissance – though the comparison is perhaps misleading, since this cultural upsurge, unlike its predecessor, did produce a specific political outcome in the successful referendum of 1997 and the consequent (re-)establishment of the Scottish parliament in 1999.

Perhaps the most significant artistic achievement of this period, however, was in the very form which was supposed – through the influence of Walter Scott – to have most insistently corrupted Scottish culture; the form in which, after Scott, Scotland's cultural weakness was most clearly revealed – the novel. The failure of Scotland's novelistic tradition had been regularly ascribed to some profound psychological defect that prevented Scots from recognising the real nature of their nation as one of the most industrialised in the world. David Craig, for instance, suggested that, 'as the country grew into a modern town-centred nation, Scottish fiction recoiled, immersing itself in the country ways which the sensitive soul . . . could use to gratify his nostalgia for that homely, rural past' (Craig 1961: 145). And in 1979, on the very eve of the Devolution Referendum, Francis Hart concluded his groundbreaking study of *The Scottish Novel* with the acknowledgment that 'There is still much truth in Edwin Muir's gloomy diagnosis of the novel in Scotland' (Hart 1978: 407). For Hart, that diagnosis pointed to three crucial areas of failure: first, a conflict between the desire to maintain local realism and, at the same time, to shape the local in terms of some universal paradigm involving 'national types and whole cultural epochs'; second, the Scottish novel's inevitable reflection of a divided history and culture, resulting in a 'dissociation of sensibility' which resulted in the inappropriate combination of contradictory genres and styles within a single work: 'romance repeatedly undercut by irony; austere realism jostling with fantasy'; and, third, the problem of how an English-writing narrator related to a community of Scots-speaking characters, producing what Hart described as a pervasively 'uncertain narrative voice' (Hart 1978: 406–7).

Hart's analysis was typical of the uncertainty about the value of Scottish culture in the 1970s. Reviewing Hart's book in *The London Magazine* in October 1979, the Scottish novelist Allan Massie suggested that it had identified the 'real problem which nobody in Scotland has answered satisfactorily. How do you write about a second-hand society?' What happened in the aftermath of 1979, however, was that these perceived weaknesses of the Scottish tradition were adapted, adopted and exploited by Scottish novelists in what, retrospectively, appears as a deliberate act of artistic devolution – if not, indeed, as a declaration of cultural independence. What were identified as the weaknesses of the Scottish tradition, when compared with the development of the English novel, were used to assert both the difference of the Scottish tradition and the validity of its particular development of the novel form.

Thus, Hart's initial problem – 'fidelity to local truth' combined with 'an intention to represent national types and whole cultural epochs' – was to be extravagantly adopted as the very medium of Alasdair Gray's *Lanark*, since it consists of two 'books' which recount the life of its aspiring Glaswegian artist, with precise 'fidelity to local truth', but then counterpoints that narrative with two other 'books' in which Duncan Thaw is translated into the figure of Lanark, who journeys through fantasy worlds that 'represent national types and whole cultural epochs'. The complex interaction of realism and fantasy is compounded by the fact that we start the novel in the fantasy world of Book 3, return to the realist world of Books 1 and 2, and conclude – after an 'Epilogue' – in the fantasy of Book 4, a structure designed to emphasise the book's deliberate combination of apparently contradictory genres and styles. Implicitly, Gray accepts Hart's definition of the contradictions of the Scottish novel but glories in their potentialities rather than retreating in embarrassment from their deficiencies. Thus in the fantasy books, Thaw's translation into Lanark invokes the 'New Lanark' of Robert Owen's nineteenth-century experiments in cooperative industrialisation, experiments which failed to 'thaw' the destructive effects of the capitalism that blights Duncan's life, but they also reveal that the realistic narrative of Duncan's experience in Glasgow in the 1940s and 1950s is equally fabulous, since he constantly encounters characters whose names – Watt, Macbeth, McAlpin – invoke Scotland's 'national types and cultural epochs'. *Lanark* situates itself assertively within the Scottish tradition by deliberately extending the possibilities of 'romance repeatedly undercut by irony; austere realism jostling with fantasy'.

Gray's strategies were to inspire a generation of Scottish novelists seeking to come to terms with the blighted economic and cultural world of Thatcherism. The typical Scottish novels of the period take place in a bleak and desolate environment in which the central character has lost all contact with the past, sometimes to the extent of being physically unconscious – as in Iain Banks's *The Bridge* or Irvine Welsh's *Marabou Stork Nightmares* (1995) – but more usually as a result of amnesia induced by psychological trauma. Lanark himself arrives in a strange city in a railway carriage with a picture of the town of Lanark on its wall from which he names himself; Jennifer in A. L. Kennedy's *So I Am Glad* 'can dig down as deep as there is to dig inside me and there truly is nothing there, not a squeak' (Kennedy 1995: 6–7); and James Kelman's Sammy Samuels in *How Late It Was, How Late* (1994) comes to consciousness aware that 'he was wearing an auld pair of trainer shoes for fuck sake where had they come from he had never seen them afore man auld fucking trainer shoes' (Kelman 1994:1). Not knowing where you are or how you got here: the central characters re-enact at a personal level the national crisis of lost identity and lost purpose, with the result that instead of maturing with time, they regress, like Margaret in A. L. Kennedy's *Looking for the Possible Dance* (1993): 'As Margaret grew her character seemed to shrink and by the time she was Gus's age she had almost forgotten what she was like' (Kennedy 1993: 85). Or they are trapped, like the drug addicts in Irvine Welsh's *Trainspotting*, in a world of sickening immobility:

> *It's a challenge tae move: but it shouldnae be. Ah can move. It has been done before . . . Ah'll move when ah'm sick enough . . . Ah jist cannae conceive ay ever being that sick that ah'll want tae move.* (Welsh 1993: 177)

Against the entrapped condition of their characters, however, the authors mobilise conventions of romance and fantasy as though, by denying expectations of realism which the Scottish tradition was accused of failing to fulfil, they could free the nation from the burden of its past. In A. L. Kennedy's *So I Am Glad*, for instance, Jennifer's relationship with a down-and-out drug addict is transformed when he claims himself to be – and appears in the novel to be – Cyrano de Bergerac, the French Renaissance poet. Fantasy's capacity to disrupt ordinary reality is parodically imaged when Cyrano deliberately insinuates himself into the photographs of tourists in Paris, so that their pictures will 'represent an honourable part of the Paris of history'. Jennifer delights in the fact that there are 'slides and videos and snapshots in the homes of all nations, each containing a small impossible addition, beaming selflessly in the background' (Kennedy 1995: 262). Post-1979, the Scottish novel delights in adding to its bleakest and most realistic narratives that 'small impossible addition' which will not only undermine the tradition of realism and reinforce those Gothic elements of the Scottish novel that celebrate the supernatural and the magical, but help make *imaginable* an alternative Scotland whose future could be fulfilled rather than deferred. The possible control over one's environment that this promised was imaged by the control that Scottish authors began to take over the visual layout of their works. In Janice Galloway's *The Trick Is to Keep Breathing*, for instance, the breakdown of the central character is expressed through a wide range of typographic devices, from mimicry of women's magazines to the representation of dialogue in playscripts. The narrative even begins to invade the margins of the page, first by writing text into them (as though the voice of the character can only exist in the margin) and then by deleting the page numbers of particular pages (as though the reader, like the character, has lost the place in the textual world). Such typographical control points in two directions. First, it underlines that the protagonist is not allowed to speak within the normal discourses of society – she can, like Scottish society in Thatcherite Britain, only exist in the margins. Second, it asserts, on the part of the author, an independence of the conventions of publishing and a control over her creative environment that sets a model for what the character lacks. *The Trick Is to Keep Breathing* focuses the double perspective of the devolutionary process of the Scottish novel. On the one hand, it is a novel of how to survive a future betrayed: 'The thing is you can spend so much time in this fantasy future you miss what the hell is going on under your nose ie The Present'. On the other, it is a novel about taking back control: 'The trick is not to think. Just act dammit. Act' (Galloway 1989: 193, 205).

If Hart's concerns about generic instability and 'dissociation of sensibility' were turned outside-in by these developments, his final concern, about the nature of narrative voice, was to be entirely rejected by a generation of Scottish writers who promptly adopted Scots not simply as the language of their characters but as the very medium of their narration. Just as Alasdair Gray accepted and extended the interaction of realism and fantasy which Hart deplored, so his close associate James Kelman adopted the conflict of standard and vernacular speech as the very identity of both his narrator and his characters. Moving back and forth between third person narrative, free indirect discourse, dialogue, and interior monologue, but with no typographic markers to distinguish them, Kelman created a style in which it seems that the character is narrating himself in the third person while commenting on that narration in the first person:

> The thing is ye see about Sammy's situation, the way he thought about things, who knows, it wasnay something ye could get yer head round. Hard to explain. Then these things as well that draw ye in then push ye away I mean fuck sake great, alright ye think alright, it's good man, it's okay, I mean who's gony fucking moan about it, there's nay moan on, it's just being practical, realistic, ye've just to be realistic, ye approach things in a down-to-earth manner. I mean Sammy was never a moaner. (Kelman 1994: 112)

In *How Late It Was, How Late*, we inhabit an indeterminate linguistic world: whose head is 'yer head'? – Sammy's, the reader's, the narrator's? Who is 'I' in the final sentence – Kelman, the narrator, Sammy himself, Sammy as narrator? The vernacular medium dissolves the linguistic distinctions that traditionally separated author/narrator from character and in so doing becomes a gesture of resistance against the dominant language of modern British society.

Vernacular Scots had always been central to the Scottish literary tradition but its imminent death had long been anticipated, so that despite its adoption by Hugh MacDiarmid as the central element of his Scottish Renaissance movement in the 1920s, and despite its deployment in working-class and historical dramas in the 1960s and 1970s, its usefulness to a modern national literature was seriously doubted. As Edwin Muir put it, 'Irish nationality cannot be said to be any less intense than ours; but Ireland produced a national literature not by clinging to Irish dialect but by adopting English and making it into a language fit for all its purposes' (Muir 1936: 178). Kelman's example, however, opened the way to a vigorous novelistic exploration of the potentialities of Scots, culminating in the international success of Irvine Welsh's *Trainspotting* (1993), with its polyphony of Scots voices phonetically rendered to emphasise their individual deviations from standard English. In the novel, the form in which English examples had most powerfully dominated Scottish creativity, the reassertion of vernacular Scottish voices forced readers into a symbolic relearning of the language of resistance and an implicit acknowledgment of Scottish writing's refusal of linguistic 'union'. *Trainspotting*'s central character, Renton, like many of Kelman's characters, can imitate standard English, but he does so only to subvert the values which it represents in Scotland. On trial with his friend Spud, he pretends contrition (in standard English), to the judge who declares that if he should

> fail to take the opportunity presented to you and appear before this court again, I shall have no hesitation in recommending a custodial sentence. Do I make myself clear?
>
>   Clear as a bell, you fuckin docile cunt. I love you, shite-for-brains.
>
>   – Thank you, your honour, I'm only too well aware of the disappointment I've been to my family and friends . . . I'm no longer indulging in self-deception. With god's help, I'll beat this disease. Thank you again.
>
>   The magistrate looks closely at us tae see if thirs any sign ay mockery oan ma face. No chance it'll show . . . Deadpan's better than dead. Convinced it's no bullshit, the doss cunt dismisses the session. Ah walk tae freedom; perr auld Spud gits taken doon. (Welsh 1993: 167)

Appearing to defer to English, he walks to freedom in Scots, and the English that seeks to suppress his vocal difference releases it back into circulation.

*

The rise of Scottish nationalism in the 1960s and 1970s perplexed political commentators. How could a nation whose general political stance was socialist or left of centre, and which regarded itself as one of the best educated and most democratic in the world, resort to the regressive fallacies of the nationalism which its people had spent the first half of the twentieth century fighting in two world wars? How could a political union which had created the most powerful empire in history, and which still played a significant role in the world, be threatened by the desire of its subordinate partner to become an insignificant northern

European nation state? Though there had been some assertion of a sense of independent Scottish culture in the folk revival of the 1950s – led by Hamish Henderson and Ewan MacColl – and signs of a new vitality in the use of Scots in the theatre in the work of writers such as Bill Bryden and Donald Campbell, even the book which did most to assert the independence of Scotland's cultural traditions – George Davie's *The Democratic Intellect* (1961) – insisted that those traditions had died in the late nineteenth century and held out no likelihood that they could be resurrected in the twentieth or twenty-first. Economists and sociologists insisted that Scotland's real difference from the rest of the United Kingdom was insignificant, so that even those inspired by the radical politics of the late 1960s envisaged a future of effective socialism rather than resurgent nationalism. The tensions of the period can be seen in the work of the most influential theatrical innovators of the 1970s, John McGrath's 7:84 Company. Their most successful works, such as *The Cheviot, the Stag and the Black, Black Oil* (1973) and *The Game's a Bogey* (1974), presented Scotland not as a partner in Empire but as itself a colonised country – a historical case argued by Michael Hechter in *Internal Colonialism* (1975) – whose salvation lay in the solidarity of international socialism. In making this case, however, the plays deployed Scottish iconography and distinctively Scottish theatrical traditions in ways that made their message, for many, one of nationalist resistance rather than socialist solidarity. As the Thatcher domination of British politics in the 1980s projected endless defeat for socialism in England, Scotland's socialist commitments came to be seen as a distinctively Scottish tradition which could be fulfilled only by real political autonomy: Scottish socialism and Scottish devolution became parallel agendas, so that almost the first act of the New Labour government of 1997 was to set up that second (and successful) referendum on a devolved Scottish parliament.

The sources of Scotland's drive towards autonomy, however, remained mysterious. The most obvious context was the decline of the British Empire, and the release of the peripheries of the United Kingdom from an unbending deferral to the needs of London as the core which held the empire together. The peripheries represented the history and experience of the British people that had been mislaid during the period when Empire required a unified culture that could be directed outwards at the rest of the world. Their re-emergence, therefore, went in parallel with the assertions of autonomy by former colonial territories that came to be identified as the 'postcolonialism' of those who wrote in English but were not the inheritors of English culture. In Ireland the postcolonial model as explanation of the success of formerly 'peripheral' cultures was enthusiastically embraced but in Scotland, with its much more ambiguous participation in colonial rule, literary critics tended to reject postcolonialism's explanatory framework for more specifically *literary* accounts of the particularity of Scottish writing, such as those offered by the 'dialogic' and 'carnivalesque' theories of the Russian theorist Mikhail Bakhtin. Ironically, it was the sudden collapse, after 1989, of the Soviet empire in which Bakhtin had worked, that revealed that Scotland's new nationalism was neither 'belated' nor eccentric.

In retrospect, what had been deferred in 1979 was not devolution: what had been deferred, but only briefly, was the collapse of the universalism, represented by the culture of English in the British Empire, that made local identity and local culture marginal to the common values of a universal history. What the Scottish vote represented was no more than a half-hearted commitment to that universalism and was an augury, therefore, of the refusal of such universalisms by the 'velvet revolutions' which overthrew Soviet communism or the 'people's revolts' which continue to resist the effects of capitalist globalisation. An era in which, in Richard Kearney's words, 'genuine internationalism (working at a global level) and critical regionalism (working at a local level) represent the two sides of a postmodern alternative' (Kearney 1997: 64) in fact turned into a new era of national self-assertion. Scotland was, in effect, a harbinger of a much vaster devolution, one in which primordial nationalisms – even if only recently 'invented' – proved far more powerful than the 'international' systems which had sought to repress them. Scotland's nationalism, which had seemed so historically inappropriate to the modern world, was revealed as only one of the many ancient identities that would emerge, like islands out of the sea, from the withdrawal of the floodtide of empires, asserting again their right to differ, refusing the deferral of their cultural traditions, and thereby becoming contributors to a modernity much more surprisingly different from any that could have been imagined in 1979.

References

Anderson, Benedict (1991) *Imagined Communities: Reflections on the Origin and Spread of Nationalism*, London: Verso

Atwood, Margaret (1972) *Survival: A Thematic Guide to Canadian Literature*, Toronto: Anansi

Banks, Iain (1986) *The Bridge*, London: Macmillan

Craig, David (1961) *Scottish Literature and the Scottish People 1680–1830*, London: Chatto and Windus

Galloway, Janice (1989) *The Trick Is to Keep Breathing*, Edinburgh: Polygon

Gray, Alasdair (1981) *Lanark*, Edinburgh: Canongate

Hart, Francis Russell (1978) *The Scottish Novel*, London: John Murray

Heaney, Seamus (1983) *An Open Letter* (Field Day Pamphlet no. 2), Derry: Field Day

Hobsbawm, Eric, and Terence Ranger, eds (1983) *The Invention of Tradition*, Cambridge: Cambridge University Press

Kamuf, Peggy, ed. (1991) *A Derrida Reader: Between the Blinds*, Hemel Hempstead: Harvester Wheatsheaf

Kearney, Richard (1997) *Postnationalist Ireland: Politics, Culture, Philosophy* London: Routledge

Kelman, James (1984) *The Busconductor Hines*, Edinburgh: Polygon

——(1994) *How Late It Was How Late*, London: Secker and Warburg

Kennedy, A. L. (1993) *Looking for the Possible Dance*, London: Secker and Warburg

——(1995) *So I Am Glad*, London: Jonathan Cape

Kuppner, Frank (1990) *A Concussed History of Scotland*, Edinburgh: Polygon

Lyotard, Jean-François (1984) *The Postmodern Condition: A Report on Knowledge*, Manchester: Manchester University Press

McCrone, David (1992) *Understanding Scotland: The Sociology of a Stateless Nation*, London and New York: Routledge

Muir, Edwin (1936) *Scott and Scotland: The Predicament of the Scottish Writer*, London: Routledge

Nairn, Tom (1981) *The Break-up of Britain: Crisis and Neo-Nationalism*, London: Verso

Noble, Andrew, ed. (1982) *Edwin Muir: Uncollected Scottish Criticism*, Totowa, NJ: Vision Press

Welsh, Irvine (1993) *Trainspotting*, London: Secker and Warburg

——(1995) *Marabou Stork Nightmares*, London: Jonathan Cape

Chapter 18

1989, Berlin and Bradford: Out of the Cold, Into the Fire

Andrew Teverson

Give me a line drawn across the world and I'll give you an argument.

(Rushdie 2002: 423)

In a 1990 interview with Blake Morrison, Salman Rushdie recalls 1989 with mixed emotions – as a source of lament and a source of celebration. His lament is for his personal situation, which prevented him from enjoying a dance on a crumbling wall. 'In normal circumstances I'd have been on the first plane to Berlin', he told Morrison:

> I envied my friends who did go . . . those images of people dancing on the Wall were quite extraordinary. And to miss the chance of being on it! I felt I'd missed out on one of the great moments of our time. (Reder 2000: 13)

His cause for celebration is a year that, personal affairs aside, might be regarded as an *annus mirabilis*:

> Those of us who were young in 1968 used to talk of 1968 as the moment when some great shift in power towards the people took place. But actually, nothing happened in 1968: a few kids ran down a street chased by the police. This time it *actually happened*. Eighty-nine does it again: 1689, 1789, and now 1989, the greatest year in European history since the end of the Second World War. (Reder 2000: 13)

The Czechs have a similar conceit, though it is expressed in more cryptic terms. '89', they point out, is '68' turned upside-down (Tismaneanu 1999: 120). Each party is dismissive of 1968 for quite different reasons. For the Czechs, 1968 was a failed year, due for inversion, because the 'Prague Spring', Alexander Dubcek's experiment in 'Socialism with a human face', was prevented from blooming into a 'Prague Summer' when Warsaw Pact tanks arrived to forcibly re-impose Soviet-style Communism. For Rushdie, 1968 was unsuccessful because the leftist student revolt against bourgeois 'authority' on the streets of Paris (and arguably, the whole utopian venture of 1960s activism) had failed to live up to expectations. Both Rushdie and the Czechs, however, are united in their reasons for lauding the achievements of 1989, for this was a year that, unlike its earlier, paler, upside-down shadow year, saw some real and enduring revolutions.

Given this, it seems extraordinary that even as late as the end of the summer of 1989, few commentators would have described the year as epochal in the terms Rushdie is able to use only a matter of months later. Significant events were unfolding in Hungary, where legislation had been passed permitting the existence of political parties to rival the Communists, and in Poland, where the once illegal trade union *Solidarnosc* [Solidarity] had gained sufficient public support to force the Communist authorities to hold elections, but no one was predicting a radical and immediate transformation in international political arrangements. Then, inspired by developments in Poland and Hungary, groups of people began to gather on the streets of East Berlin to demand similar reforms in the German Democratic Republic. Initially the GDR authorities remained inflexible. Just because your neighbour wallpapers his house, the Central Committee Secretary Kurt Hagar explained, did not mean that you had to do the same (Brown 1991: 126). As the demonstrations escalated into massive street protests throughout October, however, the position of the ailing GDR leader Eric Honecker became untenable and he was replaced by another Communist figurehead, Egon Kranz, who proposed, on 9 November, that there should be reforms, and that the borders of East Germany should be opened. In the confusion that followed, angry, ecstatic mobs on the streets took to the Berlin Wall and tore it down brick by brick, symbolically reuniting a Germany, and implicitly a Europe, that had been apportioned between the victorious allies after the defeat of Hitler in 1945 – though the wall itself was not built until 1961. This sudden removal of one kind of 'line across the world' effectively dissolved the justification for a separately constituted East German state. Egon Kranz and his politburo, accordingly, resigned on 3 December 1989, and the divided Berlin of Cold War fact and fiction ceased to exist.

By this time, hot on the heels of the dismantling of the wall, two further Eastern European revolutions were well underway. In Czechoslovakia, sizeable street protests on 17 and 18 November had forced the Communist Party Central Committee into dialogue with a Civic Forum of opposition groups, headed by the future leader of the democratic state, Václav Havel. In Romania, equivalent public protests culminated in the execution, on Christmas Day, of the Communist dictator Nicolae Ceausescu and his wife Elena. By New Year's Eve, 1989, to the astonishment of all observers, including seasoned analysts of the field, the Polish, Hungarian, East German, Bulgarian, Czechoslovakian and Romanian Communist states had gone, and the once monolithic edifice of Eastern European Communism had all but dissolved. This dramatic and precipitant political dissolution signalled the abrupt termination of the Warsaw Pact, the dismantling of the Soviet Union's 'outer empire', and, ultimately, the conclusion of the Cold War and the uneasy bi-polar power balance between Eastern Communism and Western Capitalism that had dominated and defined world affairs for four decades. When Russia itself finally declared that the Soviet Union was to be formally dissolved two years later in December 1991 this climacteric occurrence seemed only the logical culmination of the events of 1989, of which the triumphant assault on the Berlin Wall has come to stand as the most potent and enduring symbol of a people's power to rise up, resist and topple totalitarian regimes.

Authors and playwrights who habitually concern themselves with history and politics have not been slow to incorporate these events into literature. Caryl Churchill dramatises developments in Romania in 1989 in her play *Mad Forest* (1990), Howard Brenton takes the East German revolution as his subject in *Berlin Bertie* (1992), and David Edgar, in *The Shape of the Table* (1990), dramatises negotiations between former rulers and coordinated opposition groups in a country loosely based on Czechoslovakia. This latter play constitutes one of the first dramatic responses from a British left-wing standpoint to the apparent failure of the great Marxist-Leninist political experiment which began with revolutionary fervour and utopian expectations in Russia on 7 November 1917, and ended in

Eastern Europe with a fizzle, mired in corruption and discredited by human rights viola-tions on a massive scale. As might be expected from a committed socialist, Edgar's reaction is an ambivalent one. On the one hand, he clearly applauds the abrupt termination of a debased, autocratic Communist regime, and the victory of a democratically minded, populist collection of interests. On the other hand, he, and his characters, express some reservations concerning the demons that will be let loose in the wake of the collapse of Communism.

Two fears in particular trouble the political triumphalism of the moment: the fear expressed by the departing Communist leader, and Nazi concentration camp survivor, Michal Kaplan, that the European ethnic and nationalist factions that the Nazis exploited will be given new and vibrant life in the post-Communist period (a warning that the first graffiti of the new era, 'Gas All Gypsies Now', seems to reinforce) (Edgar 1990: 75); and the fear that the reaction against Communism will deliver Eastern Europe, like a lamb to the slaughter, into the hands of marauding multinational capitalists. Vera Rousova of the National Peasant's Party, for instance, while 'yielding to no one' in her delight at consign-ing the Communist Party leader 'and his associates to history's dustbin' is concerned by the implications of a clause in the opposition's demands that will allow 'foreign companies . . . a stake in national enterprises' (Edgar 1990: 60). 'You see', she explains to the discomfited student activist Zietek:

> I wonder if 'out there' they've really grasped what's going on. If they realise that they're exchanging the Red Flag for the pop song. Pravda for Playboy. The hammer and the sickle for the strip-joint, cola tin and burger-bar. To have expelled the Germans and the Russians just to hand the whole thing over to – America. (Edgar 1990: 60)

Similar anxieties are expressed by Tariq Ali and Howard Brenton in their collaboration of the same year, the play *Moscow Gold* (1990) – a Meyerholdian attempt to put the recent 'living history' of Russia onstage. The first act of the play – 'Before the Wall' – dramatises the struggle for power that brought Mikhail Gorbachev to power in the Soviet Union and the immediate effects of his policies of *glasnost* (openness) and *perestroika* (restructuring). The second act – 'After the Wall' – fictionalises Gorbachev's loss of political initiative to Boris Yeltsin as the accelerating momentum of *perestroika* and *glasnost* reveal that the Russian Communist state cannot be reformed without collapsing. Once again, while Ali and Brenton express approval at the dismantling of the KGB, and at the anti-corruption legislation passed by Gorbachev, the optimism and utopianism that led Francis Fukuyama to declare in 1989 that history was coming to an end because 'Western liberal democracy as the final form of human government' was triumphing (Fukuyama 1989: 4) is notably absent. Even as the wall is falling, the cacophonous chants of the victorious revellers – 'I want a BMW', 'I want to go shopping'· (Ali and Brenton 1990: 46) – suggest that the motivating force behind the revolution is not just a desire for social justice, freedom and democracy, but also a greed and acquisitiveness fuelled by the delusion that it will be good for Eastern Europe to become identical to Western Europe ('We want the West, we want to BE LIKE YOU') (Ali and Brenton 1990: 79).

On a more sinister note, Gorbachev fears that the thawing of the Cold War will give new life to 'the carcasses of the dinosaurs the cold has preserved all these years' (Ali and Brenton 1990: 45) – a fear that seems to be realised once the wall is down, when the stage (and by implication Russia) is hijacked by a rag-tag patchwork of neo-Nazi punks, old-school Russian fascists, Azerbaijani Islamic extremists, Moscow gangsters and Baltic nationalists. History's graduation party – as Richard Powers puts it in his representation of the wall's fall in the novel *Plowing the Dark* (2001) – may have brought about 'the end of the life-long war, the end of status quo brinkmanship, the end of the market's last alternative, the end of mutually assured destruction, of gunpoint-guaranteed safety'. Yet it had also ushered in a New World Order: 'the beginning of nuclear proliferation, the steady slide into universal factionalism, the fragmentation past any ability of power politics to control' (Powers 2002: 238). This factionalism, this disorientating sense of a loss of the taut certainties that had characterised the Cold War, has been the dominant concern of political writers in the post-Cold War international environment – as attested by David Edgar's later play, *Pentecost* (1994). This uses a debate about the provenance of a painting (and through the painting, about the provenance of the European Renaissance) to give an indication of the growing cultural, ethnic and religious disparity at play in regions like (though again it is not named) the former Yugoslavia.

A comparable sense of disorientation also figures in US drama of the period, notably in Tony Kushner's Brechtian theatrical epic of the AIDS plague, *Angels in America*. Set in 1985 and 1986, but premièring onstage in 1990 (Part One, *Millennium Approaches*) and 1992 (Part Two, *Perestroika*), the play straddles the watershed events of 1989, which it reflects in various ways. At the climax of Part One, an Angel bursts through the ceiling, scattering debris everywhere, in a breakthrough that seems to echo the sledgehammers' breach of the Berlin Wall. Heaven, which is visited in Part Two, is strewn with debris, and the Angels are disorientated due to God's having absconded. Their sense of abandonment is anticipated in the prologue of Part Two, where 'the World's Oldest Living Bolshevik', contemplating the imminent failure of the Soviet Union, asks whether it is possible 'to proceed without Theory' (Kushner 1994: 1). His question is taken up again in the epilogue, set in February 1990, after the Wall's fall, where Louis contends that 'the sprawl of life [is] . . . all too much to be encompassed by a single theory now'. This, however, is contradicted by Hannah: 'You need an idea of the world to go out into the world. . . . You can't wait for a theory, but you have to have a theory' (Kushner 1994: 98). The brief interval of *perestroika* (and of Kushner's *Perestroika*) heralds an era of indeterminacy.

The transition from the uneasy polarisation of the Cold War to the indeterminacy of the post-Communist era is also charted in the post-1989 works of the master of the Cold War spy novel, John le Carré. In le Carré's early fictions, exemplified by *The Spy Who Came in from the Cold* (1963), the world of Cold War espionage is fraught with moral ambiguity, but it nonetheless attests to what the US Deputy Secretary of State Lawrence Eagleburger was later to call 'a remarkably stable and predictable set of relationships among the great powers' (Hoffman 2001: 192). The fall of the wall and the subsequent dissolution of the Soviet Union had – as the Canadian Secret Service agent turned le Carré literary critic, Tod Hoffman recalls – cast all the assumptions made by security services and governments concerning the relationship between global powers into disarray and forced spies to start hunting around for new threats in order to justify their own existence. This, Hoffman observes, was not a difficult thing to do, '[t]hreats of varying magnitudes abounded', but '[i]t took thought to explain how Ukraine or Georgia or Kazakhstan or other Soviet successor states posed a threat to national security' and '. . . nothing presented as menacingly impressive a danger as Communism, with its promise to subvert and dominate capitalist democracy' (Hoffman 2001: 196). Le Carré's 1989 novel *Russia House* responds to this situation by forging a spy novel out of the unwillingness of the higher echelons of the secret service (especially the US secret service) to admit that '[t]he Soviet knight is dying inside his armour' (le Carré 1999b: 30). 'The old isms were dead', le Carré's narrator observes, and 'the contest between Communism and capitalism had ended in a wet whimper', but still the American strategists are struggling to prolong the Cold War 'long after the music had ended' (le Carré 1999b: 374). Their reason for doing so is expressed with commendable brevity by the CIA's head of Soviet operations: 'How do you peddle the arms race when the only asshole you have to race against is yourself?' (le Carré 1999b: 323).

Le Carré's later post-Cold War novels continue in a similar vein, with his narratives frequently turning on the efforts of British and US security services to exploit new threats to 'global security' for ideological and militaristic self-affirmation. His 2004 novel *Absolute Friends*, for instance, centres on the efforts made by the US secret services to fabricate terrorist activities in Heidelberg in order to bring Germany into line in the 'war against terror'.

*

Plays such as Edgar's *The Shape of the Table* and Ali and Brenton's *Moscow Gold* help to establish what has become the dominant response of the left in Britain to the events of 1989, one which seems to involve two common assertions. First, that although Eastern European Communism had in that heady year been comprehensively discredited, its apparent opposite, capitalism (or more specifically in Britain, 'free market' monetarist Thatcherism), had not thereby been validated. Second, that although specific Communist leaders such as Stalin, Brezhnev, Ceausescu and Honecker had been revealed to be corrupt and repressive, the original principles of Socialism – indeed, the ideals of the Socialist state – were still worth pursuing. The left-wing novelist John Berger makes an argument to this effect in an essay, while celebrating the spirited iconoclasm that led the crowds in 1989 to tear down the statues of their oppressors. 'The idols are being torn down because they embodied pitilessness', he writes. 'Yet, in the beginning, the Communists became Communists because moved by pity, Marx included. He wrote into what he saw as the laws of history the salvation of the pitiful. Nothing less' (Berger 2001: 578). Comparably, Doris Lessing, who left the British Communist Party in the 1950s in disgust at the excesses of Stalin, has insisted that it is part of the calamity of Soviet-style Communism that it has been allowed to infect and undermine potentially viable Socialist movements in Western Europe. '[T]he left-wing . . . even liberal movements of Europe', she told Edith Kurzweil in 1992, 'have been terminally damaged because the progressive imagination was captured by the soviet experience' (Ingersoll 1994: 211). In a more ideologically distanced reflection on the significance of the fall of the Berlin Wall for the British Left, in his 1992 novel, *Black Dogs*, Ian McEwan creates the character Bernard Tremaine who, in his youth, has been a Communist, but who greets the destruction of the Wall with an enthusiasm bordering on guilt. His daughter Jenny cynically observes that his hunger to be in Berlin as the Wall is dismantled is a result of his need to see 'put right' his earlier 'Big Mistake' – his youthful assumption, that is, that Communism would remain a 'benign' alternative to fascism, and not an equivalent form of totalitarianism (McEwan 1992: 70).

If the fictional Bernard Tremaine was free to go and dance on the rubble of the Berlin Wall, the wholly non-fictional Salman Rushdie was unable to do so because another international development had reached its climax slightly earlier in 1989. This development too had a relatively innocuous beginning – the publication on 26 September 1988 of the Bombay-born prize-winning British author's *The Satanic Verses*: a novel predominantly about the experiences of Asian and Afro-Caribbean migrants living in Margaret Thatcher's (or 'Maggie Torture's') Britain, but also including fantasy or dream sequences concerning the life of the prophet Muhammad. These latter scenes – particularly one in which a group of prostitutes in a brothel impersonate the wives of Muhammad to titillate customers – had led to protests by some Muslim readers and reviewers. These were noted by the Indian government, who swiftly banned the book: Rajiv Gandhi's Congress-I Party was facing an election and did not wish to risk losing the Muslim vote. In response to this ban, Rushdie wrote a public letter of protest to the Indian Prime Minister in which he argued that freedom of expression ought to be at the foundation of any democracy, and pointed out that the 'offensive' sequence concerning Muhammad 'happened in a dream, the fictional dream of a fictional character, an Indian movie star, who is losing his mind' (Weatherby 1990: 129). The ban was not revoked, however, and by now, some Muslim groups in Britain had started mobilising against *The Satanic Verses*. Dr Syed Pasha, as Secretary of the Union of Muslim Organisations in Britain, initiated a campaign to have the novel banned in the UK and demanded that the British government prosecute Rushdie. Mrs Thatcher's government declined on the basis that 'people who act within the law should be able to express their opinions freely' (Weatherby 1990: 130).

Several demonstrations were then staged by outraged Muslims in Bradford, Bolton and Hyde Park, where copies of *The Satanic Verses* were publicly burned – an act of spectacular, and highly evocative, protest that promptly made what was becoming known as the Rushdie 'affair' headline news across the globe. Rushdie declared himself to be deeply distressed by these demonstrations – not only because of their challenge to basic freedoms, but also because they were made by the very immigrant groups about whose experiences he felt himself to be writing. The worst was yet to come, however, when the Ayatollah Khomeini of Iran, a spiritual leader of Shiite Muslims, issued a *fatwa* (a decree) that demanded the execution of Rushdie and his publishers. The *fatwa* was read on Radio Tehran on Valentine's Day 1989. 'In the name of God Almighty', Khomeini declared:

> I would like to inform all the intrepid Muslims in the world that the author of the book entitled *The Satanic Verses* . . . as well as those publishers who were aware of its contents, have been sentenced to death. I call on all zealous Muslims to execute them quickly, wherever they find them . . . . Whoever is killed on this path will be regarded as a martyr, God willing. (Weatherby 1990: 154)

The following day, an Iranian cleric, Hojatoleslam Hassani Sanei of the 15 Khordad Foundation, seconded the Ayatollah's demand by placing a bounty on Rushdie's head: $2.6 million for an Iranian to kill Rushdie, $1 million for anyone else. That day Rushdie was due to attend a memorial service for his friend, Bruce Chatwin, who had died of an AIDS-related illness. After some consideration Rushdie decided to keep his appointment, pursued by the world's media, but this was to be the last public appearance he was to be able to make for several years. The service completed (and with Paul Theroux's black joke – 'you're next Salman' – to ease him on his way) Rushdie went into hiding, protected by British Special Branch Police.

The response from the literary and creative community to what was becoming known as the 'Rushdie Affair' was, with a few notable exceptions, favourable to Rushdie. Frances d'Souza and Carmel Bedford founded the International Committee for the Defence of Salman Rushdie and His Publishers (ICDSR); Tariq Ali and Howard Brenton rapidly wrote a one-act play, *Iranian Nights* (Royal Court, 1989), expressing their 'solidarity' with a 'brother author' (Ali and Brenton 1989: i); Harold Pinter organised a delegation of writers to march to Downing Street; and many others wrote publicly in support of Rushdie and his work. So many writers, indeed, were prepared to speak out in defence of Rushdie that in 1992 the German newspaper *Die Tageszeitung* 'was able to lead a consortium of newspapers in publishing a series of letters from eminent writers', subsequently collected by the ICDSR as *The Rushdie Letters* (MacDonogh 1993: 9). These letters, together with the elaboration of Muslim grievances against *The Satanic Verses* by scholars such as M. M. Ahsan, Shabbir Akhtar and Ziauddin Sardar, constitute one of the most important bodies of writing produced in recent years on the subjects of censorship, blasphemy and freedom of speech in sensitive, multicultural and multifaith environments (see Ahsan and Kidwai 1991).

For a number of writers, however, the Rushdie 'affair' was not just about blasphemy and freedom of speech, but, in Britain, reflected a developing crisis in national cultural identity – a crisis concerning what it meant to be British in the postcolonial, postmigratory period, and a crisis concerning the place of diasporic (particularly Muslim) communities within the nation. In a 1986 essay on the cultural and religious mix of Bradford, Hanif Kureishi had already attempted to capture the lineaments of developing cultural tensions both within the Asian community itself, and between the Asian community and the broader British public. For Kureishi, however, it was the 1989 'affair' that served to crystallise and clarify these tensions, especially those between the first generation of migrants from India and Pakistan 'who'd come here . . . to make a new life in the affluent west' (Kureishi 1996: 136) and their children. These children – or children's children – had grown up British, but, reacting against economic deprivation and institutionalised racism, had rejected affiliation with ideas of 'Englishness' and were seeking meaning from external (often religious) sources. Such conflicts serve as a dramatic basis both for Kureishi's later novel *The Black Album* (1995), in which Muslim responses to the Rushdie 'affair' are fictionalised, and his film, *My Son the Fanatic* (1997), the idea for which was, Kureishi claimed, 'provided by [his] thinking about the fatwah against Salman Rushdie' (Kureishi 2002: 215). The plots of both these fictions allow Kureishi to present, on one side, an argument in favour of the kinds of hybridised cultural identity that liberal-minded, secular, cosmopolitan writers like Rushdie have come to embody; and, on the other side, to seek to understand the motivations behind the backlash against figures like Rushdie from members of the Muslim community who see only collision and antagonism between white British and South Asian culture.

Similar cultural tensions are explored in Zadie Smith's first novel, *White Teeth* (2000), which, like Kureishi's *Black Album*, operates largely as an extended reflection on the state of youth in the multi-racial Britain of the 1980s and 1990s. Here the Bradford burning of *The Satanic Verses* is presented as a focus for an act of rebellion by Millat Iqbal and his 'crew' against British liberal culture and against Asians, like Rushdie, who are perceived as compromised (Rushdie is referred to by one of the characters as a 'coconut': brown on the outside but white within) (Smith 2000: 201). Millat and his crew have not, of course, done Rushdie the honour of reading his book. Echoing the Indian finance minister who had observed that it is not necessary to wade through a filthy drain to know what's in one, Millat argues that 'you don't have to read shit to know that it's blasphemous' (Smith 2000: 202). As Millat is astute enough to realise, however, the contents of the book itself, and the intentions of the writer, were no longer, by February 1989, the principle motivations behind the protests:

> Millat knew nothing about the writer, nothing about the book . . . But he knew other things. He knew that he, Millat, was a Paki no matter where he came from . . . he knew he had no face in this country, no voice in the country, until the week before last when suddenly people

like Millat were on every channel and every radio and every newspaper and they were angry,
and Millat recognised the anger, thought it recognised him, and grabbed it with both hands.
(Smith 2000: 202)

It is one of the grim ironies of the *Satanic Verses* furore that, had Millat read the book
against which he was protesting, he would also have seen his anger reflected there. For *The
Satanic Verses* itself engages in an extended and powerful protest against institutionalised
racism in the British establishment, and also includes a sympathetic thematisation of 'the
very experience of uprooting, disjuncture and metamorphosis (slow or rapid, pleasurable or
painful) that is the migrant condition' (Rushdie 1991b: 394). 'If *The Satanic Verses* is anything,' as Rushdie later protested, 'it is a migrant's-eye view of the world', designed 'to
create a literary language and literary forms in which the experience of formerly colonised,
still-disadvantaged peoples might find full expression' (Rushdie 1991b: 394). In the event,
as Millat's experience attests, *The Satanic Verses* did prove a rallying point for Muslim communities within Britain and served to bring Muslim communities and their concerns to the
attention of the broader British public – but, contrary to Rushdie's expectations, this was
achieved not in sympathy with the book but in antagonism to it.

*

The two main political developments of the year 1989 – the *fatwa* against Rushdie and the
Eastern European revolutions – are not linked in any immediate, causal sense. A number
of writers and commentators have, however, identified points of comparison between
them, not least Salman Rushdie himself. His *Haroun and the Sea of Stories* – a novella for
children written during the dark days of 1990 – includes, as one of its central images, a
'wall of force' that separates two communities. This wall has been created on the moon
Kahani by the Guppees, who are consummate talkers, in order to keep themselves separate
from (and safe from) the Chupwalas, who do not talk at all. But far from resolving the
problem of their mutual suspicion, the wall has only fostered and extended antagonisms
between Gup and Chup by making the differences between their citizens into points of
absolute enmity. The novel's youthful hero Haroun quickly realises that the moon's problems stem not from any natural or inevitable hatred between Guppees and Chupwalas, but
are the result of artificial, politicised attempts to enforce separation. These have led in turn
to the ascendance of the malignant dictator Khattam Shud, who has exploited the cultural
antagonisms implied by the wall to bring about a war between the two communities. To
resolve the situation, Haroun causes the moon, which has been stilled on its axis, to turn
so that that which has been kept separate is mixed, and the need for 'Walls of Force' is eliminated. This radical transformation in the way that the two cultures interact is prelude to
a total reassessment of their understanding of one another.

Within this story-line seem to be ravelled allusions both to the situation in Berlin, and
to Rushdie's own situation. On one hand, with his cult of silence and his fanatic's war
against the forces of pleasure, storytelling and free speech, the puritanical Khattam Shud
embodies the combined forces that Rushdie felt to be arrayed against him. On the other
hand, the polarisation of a community as a result of enforced ideological separation
involves a reflection upon the recent history of Germany. The dismantling of the 'Wall of
Force' in *Haroun and the Sea of Stories* may thus be regarded as an act with two-fold significance. It is a retrospective commemoration on Rushdie's part of something that has already
occurred in Germany (a consolation, perhaps, for his own inability to see this great

historical moment for himself), but it is also a utopian piece of wish-fulfilment in which Rushdie uses fantasy to dissolve the walls that he had seen springing up around him. In the former instance, Rushdie is saluting the termination of a form of autocracy that in 1989 had already come to grief. In the latter, he is hoping that another form of autocracy in 1989, one that seemed all too emergent, might also be blown to dust by a fantastical, intrepid child seeking to restore his father's storytelling abilities. The very fact that both forms of autocracy in Rushdie's story (residual and emergent), can be combined in the same symbolic constellation of images suggests that he perceives a comparable kind of conflict at work in both cases: the conflict between what Daniel Chirot has called 'tyrannies of certitude' (Tismaneanu 1999: 7) on one side, and pluralism, democracy, free speech on the other.

Salman Rushdie is not alone in seeing a connection between his own situation and the situation in Eastern Europe. The playwright and soon-to-be president of Czechoslovakia, Václav Havel – in a speech accepting the German Booksellers Peace Prize, and delivered in absentia (since he was still in prison) on 25 July 1989 – makes it clear that he sees his own imprisonment for dissident activities as equivalent to Rushdie's persecution for *The Satanic Verses*. In both cases, Havel argues, words are used on one side, by the Communists and Khomeini, to 'mesmerise, deceive, inflame, madden, beguile' and on the other side, by dissidents and Rushdie, to 'electrify society'. 'Words', Havel concludes, are:

> a mysterious, ambiguous, ambivalent, and perfidious phenomenon. They can be rays of light in a realm of darkness . . . They can equally be lethal arrows. Worst of all, at times they can be one or the other. They can even be both at once. (Havel 1991: 381)

Havel's emphasis on the importance of words reminds us that 1989 was also a year in which speculations concerning the functions of literature in political contexts achieved a sudden new urgency. If the abstractions of some forms of critical theory in the early 1980s had tended to detach texts from their material contexts – and if the age-old Platonic tradition that 'art' distracts us from 'reality' was still alive and well in Thatcher's Britain and Reagan's America – events of 1989 seemed to demand a reassessment. In Eastern Europe, after all, history was clearly on the move, and most commentators were agreed that dissident writers such as Václav Havel and Mircea Dinescu had had a significant role to play in that movement. The historian Timothy Garton Ash was even inspired to announce that in the 1989 revolutions 'History [had] out-done Shelley, 'for poets were the acknowledged legislators of this world' (Tismaneanu 1999: 112). Richard Powers, in his retrospective fictionalisation of the period, *Plowing the Dark*, confirms this assessment to the extent that he sees artists and image makers as having played a significant role in shaping the events of 1989. Powers's assessment, however, lacks the implicit humanism of Garton Ash's (or Shelley's) celebration of the power of art to make things better. On the contrary, the grim logic of his plot suggests that artists can be complicit in destruction as well as creation. This potentiality is concisely expressed in the novel's second epigraph, taken from Gertrude Stein's *Autobiography of Alice B. Toklas* (1933) in which Pablo Picasso, having seen a piece of military equipment that has been camouflaged using techniques developed from Cubist and Surrealist painting, observes 'C'est nous qui avons fait ça' – 'it is we that have created that' (Powers 2002: v)

Powers's novel itself is a response to an earlier fictionalisation of the period in Don DeLillo's *Mao II* which is even more sceptical about the power of the arts in the modern globalised media arena, either for good or for bad. For DeLillo, the mass-mediation of the events of 1989 (which reduces them to Baudrillardian televisual simulations), and the primacy that terrorists have gained over the art of visual sensation, have rendered the writer – one-time master of representation and spectacle – ineffectual. 'Years ago I used to think it was possible for a novelist to alter the inner life of the culture', the author figure Bill Gray complains. 'Now bomb-makers and gunmen have taken that territory. They make raids on human consciousness. What writers used to do before we were all incorporated' (DeLillo 1992: 41). A little later he adds:

> What terrorists gain, novelists lose. The degree to which they influence mass consciousness is the extent of our decline as shapers of sensibility and thought. The danger they represent equals our own failure to be dangerous . . . In societies reduced to blur and glut, terror is the only meaningful act. (DeLillo 1992: 157)

Salman Rushdie is not mentioned by name, either in DeLillo's or Powers' novels, yet the analysis of the relationship between writing and terrorism in both texts is haunted by the ghost of the death sentence passed by Khomeini (see Scanlan 1994). For DeLillo, such a death threat can only prove the powerlessness of the writer in the face of events, and confirms the ease with which books get swallowed up, beached and burned, by historical processes that overwhelm them. Powers's response is more complex: literature, like all forms of representation, may still, as the Rushdie case proves, both act upon the world and be acted upon by it. Yet that action cannot be regarded as simply 'good' or 'bad': just *complicit* or *non-complicit* with the broader trends of society and its political leaders. Literature, in either case, remains a phenomenon that is buffeted by politics – that is transformed by, subdued by, enlivened by political events; and so even as we retrospectively begin to consider how the Cold War gave distinctive form to literary endeavours between the 1950s and the 1980s, writers such as DeLillo and Powers, Brenton and Ali, Smith and Kureishi are beginning to define the political role played by literature now that it has come out of the cold and gone into the fire.

References

Ahsan, M. M., and A. R. Kidwai, eds (1991) *Sacrilege versus Civility: Muslim Perspectives on The Satanic Verses*, Leicester: The Islamic Foundation
Ali, Tariq, and Howard Brenton (1989) *Iranian Nights*, London: Nick Hern
——(1990) *Moscow Gold*, London: Nick Hern
Berger, John (2001) *Selected Essays*, ed. Geoff Dyer, New York: Pantheon
Brenton, Howard (1992) *Berlin Bertie*, London: Nick Hern
Brown, J. F. (1991) *The Surge to Freedom: The End of Communist Rule in Eastern Europe*, London: Adamantine Press
Churchill, Caryl (1998) *Mad Forest*, in *Plays Three*, London: Nick Hern, 109–81
DeLillo, Don (1992) *Mao II*, London: Vintage
Edgar, David (1990) *The Shape of the Table*, London: Nick Hern
——(1994) *Pentecost*, London: Nick Hern
Fukuyama, Francis (1989) 'The End of History?', *The National Interest*, Summer, 3–18
Havel, Václav (1991) 'A Word About Words', trans. A. G. Brain, in Paul Wilson, ed., *Open Letters*, London: Faber and Faber, 377–89

Hoffman, Todd (2001) *Le Carré's Landscape*, Montreal: McGill-Queen's University Press

Ingersoll, Earl G., ed. (1994) *Doris Lessing: Conversations*, Princeton, NJ: Ontario Review Press

Kureishi, Hanif (1996) *The Black Album*, London: Faber and Faber

——(1997) *My Son the Fanatic* London: Faber and Faber

——(2002) *Dreaming and Scheming: Reflections on Writing and Politics*, London: Faber and Faber

Kushner, Tony (1994) *Angels in America, Part Two: Perestroika*, London: Nick Hern

le Carré, John (1999a) *The Spy Who Came in from the Cold*, London: Sceptre

——(1999b) *Russia House*, London: Sceptre

——(2004) *Absolute Friends*, London: Hodder

MacDonogh, Steve, ed. (1993) *The Rushdie Letters: Freedom to Speak, Freedom to Write*, Dingle, Co. Kerry: Brandon

McEwan, Ian (1992) *Black Dogs*, London: Cape

Powers, Richard (2002) *Plowing the Dark*, London: Vintage

Reder, Michael, ed. (2000) *Conversations with Salman Rushdie*, Jackson, MS: University of Mississippi Press

Rushdie, Salman (1991a) *Haroun and the Sea of Stories*, London: Granta

——(1991b) *Imaginary Homelands: Essays and Criticism 1981–1991*, London: Granta

——(1992) *The Satanic Verses*, Dover, DE: Consortium

——(2002) *Step Across This Line: Collected Non-Fiction 1992–2002*, London: Cape

Scanlan, Margaret (1994) 'Writers among Terrorists: Don DeLillo's *Mao II* and the Rushdie Affair', *Modern Fiction Studies* 40.2, Summer, 229–52

Smith, Zadie (2000) *White Teeth*, London: Penguin

Tismaneanu, Vladimir, ed. (1999) *The Revolutions of 1989*, London: Routledge

Weatherby, W. J. (1990) *Salman Rushdie: Sentenced to Death*, New York: Carroll and Graf

Chapter 19

11 February 1990, South Africa: Apartheid and After

Louise Bethlehem

Signs of Redemption

> The man comes walking, tall and solemn and slow. One of his hands bends into a fist, an old fist, tight with stamina and ash. He raises it before the crowd, which presses in on him and takes possession of his name. (Hirson 1996: 10)

'One long ocean away' from South Africa, the expatriate poet Denis Hirson views in these extracts the global relay of images which accompanied Nelson Mandela's release from prison.

> There are only a few yards to go now, the ground widens under his feet. It is February 11th, 1990. History waits for him like a big smart car and he gets in . . . (Hirson 1996: 4, 11)

The moment, as Hirson's poem attests, was one of undeniable, even redemptive, power. So much so, that some commentators see it as having inaugurated 'the civilised twentieth century' – belatedly, yet not without consolation (Asmal, Asmal and Roberts 1997: 1). This judgement makes the slow and as yet precarious dismantling of apartheid, with its anticipation of moral repair and material reparation, into the occasion for an impromptu realignment of the century. In a stroke, the familiar invocation of the apartheid State as a powerful token of moral reproach is reversed, for 'civilisation' – or at the very least, democracy – will soon enough take up residence in South Africa. 'One more/ news programme and Mandela comes walking, behind/ him the unsealed door of an entire country' (Hirson 1996: 12).

Within that country, however, unqualified optimism would become progressively harder to sustain. In the months following the euphoria of release, massacres, political assassinations, and the daily testimony of black South Africans bore constant reminders that death had become a silent partner at the negotiating tables where South Africa's new identity was being forged. What became of the hints of redemption amid this devastation? In one tangible sense, they were concentrated in the figure of Nelson Mandela whose incisive political agency was augmented now by sheer visibility as the very incarnation of transition. A character in Pamela Jooste's post-apartheid novel *People Like Ourselves* reflects on the moment:

> For all of his young life you weren't allowed to see Nelson Mandela at all. Some or other Department put a stop to all that as if it was dangerous just to look at his face, but things have

changed now. Everyone who knows how to point a camera, how to press a button is making up for lost time. Now you can see Nelson Mandela any day of the week with any language text of your choice without even looking too hard. (Jooste 2004: 202)

Mandela's visibility was itself, the passage suggests, a lesson in the repair of the cultural sign. The making and marketing of Nelson Mandela as the definitive icon of the 'new' South Africa that was inaugurated on 11 February 1990 effectively suspended the censorship that had sought to contain Mandela's political opposition to the apartheid State by, among other things, banning his words and image. But now, the man's freedom proclaimed itself through the unrestricted circulation of its signs: a proclamation that some saw as the realisation of a prophecy. For South African literature in English had, after all, long since oriented itself towards just such a redemption of the sign, whatever the duress – or duration – of the rupture of language that was an integral part of the repressive political culture surrounding it. The euphemisms of the apartheid State were a notorious component of its social engineering. Thus the forced removals of populations from their land or the imposition of coercive regimes of land use could be designated agricultural 'betterment schemes' on the part of white bureaucrats, or the 'Natives (Abolition of Passes and Coordination of Documents) Act' of 1952 could function in defiance of its apparent meaning to extend rather than to curtail the punitive reach of the Pass Laws. From the onset of National Party rule, South African literature in English unfolded within, and against, the co-option of the sign that was itself a component of the material violence of apartheid.

The Truth about Apartheid

For many of its canonical authors under apartheid the role of South African literature in English consisted in the need to uncover the manifold falsehoods of 'separate development' through restoring to public view forms of social, historical or political knowledge that the regime, continuing the precedent of its segregationist colonial precursor, actively suppressed, distorted or denied. 'Telling the truth is bad for apartheid . . .' one local author, Rose Moss, would proclaim in the mid-1970s, in blunt articulation of the prevailing consensus. 'The primary obligation is to tell the truth' (Moss 1978: 48–9). For Moss, as for many of her more famous counterparts, to oppose apartheid through the devices of literature was, crucially, to expose it. The formula would prove to be an enduring one, whether endorsed by the moral authority of Alan Paton, Nadine Gordimer, Athol Fugard and the Afrikaans writer André Brink, or confirmed under protest by a critical tradition of black writers and intellectuals, notably Lewis Nkosi (Nkosi 1973) and, later, Njabulo Ndebele (1991), even as they questioned on aesthetic and ideological grounds the notions of 'engagement' and 'commitment' widespread among their peers.

Despite such challenges, and despite the principled deviance that J. M. Coetzee's work displays in this respect, the codes of an unadorned literary realism prevailed in prose fiction and found their counterpart in a tradition of protest poetry keyed to the 'urgency' of political resistance. Engaged literature often mobilised the resources of autobiography, also the case in literature elsewhere on the African continent. The texts of radical intellectuals such as the Nigerian Wole Soyinka (*The Man Died: Prison Notes* [1972], *Aké: The Years of Childhood* [1981], *Ibadan: The Penkelemes Years: A Memoir, 1945–1967* [1994]) and the Kenyan Ngugi wa Thiong'o (*Detained: A Writer's Prison Diary* [1981]) come to mind, as do the autobiographies of the Pan-African nationalists who led various African states to independence, including Jomo Kenyatta of Kenya (*Suffering without Bitterness* [1967]) and Kwame Nkrumah of Ghana (*Ghana: The Autobiography of Kwame Nkrumah* [1957]). The autobiographical form was also an important one for black South African women, in a lineage that includes Noni Jabavu (*The Ochre People* [1963]), Ellen Kuzwayo (*Call Me Woman* [1985]), Emma Mashinini (*Strikes Have Followed Me All My Life* [1989]), Sindiwe Magona (*To My Children's Children* [1990]) and Mamphela Ramphele (*A Life* [1995]). While Bessie Head's novels *When Rain Clouds Gather* (1969) and *A Question of Power* (1973) cannot, formally at least, be termed autobiography, they draw implicitly on Head's particular vulnerability to the classifications of race – as the illegitimate child of a wealthy white mother and a black stable-hand. Head's need to marshal writing against the dissolution of the self, it has been suggested, derived from an inescapable confrontation with the racial fetishism of the regime.

The experience of imprisonment for black or otherwise dissident South Africans elicited a similar response, evidenced by the prison memoirs of Breyten Breytenbach (*The True Confessions of an Albino Terrorist* [1983]), Ruth First (*117 Days* [1965]), Hugh Lewin (*Bandiet: Seven Years in a South African Prison* [1974]), Caesarina Makhoere (*No Child's Play: In Prison under Apartheid* [1988]), Albie Sachs (*The Jail Diary of Albie Sachs* [1966]), and D. M. Zwelonke (*Robben Island* [1973]), or the poetry of Dennis Brutus (*Letters to Martha & Other Poems from a South African Prison* [1968]) and Jeremy Cronin (*Inside* [1983]). Under conditions of marked political repression, engagement seems less a choice than a structural constraint; as the Nigerian Chinua Achebe wrote in the wake of the Biafran War,

> an African creative writer who tries to avoid the big social and political issues of contemporary Africa will end up by being completely irrelevant – like the absurd man in the proverb who leaves his burning house to pursue a rat fleeing from the flames. (Achebe 1981: 78)

But the very shape of the call to engagement itself influences the available repertoires of literary production, prescribing some and proscribing others. Oswald Mtshali, whose work prefigures that of the more radical Soweto Poets associated with *Staffrider* magazine in the aftermath of the 1976 uprising, was not being unduly provocative when he once identified 'rhyme, iambic pentameter or abstract figures of speech' as 'luxuries' reserved for 'the moment when we are free people' (Mtshali 1976: 127).

The House of Truth

The familiar presentation of the South African writer as possessed of high moral seriousness is allied to the rhetoric of urgency that Mtshali articulates, however oblique the connection between the prophetic pose of the white writer and the radicalism of the dissident. The case of Alan Paton is exemplary here, particularly in terms of his reception by an international readership. In 1948, the year that saw both the formal inception of the apartheid regime and the publication of *Cry, the Beloved Country*, the register of 'urgency' available to Paton straddled both foreboding and elegy: 'cry, the beloved country, for the unborn child that is the inheritor of our fear' (Paton 1995: 111). Paton's deliberately Biblical lyricism is counterweight to an uncompromising documentation of social devastation as the rural Zulu priest, Stephen Kumalo, travels to the black slum-yards of

Johannesburg, there to discover that his son, Absalom, has killed Arthur Jarvis, the son of the white farmer whose lands lie not far from Kumalo's village.

The journey, this particular journey, was already formulaic by the time of Paton's use of it. Douglas Blackburn, W. C. Scully and William Plomer, on one side of the colour divide, and R. R. R. Dhlomo and Peter Abrahams on the other, had all produced variants on the 'Jim-comes-to-Jo'burg' plot in response to the accelerating urbanisation of South African blacks. For Paton's protagonist, Kumalo, the trajectory is a predictably tragic one:

> The tribe was broken, and would be mended no more. The tribe that had nurtured him, and his father and his father's father, was broken. For the men were away, and the young men and the girls were away, and the maize hardly reached to the height of a man. (Paton 1995: 120)

Here as elsewhere, Paton links social disintegration to 'the sickness of the land' (Paton 1995: 52), with equivocal political effect. Admittedly, the choral 'Shanty Town' sections of the novel show Paton to be residual heir to Solomon T. Plaatje's impassioned denunciation, in *Native Life in South Africa* (1916), of the effects on the black population of the disastrous 1913 Natives Land Act. However, Paton refrains from investing the fact of dispossession with the measured political opposition provided by Plaatje, a founder of the South African Native National Congress (the forerunner to the African National Congress) whose *Mhudi* (1930) is considered to be the first novel by a black South African. *Cry, the Beloved Country* offers a cautious form of redemption instead, as the dual resources of Christian faith and a qualified liberalism on the part of the grieving white benefactor are brought to bear on the problem of renewal. 'There is ploughing in Ndotsheni, and indeed on all the farms around it' (Paton 1995: 299).

Paton's investment in truth-telling as a social remedy lingers beneath the surface of his novel – quite literally so. The killing of Arthur Jarvis interrupts the production of the manuscript, 'The Truth about Native Crime', that he was engaged in writing, but the unfolding of Paton's own text is clearly offered in compensation (Paton 1995: 170). How true to life, however, is Stephen Kumalo? J. M. Coetzee, for one, has pointed to the limits of Paton's apparently uncontrived mimesis with respect to his black protagonists, arguing that the archaic Zulu which Paton would have us reconstruct from his text is 'less the medium through which Paton's characters speak than part of the interpretation Paton wishes us to make of them' (Coetzee 1988a: 129).

Paton's nostalgia for a black pastoralism already anachronistic at the time of writing might profitably be contrasted with contemporary evidence of black South Africans' conflictual embrace of an urban identity, reflected in, say, Modikwe Dikobe's sketches of black working-class life dating from the 1950s, later compiled as *The Marabi Dance* (1973). The act of claiming the city would be a crucial component of the generational identity of the 1950s, as documented in the legendary *Drum* magazine: a photo-periodical whose sensationalism co-existed with a tradition of serious investigative journalism. *Drum* hosted many of the figures who would rise to prominence over the course of the decade: Peter Abrahams, Can Themba, Bloke Modisane, Nat Nakasa, Casey Motsisi, Ezekiel (Es'kia) Mphahlele, Arthur Maimane, Richard Rive, James Matthews, Alex La Guma and Lewis Nkosi. The African-American poet Langston Hughes was a sometime contributor, and Paton's *Cry, the Beloved Country* was itself serialised in the early issues of *Drum* (Chapman 1996: 239). But Paton's deliberate archaisms, as his critics have pointed out, ill suited the *Drum* idiom, which combined hyperbole, Americanisms, and a polyglot slang called 'tsotsi-taal' spoken by the Sophiatown gangsters – often idealised in *Drum* for their defiant insouciance which proclaimed: 'Live fast, die young and leave a good-looking corpse'. The resultant style was affectionately known as 'Matshikeze' in honour of Todd Matshikiza, *Drum*'s music columnist. It was Matshikiza who wrote the score of the jazz opera, *King Kong* (1959) based on the boxing career of the South African heavyweight champion Ezekiel 'King Kong' Dhlamini, a production that has itself become emblematic of the larger cultural moment.

Style was not solely nor simply a matter of language, however. The performance of certain kinds of selfhood was explicitly prohibited by apartheid legislation, as Marie Kathleen Jeffreys, one of the few women to write for *Drum*, presumably knew when she produced a series of essays on racial passing and interracial families under the pen-name 'Hamsi'. To be urbane, street-wise, mordantly ironic in the manner of Can Themba holding forth in his Sophiatown home, 'The House of Truth', itself defied the apartheid government's ideology of black 'retribalisation' and forced resettlement to the rural 'homelands'. Themba, it has been widely noted, claimed to speak no indigenous South African vernacular.

This hyperbolic resistance was precarious, however. By the end of the decade which saw both the codification of the Freedom Charter and crushing reprisals by the State, most *Drum* writers found themselves displaced from the land of their birth, their texts eventually banned under the Suppression of Communism Act (1966). Es'kia Mphahlele went into exile in Nigeria, Kenya and Zambia, notoriously lending support to the critique of *négritude* conducted by Wole Soyinka and Christopher Okigbo, among others.[1] Can Themba drank himself to death in Swaziland. Nat Nakasa committed suicide in New York. Following the mass removals of 1955, Sophiatown – reduced to rubble beneath the emerging contours of a white working-class neighbourhood named 'Triomf' – had become her own burial ground.

Ghost Tales

But the myth of Sophiatown lived on, consecrated in popular memory and in a variety of textual forms, including Nadine Gordimer's 1958 novel, *A World of Strangers*; one-time resident Athol Fugard's early Sophiatown plays, *No-good Friday* (1958) and *Nongogo* (1959), and the poet Don Mattera's autobiography, *Memory Is the Weapon* (1987). Nor would the physical detritus of the place remain wholly submerged. Its resurgence is one point of entry into Marlene van Niekerk's evocative and disturbing novel of white Afrikaner consciousness, *Triomf*, published in Afrikaans in 1994:

> When everything was flattened – it took almost three years – the dogs who'd been left behind started crying. [. . .] Some of the dogs died on their own, from hunger. Or maybe from longing for their kaffirs. And then they just lay there, puffing up and going soft again, until the flesh rotted and fell right off the bones. Then, later, even the bones got scattered.
>
> Even now, Lambert finds loose dog bones when he digs.
>
> Treppie says the ghosts of those dogs are all over Triomf. (van Niekerk 1999: 4)

---

[1] *Négritude*, associated with the Francophone writers and intellectuals Aimé Césaire of Martinique and Léopold Sédar Senghor of Senegal (later, her first president after independence), champions the distinctiveness of African and African diasporic culture conceived not as absence, as in racist colonial thought, but as 'refusal' in Césaire's terms. Mphahlele was critical of the reduction of *négritude* to facile forms of black romanticism. The Nigerian poet Christopher Okigbo died fighting for the independence of Biafra in 1967.

In the strange productivity accorded to death in South African literature, the corpse indeed makes its frequent return. Thus, Herman Charles Bosman's mordantly satirical short story, 'Unto Dust', first published in 1949, depicts a party of Transvaal burghers faced with the task of separating – that is to say, rending asunder, rendering into apartheid – the remains of their white companion and his black adversary:

> Stoffel Oosthuizen added that, no matter what the difference in the colour of their skin had been, it was impossible to say that the kaffir's [sic] bones were less white than Hans Welman's. Nor was it possible to say that the kaffir's sun-dried flesh was any blacker than the white man's. Alive, you couldn't go wrong in distinguishing between a white man and a kaffir. Dead, you had great difficulty in telling them apart. (Bosman 1987: 40)

The presence of the black man's dog in the vicinity of the white man's grave at the end of the story confirms the burghers' worst suspicions, neatly concretising the return of a peculiarly South African repressed.

The topos of the corpse, the wrong corpse, the missing corpse, the unidentified corpse – the *black* corpse wronged, missing, anonymous, marked by torture – is a compulsive one for the white South African writer. It surfaces – often the crucial term – in texts as varied as Bosman's detective novel *Willemsdorp* (posthumously published in 1977) or Nadine Gordimer's early short story 'Six Feet of the Country' (1953); in Anne Landsman's post-apartheid work of magic realism, *The Devil's Chimney* (1998), or in Ivan Vladislavic's playful work of metafiction, *The Restless Supermarket* (2001) which, like *Triomf*, is set in Johannesburg on the eve of the 1994 elections. But the raising of the corpse in Gordimer's *The Conservationist* (1974) is undoubtedly the paradigmatic instance here. The body of a black man, murdered and shallowly buried on the farm owned by the white industrialist protagonist is washed up again after a massive storm. This symbolism is rather overt, as the critics have noted. The black corpse which is unearthed in *The Conservationist*, Stephen Clingman famously argues, represents both an oppressed black world in white South Africa as well as a psychic state of repression for white South Africans 'bound to return to consciousness in threatening and subversive ways' (Clingman 1986: 209). When the corpse bears a name, and when that name is Steven Bantu Biko, the Black Consciousness leader brutally killed in police detention in 1977, then the regard of the white author – Donald Woods in *Biko* (1978), André Brink in *A Dry White Season* (1979), Wessel Ebersohn in the detective novel *Store Up the Anger* (1980) and, some scholars claim, J. M. Coetzee in *Waiting for the Barbarians* (1980) – also involves a certain expiation.

A Surfeit of Truth

What response might the corpse or the suffering body exact from the South African writer? J. M. Coetzee has conspicuously staked his investment in writing on this question, describing his fiction as a 'paltry, ludicrous' defence against 'the fact of suffering in this world'. The ethical standard of this fiction is the body. But it is the body in a specifically South African emplacement, suggests Coetzee:

> Not grace then, but at least the body. Let me put it baldly: in South Africa it is not possible to deny the authority of suffering and therefore of the body . . . it is not that one *grants* the

authority of the suffering body: the suffering body *takes* this authority: that is its power. To use other words: its power is undeniable. (Coetzee 1992: 248)

Coetzee's fictional strategies in the face of this authority depart from the realist preferences of South African literature in English. In his early works, *Dusklands* (1974), *Waiting for the Barbarians* (1980), *Life & Times of Michael K* (1983), and *Foe* (1986), Coetzee consistently revisits the body caught in the vectors of power, while refusing to cast the narrative of his often muted or marginalised protagonists into anything like the conventional mould of the 'liberal novel of stricken conscience', in Benita Parry's phrase (Parry 1998: 149). The coordinates of a contemporary South African setting that might denote 'urgency' are deferred, whether relegated to the past, suspended within the coordinates of an apocalyptic future, or withheld altogether. What results is a highly allegorical textual oeuvre that is nevertheless deeply responsive to the troubled politics of the late-apartheid State.

A much cited passage in *Life & Times of Michael K* is illuminating in this respect. The Medical Officer in the novel, whose temporal coordinates are deliberately vague, reflects on Michael K's incarceration in a prison camp:

> Your stay in the camp was merely an allegory, if you know that word. It was an allegory – speaking at the highest level – of how scandalously, how outrageously, a meaning can take up residence in a system without becoming a term in it. Did you not notice how, whenever I tried to pin you down, you slipped away? I noticed. (Coetzee 1983: 228)

Coetzee has widely been read as himself using allegory in order to resist incorporation into something like an overarching narrative of history. He is on record as seeking to evade those gestures which might render his fiction – or 'the novel' more broadly speaking – a mere 'supplement' to the discourse of history. Certainly, he is dismissive of the realist allegiance of South African fiction which seems to promise the reader 'vicarious first-hand experience of living in a certain historical time', opting for an ethically motivated 'rivalry' with history, instead. Rivalry carves out space for a novel which is independent of 'conclusions that are checkable by history (as a child's school-work is checked by a schoolmistress)' (Coetzee 1988b: 3).

Coetzee's debt to his European modernist and postmodernist precursors in this regard has been widely acknowledged. Within the more limited circumference of a local tradition, however, his aesthetics might be set against the slender but important precedent of formal experimentation evident in William Plomer's 1926 *Turbott Wolfe*, where the scandal of literary modernism, a feature of the work's reception for its colonial readership, was amplified by the equally scandalous depiction of sexual desire between a white woman and a black man. For all his desire to keep his distance from the ready-made formulas of a literature of engagement, Coetzee's writing does maintain significant intersections with the work of some of the South African novelist against whom he is pitted, or who pit themselves against him. Nadine Gordimer is a case in point. Her 1981 novel, *July's People*, like Coetzee's *Life & Times of Michael K* or Christopher Hope's satirical *Kruger's Alp* (1984), undoes the present in favour of an apocalyptic imagining of that which lies in wait. Barney Simon's short story 'Our War' (1974) is a beautifully evocative early example of this mode of writing. For some champions of a 'vicarious insertion' into history, these 'future histories', in Michael Green's phrase (Green 1997: 244), might be seen as evidence of precisely those 'morbid symptoms' which Gordimer invokes when she appends an epigraph from Antonio Gramsci's *Prison Notebooks* to *July's People*: 'the old is dying and the new cannot be born; in this interregnum there arise a great diversity of morbid symptoms' (Gordimer 1982).

By 1985, however, the 'interregnum' had become a fully fledged 'State of Emergency' with the nationwide imposition of emergency rule. Now, morbidity is driven against the very carapace of the body once more. Stephen Gray's 1988 text *Time of Our Darkness*, which has received too little notice beyond a South African audience, is an outstanding example of the 'Literature of the Emergency' that took shape during the period, standing alongside such works as Brink's *States of Emergency* (1988) and *An Act of Terror* (1991), Coetzee's *Age of Iron* (1990), and Richard Rive's *Emergency Continued* (1990), for example. Gray's novel describes the homosexual relationship between a white schoolteacher and his black pupil, a minor, against the background of the political turbulence of South Africa in the mid-1980s. Like Coetzee in *Age of Iron*, Gray investigates the political saturation of personal life in the late-apartheid State. The two share the recognition that the capacity to consolidate a personal identity in that time and in that place was for many, intimately bound to the fact of death or its anticipation.

Declining the Truth

It is precisely with regard to fictions or testimonies of self-fashioning and identity that the shifts and continuities of literature in the post-apartheid era may be registered. Autobiography under apartheid was rarely an individual matter, and was seldom narcissistic as Jeremy Cronin once demonstrated from prison in a deliberate, but also very literal repositioning, of the reflective surface of the autobiographical mirror:

> By holding my mirror out of the window I see
> Clear to the end of the passage
> There's a person down there.
> A prisoner polishing a doorhandle.
> In the mirror, I see him see
> My face in the mirror
>
> (Cronin 1999: 14)

A comparable imagining of social solidarity emerges from a seemingly extra-literary source in post-1994 South Africa in the institutional guise of the Truth and Reconciliation Commission. The testimonies delivered there, in the first-person voices of both 'victims' and 'perpetrators', are often regarded as individual components of a collective autobiography that coalesces around the body of the apartheid subject. Post-apartheid writing, in more recognisably literary forms, also entertains a highly confessional drive in which the narrating self seeks deliverance from the past. Rian Malan's *My Traitor's Heart* (1990) is one salient example of the autobiographical voice that chronicles a desiring betrayal of the Afrikaner volk. The gesture is sustained in Antjie Krog's *Country of My Skull* (1998), a memoir of her coverage as radio commentator on the Truth and Reconciliation Commission, and forms an implicit backdrop to Mark Behr's *The Smell of Apples* (1995), which uses the motif of sexual abuse to interrogate the ideological legacy of Afrikaner patriarchy.

The revisionist impulse does not exhaust the possibilities available to fictions of the self, however, as Coetzee's post-apartheid memoirs *Boyhood* (1997) and *Youth* (2002) richly attest. Post-apartheid literature, the scholarship has noted, seems far more willing to make provisions for an intimacy with the self which, if not exactly narcissistic, exists at a certain remove from the 'political', conceived in its historical apartheid-era form. This distance does not preclude proximity with other forms of imagined belonging: say, the homosexual identities explored in Shaun de Waal's collection of short stories *These Things Happen* (1996), or the precious and precarious solidarities of a post-apartheid urban space in Zakes Mda's *Ways of Dying* (1995), K. Sello Duiker's *Thirteen Cents* (2000) and Phaswane Mpe's *Welcome to Hillbrow* (2001). The magic realist exuberance of Mda's character Toloki transforms internal and external coordinates of being, even and especially in the face of death. The untimely deaths of Phaswane Mpe in December 2004 and K. Sello Duiker in January 2005 are, sadly, far more resistant to recuperation.

For all its vulnerability to a social landscape dominated by death, where the spectre of HIV/AIDS has yet to find sustained representation, post-apartheid literature is changing shape, and clearly so. For Achmat Dangor in *Kafka's Curse* (1997), the malleability of the self is the stuff of a literal metamorphosis. Dangor's protagonist, Oscar Kahn – or Omar Khan – is a coloured Muslim who passes as a Jewish Johannesburg architect. The narrative of passing is grafted onto the Arab myth of Leila and Majnoen, with the traditional positions of the gardener and the princess transposed into the peculiarly South African syntax of race and destiny:

> Imagine a man turning into a tree as he waits for a lover who will never arrive. A well-deserved fate, if you ask me, for a lowly gardener waiting for a princess . . . An insanity that strikes those who dare to stray from their 'life's station', that little room which you are told at birth is yours. (Dangor 2000: 30–31)

The narrative asks us to entertain the possibility that Omar, too, has become a tree. The metamorphosis is an oblique commentary on Omar's failed social metamorphosis, for the secret of his coloured birth is revealed in the wake of his mother's death. In this give and take, we see both rupture – 'I have broken the cycle of remembrance', says Oscar – and haunted intimations of continuity as the characters surrounding Omar confront the transformed social landscapes of post-apartheid South Africa (Dangor 2000: 62). This oscillation also characterises the text's relation to the literary tradition whose contours its deviance illuminates. Dangor's lifting of the codes of social or socialist South African realism in favour of a magic realist fable is one powerful index of distance travelled. But the relation to the past is altered, not suspended altogether. Dangor's text has certain ghosts, or rather the certainty of haunting, in common with Zoë Wicomb's *David's Story* (2000), whose own interrogation of coloured identity also disrupts the realist code, up to and including a dissolution of its most valued sign in South African literary culture in English. 'Truth, I gather, is the word that cannot be written' (Wicomb 2000: 136). The unwritten word is nevertheless present in its erasure, turned, tuned to what Wicomb calls 'the palindrome of Cape Flats speech': 'trurt, oh trurt, of the trurt, to the trurt, trurt, by, with, from the trurt' (Wicomb 2000: 136). The declension of the word is part charm, part restoration, part refusal. Wicomb's narrator tellingly speaks of the protagonist David's attempt to 'decline it' (Wicomb 2000: 136). But for Wicomb, as for post-apartheid literary culture more generally, no crying off is possible. Instead the conjugation of the verb 'to write' – that is to say, the very possibility of literary expression in the aftermath of apartheid – opens out onto conjuration, a word that the philosopher Jacques Derrida once exhorted us to remember means both 'solemn oath' and 'magical incantation' (Derrida 1994: 40–1). In tangible conversation with its ghosts, post-apartheid literature at the close of the twentieth century transforms a legacy of hurt into the truth of responsibility, written, unwritten and still to be written.

Acknowledgment. My debts in writing this essay date, most powerfully and most persistently, to Tim Couzens and Es'kia Mphahlele, my teachers in the African Literature programme at the University of the Witwatersrand, 1983. I wish also to acknowledge the important precedent of the 2003 anthology, *Women Writing Africa: The Southern Region* (Daymond *et al.* 2003), which brought the figure of Marie Kathleen Jeffreys to my attention. Thanks to Leon de Kock, Jonathan de Vries, Sonja Narunsky-Laden and Dan Wylie for their comments.

References

Achebe, Chinua (1981) 'The African Writer and the Biafran Cause', in *Morning Yet on Creation Day: Essays*, London: Heinemann, 78–84

Asmal, Kader, Louise Asmal and Ronald Suresh Roberts (1997) *Reconciliation Through Truth: A Reckoning of Apartheid's Criminal Governance*, Cape Town: David Philip; Oxford: James Currey; New York: St Martin's Press

Bosman, Herman Charles (1987) 'Unto Dust', in *Makapan's Caves and Other Stories*, Harmondsworth: Penguin, 37–41

Chapman, Michael (1996) *Southern African Literatures*, London and New York: Longman

Clingman, Stephen (1986) *The Novels of Nadine Gordimer: History from the Inside*, Johannesburg: Ravan Press

Coetzee, J. M. (1983) *Life & Times of Michael K*, Johannesburg: Ravan Press

——(1988a) 'Simple Language, Simple People: Smith, Paton, Mikro', in *White Writing: On the Culture of Letters in South Africa*, Sandton, South Africa: Radix, 115–35

——(1988b) 'The Novel Today', *Upstream: A Magazine of the Arts*, 6(1): 2–5

——(1992) 'Interview', in David Attwell, ed., *Doubling the Point: Essays and Interviews*, Cambridge, MA, and London: Harvard University Press, 243–50

Cronin, Jeremy (1999) 'Motho ke Motho Ka Batho Babang (A Person Is a Person Because of Other People)', in *Inside and Out: Poems from* Inside *and* Even the Dead, Cape Town: David Philip

Dangor, Achmat (2000) *Kafka's Curse*, New York: Vintage Books

Daymond, M. J., Dorothy Driver, Sheila Meintjes, Leloba Molema, Chiedza Musengezi, Margie Orford and Nobantu Rasebotsa, eds (2003) *Women Writing Africa: The Southern Region*, New York: The Feminist Press

Derrida, Jacques (1994) *Specters of Marx*, trans. Peggy Kamuf, introduction Bernd Magnus and Stephen Cullenberg, New York and London: Routledge

Gordimer, Nadine (1982) *July's People*, Harmondsworth: Penguin

Green, Michael (1997) *Novel Histories*, Johannesburg: Witwatersrand University Press

Hirson, Denis (1996) 'The Long-Distance South African', in Leon de Kock and Ian Tromp, eds, *The Heart in Exile: South African Poetry in English, 1990–1995*, Harmondsworth: Penguin, 4–12

Jooste, Pamela (2004) *People Like Ourselves*, London: Black Swan

Moss, Rose (1978) '"Telling the Truth": Interview by Jean Marquard', *Contrast* 47: 48–55

Mtshali, Oswald (1976) 'Black Poetry in South Africa', in Christopher Heywood, ed., *Aspects of South African Literature*, London: Heinemann, 121–7

Ndebele, Njabulo S. (1991) *Rediscovery of the Ordinary: Essays on South African Literature and Culture*, Johannesburg: COSAW [Congress of South African Writers]

Nkosi, Lewis (1973) 'Fiction by Black South Africans', in G. D. Killam, ed., *African Writers on African Writing*, London: Heinemann, 109–17

Parry, Benita (1998) 'Speech and Silence in the Fictions of J. M. Coetzee', in Derek Attridge and Rosemary Jolly, eds, *Writing South Africa: Literature, Apartheid, and Democracy, 1970–1995*, Cambridge: Cambridge University Press, 149–65

Paton, Alan (1995) *Cry, the Beloved Country*, New York: Simon and Schuster

van Niekerk, Marlene (1999) *Triomf*, trans. Leon de Kock, Johannesburg: Jonathan Ball; Cape Town: Queillerie Publishers

Wicomb, Zoë (2000) *David's Story*, Cape Town: Kwela Books

Chapter 20

1991, The Web: Network Fictions

Joseph Tabbi

> The Short Twentieth Century ended in problems, for which nobody had, or even claimed to have, solutions. As the citizens of the *fin de siècle* tapped their way through the global fog that surrounded them, into the third millennium, all they knew for certain was that an era of history had ended. They knew very little else.
>
> (Eric Hobsbawm, *The Age of Extremes*, 1994: 558–9)

Our age is recombinant. Not retrospective, in the way that Ralph Waldo Emerson thought of nineteenth-century culture: nobody is looking back to the classics and few look even to literature of the recent past as standards for measuring new creativity. What our age does, rather, is splice, graft and recombine the materials left lying around after the disintegration of the old orders. Since the fall of the Soviet Union in 1991, liberal democracy, no longer an embattled ideal or a provincial experiment, has become an international norm, for better or worse. The failure of socialism run by a centralised command economy, followed in Russia by the still more catastrophic failure of a purely market-driven economy, had intellectual, political and aesthetic consequences. A set of clear ideological oppositions would soon yield to a proliferation of subject positions; racial and material identities were becoming more important than national identities for both political activity and literary expression. For many commentators after the Cold War, it was not just an era of history that had ended; rather it was the 'end of history' itself (as Francis Fukuyama argued in a *Foreign Affairs* essay of 1991). Instead of a clear transition from one dominant nation or empire to another, the world found itself entering a time of generalised sovereignty, under 'a regime with no temporal boundaries and in this sense outside of history or at the end of history' (Hardt and Negri 2000: xv).

The loss of competing ideologies left many novelists and poets to explore not meanings but material constructions, down to the very 'shape of the signifier' (Michaels 2004), the lettering, the arrangements of words on a page. The page itself was also quickly becoming not an object but a process, produced electronically and capable of being linked hypertextually via computer systems to other pages, other processes, different organisations of global flows and exchanges. What was being linked, in this new media ecology, was not some 'imagined community' of consensual minds, tuned to a familiar set of texts, capable (at least in principle) of arguing *in depth*. In the absence of national and temporal boundaries, there was no need to dig in, take a stand: those with a difference of opinion could simply move elsewhere (conceptually, if not geographically); it was always possible to find other affiliations, establish new links. 'Instead of roots, we now have aerials', said McKenzie Wark, regarding such 'weird media events' as the Iraq hostage crisis (1990), the Tiananmen Square massacre (1989), and the fall of the Berlin Wall (1989). Instead of 'origins', we would be given 'terminals' (Wark 1994: xiv); and rather than 'in-depth' coverage, the objective claimed by an earlier era of broadcast news, we would be given, simply, 'more'.

The relation between literacy and the nation-state, between the stability of printed books and the sovereignty of national borders, had been well understood – at least since Benedict Anderson's classic study, *Imagined Communities* (1983). But as national sovereignty came increasingly to be replaced by open networks of communication and exchange based on the World Wide Web, and as limited conflicts among national enemies became less frequent than the unlimited policing of activist networks – both within and outside a nation's boundaries – state power itself came to resemble a network, in combination with mass media and corporate business whose non-democratic and networked power, arguably, had a greater effect than statecraft on the course of world history.

Would literary narrative, in response, have to become itself more like a network?

As literature inevitably reflects forms of power in the world (even to subvert them or to imagine alternative worlds), the sort of narrative that emerged as new and exciting, in the final decade of the millennium, was indeed capable not only of imagining networks, but of becoming itself a network: a virtual network of allusions, possible identities, embedded subjectivities, but also (in hypertext narratives) an operational network of electronic links extending to text fields and image fields throughout the Web. Increasingly, readers of fiction and viewers of media were experiencing, not an image of one another, but rather a distributed network of keywords held in common, consciously cited links, composed glosses, and marginal material thrown up automatically by search engines. In such an environment the isolated author who appeared to Emerson in his 1844 essay 'The Poet' as a 'sovereign' and 'emperor in his own right' (2006: 1640) would retain a certain uniqueness, a singularity, but this would be accomplished only in the context of other identities – women as well as men, people of colour no less than whites, machines alongside humans (alongside, but also inside, to the extent that a networked environment can influence and even create subjectivity). Traditions of individualism in American thought would remain intact, and a strain of individualism, too, persisted – beleaguered or reasserted – in English fiction: in the idiosyncratic first-person narratives which predominate in the work of authors such as Martin Amis, Julian Barnes, Angela Carter or Jeanette Winterson. Henceforth, however, the individual would increasingly find expression only through networks that all identities might now hold in common, networks through which 'Thoughts come unbidden, the mind weaving its perspectives, assembling meaning from emotion and memory' (Gibson and Sterling 1991: 2).

One name given to this networked conceptual commons is 'cyberspace' – developed as a concept in the science fiction of Vernor Vinge, brought to a literary audience by William Gibson in *Neuromancer* (1985), and to popular consciousness through the 1999 film *The Matrix*. *The Difference Engine* (a novel that Gibson produced in 1991, appropriately, not on his own but in collaboration with Bruce Sterling) gives the cyberspace network full historical substance, revealing it as having always been there, potentially, as an alternative to both the nineteenth-century Age of Empire and the extremes of twentieth-century market capitalism and state socialism. Masquerading as a 'Victorian' novel, its chapters given as 'Iterations', not detachable sections but rather serial approaches to a working solution, *The Difference Engine* is set in an imaginary London where the computer (actually worked out in principle by Charles Babbage and publicised by Lady Ada Lovelace, daughter of Lord Byron) is supposed to have been implemented as early as 1855. Byron is Prime Minister of this alternative Britain, and Ada the queen of 'clackers', so called because hacking makes noise when your computer is not electronic but mechanical, based not on silicon chips but on the punch card technology invented by Joseph Jacquard to control the patterns woven on his automatic loom. John Keats is a former medical student now working in the field of Kinotropy; and the authors find similar alternative roles for Sam Houston, former president of the independent nation of Texas; palaeontologist Edward Mallory; and spy Laurence Oliphant. Counter-history (in the science-fiction tradition of Philip K. Dick's *The Man in the High Castle* [1962], a story of an alternative America after a supposed German victory in the Second World War) is significant not only in calling attention to the ways that literary and technological personages have been, from the start, known to each other and working, in their different media, on similar problems. While acknowledging that the introduction of a new technology can be decisive, counter-history detracts from any notion of pure technological *determinism*. In *The Difference Engine*, the historical personages are made to act, not against the background of what was, but in keeping with what *could have been*: at the end of history, networked narrative takes as its material not the actual, but the potentially real.

Decentralised Intelligence

With this criterion in mind – the network as both a source and a model for an emerging narrative tradition – I want to begin with a print narrative, Harry Mathews's *My Life in CIA: A Chronicle of 1973* (2005), an authentic account of a made-up life. The book, more than most, remains scrupulously true to its title: we are given a day-to-day account of an imaginary life, though one where the imagining was done not by the author alone, but equally by a number of actual, living people. Mathews adopted the role in response to misapprehensions that he, the unattached writer, was in fact 'CIA'. (A friend tells him: 'the first thing to remember is that nobody connected with the Agency calls it *the* CIA. It's plain CIA' [Mathews 2005: 66].) The 'chronicle' itself is largely factual, many of its characters are historical, and the world events mentioned in the book are documented. The work restricts itself largely to Paris and its environs during that one internationally politically charged year, 1973 – except for a brief final section set in Berlin in 1991, that 'fateful year of the mirror' (Moulthrop 1991: 'Back to the Future'), when Mathews offers a retrospective look at events almost twenty years before. Back then, as part of his 'masquerade', he'd applied to the German academic exchange service for a year in Berlin; he's there now, in January 1991, legitimately. This soon after the fall of the Berlin Wall, his mood turns retrospective: he visits a Charlottenburg café known to be frequented by writers and artists, where he overhears his name mentioned in a conversation between two middle-aged men at a nearby table:

> 'Is it true he's CIA?'
> 'Not to listen to him talk. He used to bore people to death "explaining" his reputation. Misrepresented by a well-meaning friend in Laos. I think it was Laos.'
> 'So?'
> 'Oh, that was bullshit. I know he was CIA . . .' (Mathews 2005: 202)

In the distributed network of variously reliable witnesses, these two, anonymous and accidental contemporaries, are given the last word, overheard by the author. 'So what happened?' one asks:

> 'They had to get rid of him. In fact, they took executive action.'
> 'Executive action?'
> 'He was "terminated with extreme prejudice" – the wet solution.' (Mathews 2005: 203)

The Berlin postlude, meticulously realistic in its presentation, and the conversation, patently misinformed, recapitulate the book's persistent concern with fabrication and self-fashioning – the determination on Mathews's part to accept as truth whatever falsehoods and misapprehensions circulate around him (including the exaggerated rumour of his own death): he was a 'spook'; he was 'known' to be gay; with no visible means of support, he was surely a millionaire. His goal up to then had been 'to play a part in the grand conspiracy of poetic subversion; in fact that was how I justified my life' (Mathews 2005: 12). But those around him take notice only of real conspiracies, so fully has the fictive wormed its way into public life. As if he had come into his own expatriate version of an existential crisis, Mathews in 1973 decided, rather than correct misapprehensions (if they were indeed such), instead to embrace them and act the part of an undercover agent. To embrace the arbitrary and the accidental, and to make of *it* one's reality: that is how a simulated political memoir can become, in Mathews's hands, a peculiar yet apt account of an exemplary literary life.

1991 is an arbitrary enough date, simply the first year when a literary author could look back at the Cold War era without being caught up in the inevitable political implications of the 1970s. Reduced to its raw materiality on the page, the date however is also a numerical palindrome – a string of four numbers that reads the same backward as forward. This is cause for suspicion in Mathews, who became (in 1973, the year of his 'Chronicle') the first American member of Oulipo, the Workshop for Potential Literature, a Paris-based group of writers (including Raymond Queneau, Georges Perec, Italo Calvino, Jacques Roubaud and others) dedicated to the generation of literary forms through the application of mathematical (and, in later works, verbal and material) constraints. Mathews himself had published a number of novels based wholly or in part on Oulipian methods, including *The Conversions* (1962), *Tlooth* (1966), *The Sinking of the Odradek Stadium* (1975), and *Cigarettes* (1987), and in 2002 he would endorse 'a palindrome story in 2002 words' written by Nick Montfort and William Gillespie, and illustrated by hypertext fictionist Shelly Jackson. In *My Life*, the narrative fast-forward to 1991 offers an opportunity for recapitulation; and this reflective move is reinforced by the date which reads the same in either direction.

Mathews's tactic – to note how he is regarded by others and make that identity his own – is one way that the literary imagination, otherwise excluded, might re-enter the political realm and disturb the social sphere. The embrace of a repellent identity (the very role of CIA spy that progressives of his generation despised most) had been a way to gain 'access'; it was and is, also, a way of bringing literary devices into the lived world of 'operational' fictions. Any defence of a would-be worldly imagination, a kind of freelance surveillance, can at best involve authors in endless (and mostly futile) explanations; the imagination as an independent force at best will be regarded as 'weird' by one's contemporaries (Mathews 2005: 203); protests of political 'innocence' only produce 'a bitterness as futile as jealousy itself' (Mathews 2005: 12).

Under circumstances where consequential thought and action are denied or postponed indefinitely, where consciousness is constantly getting raised and culture is, increasingly, *pop* culture, everyone's an operative. The only difference is that Mathews makes the fictive life explicit and purposely blows his own cover. The project involves a willing suspension – not of disbelief (the basis of the romantic imagination described by Coleridge), but of one's own independent, reflective condition. In the emerging global culture, belief needn't be suspended because it has been largely *obviated*: our identities increasingly are reflected *back* on us by others, and by images of who we are, variously, expected to be. What matters is not so much what one believes (in politics or religion, for example), as how one is situated within nodes, networks and flows of information, sex and money. (Money itself, since 1973 decoupled from a gold standard and increasingly keyed to the world system of international finance, is now essentially a kind of information.) In the emerging World Literature circa 1991, national and ideological differences get rewritten as differences in 'culture', and meaning collapses, more and more often, into an expression of one's material means. Does it matter much that the characters in Haruki Murakami are Japanese, for example, or that his episodic novel of 1991, *Hard-Boiled Wonderland and the End of the World*, is set in Tokyo rather than any other brand-name city (see Miura 2003)? What force do Inuit narratives and beliefs have in the face of the tribe's relocation by the Canadian government? Is there any involvement with undeveloped nature at all, among the displaced Inuit interviewed in 1991 by William T. Vollmann, when (as part of his research for *The Rifles* [1994]) he visited an isolated village on the east side of Labrador? What matters in each case is not a character's or a people's beliefs but their positioning – their geographical, infrastructural positioning within an emerging world system.

Mirror Years: 1991, 2002

If Mathews in 1991 looks back to his own, private activity in that watershed decade, Thomas Pynchon does the same, in a more populist register, in *Vineland* (1991), his first, much anticipated, novel since *Gravity's Rainbow* (1973). Pynchon's tactic in both books is congruent – he confronts his own time through a retrospective look at past events and transfers his own, American concerns to distant settings, as Western culture (increasingly backed by American military/policing power and mass media) itself has taken root around the globe. *Gravity's Rainbow* sought origins of, and parallels to, the crystallisation of American power in 1973 by projecting its crises onto London and Germany during the final months and immediate aftermath of the Second World War, when the Allied forces and world leaders had not yet settled on the bi-polar system that erected the Berlin Wall. Variations on the same imaginative procedure can be seen in Pynchon's earlier novels, including *V.* (1963), whose chapters alternate between New York City of the 1960s and Sydney Stencil's 'impersonations' of key events at a number of crisis points in the twentieth century. *The Courier's Tragedy*, a mock-Jacobean revenge tragedy appearing midway into *The Crying of Lot 49* (1966), and the 'captivity narrative' introduced in the middle of his later novel *Mason & Dixon* (1997), are interpolations that do not parallel current events so much as recapitulate events in a recombinant narrative mode, even as the contemporary author introduces anachronism into historical forms and narratives. Eliza, the frontierswoman held hostage at a Jesuit community in *Mason & Dixon*, appears as the 'flying nun' of an American TV sitcom; elsewhere a pre-revolutionary George Washington joins Mason, Dixon and an overly perky Martha in smoking marijuana grown on his own plantation (unlike his successor, President Clinton, General Washington does appear to 'inhale').

A 'Stencil' or reproduction, a series of repetitions across eras: all feature as literary responses to a generalised culture of simulation. When in 1991 Jean Baudrillard notoriously claimed that the 'Gulf War Did Not Take Place' (Baudrillard 1995), he was of course reflecting on the first US war to be organised, from the start, in the full awareness of how the engagement would be seen by the world, in edited form, through the newly integrated media – literally a global medium, in the sense that high definition fibre-optic cables now circled the globe many times over. Image management, according to the histories and memoirs, may have been as much on the minds of generals and operatives as the proper deployment of a new generation of unmanned, 'smart' weaponry. Baudrillard's claim is in part a recognition, developed in depth and detail by American novelists over the prior two decades, that the century-long accumulation of war images, deadly 'shots' that have been replaced in popular consciousness by edited shots, would ensure that each new engagement, for the all-powerful spectator-participant, will have been felt to have *already happened*, safely, and at a geographical, temporal and existential distance. Any present carnage would be known, to the television viewer, only through repeated images of an identical rocket on its way to the point of impact; while 24-hour analysis on the Cable News Network (CNN), whose star rose with the Gulf War, broadcast a military expedition with 'the highest production values in history' (Ciccoricco 2005: 118).

The introduction of rocketry in the Second World War changed the nature of warfare fundamentally: at the appearance of a V2 rocket 'screaming . . . across the sky' over London, the narrator of *Gravity's Rainbow* could claim that there was 'nothing to compare it to' (Pynchon 2000: 3). By the year of the first Gulf War, there are *only* comparisons: to prior colonial occupations and America as inheritor of British, Roman or Spartan Empires; to Western fantasies of 'orientalism' (provoked perhaps inadvertently by Saddam Hussein on 23 August 1990, when he was seen on Iraqi state television stroking the head of a British boy, one of the Westerners being held hostage as human shields [Wark 1994: 3ff.]). There was the unavoidable comparison to the lost war in Vietnam – unavoidable if only because a number of successful movies and TV series had kept that war alive in viewers' consciousness. So it would be this war of the mid-1970s, of all others, whose 'specter' will have been laid to rest, according to the first President Bush in a radio address on 2 March 1991, at the conclusion of Operation Desert Storm in Iraq (cited by Ciccoricco 2005: 139). (Vietnam is again a primary reference in coverage of the Second Gulf War, from its inception in 2002 to the time of this writing.)

The mirror-like quality of contemporary warfare was not lost on Stuart Moulthrop, whose own fiction of the Gulf War, published in that same 'fateful year', registers a sense that *this time*, the American foray into global warfare would be accomplished without the need for allies (as in the Second World War) and without the constraints of a competing ideology (as in Korea, Vietnam, or the Cold War):

> . . . the great Return was left unfinished, and so at the start of that fateful year of the mirror, 1991, America set out once again on the torturous path of warfare. Once again, an Expedition was sent around the world, this time swift and resolute and unconstrained. (Moulthrop 1991: 'Back to the Future')

Moulthrop is one of the pioneers (along with Michael Joyce, Shelly Jackson and others) of hypertext fiction, the computer-based narrative form that exploits the capacity of electronic databases to be organised into systems of multiply linked units. In his *Victory Garden*, the hypertext form is itself grounded fundamentally in an aesthetic of repetition (see Ciccoricco 2005). Moulthrop's text, filled as it is with allusions to *Gravity's Rainbow* (on the subject of rocket technology) and Borges (on reflexive narrative), is itself a continuing reprise, or re-mediation, of the print tradition in electronic media. The title *Victory Garden* recalls (through allusions made explicit in the narrative) 'The Garden of Forking Paths' by Jorge Luis Borges, a story cited by many early practitioners, Moulthrop among them, as a literary precursor to hypertext discourse. According to the somewhat pedantic Professor Urquhart (a character in Moulthrop's work whose name is also that of a Borges character), the Argentinian late modernist had written a 'tale of murder and communication, coincidence and crossed identities . . . [a] narrative essay on necessity and the nature of time'

(Moulthrop 1991: 'The Text'). The hypertext fiction we are reading is likewise such a tale – as is, for that matter, Mathews's *My Life in CIA* and Pynchon's *Vineland*. It allows for the 'multiform' possibility that a novelist's allusiveness can be prospective as well as retrospective (Moulthrop 1997: 274); that the imagined future can be as unavoidable as the past; that certain structures of *fictionality*, if not precisely the same fictions, recur over time in response to the dominant fictions of everyday life in the developing networked world. What makes this moment of literary self-reference more than a metafictional exercise, and more than another example of modernist intertextuality, is the 'atemporally linked hypertext structure' which *activates* the sequence of fast-forwards and returns, and which involves readers manually by requiring us to select our own screens for viewing and make connections operationally, by clicking from screen to screen (Coover 1993).

The fact that one of the first, and still one of the most prominent, hypertext narratives appeared in the *same* digital medium that soldiers, commanders and journalists were employing when they conducted and simultaneously publicised the war, gives to the reading of fiction a feeling akin to the subject matter: in their own ways both operations, the narrative and the military, participate in the Command, Communications, and Control systems that characterise postmodern society generally. 'Among other things', writes Moulthrop, 'hypertextual discourse solicits iteration and involvement . . . This is certainly a property of all narrative fiction', but the driving force of iteration is different in hypertext: narrative is no longer at 'the command of *logos* or form, but driven instead by *nomos* or itinerant desire' (Moulthrop 1997: 273). The only difference between this 'nomadic invasion of narrative' in hypertext and the first-order repetitions generated by media in wartime, is that the literary 'war machine', by requiring the reader's participation in selecting and pursuing multiple narrative pathways, opposes the fatalism that is (supposedly) inherent in the single line of print, 'fostering instead an ethos of responsiveness and engagement' (Moulthrop 1997: 275).

Moulthrop is too good a critic, and too nuanced a writer, however, not to see that the 'solicitation' of reader participation has its own oppressive potential. This was already true in 1991, back before the US Communications Act of 1995 opened the floodgates to an era of spam emails, Web advertising, and gated sites requiring credit or personal data, so that our responsiveness has come to be prestructured in ways that are usually less literary than they are secretarial. Repetition in hypertext exceeds the mental recollection of sentences, motifs and verbal textures on a series of sequentially-ordered pages that is entailed in reading print narrative; it depends, rather, in no small part on the political and social organisation of the network, which is outside the reader's control but not always kept off the screen. Anticipating the *active* presence of textual and pictorial matter during the reading of literary hypertext, the novelist Robert Coover, fresh from conducting a hypertext fiction workshop at Brown University in 1991, announced 'The End of Books'. Hardly had he done so, however, than he was already forecasting the day (so soon in arriving) when writers would 'feel the need . . . even while using these vast networks and principles of randomness and expansive story line, to struggle against them, just as now one struggles against the constraints of the printed book' (cited in Moulthrop 1997: 278).

In the year 1991, Coover's near contemporary Pynchon took a different line, not resisting the printed book's page-by-page linearity but instead reasserting the power and potential of the book's medial *difference*. As critic William Paulson has perceived, in *Vineland*,

> Pynchon's ubiquitous and elastic prose describes events through other media, events already mediated by other forms: films, computer file (including text and image), video game, TV

commercial, sitcom. This pervasive *intermediality* has among its effects that of calling attention to the novel's capability to evoke so well such a wide spectrum of media activity. (Paulson
1997: 249)

In Paulson's scenario, the book 'in the age of its technological obsolescence' comes more
fully into its own; all that ends for the literary novel is its residual pretensions to be representing, rather than evoking, operational realities better left to other media. With this loss,
however comes a substantial gain in the hitherto unnoticed potential for the written word
to record and register media *effects* (Johnston 1998). The contrast between filmic and
digital technologies in *Vineland*, for example, allows Pynchon to evoke a richer, more fine-
grained contrast between the two eras it depicts: 1984, when the novel is set, and the 1960s,
when the dominant medium was film, an era recalled as 'a slower-moving time, predigital,
not yet so cut into pieces' (Pynchon 1991: 38). The narrative of *Vineland*, though focused
on one region in the Pacific Northwest (despite brief excursions to Hawaii and Japan),
alternates in time between the activism and protests of the late 1960s and 1984, the year
of Ronald Reagan's re-election, confirming the rightward movement in American political
culture and invoking the title of George Orwell's dystopian novel of totalitarianism.

A very concrete outcome of the post-1960s depoliticisation of American culture – or,
more precisely the supplanting of politics with a culture widely assertive of personal,
ethnic, sexual and racial identities – is registered by Pynchon's anti-hero, Zoyd Wheeler,
as he wheels his van into the parking lot of a Vineland roadhouse, there to meet his partner,
Van Meter:

> His old bass player and troublemaking companion had been living here for years, in what he
> still described as a commune, with an astounding number of current and ex-old ladies, ex-old
> ladies' boyfriends, children of parent combinations present and absent, plus miscellaneous
> folks in out of the night. Zoyd had watched television shows about Japan, showing places such
> as Tokyo where people got into incredibly crowded situations but, because over the course of
> history they'd all learned to act civil, everybody got along fine despite the congestion. So when
> Van Meter, a lifetime searcher for meaning, moved into this Cucumber Lounge bungalow,
> Zoyd had hoped for some Japanese-style serenity as a side effect, but no such luck. Instead of
> a quiescent solution to all the overpop, the 'commune' chose an energetic one – bickering.
> Unrelenting and high-decibel, it was bickering raised to the level of ceremony, bickering that
> soon generated its own house newsletter, the *Blind-Side Gazette*, bickering that could be heard
> even out on the freeway by the drivers of hurtling eighteen-wheelers, some of whom thought
> it was radio malfunction, others unquiet ghosts. (Pynchon 1991: 9–10)

Neither the contrasting 'oriental' reference, nor the closing media conceit, are gratuitous:
'everything' in Pynchon is famously 'connected' by way of repetitions, recurrent phrases,
allusions, and an intertext that extends beyond print culture to the newly mediated 'real
world' – 'that is to say', in Coover's characterisation, 'the world of video transmissions, cel-
lular phones, fax machines, computer networks, and in particular out in the humming dig-
italised precincts of avant-garde computer hackers, cyberpunks and hyperspace freaks'
(Coover 1992: 1). The media environment, which for many at the time promised the
book's consignment 'forever to those dusty unattended museums we now call libraries'
(Coover 1992: 1), is shown by Pynchon to have expressive consequences, attributable
perhaps to the rise of electronic media but conveyable, most effectively, through the slower,
more stable, medium of print.

The processual, operational quality of the signifier in electronic media make them effective at conveying *presences*; print fictions, by contrast, are most powerful when conveying what's *not* there. It may be no accident that we find – at the height of the digital transformation – the appearance of such prominent print titles as *This Is Not a Novel* (2001) by David Markson, or (more generally) *This Is Not It* (2002) by Lynne Tillman. The heightened differences *between* print and screen have made print narrative aware of its foundational, internalised difference *from itself*. By contrast to the floating, flickering signifier that can adjust in synch with the wider world of digitised sights and sounds, printed words are, by their very nature, *disengaged* from the things they signify. Hence a role of print fiction, one that was always fundamental but is newly emphasised in the current media environment, is to counter the media's production of presence with intimations of all that is unseen, unheard, unregistered by momentary representations. So what is presented by Pynchon as a politically inconsequential, narrowed, domestic American lifeworld is nonetheless environed by ghosts – literal ghosts of the past and also of possible futures, measurable in their effects, recordable not on tape but (partially, only evocatively) on the page. Ghostly 'presences' are sensed periodically throughout the novel, in a language whose other-worldy texture is scarcely distinguishable from the rhythms and textures of spoken discourse. But here, in the final occurrence, instead of human voices, quarrelling and alive, we are listening to voices in the underworld, where the sounds of nature blend imperceptibly into voices of the dead:

> And soon, ahead, came the sound of the river, echoing, harsh, ceaseless, remembering, speculating, arguing, telling tales, uttering curses, singing songs, all the things voices do, but without ever allowing the briefest breath of silence. All these voices, forever. (Pynchon 1991: 279)

In *Vineland*, other-worldly communications invoke nothing so much as a period when, for the first time in history, human voices could be recorded, replayed, and remixed in ways that disengage expression from its moment and context, no longer requiring the breath of human speech or song. To the lengthening list of 'posts' and 'ends', ubiquitous in cultural theory at the close of the Cold War, the term 'posthuman' was about to be added. The posthuman, in its most interesting formulations, would be concerned not only with alterations of the species by futuristic machines or genetic manipulation, but also the global distancing of humans from themselves, through an electronic archive that is already in place, here and now.

Writing under Constraint

Against the precariousness of globally mediated presences, the printed book reasserts its defining self-difference and characteristic signifying distances. Mathews for example imposes constraints on his narrative as a way of forcing his work and thought into forms and expressions outside of himself. Pynchon finds the organising form of his own retro-narrative in the media of his time, brought into the world largely by the innovations of the Second World War, but made available to a mass market only through the sustained development of a consumer society during the 1980s and 1990s. As if purposely repressing his own voice and allusive range (as William Gaddis, in his major novel of American capitialism, *J R* [1975], had repressed his own literary voice by writing exclusively in the jargon and through the media of corporate America), Pynchon restricts his range and refers nearly exclusively to content made familiar by film and TV programming, by the mid-1980s the only allusions held in common by a majority of literate Americans.

The creation of expressive freedom out of material constraints is an aesthetic common to many writers of the period immediately after the Cold War, when so many loyalties and alliances that had held world power in place seemed to be unravelling. By contrast to the 'swift and resolute and unconstrained' exercise of their government's power in the world (as Moulthrop put it in *Victory Garden*), American novelists purposely *sought* constraints, as ways of giving form to human speech and resisting media that, having become universal, were in danger of becoming formless, infinite meanings rendered meaningless by virtue of the non-judgemental equivalence of each 'bit' of information. The *Motion Sickness* referred to by Lynne Tillman in the title of her major essayistic novel of 1991 is the result not of travel exclusively; it is also, as she demonstrated in a 1993 story, 'Lust for Loss', the product of a culture whose modes of signification, post-Cold War, are shifting continually:

> She recalled Kohl and Reagan's bitter visit to Bitburg. Was the end of the Cold War a return to the beginning of the century and an undoing of both world wars? It wasn't cold now, but Madame Realism trembled. Once history holds your hand, it never lets go. But it has an anxious grip and takes you places you couldn't expect. (Tillman 2002: 146)

Bitter Bitburg? Like Pynchon's character Zoyd, wheeling his van to meet Van Meter, and like Mathews's narrator in *My Life in CIA* who devises a travel itinerary for dyslexics, listing departures only at times that read the same backward and forwards, Tillman has her narrative persona continually reflect back on her own medium, the printed word. In *Motion Sickness*, the narrator keeps track of her episodic movement through various European cities by the postcards that she accumulates: 'I want to travel light. I leave books in hotel rooms when I've finished them. I hold on only to the pictures, the postcards, my playing cards that mark presence and absence' (Tillman 1991: 88). Conventionally, postcards have value as a means of communication. They can be used (like photographs taken with a digital camera) to both document 'memories' and store them; when not hoarded the cards can help to convey impressions, visual and verbal, to friends at home or in cities left behind while travelling. By letting them accumulate, however, the author gives them a different value, in a system that (like a card game) has meaning only in itself, according to the rules of the game, not the requirements of external reference.

This shift from postcards to playing cards, while fanciful, generates material consequences as the cards take on characteristics of other, more operational, bits of paper during the course of the narrative. First, they are likened to money (the dollar had been falling in value, and even the bills look small in comparison to the Dutch Guilder): 'I have many more postcards than dollars, the postcards soothing to me as the shrunken dollars are to long-term foreign sufferers on Wall Street' (Tillman 1991: 88). Soon thereafter, the terms of comparison become political:

> my postcard is not a vote, although these days, where I come from, it ought to be part of a write-in campaign, composed of postcards from foreign places or paintings by well-known artists that would flood the capital with desire for something different. (Tillman 1991: 88)

What is here dreamed up, as a private, mass conceptual art action, would soon enough become practicable – as campaigns for both political candidates and direct action have since become a primary means of mobilising, not 'the masses' in blocks, but a herd of independent minds, each one accessible through networks that are themselves optional, not political; receptive, not broadcast. What we have here, in Tillman's essayistic fiction, is a classic instance of the condition identified by Walter Benjamin where one medium, print literature, offers an early glimpse of possibilities that would only be realised later, in a different medium (Benjamin 1969). The anticipation, in Tillman, is made through a series of literary metaphors; the realisation, in our day, would be wholly material. Given the capacity today for material realisations of what were once metaphorical explorations, what place is left for pure imagination?

No writer controls meaning, but potential meanings are everywhere, in controlling sequences, possible combinations, recombinations, returns, and reflections. The phone number 911, universally available throughout the US for contacting emergency services, is available also for other uses. In the year 1991, the same numerical sequence might be said to have marked the emergence of the global in literary culture, even as the desire to reverse it, dramatised on 11 September 2001 (9/11/01), may have been always present within the move toward globalisation itself.

References

Baudrillard, Jean (1995) *The Gulf War Did Not Take Place*, Bloomington, IN: Indiana University Press

Benjamn, Walter (1969) 'The Work of Art in the Age of Mechanical Reproduction' [1936], in Hannah Arendt, ed., *Illuminations*, trans. Harry Zohn, New York: Schocken, 217–51

Ciccoricco, Dave (2005) 'Repetition and Recombination: Reading Network Fiction', dissertation, University of Canterbury, New Zealand

Coover, Robert (1992) 'The End of Books', *New York Times Book* Review, 21 June, 1, 23–5

——(1993) 'Hyperfiction: Novels for the Computer', *New York Times Book Review*, 29 August, 1, 8–12

Gibson, William, and Bruce Sterling (1991) *The Difference Engine*, New York: Bantam Books

Hardt, Michael, and Antonio Negri (2000) *Empire*, Cambridge, MA: Harvard University Press

Hobsbawm, Eric (1994) *The Age of Extremes: A History of the World, 1914–1991*, New York: Vintage

Johnston, John (1998) *Media Multiplicity*, Baltimore, MD: Johns Hopkins University Press

Lautor, Paul, gen. ed. (2006) *The Heath Anthology of American Literature*, vol. B, Boston, MA: Houghton Mifflin

Mathews, Harry (2005) *My Life in CIA: A Chronicle of 1973*, Normal, IL: Dalkey Archive Press

Michaels, Walter Benn (2004) *The Shape of the Signifier: 1967 to the End of History*, Princeton, NJ: Princeton University Press

Miura, Reiichi (2003) 'On the Globalization of Literature: Haruki Murakami and Raymond Carver', *the electronic book review* (7 December), *www.electronicbookreview.com*.

Moulthrop, Stuart (1991) *Victory Garden*, Boston, MA: Eastgate (CD-ROM)

——(1997) 'No War Machine', in Tabbi and Wutz, eds, 269–92 *Reading Matters*

Paulson, William (1997) 'The Literary Canon in the Age of its Technological Obsolescence', in Tabbi and Wutz, eds, 227–49 *Reading Matters*

Pynchon, Thomas (1991) *Vineland*, Boston, MA: Little, Brown
——(2000) *Gravity's Rainbow*, New York: Penguin
Tabbi, Joseph, and Michael Wutz, eds (1997) *Reading Matters: Narrative in the New Media Ecology*, Ithaca, NY: Cornell University Press
Tillman, Lynne (1991) *Motion Sickness*, New York: Poseidon Press
——(2002) 'Lust for Loss', in *This Is Not It: Stories*, New York: Distributed Art Publishers, 153–7
Wark, McKenzie (1994) *Virtual Geography: Living with Global Media Events*, Bloomington, IN: Indiana University Press

Chapter 21

1993, Stockholm: A Prize for Toni Morrison

Abdulrazak Gurnah

On 24 January 1988, the *New York Times Book Review* published a letter under the heading 'Black Writers in Praise of Toni Morrison'. The letter was in two parts. The first part was an appreciation of Toni Morrison's writing in general and of *Beloved*, just published the year before, in particular. The first part appeared above the names of June Jordan and Houston A. Baker Jr, an eminent poet and an eminent academic, both African-American. The second part, which was preceded by the word 'STATEMENT', took the more recognisable form of a letter to a newspaper with its 'We, the undersigned'. The undersigned lamented the 'oversight and harmful whimsy' of failing to award Morrison either the National Book Award or the Pulitzer Prize, the 'keystone honors' of national recognition in the US, and offered their own tribute as an affirmation of 'our pride, our respect and our appreciation' for the writer and for *Beloved*. The letter was signed by forty-eight African-American writers and academics of varying ages, achievements and persuasion, including Maya Angelou, Toni Cade Bambara, Amiri Baraka, Angela Davis, Henry Louis Gates Jr, Rosa Guy, Paule Marshall, Alice Walker and John Edgar Wideman. The letter became notorious in some circles as an example of the special pleading that accompanied discussions of 'race' and writing. When Toni Morrison's *Beloved* did go on to receive the Pulitzer Prize three months later, the Prize spokesman was constrained to deny that the letter had had any influence on the decision. Morrison herself expressed some relief at the Pulitzer Committee's decision. *Beloved*, she said, 'had begun to take on a responsibility, an extra-literary responsibility that it was never designed for' (Mitgang 1988: 5).

Prizes are almost always contentious, which is what makes them compelling to the media and as public events. Even when the award of the prize reflects a consensus, someone will feel compelled to ginger up the story with derision or hyperbole. The 1993 award of the Nobel Prize for Literature to Toni Morrison was thought to have settled the issue about her greatness, although it briefly revived the letter episode. To those who had got round to reading Toni Morrison's writing, and particularly for her African-American readers, the controversy about prizes and tributes would have seemed thoroughly pointless, as the writing's power and originality was self-evident.

In the case of Morrison, and perhaps of other African-American reputations, issues of 'race' are tangled with an unease that affirmative action in this context is unnecessarily assertive. There is a perception, declaimed sometimes nervously, sometimes with bravado, that what constitutes the canon is being enlarged for conscience-stricken reasons. This is not necessarily a matter of 'race'. Ralph Ellison, for example, himself a winner of the National Book Award for *Invisible Man* in 1953, thought the letter a mistake, and imagined that Toni Morrison would be embarrassed by it (Mitgang 1988: 5). On the other hand, and to those who are not persuaded by this opinion, there is a conviction that behind such high-minded objections is, at best, a delusion about the possibility of impartial judgement, or at worst, a desire to exclude out of an unacknowledged habit of cultural egotism. It is significant, in relation to this idea of unacknowledged bias, that the African-American writers' letter cites James Baldwin, just recently dead in 1988, as the most extreme example of what it calls 'national neglect'. It sees his neglect (in the sense of not being awarded one of the 'keystone honors') as an 'emblematic death', not only of Baldwin but of 'every black artist who survives him in this freedom land'.

The award of the Nobel Prize to Toni Morrison in 1993 might at a quick glance, then, seem a good moment to look back at the struggles of black writers to win admission into the canon. However, there are two considerations which lead us away from this direction, and the ensuing discussion will take these up. The first one is a general point. The emphasis on public recognition of this kind for writing – national and international prizes, the media acclaim that accompanies them, the national self-congratulation – is also a distraction. The significance of such recognition to the writing context is not clear-cut or permanent, especially if it is glibly taken that the award of the Nobel Prize to an African-American writer indicates a dramatic change for non-European writing in English in a wider sense. The second consideration is the specificity of African-American writing culture and the contrasting trajectory of non-European British writing.

The production and reception of African-American writing in the United States is profoundly tied up with the history and culture of that country, of course. The celebration of Morrison's award is, in a sense, the culmination of a phase of that writing, beginning with Richard Wright and running through to Morrison herself, and taking in, among many others, Ralph Ellison, James Baldwin, Maya Angelou, Alice Walker (the first African-American Pulitzer prizewinner) and August Wilson, Pulitzer prizewinner for drama in 1986 and again in 1990, for two of the plays from his ambitions ten-play cycle on African-American history in the twentieth century. The themes of African-American writing arise out of a history of denial of justice and opportunity, and the wounds that are inflicted and are self-inflicted when anyone is forced to live in such a condition. The monstrousness of Richard Wright's Bigger Thomas in *Native Son* is a malevolent expression of humanity distorted by racial terror. Ralph Ellison's narrator in *Invisible Man* has to tolerate invisibility so that he can live sanely: in other words, he has to be ambivalent about racial hostility to keep his sanity. This is also a theme of much of Baldwin's writing, when he repeatedly refers to the superior form of tolerance by victims of racism which made the United States function.

It is tempting to link this phase with other developments of the postwar period: the formal integration of US armed forces and other domestic rumblings towards the Civil Rights campaign, and in a wider context, the Pan-African movement and the beginning of decolonisation. Both Richard Wright and James Baldwin attended the *Présence Africaine* conference organised in Paris in September 1956 by Alioune Diop, Léopold Sédar Senghor and Aimé Césaire, at a time when the revival of Civil Rights in the United States was finding an international context (Leeming 1994: 120–1; Gayle 1980: 264–74). W. E. B. Du Bois, the great African-American 'educator', was refused permission to travel by the United States government, and his telegram to the conference specifically linked this act to a desire by the State Department to prevent him from speaking about the 'Negro-American' struggle for equality to an international audience. Yet what is interesting in Baldwin's account of the conference and its dramas is his sense that the Africans had no idea of the African-American experience. It is also just as clear that Baldwin himself has no sympathy for the *négritude* project which this event was part of (Baldwin 1964: 24–53). He also hints that Wright got the tone wrong when speaking to the African delegates about the benefits of European colonialism. So the Americans too had an uncertain idea of the African experience of colonialism the delegates were gathered there to speak about. Members of the African-American delegation were apparently shocked to hear Aimé Césaire describe them as 'colonised' (Gayle 1980: 268). African-American writers of this period wrote about their world with a new candour about its brutality, its history of degradation and corrupting intimacies, its unresolved dependencies. The *négritude* movement sought celebration and self-affirmation of culture and of the intellectual life of 'the people', a Pan-African Romanticism that sought to applaud the virtue of the despised in terms of nature and feeling. African-American writing culture, then, had its own concerns and agendas which were distinct from those of the largely African and Caribbean intellectuals of *négritude*, despite the desire in some quarters (Césaire's address at the conference, for example) to blur the distinction in favour of a community of the historically-wronged.

In any case, the radicalisation of the Civil Rights movement into the violent resistance of the Black Panthers also radicalised the language of race in the 1970s. It was out of this charged context that the Black Arts movement arose, to identify and promote modes of expression that grew out of the real experiences of African Americans and to describe a 'Black Aesthetic', a way of producing and consuming art that was 'black'. At its extreme, the Black Arts rhetoric turned its revolutionary rage on African Americans for self-treachery, for betraying their 'authentic' selves for acceptance. Eldridge Cleaver attacked James Baldwin for writing about gay love with 'white' men, seeing that as self-hatred (Cleaver 1969: 100). Cleaver himself was in jail for serial rapes of white women, after first 'refining his technique' on black women. In justification of his crimes, which he describes as a pathology he is helpless to resist because of racial oppression, Cleaver quotes Leroi Jones on black rage (Cleaver 1969: 14). Poet, playwright and activist Leroi Jones/Amiri Baraka was himself later to describe Ishmael Reed (author, among other novels, of *Mumbo Jumbo* [1972] and *Flight to Canada* [1976]) as 'a house nigger' for making critical remarks about Malcolm X, and generally for refusing the monocultural argument of the Black Arts movement (Baraka 1980: 12). In a sense, the argument has neither been resolved nor run its course, but it has mutated and continues in contemporary afrocentric forms.

The 1980s saw the appearance of important African-American women writers. Alice Walker, Maya Angelou and Toni Morrison herself bring an intensified gender focus on issues of history and justice, opening up a debate about gender roles within the American debate about race. Among the central themes of their writing, and particularly of Morrison's, is how African-American men wrong their women, and how critical women's work is in preserving and transmitting the intimate knowledge of the community. It might be argued that the latter of these themes is an expression of an impossible desire for a homogeneous story of African-American life. For example, in *Song of Solomon* (1977) Pilate carries a sack of bones with her throughout her wandering, a preserver of ancestral memories in this literal sense as well as in her song and her knowledge of herbs and lore. Milkman, at first an abuser of women like his father before him, discovers the true gold of his heritage in the Deep South, the site of ancestral suffering. Morrison problematises this desire in that Pilate's bones turn out not to be an ancestor after all, and her song is misremembered, and Milkman's discovery ends with an ambiguously miraculous 'flight', but in both cases the desire is healing. It is probably the case that the privileging of these themes of male guilt and women as preservers of African-American life come late in the 1980s as a response to the earlier masculine ethos of African-American resistance in the postwar period.

So the Nobel Prize for Toni Morrison in 1993 can be seen to bring to a successful conclusion a struggle to achieve recognition, and admission into the canon, for non-European
writers hitherto excluded from the intellectual fold. Though this struggle clearly has global
dimensions, these should not be allowed to place too much or too exclusive an emphasis
on the United States and its internecine cultural and historical wars. This is an emphasis
we are nevertheless familiar with: even Paul Gilroy, in his excellent *The Black Atlantic*
(1993), cannot resist using the term 'African diaspora' to mean the United States, the
Caribbean and Europe (and chiefly the United States), when the largest 'African diaspora'
is to be found further south, in Brazil. The consequences of dispersals and survivals, in
Brazil, perhaps also offer a complicated counterpoint to the 'double consciousness' argument that figures so prominently in Gilroy's account.

Furthermore, to make 1993 and the award of the Nobel Prize such a dramatic moment
of recognition for African-American writing is to overestimate the meaning of the Prize.
After all Winston Churchill was awarded the Nobel Prize for Literature ('for his mastery
of historical and biographical description as well as for brilliant oratory in defending
exalted human values', Nobel Prize 1953), and when Sartre's moment of recognition
arrived, he declined it. In any case, the Nigerian writer Wole Soyinka was awarded the
Prize in 1986, and Derek Walcott, the St Lucian poet, in 1992, both of them writing in
English. So Toni Morrison's 1993 award was not the dramatic triumph for black writing
that the United States media made it out to be, a great triumph though it was.

Perhaps it is time to turn away from prizes for the moment and cast a retrospective look at
non-European writing in English in the British context and in a comparable period to that
for which 1993 seemed such a triumphant climax. The period in question is the second half
of the twentieth century, post-1945. We have become used now to think of 1945 as the starting-point for many observations about the postcolonial phenomenon, and there are good
reasons for doing this despite the inevitable simplification behind it. It is a period which
inaugurates great changes in the colonial world: decolonisation and imperial retreat in Africa
and Asia, and a dramatic new dimension to migration patterns. In the postwar period, millions still pour out of Europe to settle in the lands acquired through empire and its aftermath,
but now, for the first time on such a scale, millions from the colonised and decolonising world
pour into Europe. Some are extricated from the decolonising shambles because of their complicity with colonial rule, as was the case with thousands who fled Indonesia after the collapse of the Dutch empire in South Asia. Some are seduced or summoned to work in French
factories and British building sites to plug the labour gap in the postwar boom. It is not millions all at once, despite panicked predictions at the time, but they become millions in good
time and spread into every nook and cranny where there is a living to be made. For Britain,
a new voluntary 'diaspora' begins to take shape, most notably imaged in the photographs of
men in thin suits descending from the *Empire Windrush*, the ship famous for bringing the first
substantial influx of immigrants from the West Indies. They have come to Britain to work.
They take themselves seriously. They are dignified. This is not the complete image, of course,
even of the Caribbean dimension of this arrival. These are all Jamaicans, and there will be
Trinidadians and Barbadians and Guyanese, not to mention Montserratians, half of whose
entire population leave for Britain in these early decades of the second half of the twentieth
century. There will be Indians and Pakistanis, and later Bangladeshis, and other numerically
less significant populations: Nigerians, Turks, Somalis, even a few Zanzibaris.

Among them were writers, and the ones who made the greatest impact in these early
days were West Indian writers: Sam Selvon (*A Brighter Sun*, 1952), George Lamming
(*In the Castle of My Skin*, 1953), V. S. Naipaul (*The Mystic Masseur*, 1957) and Wilson

Harris (*Palace of the Peacock,* 1960). These were writers who were ambitious, who took themselves seriously, who were published by major British publishers, and whose work was received with acclaim. Naipaul, the most well-known now out of this group, picked up prize after prize even before prizes were major media events. Richard Wright wrote an introduction to the McGraw-Hill American edition of *In the Castle of My Skin* (1954). Wilson Harris criticism is now a small academic industry in itself, and Selvon's *The Lonely Londoners* is likely to be the opening text in any British undergraduate module on migrant writing in English. In other words, these writers and their texts made swift progress into the canon long before 1993. There were many others in addition to these, most notably the reappearance of West-Indian born Jean Rhys in 1966 with *Wide Sargasso Sea* and Barbadian Edward Brathwaite's remarkable *The Arrivants* in 1967.

How can we account for this rich creativity out of nowhere? In the first place, it was not really out of nowhere. As any study of the writing will show, a major strand of Caribbean writing of earlier periods saw itself in the tradition of canonical English writing. It was schooled in the Classics, in the Metaphysical poets and in the Romantics, and relished the knowledge and use of this tradition. In the poetry of someone like Una Marson and Walter Adolphe Roberts, whose 'The Maroon Girl' begins as an echo of Wordsworth's 'The Solitary Reaper', this is evident in both the philosophy of emotion and in the diction. Derek Walcott acknowledges and debates his engagement with this canonical English tradition throughout his poetry and his essays, although in his case he also has W. H. Auden and T. S. Eliot to contend with (Walcott 1998). Impatient with the debt to English that he sees disabling creativity, Brathwaite takes Caribbean poetry in a different direction. He urges West Indian poets to describe the palm tree rather than the elm, to get away from an English voice and to hear instead the 'folk' voice of that other insurrectionary tradition in West Indian culture: the song (Brathwaite 1984).

Wilson Harris has to shake off the nineteenth-century novel in order to write his own, and he formulates his ideas on this in one of his early essays 'Tradition and the West Indian Novel' (Harris 1999). The subject and its resolution figures centrally in Harris's critical writing, and this essay is the earliest attempt at it. Harris uses the phrase 'the novel of persuasion' to describe the nineteenth-century novel, and to him it seems a directive and duplicitous method, offering an ensemble of half-truths to achieve verisimilitude:

> The novel of persuasion rests on grounds of apparent common sense: a certain 'selection' is made by the writer, the selection of items, manners, uniform conversation, historical situations, etc., all lending themselves to build and present an individual span of life which yields self-conscious and fashionable judgements, self-conscious and fashionable moralities. (Hari 1999: 140–1)

To some extent, Harris writes about the nineteenth-century novel as if it was still the hegemonic novel mode, as if modernism had not happened, or as if it was only a muted affair so far as novelistic trends went. Harris's technique *looks* modernist: its non-linear narrative, the shifting identities of its figures, the overlapping temporalities of its setting. But for Harris, modernist writing had only gone part of the way in resisting 'the novel of persuasion', in refusing unities of style and theme, in destablising the narrative voice, in regarding the unregarded; but it was trapped in disappointment and disillusion and was not capable of liberating the 'simultaneity' of the imagination.

He finds the West Indian novel of his time (1964) 'belongs – in the main – to the conventional mould', following closely on his description above of 'the novel of persuasion'. In this description, he specifically includes the work of George Lamming, whom he sees as a realist who restlessly over-elaborates without breaking through the ruling framework. He applauds Lamming's interest in 'the folk', but doubts that 'realism', with its stony linearity will allow him to penetrate to 'the tragic premises of individual personality' (Harris 1999: 146). For Naipaul's *A House for Mr Biswas* (1961), Harris has even less sympathy. The novel had been praised for the sensitivity and pathos of its account of the troubled and troublesome central figure who has to 'learn to paddle his own canoe'. His stubborn triumphs and farcical defeats construct the classic 'little man' who hangs on, malingers and dreams of escape and fulfilment. The novel presents this figure with affection for its eccentricities. As is well known, Mr Biswas's history closely parallels that of Naipaul's own father. Mr Biswas's rebellion is comic because it is so frantic, but the comedy is made bitter because the oppression he resists is so detailed and so intimate, and he is so apparently helpless before it. The Tulsi family, into which Mr Biswas casually marries, crushes and contains the individual for the greater good of the family ethos. In this respect and in many others, the novel evokes its dislocated Indian context in detail, and is precise about its tragic dimensions.

But Harris is not persuaded. He finds that 'the sad figure of Mr Biswas lends itself to a vulgar and comic principle of classification of things and people which gives the novel a conventional centre (Harris 1999: 147). On this count, Harris finds the novel's comedy to be clichéd, and therefore the shape of the whole can only be 'conventional'. The novel is, Harris says in the same essay, 'devoid of phenomenal . . . sensibility', by which he means, I think, that it shows no interest in different ways of seeing phenomena. It is anchored in the material and ignores the numinous, and offers no challenge to 'preconceptions of humanity'. There is an echo here of the argument that Leavis made famous about Dickens, that the comedy in his writing denied his characters imaginative and emotional depth. It is not an unlikely echo, given that early reviews of *A House for Mr Biswas* made the Dickensian comparison (*The Times*, 5 October 1961: 16). Harris no doubt wished to show that being compared to a great nineteenth-century novelist was not as straightforward an approbation as it might seem.

What is apparent in Harris's analyses of Lamming and Naipaul is the implicit account of the novel Wilson Harris was writing and continued to write. Between 1960 and 1964, Harris had published five novels which had baffled reviewers and sometimes exhilarated them. Over the years, Harris has produced twenty-two novels altogether and an impressive stream of critical reflections on what writing should aspire to achieve. That aspiration is nothing less than a new beginning, not one that does away with the past or with difference, but that brings everything together in 'a confluence of spaces'. In a 1998 essay titled 'Creoleness, the Crossroads of a Civilisation', Harris says:

> we need a narrative that helps us to sense the partiality of linear progression and brings home to us in genuine stages of creativity . . . the simultaneity of the past, the present, and the future in the unfinished genesis of the imagination. (Harris 1999: 244)

He has said something similar countless times in his essays and in his fiction. This faith in the subtle hidden connections in phenomenon, the interconnectedness between the 'live' and the 'fossil' through language, is exactly what he found missing in *A House for Mr Biswas*.

The comparison of *A House for Mr Biswas* to Dickens was not the invention of one reviewer. Other readers saw the likeness, and Naipaul acknowledges the influence of Dickens, although this is not a straight forward matter. Dickens offered as much an example as a tradition to reject, Naipaul commenting that he rejected 'all Dickens's descriptions of London . . . Dickens's rain and drizzle I turned into tropical downpours' (Naipaul 1972: 24).

Naipaul acknowledges a much more clear-cut debt to Joseph Conrad, although this too is not to suggest that the latter was an example or a model either. If anything, what Naipaul describes in 'Conrad's Darkness' is a degree of resistance, through which he comes to understand a shared vision with him (Naipaul 1980). Naipaul has analysed his own 'insecurity' as arising from the limited vision of a colonised society. To live as 'a colonial' is 'to inhabit a fixed world,' he argues, with simple beliefs and simple actions (Naipaul 1980: 207). He sees how Conrad has attempted to understand the limited vision of people who live in such places and in such ways, that he had understood how precarious their existence was because it was without reflection or hope. He had grasped the profound nihilism of their existence. These, Naipaul says, 'were the things that began to preoccupy me', the ramshackle fantasy of nationhood in 'the half-made societies that were doomed to remain half-made', and he saw that Conrad had already been there ahead of him. Conrad's vision, as Naipaul sees it, is of an unstable world which re-made itself daily, without goal or reason but to repeat itself. He thinks he shares with Conrad a knowledge of the precariousness of this 'half-made' world, the colonial one for Conrad, and, in the 'new politics,' the postcolonial one for Naipaul (Naipaul 1980: 27). He comments on Conrad's effort to utter these unpalatable truths, and it is implicit here that he thinks that is what he does too. He not only shares a vision with Conrad, he also shares a moral attitude.

Naipaul has travelled a long way from being a writer of biting comedies about rural and small-town Indians in Trinidad to one who pronounces with impossible assurance on the state of the world: on Africa, on India and on Islam. He has the authority to speak on these matters, from a certain way of thinking about authority, because he is an Indian from the Caribbean who has travelled and lived in Africa and has made a special project of Islam. In the recent phase of his long writing career, he has turned more definitely, and with some sympathy, towards India. In return, India has welcomed back another prodigal. His award of the Nobel Prize for literature was celebrated in India as a minor state occasion, with Naipaul himself in attendance at formal banquets and press briefings. Yet Naipaul's writing has followed a different trajectory altogether from that of the Indian writing of the diaspora which has seen such a remarkable efflorescence in the last three decades. In many ways, despite his late turn to India in recent times, Naipaul is still a Trinidadian writer who came to Britain in the 1950s and long continued to sort out the consequences of that move, still charted in *The Enigma of Arrival* (1987) and beyond. It is time now to turn to that diasporic Indian writing in the British context.

In 1948, G. V. Desani published his first and only novel, *All about H. Hatterr*, later frequently revised. Introduced in this way, it might seem that the invitation is to see this publication as a point of origin, and in some ways it is – of a certain style and attitude to writing and to English. Indian writing precedes this moment by thousands of years, of course, and even Indian writing in English by several decades (see Innes 2002; Nasta 2002). Desani's novel was written and published in the same era as some of the great names of twentieth century Indian writing in English – Raja Rao, Mulk Raj Anand, R. K. Narayan – all of whom had their concerns and styles, and were different from each other in important ways. But Desani's novel was dramatically different in style from its contemporaries. And even though the subject matter overlapped to some extent – caste, the search for spiritual meaning, Europe, colonialism – Desani's treatment is frantic and comically grotesque. The bulk of the text (pp. 21–278) is narrated by H. Hatterr himself:

> The name is H. Hatterr, and I am continuing . . .
>   Biologically, I am fifty-fifty of the species.

> One of my parents was a European, Chistian-by-faith merchant merman (seaman). From which part of the continent? Wish I could tell you. The other was an Oriental, a Malay Peninsula-resident lady, a steady non-voyaging, non-Christian human (no mermaid). From which part of the Peninsula? Couldn't tell you either. (Desani 1972: 31)

Hatterr, then, is of European–Asian ancestry. His father 'the merchant merman', takes him away from his mother, and he never sees her again. The father dies within the year of 'chronic malaria and pneumonia-plus', and Hatterr is adopted and brought up by the English Missionary Society as an orphan-ward: 'thus it was I became a sahib'. Being a sahib also allowed Hatterr a claim to English, which he then proceeds to use with hilarious freedom and eccentricity. At the opening of his narrative, he has just decided (on the toss of a coin) to go to England:

> All my life I wanted to come: come to the Western shores, to my old man's continent, to the Poet-Bard's adored Eldorado, to England, to God's own country, the seat of Mars, that damme paradise, to Rev. the Head's mother and fatherland, to the Englishman's Home, his Castle, his garden, fact's, the feller's true alma mammy and apple-orchard. (Desani 1972: 35–6)

Hatterr's naivety about England is Desani's irony about English self-constructions, a method other migrant writers have used to puncture the pompous meanness they encountered on arrival. *All about H. Hatterr* was accompanied with a foreword by E. M. Forster when it was first published. Writings by Indian authors still needed this kind of endorsement in 1948 if they were to make an impact. Raja Rao's *Kanthapura* (1938) also had a foreword by E. M. Forster, as did Mulk Raj Anand's *Untouchables* (1946).

Desani himself was born in Nairobi, Kenya Colony in 1909. His parents came from Sind and his father sold wood to the newly built railway that was to serve the white settler colony established four years earlier. In 1918 the family returned to Karachi where Desani lived until he fled to Britain to escape marriage to a child-bride in 1926, aged seventeen. He returned to India after two years, and then came back to Britain in 1939, just weeks before war broke out, and worked for the BBC Eastern Service throughout the war years where he encountered E. M. Forster, T. S. Eliot and George Orwell, among others.

There is something of the modern migrant's experience in this profile of multiple homes and extended dislocations. The style of Desani's novel reflects some of this hybridity and ambivalence, the sense that 'home' requires negotiation, as does 'language'. Hatterr describes the language of his narration in the novel as 'rigmarole English', a hybrid form authentic to India. We are familiar now with the argument about the legitimacy of hybridised forms of English as writing languages, and Desani's use too is both a refusal and an affirmation. It refuses to defer to a monoculturally-inflected language and worldview, and its hybridised forms are also an affirmation of the 'unofficial', the undervalued and the colonised

Remarkably, *All about H. Hatterr* was a great success. It was reissued in 1950 and published in an American edition in 1951. Desani never wrote another novel, but revised *Hatterr* again and again, the last time in 1986. The novel's reputation declined over the years as it faded from view, until Salman Rushdie's citation of it as an ancestor turned out to be the start of a revival. It will be clear to any reader of his oeuvre why Rushdie might have cited this novel as an influence, but Rushdie also spelled it out some years ago, in an article written soon after his own great triumph with *Midnight's Children* (1980):

> As long ago as 1948, within months of the independence of India, G. V. Desani published *All About H. Hatterr* and showed how English could be bent and kneaded until it spoke in an

authentically Indian voice . . . Desani's triumph was to take babu-English, *chamcha*-English, and turn it against itself: the instrument of subservience became a weapon of liberation. It was the first great stroke of the decolonizing pen. (Rushdie 1982: 8)

And Rushdie's writing was itself the beginning of a great era of South Asian writing in English, 'decolonizing' the English canon in a way he predicted in his 1982 article cited above, but in which perhaps he would not have imagined his writing would play such a crucial part. *Midnight's Children* won the Booker Prize in 1981, the first prize ceremony to be televised, winning a huge audience for the novel. The *fatwa* issued against Rushdie on account of *The Satanic Verses* (see Chapter 18) made him known across the world. At the height of the affair, his presence on newspaper front-pages and on TV for weeks on end, made him a liberal image of what writing dares to do and put his texts on reading lists for literature degrees. Above all, Rushdie was able to achieve in this novel what he praised Desani for doing, to write English in an Indian voice, and to charge it with dynamism and energy that was irresistible. Other writers who preceded and followed Rushdie in this great era include Anita Desai, Amitav Ghosh, Vikram Seth, Rohinton Mistry and most recently Hari Kunzru. Not all of them are Indian writers of the British diaspora – Ghosh lives in New York and Mistry in Toronto – but they come out of the English novel tradition as it was transmitted in India and to Indians.

What this writing has done with its subject is distinctly of itself, recognisable in its themes and concerns: the tragedy of partition, the tyranny of the family, living in the diaspora, religion and politics and history of modern India. It is less easy to make a broad statement like this about a distinct style and method. Rushdie's style draws attention to itself, not only because of its large gestures and exhibitionism, but because it is so restlessly innovative and relentlessly intertextual with popular cinema and music. From an academic point of view, Rushdie's texts repay investment. In addition to the vibrancy and variety of Indian writing in English, what can be said about it is that it developed along quite a different route from African-American writing. I have argued something similar about the trajectory of writing by Caribbean migrants. None of these contexts and details can be safely simplified. All these writings intersect at some important points, and seem to invite a generalised grouping, but it is an invitation to be taken up with caution.

References

Baldwin, James (1964) 'Princes and Power', *Nobody Knows My Name*, London: Penguin, 24–53

'Black Writers in Praise of Toni Morrison' (1988) *New York Times Book Review*, 24 January, 36

Baraka, Amiri (1980) 'Afro-American Literature and Class Struggle', *Black American Literature Forum*, 14.1, Spring

Brathwaite, Edward Kamau (1984) *The History of the Voice: the Development of Nation Language in Anglophone Caribbean Poetry*, London: New Beacon Books

Cleaver, Eldridge (1969) *Soul on Ice*, London: Jonathan Cape

Desani G. V. (1972) *All about H. Hatterr*, Harmondsworth: Penguin

Gayle, Addison (1980). *Richard Wright: Ordeal of a Native Son*, New York: Anchor Press/Doubleday

Gilroy Paul (1993) *The Black Atlantic*, London: Verso

Harris, Wilson (1999) 'Tradition and the West Indian Novel,' in Andrew Bundy, ed., *Selected Essays of Wilson Harris*, London: Routledge, 140–51

Innes, Lyn (2002) *A History of Black and Asian Writing in Britain, 1700–2000*, Cambridge: Cambridge University Press

Leeming, David (1994) *James Baldwin: A Biography*, London: Michael Joseph

Mitgang, Herbert (1988) 'For Morrison, Prize Silences Gossip', *New York Times Book Review*, 1 April, Section B, 5

Naipaul, V. S. (1972) 'Jasmine' [1964], in *The Overcrowded Barracoon*, London: André Deustch, 23–9

——(1980) 'Conrad's Darkness' [1974], in *The Return of Eva Peron*, London: Andre Deutsch, 197–218

Nasta, Susheila (2002) *Home Truths: Fictions of the South Asian Diaspora in Britain*, London: Palgrave

Nobel Prize (1953) http://nobelprize.org/literature/lauroater/1953

Rushdie, Salman (1982) 'The Empire Writes Back with a Vengeance', *The Times*, 3 July, 8

Walcott, Derek (1998) 'The Muse of History' [1974], in *What the Twilight Says*, London: Faber and Faber

Coda

11 September 2001, New York: Two Y2Ks

Brian McHale and Randall Stevenson

Senses of an Ending

Ending a literary history at the end of one century and the beginning of a new one is arbitrary, but at least it has the virtue of being *transparently* arbitrary – all the more so when that end and beginning also coincide with the onset of a new millennium. Centuries and millennia are convenient fictions, and using them to frame a history is a way of acknowledging that there is no 'natural' place to stop – as there is no 'natural' place to start. Developments begun on one page of the calendar continue on the next page, and the conditions prevailing before New Year's Eve also persist after it. Conversely, thresholds can be crossed at any time, regardless of what the calendar says, and we can find ourselves abruptly in a condition of unheralded newness, for better or worse. The end of the twentieth century, or rather its *endings*, in the plural, offers a kind of parable of history's continuities and discontinuities, its lingering sameness and catastrophic newness.

'Every New Year's Eve is impending apocalypse in miniature', writes Zadie Smith in her end-of-millennium novel, *White Teeth* (Smith 2000: 412). Seldom are they as apocalyptic, in prospect at least, as New Year's Eve 1999. Computer engineers were predicting widespread failures when computer systems whose internal calendars were designed to work with dates beginning in '19__' tried to roll over to '2000'. This 'millennium bug', it was predicted, would jeopardise air traffic control and the proper operation of power stations, telecommunications, banking, perhaps even nuclear armaments. The popular imagination seized on visions of modern technologised society grinding to a halt. Survivalists stockpiled goods and weapons, planning to retreat into the hills in expectation of a breakdown of social order. The post-apocalyptic scenarios of living on amid the ruins of the twentieth century, rehearsed so often in science-fiction novels (e.g., Walter M. Miller's *A Canticle for Leibowitz* [1959], Russell Hoban's *Riddley Walker* [1980]) and Hollywood films (e.g., *On the Beach*, *A Boy and His Dog*, *The Omega Man*, the *Mad Max* trilogy), seemed on the verge of coming true.

In the event, the survivalists were disappointed. In the years leading up to what, in computer-era jargon, we learned to call 'Y2K', many thousands of programmer man-hours and many millions of dollars were expended on forestalling the millennium bug. Apocalypse was narrowly averted – or so the engineers claimed, and who knew enough to contradict them? A sense of anti-climax set in, coloured by cynicism and resentment: were the catastrophic scenarios merely media hype? Even a marketing ploy? Nothing about Y2K was certain or unambiguous, except that nothing catastrophic happened.

How does a century end? On New Year's Eve 1999 it ended (or failed to end) with the muted whimper that T. S. Eliot had anticipated as long ago as 1925, and not with any apocalyptic bang. Then, nearly two years later, on 11 September 2001 it appeared really to end, this time explosively. As everyone knows, in the middle of the morning on that day, two hijacked airliners were crashed into the World Trade Center towers in Manhattan; another was crashed into the Pentagon; a fourth, evidently en route to another target in Washington, came down in a field in Pennsylvania. The burning and ultimate collapse of the twin towers was viewed around the world 'live' on television, to be etched in the global consciousness. Here was the catastrophe that conspicuously failed to transpire on Y2K – 'apocalypse in miniature'.

9/11 (to use the shorthand designation that sprang up almost immediately) was everything that Y2K was not. It came as a shock, literally 'out of the blue', whereas Y2K was tediously anticipated; it was a media spectacle, where Y2K was invisible, a non-event; it was horrific, involving the loss of nearly 3,000 lives, where Y2K was merely bathetic. Y2K existed in the dimension of prospection – we 'looked forward' to it, many with dread, some with apocalyptic glee. 9/11, by contrast, existed in the dimension of retrospection. Once it had occurred, we began piecing together, retrospectively, the developments that had led up to it: the threats, clues, and foreshadowings that intelligence organisations had failed to recognise; the larger historical tendencies that led jihadists to sacrifice their lives to destroy symbols of First-World power in the full glare of the media spotlight; and the imaginative anticipations of disaster that form a strand running throughout twentieth-century cultural expression. For the 'apocalypse in miniature' of 9/11, if it was in one sense unimaginable and unthinkable, was also, in another sense, immediately *recognisable*. We recognised it from the many representations, in verbal fictions, but especially in films and on television, of the way the world ends. The televised images of the morning reminded many of us of movies, or were even mistaken *for* movies, at first. The real event was almost, but not quite, pre-empted in our imaginations by the abundant media images of staged disaster that we had already viewed over and over. 9/11 appallingly fulfilled the century's imagination of disaster.

How does a century end? Y2K and 9/11 yield two alternative end-points and thresholds, one artificial and anticipated, the other unanticipated, imposing itself on our imaginations by acts of violent will. They also yield two alternative ways of thinking about ends and beginnings in cultural history. There is the *scheduled* end-point, the one marked on the calendar: the end of a decade, a century, a millennium, as arbitrarily measured by the calendar. (Even in calendrical measurement, ambiguity abounds: did the new century 'really' begin on New Year's Day 2000, the date embraced by the popular imagination, or on New Year's Day 2001, as purists insisted?) Having been determined in advance, the scheduled end-point shapes expectations and behaviour, becoming a self-fulfilling prophecy; we expect the end, so we behave as though it were nigh. Hence the *fin de siècle* consciousness of the last decade of the nineteenth century, and the millennial anticipations in the last decades of the twentieth. The alternative model is the one exemplified by the events of 9/11: the irruption of historical contingency into the measured sequence of calendrical time. Unlooked for by anyone, the event, once it has actually happened, becomes inevitable, a threshold. We range backwards in time from it, reinterpreting and reordering the sequence of events to make the unanticipated end-point an inevitable outcome of what came before. This, too, is a way of thinking about ends in cultural history, backwards rather than forwards.

Looking Backward, or, the Angel of History

Looking backward, the Edwardian and interwar 'long weekends' come to be read in the light of impending crises, just as the last decades of the twentieth century have come to be read in the light of an unanticipated 9/11. Avant-garde gallery-goers whom Virginia Woolf might have been thinking of when, in her 'Mr Bennett and Mrs Brown' essay (1924), she dated the change in 'human character' to 1910, would of course have known perfectly well that they were attending a *Post*-Impressionist exhibition. But they could only have guessed that they belonged to a *pre*war age. Nor could they have anticipated that some of the art they witnessed, and even the whole society they lived in, would come to seem products of an Edwardian *belle époque*, calm and sunny by comparison with dark years so soon to follow. During those years, the allure of that *belle époque* was often recalled exactly in terms of its happy ignorance of what would come after. Contrasts of almost Edenic innocence with later experience were sharply accentuated by Marcel Proust, who located his hero's idyllic childhood, in *A la recherche du temps perdu* (1913–27), in what would become catastrophic battlefields of the First World War. Similarly ironic contrasts and divergent states of mind figure in *To the Lighthouse* (1927), highlighted by Woolf's juxtaposition of the Ramsays' sunny holiday around 1910 with the disasters of the war, and the uncertainty of its aftermath, described in the novel's second and third sections.

Interests in recovering the splendours of the prewar period were widely shared by modernist contemporaries of Proust and Woolf. Though Ezra Pound's modernist motto 'make it new' insisted on fresh artistic technique, the most striking innovations of the 1920s were often dedicated to literary recovery of the past, to juxtaposing memory with present experience through new structures for fiction, or new styles of stream of consciousness, in the work of Joyce and others. In *The Great Gatsby* (1925), F. Scott Fitzgerald offered another motto for the 1920s, in his narrator's conclusion that even when looking towards the future, Gatsby's compatriots are forced to 'beat on, boats against the current, borne back ceaselessly into the past' (Fitzgerald 1968: 188). Similar attitudes remained in evidence in the next decade, especially clearly in George Orwell's *Coming Up for Air* (1939). Orwell's hero flees an impending second war by returning almost literally to the years before the first – to '1911, 1912, 1913 . . . a good time to be alive . . . always summer' (Orwell 1962: 102–3). A few months after the long-expected Second World War finally broke out, the German-Jewish critic Walter Benjamin captured the modernist era's sense of history in his arresting image of 'the angel of history', whose

> face is turned toward the past . . . A storm is blowing from Paradise . . . This storm irresistibly propels him into the future to which his back is turned, while the pile of debris before him grows skyward. This storm is what we call progress. (Benjamin 1969: 257–8)

Debris grew substantially further 'skyward' during the Second World War. The years that followed did little to reduce the pile, or to encourage confident re-direction of vision upon the future. Benjamin's angel makes a half-covert reappearance half a century later in Tony Kushner's *Angels in America* (Part One, *Millennium Approaches*, 1990–1; Part Two, *Perestroika*, 1992), a play that mourns history's casualties as it anxiously anticipates the approaching millennium. Throughout the intervening period, literary imagination remained much inclined to look back in anger over the first half of the century, and significantly often, with particular regret for the paradisal lost promise of its opening years, or of late Victorian ones. As late as 1980, in 'Playing Through Old Games of Chess', Andrew Waterman still lamented not only the 'long lost summer' of this idyllic age, but also its innocent sense of progress and the future, consolidated at a time when 'Pax Britannica,/ and Europe's chordage held the world enthralled' and

> all history seemed a sort of sunlit incline upwards,
> with problems like the Balkans, abolishing cholera, crime,
> certainly soluble, and change meant improvement,
>
> hygiene, gas cooking, fast travel, the bioscope.

Yet as Waterman's poem indicates, images of 'sunlit incline' offer an incomplete picture, even a 'dream', of an age that was also characterised by high infant mortality, 'old dynasts' and a Pax Britannica which kept 'countless hordes' around the world thoroughly enthralled, along with much of the population at home (Waterman 1980: 11, 12). *Coming Up for Air* likewise acknowledges the partial 'delusion' of summery images of 1911, 1912 and 1913, and the sentimentality likely to colour all such recollection. While praising a lost Edwardian 'feeling of continuity' – in a period which 'didn't think of the future as something to be terrified of' – Orwell nevertheless admits that 'people on the whole worked harder, lived less comfortably, and died more painfully' (Orwell 1962: 103, 106–7). As each author suggests, anyone – surely any angel – looking back over the twentieth century might acknowledge not only loss but a number of genuine 'inclines upwards', scarcely confined to the Edwardian period. These might include the extensive enfranchisement of populations in the West, the retreat from empire, and the liberation of women (simultaneous, Woolf suggests in *To the Lighthouse*, with the anguish of the First World War); or, for that matter, improvements in hygiene, the treatment of cholera, and the infant mortality rate – to take only a couple of examples among very many.

   Any view of the twentieth century, in other words, is shaped by recollection not only of war, disaster and loss, but of piles of such 'debris' accumulating at a time when there seemed such good opportunity of removing or avoiding them. An epochal image more apt even than Benjamin's angel may therefore appear in one of the outstanding English-language novels of mid-century, *Under the Volcano* (1947) – in Malcolm Lowry's characterisation of Geoffrey Firmin, who determinedly damns himself to death and darkness while still enjoying full, clear awareness of the light. Set on the brink of the Second World War, Lowry's novel provides in its middle chapter a figure for the century's situation in its image of Firmin's entrapment on a *máquina infernal*: a Ferris Wheel which leaves him upended in mid-air when it stops at the height of its arc. The moment suggests uneasy tension between contrary impulses, or between inclines upwards and downwards – towards progress and regression; hope and disaster. Any equilibrium between them is nevertheless no more than momentary. The rest of Lowry's novel follows a disastrous downrush towards oblivion – for its hero, and by symbolic extension for the century itself. Mindful of the recent use of nuclear weapons, Lowry repeated on his novel's last page its regular warnings about eviction from a garden, emphasising in a letter early in 1946 that Firmin's 'fate should be seen also in its universal relationship to the ultimate fate of mankind' (Lowry 1985: 66).

Millennium Approaches, or, Slouching Towards Bethlehem?

Lowry's novel is thus firmly located within that other tradition of twentieth-century literature, in fiction and film, mentioned above – one that reacts to 'the future as something to be terrified of' not through alternatives of nostalgic or Edenic retrospection, but through apocalyptic scenarios, the imagination of disaster. As the century wore on, and *belles époques* were displaced from living memory by the mounting debris of war and disaster, it was perhaps inevitable that the tradition of apocalyptic anticipation should partly replace the backward look. Lowry's mid-century image of Firmin arrested in mid-air before resuming his fall is echoed a quarter-century later by the missile suspended above the roof of the cinema at the end of Pynchon's *Gravity's Rainbow* (1973) and then, as millennium approaches, by the popular imagination's vision of civilisation brought to a grinding halt by the Y2K computer bug – a vision decisively eclipsed, though also partly fulfilled, by the fiery reality of 9/11.

Certainly, responses to the events of September 2001 were characterised less often by a backward-looking sense of lost innocence than through reference to the century's tradition of apocalyptic anticipation. Several critics – notably Terry Eagleton in *Holy Terror* (2005) – remarked that the events in New York, and still more those in Madrid in 2003, and London in 2005, made Joseph Conrad's *The Secret Agent* (1907) into one of the most prescient novels of our era, even though its narrative derives from an obscure outrage in the 1890s. Commentators in 2000 had often expressed millennial anxieties through W. B. Yeats's anticipation, in 'The Second Coming' (1921), of a return to the 'twenty centuries of stony sleep/ . . . vexed to nightmare by a rocking cradle' when some 'rough beast, its hour come round at last,/ Slouches towards Bethlehem to be born' (Yeats 1971: 211). After September 2001, T. S. Eliot's *The Waste Land* (1922) also seemed to provide anticipatory imagery – of cracks bursting across the air, and of cities of falling towers. Fears that W. H. Auden expressed on the eve of the Second World War seemed if anything still more contemporary, in 2001, than the apocalyptic dreads that Yeats and Eliot had extrapolated from recent experience of the First. Auden's 'September 1, 1939' became the most widely quoted English-language poem in the aftermath of September 2001. Uncanny resonances were immediately available in Auden's reflections on a New York where 'the unmentionable odour of death/ Offends the September night', where 'blind skyscrapers use/ Their full height to proclaim/ The strength of Collective Man' and where 'those to whom evil is done/ Do evil in return' (Skelton 1975: 280–1).

'Uncanny resonance' is, of course, one of literature's perennial qualities, whether in times of crisis or otherwise; or, to adopt a jargon appropriate to the beginning of the twenty-first century, we might call it 'pattern recognition'. Registering such resonances and recognising such patterns is one of the perennial tasks of literary history. It is no easy task to undertake, especially at times when the patterns seem to have been obscured by the flux of historical change, and the resonances to have been overwhelmed by noise. Writing out of just such a moment, in the immediate aftermath of the First World War, T. S. Eliot, in one of the century's most celebrated critical essays, 'Tradition and the Individual Talent' (1919), seeks to re-establish a sense of historical coherence, of individual intelligence engaging with wider cultural patterns, while at the same time acknowledging that these patterns are themselves continually reshaped by the vision of the present. This is one model for how literary history might understand its task in the face of the continuing historical crises of the twentieth and twenty-first centuries. But the task becomes no easier, the patterns, if anything, harder to recognise as the pace of historical change accelerates and millennium approaches.

Evidence of how much harder it is now even than in Eliot's time is to be found in one of the first novels to register the events of 9/11, called, appropriately enough, *Pattern Recognition* (2003). Its author, William Gibson, is known for his innovations in the science fiction genre, but *Pattern Recognition* is a novel of the immediate present; or, to put it another way, here the present seems to have caught up with the future we once could only imagine, and the gap between present reality and science fiction seems to have closed. 'For us . . . things can change so abruptly, so violently, so profoundly that futures . . . have insufficient "now" to stand on', says one of Gibson's characters. 'We have no future because our present is too volatile . . . We have only . . . the spinning of the given moment's scenarios. Pattern recognition.' Even 'the past changes', another character concurs (Gibson 2003: 57).

Can literary history offer anything more than 'the spinning of the given moment's scenarios', the present's preferred versions of a past that changes as we look back upon it? Scepticism about strong claims to have grasped the patterns of literary history seems very much in order. Yet such scepticism can be at least partly offset, on the one hand by taking fully into account the ways the present shapes the past (as well as vice versa) – as in Eliot's 'Tradition and the Individual Talent' – and on the other hand by scrupulous attention to historical particularity. Conrad's crises, or Auden's, resonate in our own moment of crisis, but just as it is important to register that resonance, so it is also important to identify what, in their moments, resists assimilation to our own – what is irreducibly *theirs*; shaped by their historical circumstances, and not ours. Relevant as *The Secret Agent* is to the events of 2001, 2003 and 2005, Conrad is responding to late-nineteenth-century terrorism, not that of the early twenty-first, and the differences matter. Auden is reflecting on the onset of the Second World War in 'September 1, 1939', not the events of 9/11, uncanny though the resonances might be.

This is part of the understanding that the *Companion* has sought to provide. Discontinuous but particular, it corresponds to Auden's hope that 'dotted everywhere/ Ironic points of light' might illuminate a century's problematic history. Or, to return to our introduction, it corresponds to the image from Pynchon's *V.* of streetlamps intermittently throwing light on the dark street of the twentieth century. The 'far end or turning' of the street of the twentieth century offers little of the safety Pynchon hoped for, and little opportunity for return to an idyllic past; even to dreams of one. All the more reason, then, for scrupulously attending to such illumination as has appeared on the street behind, and to the light it can shed on where we stand now.

Macclesfield – Amsterdam – Edinburgh, 2003–2005

References

Benjamin, Walter (1969) *Illuminations: Essays and Reflections*, ed. Hannah Arendt, New York: Schocken

Fitzgerald, F. Scott (1968) *The Great Gatsby*, Harmondsworth: Penguin

Gibson, William (2003) *Pattern Recognition*, New York: G. P. Putnam's Sons.

Lowry, Malcolm (1985) *Selected Letters*, ed. Harvey Breit and Margerie Bonner Lowry, Harmondsworth: Penguin

Orwell, George (1962) *Coming Up for Air*, Harmondsworth, Penguin

Skelton, Robin, ed. (1975) *Poetry of the Thirties*, Harmondsworth: Penguin

Smith, Zadie (2000) *White Teeth*, New York: Random House

Waterman, Andrew (1980) *Over the Wall*, Manchester: Carcanet

Yeats, W. B. (1971) *The Collected Poems of W.B. Yeats*, London: Macmillan

Notes on Contributors

Chris Baldick is Professor of English at Goldsmiths' College, University of London, where he directs the MA programme in Twentieth-Century Literature. Among his published works are *Criticism and Literary Theory, 1890 to the Present* (1996) and *The Oxford English Literary History, volume 10 (1910–1940): The Modern Movement* (2004).

Louise Bethlehem lectures in the Department of English and the Program in Cultural Studies at the Hebrew University of Jerusalem. She has published widely on South African literary and cultural historiography, postcolonialism and gender theory. She recently completed a book-length study, *Skin Tight: Apartheid Literary Culture and its Aftermath*, which is due to be published by Unisa Press, South Africa.

Cairns Craig is Director of the Centre for Irish and Scottish Studies at the University of Aberdeen. His books include *Yeats, Eliot, Pound and the Politics of Poetry* (1982), *Out of History* (1996), and *The Modern Scottish Novel* (1999). He was general editor of the four-volume *History of Scottish Literature* (1987–9) and an editor of the Canongate Classics series.

Jane Goldman is Senior Lecturer in English and American Literature at the University of Dundee. She is General Editor, with Susan Sellers, of the Cambridge University Press edition of the writings of Virginia Woolf. She is author of *The Cambridge Introduction to Virginia Woolf* (Cambridge University Press, 2006), *Modernism, 1910–1945: Image to Apocalypse* (Palgrave, 2004), and *The Feminist Aesthetics of Virginia Woolf: Modernism, Post-Impressionism, and the Politics of the Visual* (Cambridge University Press, 1998), and editor, with Vassiliki Kolocotroni and Olga Taxidou, of *Modernism: An Anthology of Sources and Documents* (Edinburgh University Press and University of Chicago Press, 1998). She is currently editing the Cambridge University Press edition of Virginia Woolf's *To the Lighthouse*, and writing a book entitled *Virginia Woolf and the Signifying Dog*.

Abdulrazak Gurnah is Professor of English and Postcolonial Literatures and is Head of the School of English at the University of Kent, England. He is the author of seven novels, most recently *Desertion* (2005). He is currently editing a collection of essays on the writing of Salman Rushdie.

Ursula K. Heise is Associate Professor of English and Comparative Literature at Stanford University, where she teaches contemporary literature and literary theory, with special emphasis on theories of modernisation, postmodernisation and globalisation, as well as on ecocriticism. Her book *Chronoschisms: Time, Narrative, Postmodernism* appeared from Cambridge University Press in 1997; she is currently completing a book called *Sense of Place and Sense of Planet: The Environmental Imagination of the Global*.

John Hellmann is Professor of English at the Ohio State University. He is the author of *Fables of Fact: The New Journalism as New Fiction* (1981), *American Myth and the Legacy of Vietnam* (1986), and *The Kennedy Obsession: The American Myth of JFK* (1997). He has been the recipient of a major grant from the American Council of Learned Societies (ACLS). During 1992–3 he served as a Senior Fulbright Lecturer at the University of Bonn, Germany.

Linda A. Kinnahan is Professor of English at Duquesne University in Pittsburgh, PA. She is the author of articles and books on modernist and contemporary poetry, including *Poetics of the Feminine: Authority and Literary Tradition in William Carlos Williams, Mina Loy, Denise Levertov, and Kathleen Fraser* (1994) and *Lyric Interventions: Feminism, Experimental Poetry, and Contemporary Discourse* (2004). She is currently exploring intersections between modernist women, poetry and economics.

Vassiliki Kolocotroni is Lecturer in English Literature and Acting Director of the Graduate School of Arts and Humanities at the University of Glasgow. She is the co-editor of *Modernism: An Anthology of Sources and Documents* (Edinburgh University Press, 1998), *Nicolas Calas: Sixteen French Poems and the Correspondence with William Carlos Williams* (Ypsilon Books, 2002) and *In the Country of the Moon: British Women Travellers in Greece 1718–1932* (Hestia Publishers, 2005). She has published articles on Julia Kristeva, James Joyce and Virginia Woolf, and is currently working on a study of Modernism and Hellenism.

Brian McHale is Distinguished Humanities Professor in English at the Ohio State University. For many years an editor of the journal *Poetics Today*, he is the author of *Postmodernist Fiction* (1987), *Constructing Postmodernism* (1992), and *The Obligation Toward the Difficult Whole: Postmodernist Long Poems* (2004), as well as many articles on modernist and postmodernist topics, science fiction, and narrative theory.

Philip Mead is a Senior Lecturer in English at the University of Tasmania. He has been associated with poetry publishing, particularly in little magazines, since 1972. From 1987 to 1994 he was Poetry Editor of *Meanjin Quarterly* magazine. He has published widely on poetry in magazines and newspapers and edited, with John Tranter, the *Penguin Book of Modern Australian Poetry* (1992). His edited collection of essays, *Kenneth Slessor – Critical Readings* appeared with University of Queensland Press in 1997, and *Frank Wilmot: Selected Poetry and Prose* was published by Melbourne University Press in the same year.

Tyrus Miller is Associate Professor of Literature at University of California at Santa Cruz. He is the author of *Late Modernism: Politics, Fiction, and the Arts Between the World Wars* (University of California Press, 1999) and a forthcoming study of Anglo-American avant-gardes after the Second World War entitled *Singular Examples: Artistic Politics of the Post-War Avant-Garde*.

Alan Nadel, Bryan Professor of American Literature at the University of Kentucky, is the author of several books on American literature, culture and film, including *Containment Culture: American Narratives, Postmodernism, and the Atomic Age* (Duke University Press, 1995), *Flatlining on the Field of Dreams: Cultural Narratives in the Films of President Regan's America* (Rutgers University Press, 1997), and, most recently, *Television in Black-and-White America: Race and National Identity* (2005).

Cary Nelson is Jubilee Professor of Liberal Arts and Sciences and Professor of English at the University of Illinois at Urbana-Champaign. Among his many books are *Repression and Recovery: Modern American Poetry and the Politics of Cultural Memory, 1910–1945* (1989), *Manifesto of a Tenured Radical* (1997), *Academic Keywords: A Devil's Dictionary for Higher Education* (1999), and *Revolutionary Memory: Recovering the Poetry of the American Left* (2004).

Michael North is Professor of English at the University of California, Los Angeles. His most recent books are *Camera Works: Photography and the Twentieth-Century Word* (Oxford University Press, 2005), *Reading 1922: A Return to the Scene of the Modern* (Oxford, 1999) and the Norton Critical Edition of T. S. Eliot's *The Waste Land* (2001).

Rick Rylance is Professor and Head of the School of English at the University of Exeter. His research interests cross between the nineteenth and twentieth centuries and he is particularly interested in the relations between intellectual and literary history. He is author of *Victorian Psychology and British Culture 1850–1880* (Oxford University Press, 2000) and is currently completing the mid-twentieth-century volume of the Oxford English Literary History, *Literature among the Wars: 1930–1970*. Future projects include books on Darwin and D. H. Lawrence.

R. Clifton Spargo, a fiction writer and critic, is Associate Professor of English at Marquette University and formerly the Pearl Resnick Fellow at the Center for Advanced Holocaust Studies of the U.S. Holocaust Memorial Museum. He is the author of *The Ethics of Mourning: Grief and Responsibility in Elegiac Literature* (Johns Hopkins University Press, 2004) and *Vigilant Memory: Emmanuel Levinas, the Holocaust, and the Unjust Death* (Johns Hopkins University Press, 2006). He is also the author of articles on American literature and the cultural memory of the Holocaust in journals such as *Representations* and *PMLA* and is a completing a monograph on that subject.

Randall Stevenson is Professor of Twentieth-Century Literature and Deputy Head of the Department of English Literature in the University of Edinburgh. His publications include *The British Novel since the Thirties* (1986); *A Reader's Guide to the Twentieth-Century Novel in Britain* (1993); *Modernist Fiction* (1998); *Oxford English Literary History* vol. 12: *1960–2000 – The Last of England?* (2004); along with many articles and book-chapters in the areas of twentieth-century literature and drama. He is General Editor of the *Edinburgh History of Twentieth-Century Literature in Britain* series, to be published by Edinburgh University Press.

Joseph Tabbi is the author of *Cognitive Fictions* (Minnesota University Press, 2002) and *Postmodern Sublime* (Cornell University Press, 1995). He edits *the electronic book review* and has edited and introduced William Gaddis's last fiction and collected non-fiction, *Rush for Second Place* (Viking/Penguin, 2002). His essay on Mark Amerika appeared at the Walker Art Center's phon:e:me site, a 2000 Webby Award nominee. Also online (at the Iowa Review Web) is an essay-narrative, titled 'Overwriting', an interview, and a review of his work. He is a professor of English at the University of Illinois, Chicago.

Andrew Teverson is a lecturer in English at Kingston University. He has recently completed a monograph on the fiction of Salman Rushdie for Manchester University Press and is currently preparing research on the uses of fairytale and folklore in colonial and post-colonial contexts.

Patrick Williams is Professor of Literary and Cultural Studies, and director for the Centre for Diaspora and Migration Studies at Nottingham Trent University, where he teaches courses on race, national identity, diaspora and postcolonial studies. His publications include *Colonial Discourse and Post-Colonial Theory* (Harvester/Pearson, 1993), *Introduction to Post-Colonial Theory* (Prentice Hall/Pearson, 1996), *Ngugi wa Thiong'o* (Manchester University Press, 1999), *Edward Said* (Sage, 2000) and *Post-Colonial African Cinemas* (Manchester University Press, 2006).

Patricia Waugh is Professor of English at the University of Durham. She has published extensively in the field of modern fiction and criticism. Book-length publications include *Metafiction: The Theory and Practice of Self-Conscious Fiction* (Routledge, 1984), *Feminine Fictions* (Edward Arnold, 1989), *Practising Postmodernism/Reading Modernism* (Edward Arnold, 1992), *The Harvest of the Sixties* (Oxford University Press, 1995), *Revolutions of the Word* (Oxford University Press, 1997) and with David Fuller, *The Arts and Sciences of Criticism* (Clarendon, 1999). She is the editor of the *Oxford Guide to Criticism and Theory* (Oxford University Press, 2006) and is currently completing a book entitled *Science, Literature and the Good Society*. She is also writing the *Blackwell History of British and Irish Literature 1945– Present*.

Index